5.00

DATE DUE

Commonplace Book

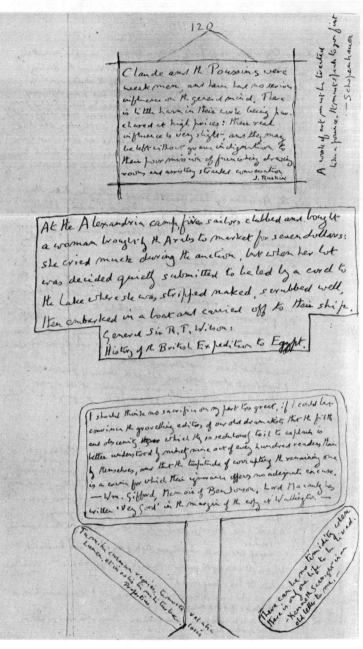

Commonplace Book, p. 120. See page 113 of this edition.

E. M. FORSTER
Commonplace Book

edited by

PHILIP GARDNER

Stanford University Press

STANFORD, CALIFORNIA

1985

Stanford University Press
Stanford, California
Originating publisher: Scolar Press, London
First published in the U.S.A. by Stanford University Press, 1985
ISBN 0-8047-1280-8
LC 85-50099

E. M. Forster's text first published in
manuscript facsimile, with an introduction by
P. N. Furbank 1978

Typeset by Gloucester Typesetting Services
Printed and bound in Great Britain
at the University Press, Cambridge

Contents

Preface, vii

Introduction, xiii

COMMONPLACE BOOK

Notes, 260

Index, 363

Publishers' acknowledgements, 370

Preface

Throughout this transcription and edition of Forster's Commonplace
Book, my aim has been to present the text in a form as close as the
medium of print allows to that of Forster's original: that is, while
reproducing its matter faithfully, I have also tried to retain as much of
its manner as is practicable, and thus avoid reducing it to the uniform
appearance of a book destined by its author for publication. Those
scholars and general readers who wish to establish the extent to which
this edition diverges from the original may do so by consulting either
the original itself, housed in the library of King's College, Cambridge,
or the facsimile edition published in 1978 by Scolar Press in a limited
edition of 350 copies.

Forster's original text is a fascinating document. Much of its format, however, exhibits a freedom and variation which it would have
been impossible to reproduce without prohibitive typesetting costs,
wastage of paper, and in some cases a degree of oddity, in print, which
would have both irritated the reader and, in spirit if not in the letter,
betrayed the 'feel' of Forster's holograph. Forster's pages are wider,
and much longer, than those of this book, and he makes full use of
them, packing a great deal on to each page in middle-age, and less,
often in bigger writing, in old age. He encloses some sentences in
'boxes', quotes poems side by side, makes interlinear and marginal
additions, writes diagonally, links related passages by lines across the
page or across facing pages, thickens pen-strokes or enlarges words
for emphasis, occasionally uses red ink, and employs indentation with
a finesse that suggests the fluid inflections of talk. To separate topics,
he sometimes leaves large spaces, and less often whole pages, blank;
on one occasion (p. 170 of this book) he isolates a single couplet
poignantly at the centre of an otherwise empty page. On another
page (p. 113 of this book) he arrays a group of quotations pictorially:
the top one, from Ruskin, is appropriately placed in a picture frame
to which the lines of a hanging cord have been attached; the bottom

one, from William Gifford, is enclosed as if in the branches of a square 'tree' beneath which he has drawn a pedestal-like trunk. Enhanced by the rapidity of his fluid-cum-sharp handwriting, Forster's original is more intimate, more dramatic, and more versatile than a printed edition is capable of being. A few of Forster's simpler 'shapes' have been retained, however, additions intended by him as footnotes have been placed within ruled lines in the text, and I have drawn attention in individual notes to any characteristic, eccentric, or felicitous modes of addition and linkage.

But, while larger aspects of Forster's presentation have perforce had to be regularised, I have tried in such matters as punctuation and spelling not to tamper unduly. In the majority of instances, Forster's spelling is correct; where it is not, and the error is no more interesting than a schoolboy howler ('desparate' for 'desperate', 'weild' for 'wield'), I have silently corrected it. Sometimes, however, Forster's mis-spellings have an air of deliberation, archaic, joky, irreverent; these – such as 'reckognise', 'Ouverture', and 'cieling' (written in such a firm hand that I felt emendation would be mere discourtesy) – I have retained. And in the computer age, it is perhaps both humane and refreshingly subversive to cherish Forster's 'computor'. I have also preserved, for their informality and occasional debunking humour, Forster's erratic spellings of personal names. The reader, therefore, may reasonably assume that any 'errors' still in the text are not compositors' blunders or proof-readers' unconsidered trifles, but represent the editor's wish to stick to his author.

Forster is normally careful about punctuation. Sometimes, though, he omits commas and periods, occasionally letting the margin of his page act in their capacity. Where, in print, adherence to his practice would look odd, I have preferred to restore missing punctuation silently. He sometimes fails to close brackets, or to supply final quotation-marks; I have added these. Where he allows a final bracket to do double duty as a period, I have normally done so too; but I have sometimes capitalised the initial letters of sentences when he has failed to do so.

Very rarely, Forster repeats a phrase immediately after its first occurrence; I have deleted such repetitions, feeling they would merely irritate. But some instances of ungrammatical usage and some *lapsi calami* I have let stand, since they provide graphic instances of mistakes in writing (cf. 'instance' for 'insistence' on p. 63) on which Forster himself sometimes comments. I have also – a larger matter – made no attempt to tidy up Forster's order of presentation on those few occasions when he makes an entry out of chronological sequence, since he normally remarks on this himself. For instance, an entry on the film of *Richard III*, made in 1964, is written, on a page previously left blank, among entries for 1963 (p. 246); and the placing of an entry for October 1960 (p. 227) among, and interrupting, two entries made in 1961 clearly came about because Forster inadvertently turned over two leaves instead of one in 1960, and then went back to use up the intervening space. For an editor to 'correct' errors like this would be to substitute false, mechanical regularity for true, human fallibility.

Forster is not invariably accurate when quoting from other writers. I have left any such misquotations uncorrected in the text, since the Commonplace Book is a record of Forster's reading and memory and not his editor's; I have, however, usually indicated the proper versions in my notes. These are secluded at the back of the book, since I did not wish to spoil the reader's enjoyment, or interrupt Forster when he was talking, by annotations at the end of entries or the foot of the page. For the same reasons I have not used footnote numbers: any marks in the text – asterisks, crosses – are Forster's own, as are all bracketed phrases, except a minute number which are either self-evidently mine or explained in the notes. Instead, the notes are keyed to page numbers, and will, I hope, provide adequate explanation or amplification of any reference in the text which the reader may find puzzling or intriguing; translations are also to be found in the notes. If I have not been able to explain everything, this has not been for want of trying, or for want of the help of fellow-scholars, which has been generously given me.

Some other editorial procedures need to be briefly mentioned. This transcription of Forster's text employs two sizes of type: normal, for his own words; smaller, when he is quoting or summarising other writers or copying out his own letters. This simple distinction was impossible to maintain in a few passages (such as those concerning the Church Fathers) when Forster moves quickly to and fro between quotation and comment. Where Forster uses terms like 'overleaf' and 'opposite', these have generally been replaced by phrases more appropriate to the text as printed here; similarly, Forster's occasional numerical references back or forward have been re-numbered to fit this edition. In order to give the reader an indication of chronology, I have supplied a year date, at the top of the relevant page, for each point of transition forwards. And, finally, a few references to people, which might give hurt or offence if left in the text, have been omitted and blanks substituted for them.

I am grateful to the Provost and Fellows of King's College, Cambridge for making me a Visiting Member of High Table during the academic year 1980–81, and for allowing me unrestricted access to Forster's unpublished papers both then and later. The work I did at King's College Library was made possible, and very enjoyable, as a result of the unstinting help I received from its staff, notably the then Librarian, the late Peter Croft, the Sub-Librarian, Mrs Elizabeth Russell, and the Modern Literary Archivist, Dr Michael Halls. I should also like to thank the staff of Cambridge University Library.

Funds were generously provided to aid my research by the Social Sciences and Humanities Research Council of Canada, which awarded me a Sabbatical Leave Fellowship for 1980–81; and on a number of occasions by the Memorial University of Newfoundland. I am deeply indebted to both institutions.

I acknowledge with gratitude the information and the various forms of help I have received over the past six years from the following individuals: at King's College, Cambridge, Dr George Rylands, Dr Donald Parry, the late Peter Croft, Dr Michael Halls, Mr P. N. Furbank, the late Oliver Stallybrass, Dr Elisabeth Heine, Mr D. W. Lucas, Mr Ian Stephens; in Cambridge, Mrs H. W. Leakey; at the University of Reading, Professor W. D. Redfern, Dr Alan Wardman, Mrs Judith Wardman; at the Memorial University of Newfoundland, my colleagues the late E. R. Seary, Dr David G. Pitt, Dr Iain Bruce, Dr John Whittaker, Mrs Lieda Bell, Dr Raymond Clark, Mr Roger Clark, Mr Tony Chadwick. Mrs Cathy Murphy and Mrs Cathy Kielley, departmental secretaries, typed my original manuscript. I owe, as always, a special debt to my wife and colleague, Averil Gardner, to whom I have never turned for advice and help in vain.

I am grateful for the encouragement I have received from two eminent Forsterians in the United States, Professor Wilfred Stone and Professor Frederick MacDowell. I should also like to express my appreciation to my publishers, whose kindness, patience, courtesy and punctilious concern for standards have been exemplary.

I wish, finally, to express my thanks to the four men at King's who, after the death of Oliver Stallybrass in 1978, invited me to edit Forster's Commonplace Book in his stead: Dr George Rylands and Dr Donald Parry, the Trustees of Forster's Estate; Mr P. N. Furbank, Forster's official biographer; and Professor Frank Kermode, Fellow of King's and at that time King Edward VII Professor of English at Cambridge. Deeply sensible of the honour their invitation did me, I can only hope that I have responded adequately to it. To know

Forster personally, as I did when an undergraduate at King's in the nineteen-fifties, was to become aware of humane values, distinction and quickness of mind, and warm human sympathy. To edit his Commonplace Book has been a liberal education.

Philip Gardner
May 1985

Introduction

More completely than for most writers, E. M. Forster's work is his monument. It is not possible for readers of it to commune with a gravestone, or to imagine from a distance a place where, as after the funeral of Mrs Wilcox in *Howards End*, 'hour after hour the place of the interment remained without an eye to witness it.' Born near a London main-line railway station, transient all his life through a succession of houses and rooms not his own, Forster finally died in the semi-detached house of his old friends Bob and May Buckingham in the suburbs of Coventry – a city much of whose past, like his own, had been obliterated. His body was cremated, and its ashes scattered over the rose-bed in the Buckinghams' garden.

After his death, on 7 June 1970, a great deal of unpublished material was found in his rooms at King's College, Cambridge, the last and longest of his temporary homes, and the one where he had been able to curve his ninety-one years of life into a kind of circle. For all his physical rootlessness, Forster set much store by continuity, and at King's it was almost possible for him to say, with T. S. Eliot, 'in my beginning is my end'. Some of the unpublished writings – the homosexual novel *Maurice*, the homosexual short stories collected in *The Life to Come*, the unfinished *Arctic Summer* and other fragments including Forster's very last story, 'Little Imber' – have already appeared, and have both widened and modified for the general reader the public image of Forster which was given a late boost in 1969 by his appointment to the Order of Merit. It is easier now than it was in Forster's lifetime to see him not just as a skilful, indeed an immensely skilful, professional writer, but as a person of passionate if circumspectly unleashed instincts, and as a 'foolish, fond old man' as well as a wise spokesman for liberal humanism.

Much greater insight into Forster the man is furnished by two non-fictional documents at King's at his death. One is his locked Diary, which he kept from 1909 to 1967; it was in this that he noted, on 28 August 1964, listening with a friend to a recording of T. S. Eliot reading *Four Quartets*, and commented that 'despite his priestliness he held us'. There are, however, no plans at present to publish this fascinating though not voluminous book. An even fuller view of him emerges from the other document, his Commonplace Book, which he began in 1925 and rounded out towards the end of 1968. In this, in 1962, he recorded having read Eliot's *Little Gidding* aloud to himself ('a good experience'), and went on to compare himself with Eliot, to his own advantage. At various points in the Commonplace Book he assessed his own characteristics in terms of other writers – Coleridge, Voltaire, Gray, Ruskin, even St Jerome – and ended by relating himself to King Lear: 'old, idle, and trustful, and so far like myself'. Forster's Commonplace Book, issued in a limited facsimile edition in 1978, and now transcribed and annotated, offers far more than a dictionary-defined compendium of striking 'quotations, poems and remarks'; rather, following on from Forster's last novel, *A Passage to India*, it provides a commentary – sharp, wry, and frequently very moving – on the second half of Forster's life. And since Forster was essentially writing for himself, one can apply to it, with even more truth, an admission he made in it in 1932, just before copying out a letter he had written to Goldsworthy Lowes Dickinson: 'it is only in letters that I say what I feel; not in literature any more, and I seldom say it, because I keep trying to be amusing.' Parts of the first three-quarters of the Commonplace Book may be fruitfully set beside *Aspects of the Novel* and the polished public essays collected in *Abinger Harvest* and *Two Cheers for Democracy*; its final quarter, a literary, aesthetic and spiritual diary, presents a picture of Forster available nowhere else.

His decision to keep a Commonplace Book was an act of conscious continuity. In 1924, he inherited from his aunt Laura Forster her house above the village of Abinger Hammer in Surrey. First called Laura Lodge but later renamed West Hackhurst, it had been built for her, on leasehold land, by Forster's architect father. Having moved in, he discovered there a very large notebook, size 12 inches by 8, bound in boards and leather, and containing some four hundred pages of fine quality paper. It had been bought in 1804 for use as a commonplace book by John Jebb, a Church of Ireland rector who began making entries in it at Cashel. Jebb later became Bishop of Limerick and, having filled only eighteen of its pages (half of them in Latin and some Greek), he eventually bequeathed it to his chaplain, Forster's grandfather. Neither the Rev. Charles Forster nor his daughter Laura, to whom it passed in 1871, made any use of its blank pages.

Forster recorded his find in his diary, and on the same day proceeded to annex it with a confident hand, writing under Jebb's inaugurating date and signature on the flyleaf: 'Continued it at Abinger Hammer, Wednesday October 21, 1925, E. M. Forster'. By the bottom of his first page, after three entries of a general nature – on Commonplaces, Isolation and Resentment – he was already recording a 'Change of Plan', by which he would abandon 'this awful arrangement by topics'. He found it too preconceived and dictatorial, being unable to tell what he thought till he saw what he said; but he determined to adhere to the Bishop's system of ruling a margin and straddling it with the first word of each entry, so that 'the letter may be retained while the spirit is killed'. He also made regular use of Jebb's handsome index, though, oddly, he stated in his essay 'Bishop Jebb's Book', (1940) that he had 'disdained it'. Jebb had devoted two facing pages to a sequence of the letters of the alphabet (omitting as a good classicist 'J' and 'V'), each letter accompanied by a five-fold subdivision by vowels. He himself made little use of it, whereas Forster listed in it page references for no fewer than 196 entries by subject.

A last attempt at continuity was made when Forster, having reopened the book in 1968 after a three years' silence, balanced Jebb's original flyleaf inscription – whose date he had recorded in 'Bishop Jebb's Book' as 'Wednesday, November 11th, 1804' – with his final instruction about the book's disposal: 'To be given to the College Library, Nov. the 11th 1968'. The claim for the book of exactly 164 years of life (with 110 pages still left to fill) was in fact three days out: Jebb's faint brown ink reads 'November 14'. The pious wish for historical symmetry is touching; its near miss would have appealed to Forster's sense of irony.

Broadly speaking, Forster's Commonplace Book gives the impression of revealing his reading in the earlier parts and the man himself in the later. To put it another way, one seems to approach ever closer to Forster as his intellectual responses are replaced by emotional ones and opinions give way to instincts. In part this is an optical illusion created by the initial preponderance, in the years 1925 to 1930, of entries relating to books. On 17 May 1926, having been invited to give the Clark Lectures for 1927, and being 'a good deal hung up', Forster wrote to Virginia Woolf for advice about the best novels to read, admitting his own limitations with a wry frankness: 'I have only just read Tristram Shandy and Moll Flanders, so you see.' The first seventeen pages of the Commonplace Book thus contain material that was to surface, reorganised and sometimes altered, in *Aspects of the Novel*. And the peak single year for Commonplace Book entries, 1930, is largely occupied with notes on Forster's reading of plays by Dryden and Corneille, and on his investigation of the literary theories and criticism of Dante, Swift, Boileau, Samuel Johnson, Wordsworth and Coleridge, on all of whom he had stimulating things to say which he did not repeat elsewhere.

But his later years, too, were much exercised by books. Sometimes he was provoked to admiration by the work of writers much younger than himself, like William Golding, Penelope Mortimer and John Knowles. Sometimes, as with the poetry of Edwin Muir which he read in the 1950s, he was moved to tears by an emotional affinity sensed beneath different attitudes and circumstances. And in his engagement with certain works – Yeats's 'The Magi', Eliot's *Four Quartets* and Tolstoy's *Anna Karenina*, his second reading of which, in 1964, prompted his last entry devoted to a novel – one is aware of an urge to do justice to the genius of writers whose personalities were not especially congenial to him: the literary equivalent of the gratitude he felt in old age for the diversity of the phenomenal world and expressed in a remark of 1951: 'So all the time objects are calling to me, whether I answer them or not.'

But if, in fact, responses to literature are to be found throughout the Commonplace Book, so too are responses to 'life', ranging from the dry notation of absurdities overheard in conversations or read in newspapers to passages (perhaps more uniformly eloquent than his entries of any other kind) indicating Forster's sense of alienation in a twentieth-century landscape increasingly mechanised, built over, and unamenable to being understood by means of the notions of 'Pan' and 'Wessex' which had underlain his early short stories. Perhaps one reacts to the later manifestations of Forster's regret with a deeper sympathy simply because he is older, and England that much further gone; as when, writing in 1963 of 'fragile Tennysonian Lincolnshire', he remarks that: 'The death of our countryside [which will *never* be renewed] upsets me more than the death of a man or of a generation of men which [will] be replaced in much the same form.' Yet no less moving are his laments expressed between 1928 and 1930 for the 'collapsing countryside' of Surrey, of which there is 'too little . . . to hide me, even at night, or to go round.' His remedy at that time for a changing world was a brave attempt to encompass the post-Einsteinian explanatory books of Sir Arthur Eddington; and in the 1950s and 1960s he dipped into similar books by Fred Hoyle. But essentially he remained stranded between past and present, and for much of the Commonplace Book his voice is elegiac, with overtones of bitterness (often self-reproachful) and of an exhausted calm.

There is little about Forster's own fiction in the Commonplace Book. In 1930, he reproached himself with 'only paring away insincerities', in contrast to Joyce and Shaw who had 'something to say'; and in 1958 a brief glow of approval for his achievement in *Howards End* was chilled by the realisation that he 'cannot love' the novel because (unlike his other novels, and 'The Other Boat' which he had recently finished) it contained 'not a single character . . . for whom I care'. From time to time he pondered the possibility of another novel, but did not begin one. In 1927, approaching fifty, he toyed with the idea of trying to depict the peculiar essence of middle age, that one was doing things done many times over and realising, 'without pathos or bitterness', not merely that one's former passions had become habits but that the realisation 'had itself the force of a passion'. It was a difficult state of mind to capture, and in his 'Pensée' of a few months later he expressed a reluctance to spoil emotions by trying to embody them in characters. In 1930 he considered a 'mother and son' novel, clearly cognate with his own close ambivalent relationship to his mother, but discarded it in favour of the 'only serious theme worth treating', that of 'two people pulling each other into salvation'. (This theme was to some extent realised in 'Little Imber', written in 1961, and seems to surface again in 1965 in his 'Dream of Saint Cerf'.) And in 1943 a forceful suggestion from Bob Buckingham prompted an inconclusive entry which Forster headed 'One More Novel?'.

To Buckingham, it did not matter whether Forster repeated himself. 'Say again', he urged, 'that you believe in human relationships and disbelieve in power.' Forster still held both views, despite writing in 1928 that 'personal relationships no longer seem to be a serious branch of study.' As the Thirties had worn on, and had increased his pessimistic belief that a war would bring all sorts of unpleasant characters out of the woodwork and the post-war world (as he said at the Writers' Conference in Paris in 1935) would be inherited by 'people whose training has been different from my own', a concomitant wish to reassert his humanistic credo had grown in him. Despite his gloomy and at the time not unnatural certainty, expressed in his diary for 22 August 1940, that 'WE HAVE LOST THE WAR', a defiant resolve is recorded the same year in his Commonplace Book: 'My duty is plain enough: to talk this late nineteenth century stuff [civilisation as being greater than 'the ancestral wisdom of barbarians'] in a twenty [*sic*] century voice, and not to be shoved out of believing in intellectual honesty and the individual.'

The six years of war from 1940 to 1945 occasioned in Forster a fuller use of his Commonplace Book than any equivalent period over the four decades he kept it. Affection for a now inaccessible France which he feared he might never see again seems likely to lie behind his copying out of so many extracts from French authors – Cocteau, Gide, Balzac, Madame de Sévigné; and to this was certainly added the nostalgia of friendship as he transcribed on to three of his large pages old letters from his translator Charles Mauron. But the largest amount of space was devoted to material of a kind which reinforces the truth of his statement in 1929 that 'I don't belong automatically [to 'Bloomsbury']'. Though an agnostic, who insisted in 1958 that he wished to avoid the over-generous death-bed clutches of the Church, and left instructions that no religious ceremony was to accompany the disposal of his body, he gave up some pages during the war years to listing opinions about Christ and to setting down in parallel columns the four accounts of Easter in the Gospels. He also returned at much greater length to an interest in the early Church Fathers originally demonstrated in essays in *Pharos and Pharillon* (1923). His first motive, to seek in the reactions of St Augustine and St Jerome to the Fall of Rome 'wisdom with which to bear [our disaster]', developed into an 'interest in the past' which embraced a wide range of late Latin and Greek writers, Patristic and secular, and led him to consult (perhaps in the London Library) the magnificent pictorial records of Byzantine Art assembled by Peirce and Tyler and by the German, Joseph Wilpert. 'These fragments', one may feel as Forster sees the London Docks burning in 1942, 'I have shored against my ruins'. The student of Forster's fiction may, nevertheless, derive pleasure from establishing a likely date of composition (1942) for his hitherto not precisely dated story 'The Torque': in noting his wartime reading, Forster mentions the real St Perpetua, together with a Marcian and a Euric – the names he used for his characters in that escapist homosexual fantasy of a collision between early Christians and a Goth.

The end of the war indeed brought Forster a different world. In his diary (15 July 1944) he had referred to his home as 'eternal West

Hackhurst, which I connect with no acute joy'; but when the follow-ing month in the Commonplace Book he recorded a premonition that he might soon lose it 'perhaps by my own death', his tone evinced no feeling of relief. The death, in fact, was his mother's, in March 1945. It was followed, on his return from a trip to India which he wrote up in a separate diary, by a request that he vacate West Hackhurst, whose lease had been extended only for his mother's lifetime. His entries in the Commonplace Book at this period – quotations from Samuel Henley and Ruskin, a description of an evening spent beside Paddington pool, a detailed plan he drew of the kitchen garden at West Hackhurst in 1946, 'the year I was driven out' – are of an almost unbearable poignancy. Concluding a comment on Wordsworth's sonnet 'The world is too much with us' with the remark 'I will be less forlorn', he nevertheless added underneath, in capitals, 'the last entry'.

The Commonplace Book was large and heavy, and Forster had been uncertain where he would go. Providentially his old Cambridge college, King's, appointed him an honorary Fellow and, on the initiative of George Rylands, he was invited to reside there. He arrived in November 1946, and re-opened his Commonplace Book on Tuesday, 13 January 1947, making an entry on the flyleaf to that effect and writing in an elegiac couplet, which stands by itself on page 183 in the original. In fairness one should say here, though, that he found at King's rather more than the autumnal withering which was all that he expected, and to which his earliest Cambridge entries, from the more obscure plays of Beaumont and Fletcher, refer. King's gave him the company of the young, and a number of entries in the Commonplace Book mention undergraduates with whom he formed friendships. It also gave him proximity to his earliest home, Rooks-nest in Hertfordshire, now only 25 miles away: one of his earliest visitors at King's was William Taylor, the second of the garden boys who had worked at Rooksnest when Forster was a child. Forster often travelled down to visit the place and, though no longer feeling the 'magic' it had had for him up until the 1920s, did what he could in 1960 to avert the danger to it posed by the extension of Stevenage New Town. The establishment of this in 1946, and all it entailed for Forster's memories of the past, seem to lie behind his grave paragraph of 1947 beginning 'I have always wanted to share my advantages with others' (p. 172), though he was consciously prompted to write it by a difference of opinion between 'town' and 'gown' over indus-trial development for Cambridge.

The original entries which Forster made in his Commonplace Book between the ages of sixty-eight and eighty-six, and the quotations he copied out, convey a blended preoccupation with change, death, and moments of acute vision which brought him tranquillity and inspired his gratitude. Between 1927 and 1946 he noted four times the fact that his 'three nibblers', diminishing him and distracting his concentration, were 'kindness, lust and fun'. In old age he seems to have come to terms with them: though, in 1961, he watched himself being unable to obey a resolution to get out of his morning bath promptly, he was able to write a final story, 'Little Imber', that year, and his undiminished awareness of natural beauty and increased sensitivity to the literary style of others are expressed with the ease and beauty of a master.

All that falters is the handwriting. One follows it, in the original, with admiration and sympathy, as one might accompany an octogenarian walking, putting out a hand in case he stumbles but not quite presuming to touch his arm. In view of the many dreams, and sentences from them – comic or mysterious – which Forster recorded there, the homage of a rational man to what lies beyond reason, it is appropriate that his last quotation in the Commonplace Book, made in 1965, was from Philo of Alexandria's disquisition on dreams. Having written it out 'with some trouble', he added the declaration that 'I would like sense-perceptions to attend me to the end'. In his diary (April 1967) he noted their decline: 'I can see scarcely at all by my left eye and very little by my right. Total blindness cannot be far off. But I shall continue writing though with little to say.' Only one entry followed this, however, on 6 June 1967, recording the death of his friend J. R. Ackerley (which he had not fully taken in), and concluding: 'I am probably close to the end of my own life, which has been a sucessful [*sic*] one an[d] to the end a happy one. – And now for dinner!' Given the jauntiness of this, it is rather sad – though a sense-perception – that the final phrase in Forster's Commonplace Book, re-opened in November, 1968, should be 'How it rains!' The entry occurs, in the original, on page 291. Nine further pages, numbered by Forster to 300 and with margins ruled, remain unfilled.

Forster was as far from behaving like a celebrity as one could imagine. Yet he had a clear enough sense of his own contribution to literature. If in 1930 he felt a momentary inferiority to Joyce and Shaw, in 1948 he confided to the Commonplace Book his feeling of superiority as a writer to Edward Fitzgerald and Thomas Gray; and in 1962 he pronounced himself to be 'as far ahead of [T. S. Eliot] as I was once behind'. He did not, however, invest his good opinion in the Commonplace Book, inserting a reminder to himself in 1943 to the effect that 'this book and pensées [are] not important and the temptation to mistake them for Creation must be resisted.'

Did he intend, or imagine, that others would read it? The use of its earlier pages as a repository for notes towards his Clark Lectures suggests that he did not; though the note form he employed for his comments on novels, rapid in effect if not necessarily in composition, in no way limits the interest of the opinions expressed. Other material from it, concerned with his response to the area around West Hackhurst when he first came there to live, and just before he left, was published almost *verbatim*, as 'The Last of Abinger', in *Two Cheers for Democracy* in 1951. But one notices a difference in 'inwardness' from his other published essays: one seems to be admitted by afterthought to private ruminations, unstiffened to support any kind of *persona*. The idea of a possible reader did cross his mind in 1961, when he was copying out passages from John Addington Symonds's memoirs, lodged in the London Library. Public reference to them was prohibited at that time, and he felt the need to put what is clearly, from his underlining of it, a request rather than a wistful hope-againsthope: 'The above, and all that follows, is in J. A. S's unpublished autobiography in the L.L. which may not at present be quoted from, nor I think referred to. *Will anyone who reads this remember that?*' And in 1968, when he consigned the Commonplace Book to King's College Library, he must have envisaged the possibility of its being read.

These, however, were late thoughts. It is not easy to conceive that, at the point of writing in 1948, he took his frank examination of his own physical decay (pp. 178–9) to be other than a chastening exercise in private stocktaking, and all in all one may reasonably feel that the Commonplace Book was intended by Forster as a personal record for his eyes only. Nevertheless, of much of it may be said what he said of *Maurice* on its completion in 1914: 'I wrote it neither for my friends or [*sic*] the public . . . but . . . my previous training made me write it as literature.' For someone as wedded to the written word as Forster was, the shaping of experience – what in a disparaging moment he once described as 'putting things' – came as naturally as leaves to the tree.

Thus, when he said in 1960 (p. 219) that his reason for not writing in the book every day was 'partly because I feel I ought to write well and know I can't', it was hardly a few phrases before he disproved his under-estimation, in a sentence whose unobtrusively musical syntax is equalled by the sense it gives of an individual perfectly still at the centre of an apprehended universe:

On either side doors threaten, for I do not feel my peace important enough to be locked in, steps sound on the stairs, there's a faint car, a fainter plane, a doubtful bird, the weather odious since my return, has again clouded over after the thunderousness, and my own hand, not writing so badly, moves over this paper which is 159 years old, and presses this book whose covers have come loose.

One could multiply examples of such felicity; here is just a phrase from the meditation which Forster wrote in 1946 about Paddington pool, before leaving West Hackhurst: 'The fish moved, the trees regrouped, the lovely summer night came on' (p. 168).

Sentence-rhythm is not the only element that gives the Commonplace Book a claim as literature. The book's linear unfolding reveals larger patterns, not always consciously intended, perhaps, but there to be recognised. The quoting of Housman's letter of 1925 to the Master of Trinity College, declining to give the Clark Lectures at Cambridge, is balanced in 1960 by Forster's own letter to the Mistress of Newnham, declining an invitation to give the Sidgwick Lecture (though the reasons are different). Two quotations made by Forster in 1937, from *The Life and Death of Mr. Badman*, are separated by a quotation from La Bruyère which comments on the heart's ability to admit the 'incompatible' appeal of works of devotion and of gallantry: was Forster the agnostic perhaps making a slightly shamefaced admission here, before continuing to be 'touched' by the content, as well as the style, of Bunyan? Twice Forster quotes, from Melville's poem 'Bridegroom Dick', lines which end 'And who can keep the tally o' the names that fleet along?'; the second time (p. 189), they follow extracts from the Journals of Denton Welch, whom Forster admired and who had recently died. Was the repetition merely an oversight? And in 1959, his fine description entitled 'Eastern Sunset' is followed, a month later in time but immediately in space, by an equally fine passage he entitled 'Western Radiance': a diptych celebrating the transcendent surprises of the created world, which is itself a form of creation.

Writing in 1940, in his essay 'Bishop Jebb's Book', of his discovery of the vehicle which, in the event, carried his self-expression along for almost the rest of his life after 1925, Forster went on to speak a

little of what he was then using it for – 'scribbling notes about Marx
. . . copying extracts from Madame de Sévigné.' What would the
Bishop have thought of this, Forster speculated? He was too far
away to have any views, Forster answered. Elsewhere in the essay
Forster expressed his own opinion of his and the Bishop's joint
efforts: 'It would do his reputation no harm if the whole collection
was published, and mine no good.' The transcription offered here
does not include the Bishop's small portion, so readers can make no
judgement; but with the second half of Forster's verdict I am
confident that they will disagree.

St John's, Newfoundland   Philip Gardner
Easter, 1982

Commonplace Book

<u>Western Radiance</u> A month after the overleaf entry I find myself in the same mood wanting to record the same sort of thing: this time the view from the Combination Room towards the Backs — tender green, sunlight, blue and black sky, all in themselves agreeable but pulled out of themselves by the bright orange brown of an advancing jersey. The effect only endured for the half of a second, for the jersey advanced out of sight and was lost, and whether it was on a man or a woman and whatever was its exact colour I forget. But there was a definite statement. I called my colleague Jasper Rose to enjoy the sight with me, but he was too late. He paints, and might have liked it. But the incident drew us together and bred warmth. I spoke of the tiny cherries on the Michael Schweets in the National Gallery years ago, and could have mentioned Arthur Smith poll's canary-coloured shirt which brought its wearer to prison; J.R. of the matted box get which a painter introduces to see the picture alight (the short his, the power lacks) We agreed that we are intolerant because we have too many ideas. What indeed have I secured from that split second beyond the idea of its importance? It dissolved into nothing as soon as the jersey passed behind the stone work to my right, and is now nowhere — leaving me back in the world of boredom and laughter which it can cancel during its passage.   27-2-59

Commonplace Book, p. 228. See page 212 of this edition.

Commonplaces   My difficulty in making them is that I shall not know
what they are about until they are finished. Bp. Jebb seems to
have known and never to have been surprised by any development in his own thought. This, even more than neatness of
handwriting and aptness of quotation, separates him from his
successor, who continues his work after an interval of a hundred
and twenty one years. Apparently, if he had an idea he could put
it down as he had it. But perhaps what he had were not ideas but
certified topics that could be carried about intact. I must know
what is inside me before I can tell what I am after. Perhaps, if I
get through a dozen pages of this book, I shall tell, and my New
Ethic result. Each commonplace will be very short: how pleasant
it would be to feel copious as well as fluid! the modern mind
takes such small flights.

Isolation is the sum total of wretchedness to man. To be cut off, to
be left solitary: to have a world alien, not your world; all a hostile
camp for you; not a home at all, of hearts and faces who are
yours, whose you are? It is the frightfulest enchantment; too
truly a work of the Evil One. To have neither superior, nor
inferior, nor equal, united manlike to you. Without father, without child, without brother. Man knows no sadder destiny. 'How
is each of us' exclaims Jean Paul, 'so lonely in the wide bosom of
the All!' Encased each as in his transparent 'icepalace'; our
brother visible in his, making signals and gesticulations to us; –
visible but forever unattainable: on his bosom we shall never
rest, nor he on ours. It was not a God that did this: no! – Carlyle,
Past and Present IV. 4.

Resentment is a plant of tortuous growth. Middleton Murry patronises and attacks my work, and at first I seem uninfected by this

contact with him, and see clearly enough that he is lamenting not
my troubles but his own. And I think that my feelings remain
friendly towards him, and that I pity him. But the pity is not genuine, and, having led me to take unusual interest in Middleton
Murry, it evaporates. I now discover that my unusual interest has
a hostile tinge, and my heart beats quicker in the hope of him
making a mistake, and I enjoy hearing his enemies speak against
him, and am even happier when he loses another of his former
friends. But for appearing petty, I would patronise and attack him.
Resentment: not a strong or freely growing plant, though its roots
run deep: a small sucker from Blakes Upas Tree. It is so far evil
that it makes for self consciousness, and it can only be killed by
crowding it out with healthier growths. Middleton Murry – to
complete my little circle! – makes the mistake of trying to pull out
of himself what he considers bad.

Change of Plan. It will prove impossible to keep to the bp's scheme in
this book, nor do I find that he has been truly conscientious himself. I must scrap this awful arrangement by topics, and put down
whatever I like, allowing the first word of each instalment to pro-
trude beyond the margin, so that the letter may be retained while
the spirit is killed.

Tristram Shandy

Gravity

Sometimes in his wild way of talking he would say, That Gravity was
an errant scoundrel, and he would add of the most dangerous kind
too, because a sly one: And that he verily believed more honest well
meaning people were bubbled out of their goods and money by it in
one twelve-month than by pocket-picket and shop lifting in seven. In
the naked temper which a merry heart discovered, he would say there
is no danger but to itself: whereas the very essence of gravity was
design and consequently deceit: 'twas a taught trick to gain credit of
the world for more sense and knowledge than a man was worth; and
that with all its pretentiousness it was no better and often worse than
what a French wit had long ago defined it – viz. A mysterious carriage
of the body to cover the defects of the mind

– *Tristram Shandy* I. 11. Insight vitiated by instinct of self defence –
probably typical of Sterne, whom I have begun to read. How did
he discover the art of leaving out what he did not want to say? And

why was it lost again until our own time. Can nothing liberate English fiction from conscientiousness? S. clearly a g^t writer and his philosophy of life almost good and quite good in quotations: 'Look at little me' spoils it in the bulk.

But (now finishing T.S.): what character drawing! The 'humours' or 'ruling passions' are done from within and become obsessions instead of labels. Association of ideas; psychological importance of puns. Disbelief in system: –

It is a singular blessing, that nature has formed the mind of man with the same happy backwardness and remissness, which is observed in old dogs – "of not learning new tricks." What a shuttlecock of a fellow would the greatest philosopher that ever existed be whisk'd into at once, did he read such books and observe such facts, and think such thoughts, as would eternally be making him change sides! – [cf. Erewhon: 'there were some who seemed to devote themselves to the avoidance of every opinion with which they were not perfectly familiar, and who regarded their own brains as a sort of sanctuary, to the which if an opinion had once resorted, none other was to touch it.']

I am convinced that there is a North-west passage to the intellectual world; and that the soul of man has shorter ways of going to work on knowledge and instruction than we generally take with it.

His lubricity very intelligent. Birth then – as still now – an unexplored field for the novelist. Love a tickling feeling. Unreality of time. Supremacy of indecision in human life. All these make him 'modern' – cf. Proust & Joyce as well as Butler. – But he didn't take a view of human life – (his sentiment only flocks of cotton wool stuck on the pulpit).

Floppy yet tenacious. His charm, when it did not subdue, must have given the shudders.

Always a bit muddled in the head.

More I reflect on the novel the higher I place it: attempts to read Swift, Miss Burney, Smollett, place it on a pinnacle. More quotations from it: –

Shall we be destined to the days of eternity, on holy days as well as working days, to be shewing the relicks of learning, as monks do the relicks of their saints, without working one, one single miracle with them?

Chastity, by nature the gentlest of affections – give it but its head, tis like a ramping and a roaring lion.

'Nothing odd will do long. Tristram Shandy did not last' said the unfortunate Dr. Johnson in 1776.

Moll Flanders a great novel of adventure, Peregrine Pickle a silly one, because it was not Defoe's deepest impulse to tell a story. Moll physically a character, with hard plump limbs, which got into bed or pickpockets. So real that the repentance does not seem super-imposed, and Defoe manages to be ribald and pious with equal sincerity. I should not have thought this possible, unless one was writing one's autobiography, or photographing someone else's. A puzzling book – gynomorphic, not one stitch of the man-made. Attractive as she is, the heroine always keeps to the rules of her game, and never tries to capture our sympathy. When she and her 'Lancashire husband' discover each other to be a penniless cheat, instead of recriminating like

Truly, said I to him, I find you would soon have conquered me; and it is my affliction now, that I am not in a condition to let you see how easily I should have been reconciled to you, and have passed by all the tricks you have put upon me, in recompense of so much good humour; but my dear, said I, what can we do now? we are both undone, and what better are we for being reconciled, seeing we have nothing to live on.

We proposed a great many things, but nothing could offer, where there was nothing to begin with. He begged me at last to talk no more of it, for, he said, I would break his heart; so we talked of other things a little, till at last he took a husband's leave of me, and so went to sleep.

Which is both truer to life and pleasanter to read then Dickens. The couple are up against facts, not against the author's theory of moral-ity, and being sensible good hearted rogues they don't make a fuss. Yet all the time Defoe does think it wrong to steal or get into a fresh person's bed. (? thinks it wrong to be caught)
Moll's decency funnier than he intended? How just her reflections when she robs of its gold necklace the little girl returning from her dancing class. No hypocrite. We laugh without bitterness or sup-eriority. 'I spoke with a melancholy air, and said No, the boy is gone for a pint of ale for me' seems consummate comedy, yet part

of its effect accidental (she is about to steal a tankard). Intelligent cockney fun – cf. Reg: Palmer – with Sich is life for a philosophy, and Newgate in the place of Hell.

An untypical passage:

Let them say what they please of our sex not being able to keep a secret, my life is a plain conviction to me of the contrary: but be it our sex or the men's sex, a secret of moment should always have a confidant, a bosom friend to whom we may communicate the joy of it, or the grief of it, be it which it will, or it will be a double weight upon the spirits, and perhaps become even insupportable in itself; and this I appeal to human testimony for the truth of. And this is why many times men as well as women, and men of the greatest and best qualities other ways, yet have found themselves weak in this part, and have not been able to bear the weight of a secret joy, or of a secret sorrow: but have been obliged to disclose it even for the mere giving vent to themselves, and to unbend the mind, oppressed with the weights which attended it; nor was this any token of folly at all, but a natural consequence of the thing; and such people, had they struggled longer with the oppression, would certainly have told it in their sleep –––

Moll still speaks, but scarcely with Defoe's voice. As a rule he says 'Of course I believe in Infinity', like the bus drivers when pressed – and there is no more to be said; it shuts the door more strongly than denial.

To cheat a man, and to tell him so pleasantly afterwards at the right moment, is to slide further into his good graces. A pretentious psychologist would labour long ere he grasped this truth, but D. knows it straight away. What happened to him in Newgate? was it the creative germ?

Form of the book springs out of its subject: Moll turns from husbands to shop-lifting as the years pass, then is punished and repents. Also a slight attempt to make her brother-husband the centre of a plot, but no emphasis falls here in the end: when she and her Lancashire h. encounter him, he is deprived of eyesight and intellect to save trouble, and the episode closes amid the commercial urbanities of her misbegotten son. The tradesman-hu, the legal one, contributes nothing after his disappearance. – Evidently Defoe wrote ahead, leaving a thread here and there such as a child on the chance of requiring it after, but really carried through on his impulses.

Style:

> A gentleman on horseback, and a page with a feather in his hat upon another horse.

> I could make but little of my trade, only at a little country opera house I got a gold watch from a lady's side, who was not only intolerably merry, but a little fuddled, which made my work much easier.

> I say, there was no room to question the truth of it, I knew his clothes, I knew his horse, and I knew his face.

> the dress was indeed exceedingly surprising, perfectly new, very agreeable, and wonderful rich.

> [Roxana. Is 'wonderful' intentional?]

Novels

(1) *Living Character* in a novel best discovered by negative tests. If it is always startling us into approval it is a proof that it dies between the sentences. If a character lives, much else is apt to follow: we are distracted from deadness elsewhere. – All characters alive, up to the edge of the book? Possible? Desirable? Happens in War & Peace, but that has no edges. Many books they might split, so a novelist's sterility may serve him well as well as badly.

Axiom: Novel must have either one living character or a perfect pattern: fails otherwise. (Though what about Moby Dick?)

(2) *Telling the Story:* atavistic element; shock-headed public gaping round the camp-fire, and only kept awake by *suspense* (or by *surprise* and the hope of further surprises. But this assumes a subtler audience, and leads us nearer to literature.) – If story is about living beings, well and good, but public seems equally thrilled by dummies, indeed prefers them because they recall the other stories that lie piled in his mind. ['Oh no, that won't do, it's what we should say ourselves' they complained about the 'Prisoners of War' at Woolaston] N.B. – Story teller needn't pick up loose threads. As long as he keeps his shock-heads excited he needs no plot. Films. Reading aloud – Scott said to seem better then.

(3) *Pattern* or Rhythm seems to me the third great element in a novel,

but these are words easier to use than to define. They have some connection with the Story (which must in its turn have some connection with Living Character). The Pattern may be the Plot–in the Bros. Karamazov they run together so far as either is present: strengthens the book when this happens. Or they may run in different directions, as in Bleak House, where the plot is a complicated maze only of interest to detectives, and the pattern little more than the drifting of the London fog. [Mem.: read The Golden Bowl; one can approach the meaning of pattern by seeing what J. sacrificed to attain it ––– snipping beetroots and spring onions for his salad: for I know he would keep among the vegetables, if only because their reproductive organs are not prominent –––––]

P. Lubbock's Roman Pictures has a competent machine made pattern. He thinks ['The Craft of Fiction' – a sensitive yet poor spirited book] that the aim of a novel should be capable of being put into a phrase, 'ten words that reveal its unity', and so boggles at War & Peace, though he 'duly' recognises its vitality. So Pattern or Rhythm shouldn't be difficult to define for him: for he connects them with the plot, and thinks that can be tersely stated. Must I read him through?

Immediate Past is like a stuffy room, and the succeeding generation waste their time in trying to tolerate it. All they can do is to go out, leaving the door open behind them. The room may be spacious, witty, harmonious, friendly, but it smells, and there is no getting round this. Hence letters to The Times on the one hand and broken windows on the other. 'What a pity the young are not more tolerant.' Quite so. But what a pity there is such a thing as death, for that is the real difficulty. The apartments occupied by the succeeding generation will smell equally in their turn. [Writers whom I find smell: H. James, Meredith, Stevenson: and if Hardy doesn't it's not because his novels are better than the other three: – they are not so good – but because of the injection into them of great poetry.] Ladder of the shocked, starting from Adam. M. Arnold shocked people by Empedocles on Etna and was shocked in his old age by Mr. H. A. Jones, who is now shocked by everything himself and whom I have difficulty in conceiving as a fresh young thing – easier to enter into the youth of M.A. who is now shocked.

Thus the literature of the immediate past cannot free us from the tyranny of time. Its limitations evoke our own, date us, and we retort by accusing it of dating. Impossible to read a Meredith as simply and fairly as a Fielding, with one eye fixed on the author's interests and the other on his achievement. [read Tom Jones & Evan Harrington when I had chicken pox, 19, and felt this strongly]

Virtue, alas, is no more like the thing that is called so than 'tis like vice itself. Virtue consists in goodness, honour, gratitude, sincerity and pity: and not in peevish snarling strait-lac'd chastity. True virtue, wheresoever it moves, still carries an intrinsick worth about it, and is in every place and in each sex of equal value. So is not continence; you see: That phantom of honour, which men in every age have so contemned, they have thrown it amongst the women to scrabble for.'

Vanbrugh – *The Provok'd Wife* III, 1.

H.C.D. – Novels, *because they are written in prose*, all make some pretence of representing ordinary life. This is their H.C.D. – low and uninteresting: but above it they begin to differentiate. Not a bad plan to think a novel's going to be a letter. Think of novelists all writing letters at once in a sort of B.M. Reading Room and getting books at the same time on various subjects.

Ordinary daily life is full of the time sense 'She rang the bell and the footman answered it'. 'The general gave orders to cease firing.' 'H.R.H. pulled the string which released the Union Jack and Mr. Tweedie's monument was at once exposed to view.' – We don't learn why the Prince was there or what the monument was like: to answer such questions requires other apparatus: but we do learn that one thing happens after another, and this obsession with the time-sequence fills our daily life and is the sorry common unit of the novel.

[If the time-sequence is taken seriously it produces a sad effect – *Old Wives Tale* – but not a tragic one: War and Peace depends for its effect on something else. If taken either lightly or instinctively it leads to a slackening of emotion and a shallowness of judgement. Consequently many novelists have been inclined to play tricks with time. Proust, Emily Bronte, Sterne, Conrad, all discovered that he was not exactly their friend, or only friendly for moments, and that he must be kept in his place if they were to do what they wished.]

Old Wives Tale, like Couperus 'Old People and the Things that
Pass' fails of greatness because its main theme is 'people get old.'
Of course they do. Daily Life is the business of getting old – that is
the time sequence as it touches humanity and all creation. And a
great book must rest on something more than an 'of course.'

Then have they also the same H.C.D. as plays? Perhaps I am
altogether on too vague a track, and this pretence of a time sense
may be common to the whole of literature and may be implied
when one word is written after another. Yet it is *not* implied in
music nor in words under their musical aspect: these have nothing
to do with the time sequence of ordinary life.

Robinson Crusoe an English book, and only the English could have
accepted it as adult literature: comforted by feeling that the life of
adventure could be led by a man duller than themselves. No gaiety
wit or invention. (Contrast Friday with Amy in Roxana: or the two
storms). Boy scout manual. Unlike Moll or Roxana or Selkirk
himself, Crusoe never develops or modifies. As much bored as I
was 30 years ago. Its only literary merit is the well contrived cres-
cendo of the savages. Historically important, no doubt, and the
parent of other insincerities, such as Treasure Island. Nearly as bad
as Captain Singleton, and I shan't read Part II.

I took it up by another handle and asked him who made the sea, the
ground we walked on, and the hills and woods. He told me it was one
old Benamuckee that lived beyond all; he could describe nothing of
this great person, but that he was very old, much older he said than
the sea or the land, than the moon or the stars. I asked him, then, why
did not all things worship him? He looked very grave, and with a
perfect look of innocence said, All things say O to him. I asked him
if the people who die in his country went away anywhere? He said,
Verily all went to Benamuckee; then I asked him whether these they
ate went thither too? He said Yes.

Friday then

listened with great attention and received with pleasure the notion of
Jesus Christ being sent to redeem us.

But without surprise. Defoe never really leaves Newgate or Bar-
tholomew Close, though I must grant him an occasional triumph

in the realm of the half-sincere. For the above passage is good
though silly – how silly when we place it by

> his art is of such power
> It would control my dam's god, Setebos.

Defoe never makes that accidental approach to science that is one
of the achievements of poetry. Crusoe's island differs from Prospero's because there are no real savages in it, and not a glimmer of
primitive religion, and this difference is connected with an
imaginative gulf.

I intended to do a note on *Roxana* too. It's as good as Moll, but
lacks the thieving, and consequently suffers in its form, and in its
morality also, which becomes purely sexual and therefore dates. [by
the way why is D. only keen on the sexual life of women? His
approach to men's – in Col. Jack – is quite perfunctory. Only when
there is a woman in the case does he warm up] The raping of Amy
and the storm going to Holland: best I ever read.

Virginia says: 3 cardinal points of perspective, God, man, Nature,
and Crusoe snubs us on each and forces us to contemplate 'a large
earthenware pot' – i.e. Defoe has 'a sense of reality' which she also
calls 'common sense'. Passing on to the dreary Bloomsbury conclusion that the pot's perspective may be as satisfying as the universe if the writer believed in a pot with sufficient intensity. I say
such a writer's a bore merely.

Gulliver is Robinson Crusoe in Fairy Land. People are smaller than he
is, or larger, or horses, and he works out the consequences. He has
a bad temper in the place of R.'s none, and moral indigestion
pushes him towards fantasy in 'Laputa', the most successful of his
voyages. Inferior to Erewhon and even to the Memoirs of a Midget,
because he never succeeds in making the reader think that he deals
with living stuff. Indignation isn't a creative force: 'come you're
cross, and what for?' we exclaim. The book is illustrated with
maps. Did Swift compose these? They are not inspiring.

He said the *Struldbrugs* commonly acted like Mortals till about thirty
Years old, after which, by Degrees, they grew melancholy and dejected
– etc. --

but I will transcribe this passage into my anthology, under Old Age:

here observing that it is Swift at his best. Perhaps too there is a sort of dried poetry in these 18th cent. writers, which is nearer the true thing than the upholstery of Scott. If steeped in the right liquid Crusoe and Gulliver and Tristram might expand – they wouldn't rot. But the Romantics thought it was the right thing to be poetical. They w'dn't tolerate us.

Dates of 18th cent. novels: –

1722 Moll Flanders,⎫ and a gap of about 20 years before Richard-
1726 Gulliver   ⎬ son Fielding and Smollett all get going
                      ⎭ together while Sterne & Goldsmith start
                        off in the 60s.

Border Cases: are these novels? – Pilgrims Progress, Marius the Epicurean, the Bible in Spain, the Adventures of a younger Son, the Journal of the Plague, Zuleika Dobson, Rasselas, Green Mansions.

And if we answer this question do we appreciate them better or not so well?

I can reply to neither, nor to that other question of subject versus treatment, and my temperament is to dismiss all this sort of stuff as the product of the examination-system or as the need of talking seriously which people seem to experience after they reach a certain age. The desire to appear weighty often disguises itself as disinterested curiosity.

Clarissa Harlowe. Have read 1/3 of. Long books, when read, are usually overpraised, because the reader wants to convince others and himself that he has not wasted his time. cf. St. Paul's argument for immortality. Certainly I am bored, but the book is not tedious through repetition – the endless variety and modulations are not in themselves interesting enough – its that. I never mock. Granted her premises about copulation and relations, Cl. deduces with delicacy and truth. Within her conventions, she is sound. She is tragic and charming. Rich. had a tragic mind.

I don't know what to do – not I! God forgive me, but I am very impatient! I wish – but I don't know what to wish without a sin. – Yet I wish it would please God to take me to his mercy! – I can meet with none here. – What a world is this! – What is there in it desirable?

The good we hope for so strangely mixed, that one knows not what to wish for! And one half of mankind tormenting the other, and being tormented themselves in tormenting (ii, 46)

cannot come out of shallowness. cf. Kath. of Arr.

The book raises the question of subject-matter. Within its limits its great. But what limits!

Provincialism. We must remember the mountains that lie outside our territory, but not below our horizon – Tolstoy, Dostoevsky, Proust. They will give scale to our criticism and stop us from being too grave over the Heart of Mid Lothian or pottering too long over Cranford. The great English novelists – Defoe Richardson Sterne Dickens Jane Austen, E. Bronte – are either not great enough, or perhaps not of the particular greatness, that keeps the small fry in awe. Which is well enough for literature, but harmful for criticism. English poetry excels in quality as well as quantity. English fiction, though profuse, does not contain the best stuff yet written, either in vitality or intensity.

To Take the reader into your confidence about your *characters**: always means intellectual and emotional lowering. You try to cover up your deficiences as a creator by turning friendly. Like standing a man a drink that he may not criticise your opinions. Provincial chattiness. Fielding & Thackeray. Scott when he tries it is awful. Always leads to facetiousness and an invitation to see how the figures hook up behind. 'Doesn't A. look nice.' 'Let's think why B does that.' 'C. always was a mystery.' Intimacy is gained at the cost of illusion and of nobility. Nothing has dragged the novel down more [though what about Tristram Shandy?]

Confidences about the *universe* are a less serious matter. Does it hurt the character if the novelist steps outside them and generalises on the conditions under which life, he thinks, is carried on? Tolstoy, Hardy, Conrad.

*Now, what about intermittent knowledge? The average novelist is omniscient when it suits his book, then shamelessly draws a curtain and shakes his head. Condemned by purists. I see no objection if he bounces the reader successfully. Far less fatal than chatting. Indeed this ability to expand or contract perception without being detected is one of the advantages of the novel form,

and has a parallel in our perception of life: we are stupider at
some times than at others, and this intermittence lends variety
and colour to the experiences we receive. Nothing to make a fuss
over here.

[All the same this important subject must be pursued, the academic
divisions examined and a few novels analysed. And the more
general question is raised. Why is it right to deceive the readers in
some ways and wrong in others? cf. The Fiction Factory in my
scrap book, p. 84.]

The Ambassadors (analysed in Craft of Fiction. p.   )
Pattern exquisitely woven. Strether and Chad change places, like
Paphnuce and Thais in A. France, but with qualifications. S. –
sent to rescue C. to *commonplace and commerce* from going to the
bad in Paris finds that C. hasn't gone to the bad, but has been
redeemed and enlarged by Mme de Vionnet: (and ends through
appreciation of this), he gives up his mission and hopes of marrying Mrs Newsome, he fights for *Paris* instead of against it. Then,
out in the country, he encounters C. & Mme de V. out on the
spree – and that they should be ashamed of it and tell him lies
shows him that they are *vulgar* and that the force of his imagination has more spiritual value than their youth. C. will tire of her,
he will go back to America. S. will have lost – and gained –
everything.

As a child, as a 'bud' and then again as a flower of expansion, Mamie
had bloomed for him, freely, in the almost incessantly open door-
ways of home; where he remembered her as first very forward, as then
very backward – for he had carried on at one period in Mrs Newsome's
parlours, a course of English literature reinforced by exams and teas –
[p. 322, 324] and once more, finally, as very much in advance, ...
She was dressed, if we might so far discriminate, less as a young lady
than as an old one – had an old one been supposable to Strether as so
committed to vanity; the complexities of her hair missed moreover
the looseness of youth; and she had a mature manner of bending a
little, as to encourage and reward, while she held neatly in front of her
a strikingly polished pair of hands

[typical examples of H. J.'s power of indicating instantaneously
and constantly that a character is second rate, deficient in sensitiveness, abounding in the wrong sort of worldliness. The vitality

with which he endows such a character always increases its absurdity]

His greatest uneasiness seemed to peep at him out of the possible impression that almost any acceptance of *Paris* might give ones authority away. It hung before him this morning, the vast bright Babylon, like some huge iridescent object, a jewel brilliant and hard, in which parts were not to be discriminated nor differences comfortably marked [p. 67]. It twinkled and trembled and melted together, and what seemed all surface one moment seemed all depth the next. It was a place of which unmistakably, Chad was fond; wherefore if he, Strether, should like it too much, what on earth, with such a bond, would become of either of them?

She had but made Chad what he was – so why should she think she had made him infinite? She had made him better, she had made him best, she had made him anything one would; but it came to our friend with supreme queerness that he was none the less only Chad. . . . . . . [p. 428] The work, however admirable, was nevertheless of the strict human order, and in short it was marvellous that the companion of mere earthly joys, of comforts, aberrations – however one classes them – within the common experience should be so transcendently prized.

Pattern woven – at what sacrifice? Most of human life has to disappear – all fun, all rapid motion, carnality, etc., and 9/10ths of heroism. Maimed creatures can alone breathe in his pages – maimed yet specialised: cf. the exquisite deformities that appear in Eg. art under Akhnaton – all heads and no legs, but nevertheless charming. Is this maiming of the human worthwhile except in the interests of the super human? The curtailment and specialisation of our fabric with H.J. doesn't give a religion or a philosophy, only a pattern into which cock tails and stands won't fit. When his characters say to each other 'But you're wonderful' 'But you're magnificent' they are right in the first case, wrong in the second. H.J. v. intelligent, self denial and timidity with him almost the same thing. His art so sure and dominating that it pacifies us while we read. But it doesn't satisfy us. We still say 'this won't do' and still he replies Perhaps not, but it does for my poor book.

Style. However hard you shake his sentences, no banality falls out. But he is rather apt to have a good sentence, and round it, like suckers, others that are less good and connected with their parent by verbal misunderstandings.

Characters. Main one usually an observer who tries to influence the action and who through his failure to do so gains extra opportunities for observation. (Strether, Fleda in The Spoils of Poynton). Often has a mother in a background and a *nameless* disease. Then the vulgar comics as above (Henrietta Stackpole an early ex.). And other characters such as such an observer can observe – through lens procured from 1st class oculist. Introduce Emma or Tom Jones into a H.J. they would become not unsuitable but invisible.

N.B. How he hates naming anything! Contrast the anonymous article manufactured by the Newsomes with Tono Bungay. cf. The Pattern on the Carpet.

N.B.B. Not a nice character.

and listen to the uncomfortable words of H.G.W. himself: –

James demands homogeneity. Why should a book have that? For a picture it's reasonable, because you have to see it all at once. But there's no reason to see a book all at once, . . . He begins by taking it for granted that a novel is a work of art that must be judged by its oneness. Someone gave him that idea in the beginning of things and he has never found it out. He doesn't find things out. He doesn't even seem to want to find things out. He accepts very readily and then – elaborates . . . . . . [and selects until . .] . . The only human motives left in his novels are a certain avidity and an entirely superficial curiosity . . . . His people nose out suspicions hint by hint, link by link. Have you ever known living human beings do that? The thing his novel is *about* is always there. It is like a church lit but with no congregation to distract you, with every light and line focussed on the high altar. And on the altar, very reverently placed, intensely there, is a dead kitten, an egg shell, a bit of string . . . Like his 'Altar of the Dead' with nothing to the dead at all . . . For if there was, they couldn't all be candles, and the effect would vanish.

– Boon, p. 102–106.

and to H.J.'s reply:–

Round versus Flat characters – types, 'humours'. One of my lectures on people will turn on this distinction. Tolstoy the 'rounder'. And *Jane Austen* – infelicitously described as a miniaturist on ivory. Carves cherry stones if you like. But even Miss Bates has a mind, even Elizabeth Eliot a heart. Discovery that Lady Bertram has a moral outlook shocked me at first. I had not realised the solidity of an art which kept such an aspect in reserve, and placed her always on the sofa with pug.

Dickens' characters are types, but his vitality causes them to vibrate a little, so that they borrow his life and appear to live their own. Mr Micawber, Pickwick, Mrs Jellaby, live, but not in the sense that we can turn them round and see new aspects. Contrast Pickwick with Falstaff.

Wells – like Dickens – doesn't really create: Kipps and the aunt in Tono Bungay the chief exceptions. Author's vitality again.

Parallels between *Dickens and Wells*: Low birth, cockney outlook, comedy, social problems – relish indignation. Put people into their books and deny they have done so afterwards. W's power of observation stronger – he photographs those he meets and agitates the photographs. D. relies more on types.

Flat character can always be reckognised by the reader whenever it reappears. Hence its advantage for story telling. And authors who do work in the round, like Proust with M. de Charlus, often have their minor characters flat – Comtesse Molé. Useful in social pictures. It is incidentally condemned by *Norman Douglas*: –

I spoke just now of the novelist's touch in biography. What is this touch? It consists, I should say, in a failure to realise the complexities of the ordinary human mind; it selects for literary purposes two or three facets of a man or woman, generally the most spectacular and therefore useful ingredients of their character, and disregards all the others. Whatever fails to fit in with these specially chosen traits is eliminated; must be eliminated for otherwise the description would not hold water. Such and such are the data; everything incompatible with those data has to go by the board. It follows that the novelist's touch argues, often logically, from a wrong premise; it takes what it likes and leaves the rest. The facts may be correct as far as they go but there are too few of them; what the author says may be true and yet by no means the truth. That is the novelist's touch. It falsifies life.

– A Plea for Better Manners
(attack on D. H. Lawrence).

N.B. Modern tendency to *pseudo-roundness*. Something contra-dictory or incredible is said towards the end of the book about a flat character, in order to persuade the reader of its profundity and rebuke the shallowness of his previous judgements.

H. Melville

Evil Feebly envisaged in English fiction, which seldom soars below misconduct or evades the clouds of mysteriousness. *Either* sexual and social; *or* a special style, with implications of poetry is thought necessary when describing it. I don't believe evil exists: but most writers think it *ought* to exist and form the backside of their plots: and one or two think it does exist. Dostoevsky. *Melville*:

> The great power of blackness in him (Hawthorne) derives its force from its appeal to that Calvinistic sense of Innate Depravity and Original Sin from whose visitation in some shape or other no deeply thinking mind is always wholly free. For in certain moods no man can weigh this world without throwing a something, somehow like original sin, to strike the uneven balance.

This is playing the clean game as against the muddled or moral ones which were all that Hawthorne (as a matter of fact) knew. *Billy Budd* has goodness – faint beside Alyosha's and rather alloyed by H.M.'s suppressed homosex:! Still he has goodness, of the glowing agressive sort which cannot exist unless it has evil to consume: goodness

> dropped into a world not without some man-traps and against whose subtleties simple courage lacking experience and address and without any touch of defensive ugliness, is of little avail; and where such innocence as man is capable of does yet in a moral emergency not always sharpen the faculties or enlighten the will (p. 38).

Speaking of Claggart, whom Billy kills:

> Civilisation especially if of the austerer sort is auspicious to it [i.e. to Natural Depravity]. It has its certain negative virtues, serving as silent auxiliaries. It is not going too far to say that it is without vices or small sins. There is a phenomenal pride in it that excludes them from anything – never mercenary or avaricious. In short the character here meant partakes nothing of the sordid or sensual. It is serious but free from acerbity.

Don't know what H.M. means, but he knows, and what grand conception of characters are consequently possible for him. *Moby Dick* also a struggle, and of course a bigger one than Billy

Budd's, but Ahab and the whale – what do they stand for? 'Oh what quenchless feud is this, that Time hath with the sons of men.' (Pierre) and perhaps that is all.

Other claimants to Satanic intimacy: the Pan school, petering out in Hichens and E. F. Benson. Hawthorne's Marble Faun an early specimen of it: and Forrest Reid.

Conrad? – scarcely claims. H.J. in The Turn of the Screw is merely declining to think about homosex, and the knowledge that he is declining throws him into the necessary fluster.

Only a writer who has the sense of evil can make goodness readable. I come back to Melville and Dostoievsky. Villains I havn't the spirits to give a separate note to, tho' they could form the basis of a long literary chat. Richardson. Dickens: influence of Germany; on and on.

Melville's apprehensions free from that personal worry that contracts Hawthorne or 'Mark Rutherford'. We are bigger not smaller after sharing them.

Boredom avoidance of by modern writers. Leads them into flimsiness. Bunny Garnett, though he has central conception works thinking of the surface. A point of honour not to be a bore. Boredom less prevalent in the age of faith. Dickens so far modern that he's only a bore when he is bad. But C. Bronte and G. Elliot positively progress while they massacre us. Psychology of B'm? ask Heard. Bores and romanticism – not 18th cent.

Great Expectations. Alliance between atmosphere and plot (the convicts) make it more solid and satisfactory than anything else of D. known to me. Very fine writing occasionally (*end of Pt. I.*). Pip adequate, Joe Gargery not a stick. Occasional hints not developed – e.g. Mrs. G.'s and Jagger's character *does* nothing, Herbert Pocket's has to be revised: But all the defects are trivial, and the course of events is both natural and exciting. Now and then (e.g. in the return of Magwitch) D. grasps at subtleties which would impede him if he grasped them always. Pip's cold disgust and fundamental decency.

Beating heart – instead of good digestion of Scott.

Chilly mist – chill without mist in D. Copperfield. Autumnal England.
And the river – cf. Our Mutual Friend.
Cannot express its merits properly. One of the few masterpieces in my copious catalogue.

I walked away at a good pace, thinking it was easier to go than I had supposed it would be, and reflecting that it would never have done to have had an old shoe thrown after the coach in sight of all the High Street. I whistled and made nothing of going. But the village was very peaceful and quiet, and the light mists were solemnly rising as if to show me the world, and I had been so innocent and little there, and all beyond was so unknown and great, that in a moment with a strong heave and sob I broke into tears. Twas by the finger post at the end of the village and I laid my hand upon it, and said. "Goodbye oh my dear dear friend." . . . . . . We changed again, and yet again, and it was now too late and too far to go back, and I went on. And the mists had all solemnly risen now and the world lay spread before me.

THIS IS THE END OF THE FIRST STAGE OF
PIP'S EXPECTATIONS

Novels

Worse at the end Nearly all novels go off at the end. Exceptions: the artists – Jane Austen, Richardson, Henry James, D. Garnett: the fantasists – Sterne. 'Nor can I go on, without a reflection on those accidental meetings, which, though they happen every day, seldom excite our surprise but upon some extraordinary occasion.' – Vicar of Wakefield. Nor could he indeed. Pity there isn't another convention, which allows a novelist to stop when he's getting out of his depth. V. of W. gets out of his 1/2 way through – after the painting of the family group with Mrs Primrose as Venus all the grace and wit vanishes. Olivia's elopement breaks the comedy, and the happy ending to the tragedy makes all worse than ever. cf. Lolly Willowes too – how silly the book becomes when the witchcraft starts, how worse than silly when it culminates.

Bunny's books are so good because they *don't* go off. A Man at the Zoo fails at the end because the author darent put the lady into the cage as well as the man. But Fox and Sailor strengthen steadily.

Time bears all its sons away unless they look sharp. Something
numbing in the numbing sequence of birth, days, nights, death
and consequently something unsatisfactory in a *Story* which is
essentially a narrative in time, tempered by reminiscences and
prophecies, and must be either insincere or depressing. A story is
the basis of all novels but it can't alone form a great book, because it is tethered to time. Supposed the healthiest form of art,
its real moral is decay, and various *escapes* are attempted besides
the insincere 'they all lived happily ever after' and the sincere but
terrible grasping of the River of Time by the horns (Old Wives'
Tale). Interest the reader in *people* – not in what happens next. Or

seems obvious yet as soon as we have admitted the importance of
people we have struck a blow at story telling pure and simple.
'A story is a narrative in time about ninepins' is an easier thesis
than 'a story is a narrative in time about people', because people
are so arresting that they can survive their own decay.

in the scenes through which the people pass. Or get an emphasis
other than the time one – *plot or pattern* [have not worked this

say – plot intellectual, pattern aesthetic: you have to think out the
peripateia of Bleak House, but must have taste to appreciate that
of Thais or Together.

out yet: arrival of art]. Or reveal or imply incidentally something
that transcends – Moby Dick. Or play about – Sterne, Peacock,
de la Mare, N. Douglas.

Human Nature less mysterious than it was to any one who has the
inclination to observe it. We know fairly well now – not *what*
people are going to do but why they have done it. Man's destiny
will always be an object for speculation, but his nature (like his
origin) is getting pinned down [e.g. Denis Mansfield's conceit is
clearly not an extra defect but an attempt to conceal his imbecility]

Does it develop – except by its power of observing itself?

Aims and Achievements The scientist aims at truth, and succeeds if he
finds it. The artist aims at truth and succeeds if he raises the emotions. The orator aims at raising the emotions and succeeds if he

raises them. This is true even of books that are planned before hand: writer may hope that fire will descend on his skeleton, yet his concern is anatomy, not the striking of a match. Still truer of books that are not planned before hand, but grow.

From which spring 2 questions.

(i) Bad aims – i.e. to make money or give pain to living people or to deceive: only a moralist can assert these always lead to bad results. Defoe's Novels are morally on the level of Opal Whitely or the Diary of a young lady of fashion – designed to take in the ill informed, for money. Trollope wrote for money –   words before breakfast. Joseph Andrews caricatures. Wells in New Machiavelli etc.

(ii) Have forgotten what it was to be.

Her Business is not half so much with the human heart as with the human eyes, mouth, hands, and feet. What sees keenly, speaks aptly, moves flexibly, it suits her to study; but what throbs fast and full, though hidden, what the blood rushes through, what is the unseen seat of life and the sentient target of death – that *Miss Austen* ignores.

– Charlotte Bronte Quoted by H. Read.

Aristotle versus Alain on Character, etc.

All human happiness or misery takes the form of action; the end for which we live is a certain kind of activity, not a quality. Character gives us qualities, but it is in our actions – what we do – that we are happy or the reverse. In a play accordingly they do not act in order to portray the characters; they include the characters for the sake of the action . . . . . .

Four points to aim at in a character (in Tragedy): good – appropriate – real, 'which is not the same as good and appropriate in our sense of the term – and consistent: if inconsistent, consistently so.

Housman, A. E., letter from, Trinity College, 22 February, 1925

My dear Master,
    I take up my pen in a rather sorrowful mood, because I recognise the compliment implied in the Council's offer of the Clark Lectureship, and am grateful for their friendliness and for yours, and therefore I cannot help feeling ungracious in making the answer which nevertheless is the only answer possible.

I do regard myself as a connoisseur; I think I can tell good from bad in literature. But literary criticism, referring opinions to principles and setting them forth so as to command assent, is a high and rare accomplishment, and quite beyond me. I remember Walter Raleigh's Clark lecture on Landor: it was unpretending and not adorned or even polished, but I was thinking all the while that I could never have hit the nail on the head like that. And not only have I no talent for producing the genuine article, but no taste or inclination for producing a substitute. If I devoted a whole year (and it would not take less) to the composition of six lectures on literature, the result would be nothing that could give me, I do not say satisfaction, but consolation for the wasted time; and the year would be one of anxiety and depression, the more vexatious because it would be subtracted from those minute and pedantic studies in which I am fitted to excel, and which give me pleasure.

I am sorry if this explanation is tedious, but I would rather be tedious than seem thankless and churlish.

I am

Yours sincerely

(Sd.) A.E.H.

Preceding 16 pages all refer to my own course *Aspects of the Novel*. Housman came to two and I called on him on the strength of this, but he took no notice.

Train Talks

[Strikes] They all come out like a flock of sheep. (s.v.) I think the army as ad a lot to do with that. Dissipline as its shortcomings as well as its long goings. The very word dissipline means obey. As a matter of fact if some society was to drop about 1000 footballs in the East End of London it would do a lot of good – that; their little tin god, football.

I've been in South Africa Sudan Basutoland West Africa Grand Canary and I've never seen a country in the state of this. And I've been to Turkey Egypt Ishia Minor – –
That isn't the point. Look at them apple trees – God's book apple trees planted every twenty yards along the road where they improve the land in Germany. The people in this country – they ought to be collected every morning in vans – all non-entities – they put away four meals every day and cant produce anything but a turd and that they do with difficulty.

The stye in his eye went right away yesterday and came back this afternoon. Peculiar isn't it. [expressionless woman to her husband re. their child]

He's a funny chap until you get to know him, but when you know
him he's as right as rain [expressionless professional cricketer.]

[culture disapprobant administration and tentative] Ander – a very
interesting figure – something to work on – results – ander – one has
seen her record – we must try to be as human as we can – we can't
make a very great mistake.

Self The attempt to escape from the *s.* probably identical with the
attempt to discover it: that is to say, they are attended by a similar
malaise. Ibsen (Peer Gynt) and M. Arnold are searchers; Indians,
and the more-mysticals, are shunners. The moderns – Sebastian
let us say – regard either movement as romantic nonsense, and

> make no claim
> On life's incognisable sea,
> To too exact a steering of our way;
> Let us not fear and fret to miss our aim
> If some fair coast has lured us to make stay,
> Or some friend hail'd us to keep company.

and would deny the poem's conclusion:

> Even so we leave behind,
> As, chartered by some unknown Powers,
> We stem across the sea of life by night,
> The joys which were not for our use designed; –
> The friends to whom we had no natural right,
> The homes that were not destined to be ours.

or would shift the emotional balance by destroying every reference to an external control, and by regarding it just as one of the
many devices which the individual employs to enhance his own
importance.

Lover A considerate ingratiating person not expected to be an L.
The kindness which he shows and receives is a double barrier
between him and the right to be passionate. If he crosses it, a
feeling of disillusion and disappointment comes over his friends.
Having held him as superior to themselves, they despise him as
inferior and find him lecherous, grotesque, and deceitful.

Note also how readily we deny passion to *all* to whom we are
accustomed. Relatives particularly. The worlds of habit and of

adventure are very different, and we expect the people we meet in them to function differently.

Sketch for a character: a highly civilised man who has deep emotions but has prepared no one to respect them when they come out. Consequently he is reduced to casual lust where he is satisfied and happy until his civilisation has an elevating and redeeming influences upon his bedfellows. The 'better' he makes people the lonelier he feels. He need not be unattractive physically.

St. Michael's, Coventry, inscriptions under the tower.

On Sunday Morning the 6th Sept. 1807 was rung in this Steeple by the following persons belonging to the Society of Coventry Youths a Compleat Peal of Bob Major Royal containing 6140 Changes in 4 hours & 23 minutes composed and called by Joseph Keene.

The unknown Arts, despised by the Ignorant

[also recorded: Oxford Treble Bob Royal to celebrate Salamanca in 1812, and Grandsire Cators on the marriage of the Prince of Wales, 1867.]

Terrors from Ecclesiasticus

All bread is sweet to a whore-monger, he will not leave off till he die. 23.17.

= surely there are so many different sorts of personal relationship.

As one that letteth a bird go out of his hand, so hast thou let thy neighbour go, and shalt not get him again. Follow after him no more, for he is too far off, he is as a roe escaped out of the snare. As for a wound, it may be bound up, and after reviling there may be reconcilement, but after betraying secrets there is no hope. 27.19.

It is a tempest which no man can see, for the most part of his works are hid. 116.21.

He gave them few days and a short time, and power also over the things therein. He endued them with strength by themselves. 17.2.

Terrors peter out here and book all through is more alarming to quote from than to read. The more serious thoughts of a married tradesman. Why it appealed to Richardson who read in it while writing Clarissa. I still hunt for his:

And let the counsel of thine own heart stand, for there is no man more faithful to thee than it. For a man's mind is sometimes wont to tell him more than seven watchmen that sit above in a high tower:

or was it Ecclesiastes?

Inferior to Wisdom, but has its own tart flavour.

Cat in Wood washing its face on the grand new oak stump with amphitheatre of hollies behind it. After a time turned and saw me – cat I knew slightly but not in that place. We stared, motionless, but it gradually lowered its head after a bit. I guessed what was up – it wouldn't take its eyes off mine yet wanted to get them down to a place where they couldn't be on them. A frond of fern was enough and cat bolted.

Mem: do not want to stroke cat's genitals. Didn't know anyone did until last week.

Wee Tots, complains a Mr Ardeen Foster in a letter to the Times, use expressions like

Daddy h'ain't writ home for a whole week
Who writ the last letter?
It don't matter do it?
He done it.

and distress him very much.

And he me for I am in a bad temper this morning and looking round right and left to cause pain: cf. Samuel Butler passim. I have sent Mr Foster an arnonymous post card.

Mrs Stanley Baldwin says: We can be too lady-like – we have got to put our pride in our pocket and talk to more people more intimately. It is up to every one of us to drive things home by speaking to people wherever we meet them.

The Party subsequently proceeded to a rhino camp where the Duke shot a fine specimen of a white rhinoceros. After the Duke had secured the Duchess refused to take advantage of her permit to shoot another, being informed that the rhinoceros was a rare animal and comparatively harmless. The Duchess' action has created a very favourable

impression here, owing to the large number of applications for permits
to shoot a white rhinoceros, which is threatened with extinction.

Times 17.3.25

Chartres Cathedral, walking from S. transept to N. I noted the order
in which the windows came into sight. The Rose of France was
in front; added to it (i) hints of two tiers in nave and choir
clerestory (ii) glimpses of red & blue 13th cent. stuff in choir aisle
(iii) sudden burst of 7 great lancets in apse and 12th cent. blueness-
into-gold in the west. My note is nearly useless. The fact of writing the order down on the spot seems to exempt my imagination.
Only what is seen sideways sinks deep. There is a small square at
Bourges (12th cent. – the 3 Kings) which I looked at because I
thought Gerald Heard told me to. They had blue or green crowns.

Principle? What is principle to me? I am a Pitt. – Lady Hester Stanhope.
Copyright? What is copyright to me? I am a Beerbohm – Max.

[Letter from Max to Lytton]

Dryden's Epistles

To Doctor Charleton,
who ascribed Stone-
henge to the Danes,
whereas Inigo Jones
declared it to be
Roman.

The longest tyranny that ever swayed
Was that wherein our ancestors betrayed
Their free-born reason to the Stagyrite
And made his torch their universal light,
So truth, while only one supplied the state,
Grew scarce and dear, and yet sophisticate;
Until 'twas bought, like empiric wares or
    charms,
Hard words sealed up with Aristotle's arms.

To George Granville
who wrote Heroic
Love and became
Secretary of State.

Thus they jog on, still tricking, never
    thriving,
And murdering plays, which they miscall
    reviving.
Our sense is nonsense, through their pipes
    conveyed,
Scarce can a poet know the play he made,
Tis so disguised in death; nor thinks 'tis he
That suffers in the mangled tragedy.
Thus Itys first was killed, and after dressed
For his own sire, the chief invited guest.

To John Driden
his cousin, of
Chesterton, Hunts.

> The hare in pastures or in plains is found,
> Emblem of human life; who runs the round,
> And, after all his wandering ways are done,
> His circle fills and ends where he begun,
> Just as the setting meets the rising sun

An hour won. Dryden's Epistles read for pleasure September
night windy, dark, warm, and I have read the Epistles of Dryden

Reading these Epistles which have no connection with my work
and little with my ideas, have given me a happy sense of my own
leisure. Who has the necessary time and vacancy of mind to read
Dryden's Epistles for pleasure in 1927? or to copy out extracts
from them into a Commonplace Book? Or to write out more often
than is necessary the words: Dryden, Epistles, Dryden's Epistles?
No one but me and perhaps Siegfried Sassoon.

Public Bores H. M. Tomlinson, Edward Thomas (Bore-Laureate),
Cunningham Graham, W. H. Hudson, C. E. Montague, F. S.
Marvin, Albert Mansbridge (both of these last live in the Welwyn
Garden City), Edward Thompson of Boars Hill itself, though he
cannot be counted among true boars until borne in silence.
Baughan-Williams?

Add to their list; trace their descent Pope says from Heywood
(Dunciad I, 98) from Addison via Lord Morley of Borley, note
the influence of journalistic friendships on the emasculation of the
public mind. Ask the question Is any harm done? Answer
reluctantly Not much. Readers with any guts always manage to
keep them, and to rage over the fate of those who havent, as
Samuel Butler spent most of his life in doing – can't finish sentence. My objection to Salt Junk and Edward Eastaway resolves
itself into a comment on civilisation – comment of an *educational*
nature and therefore of the second class.

[here is important point can't get clear on, except that *education*
must have a bad effect upon the educator. Connection or antithesis between education and creation? what is it? We creatives
are never sincere here and always imply that good work corrects
public abuses – at all events ultimately – leading to another point,
most important: the connection between influence and merit, the

'Christ is widely worshipped therefore he must have been great'
argument, which in the case of Christ is regarded as clinching.]

Time (Thomas Mann):

> Vacuity, monotony, have the property of lingering out the moment
> and the hour and making them tiresome. But they are capable of con-
> tracting and dissipating the larger, the very large time-units, to the
> point of reducing them to nothing at all. And conversely, a full and
> interesting content can put wings to the hour and the day: yet it will
> lend to the general passage of time a weightiness, a breadth and solidity
> which cause the eventful years to flow far more slowly than those poor
> bare empty ones over which the wind passes and they are gone. Thus
> what we call tedium is rather an abnormal shortening of the time conse-
> quent on monotony . . . . . Such is the purpose of our changes of air
> and scene, of all our sojourns at cures and bathing resorts; it is the
> secret of the healing power of change & incident. Our first days in a
> new place, time has a youthful, that is to say a broad and sweeping
> flow, persisting for some six or eight days. Then, as one "gets used to
> the place", a gradual shrinkage makes itself felt. On the other hand,
> the quickening sense of time will reassert itself after the return to
> ordinary existence, but only for a few days, for one adjusts oneself
> more quickly to the rule than the exception; and if the sense of time
> be already weakened by age, or – and this is a sign of low vitality –
> was never very well developed, one drowses quickly back into the old
> life.

– Thomas Mann, *The Magic Mountain*: contains much on the
connection between the perception of time and the sense of life;
expressed from a poetic standpoint though not poetically –

Music's peculiarly life enhancing method of measuring time imparts a
spiritual awareness and value to its passage. Music quickens time, she
quickens us to the finest enjoyment of time.

Thomas Mann a bore, but from a sense of literary duty rather
than personally. The German never gives that anxious look
behind to see whether trails of unnecessary words are not clinging
to his skirts – an anxious look habitual with me, and entailing
expenditure of vitality which might have been employed otherwise – i.e. be very tolerant with bores who have something to
say. If they did not bore they might not say it.

Novel, beginning one: any subterfuge seems preferable, even those
adopted by Lytton for not finishing his life of Queen Elizabeth.

Yet a *middle-aged* novel, i.e. by myself as an M.A., does attract.
Would anyone want to read it though?

Robust alert character of 50 – not sympathetic to the 20s except
through duty or lust. Not hard on the young or consciously
thwarting them, but unable to adopt their attitude. Which was?
Well he isn't very clear. He only notices them occasionally. To
show M.A. as measuring itself against youth: a mistake. A tolerably married pair with no children perhaps. At the end of the book
they are still tolerably married. Often absent from each other
through diversity of interests ———: no this doesn't satisfy me.
I must get nearer myself, but how? how get out my wit and
wisdom without this pretence that it is through the young and on
behalf of the young. Puberty-sauce – hiding the true flavour of
M.A. dishes. I'm not sad or mellow either. Eternal well being
much more the note, into which some little ache might be
insinuated finally, heralding decay and its possible revelation.

Would any one want to read this though? – a public in any good
sense? I see another interesting book, and therefore one which
has no future life except an intellectual one. Yet M.A. is more
than interesting – there is an emotion in contemplating the shades
of the prison house that *have* fallen – a specific emotion. To realise
our passions have become habits has itself the force of a passion:
and perhaps the awe with which M.A. occasionally realises that
his apparent range is really a tether of his own weaving may give
me the clue I seek, though I have to realise Henry James might
be seeking it too [my ability to write fuck may preserve me from
too close contact with H.J. however]. The occasional feeling that
e.g. one's sexual outlook was not inevitable brings a gloomy
reality into the cell – which cell is the proper abode of man and
cannot be abandoned by him after 50, without dissolution. How
again render this readable? for either pathos or bitterness will
destroy the novel at once. How get down the first hand experiences of my life – today I heard F.V. was not going to prison,
helped to lift garden seats, planted tulips, ate Scotch   inside
bread & butter, read Thomas Mann, fear the elm will be blown
down – I might have spent such a day twenty years back, here it
is, and what can I do with it? Digested by my literary mind, it
will tend to reappear as a young man's day, and all the incidents
will be haloed with a spurious novelty and wonder, they will be
falsified by "oh this was the first time he . ." which insensibly

perverts and pervades modern literature, and turns the numerous and fascinating noises of life into a mechanical morning song. Abjure freshness, underemphasise surprise. Each incident should fall on to a thick bed of previous impressions, like the tree on to mould that has been formed by its own dead leaves: the M.A. can be unprepared if necessary, but not surprised, except when he has to be exhibited as a fool.

If M.A. stands for Middle Age book is narrowed and dull, and if it exhales life's mellow wisdom it is flattened and dead. By what handle shall I hold the bloody thing, or prevent, despite obscenities, my troubles approaching H.J.'s?

My 'robust alert character of 50' – I think he had better be lecherous, and get only incidental rebuffs. The curtain might rise upon him and wifie in their bed. Here again, how present this as anything but dreary? And it might fall on him as still capable of a carnal meal.

Nothing indeed can make me feel him anything but a bore. I fall back defeated this time, but, even while writing this commonplace, ideas came to me which I forgot – I, an M.A., I had them:

i That a high threnodic note should be avoided was I think one; the note occurs in Mann and much in Conrad, two writers who face or half-face my problem. [Mann has indeed led me back to think it over]

ii Good health of the set-fair type, illness bounces off disregarded as the railway train pounds away through landscapes that keep repeating themselves

But again one returns, more forcibly than in youth, to one's own life; to the elms in the storm outside and to the particular quality of my fear that the dangerous one will fall and crush my house and my mother, over 70, now listening to wireless in the drawing room, with cat on sofa; to the problem of transferring on to paper experiences (which however ardent and insistent are not new) without giving them a spurious newness and making them booky.

I go on. Antithesis between the *interesting* and the created. An interesting lecture: an int. commonplace, but no novel coagulates in its swish because a novel must begin with *incidents* – living beings are incidents, nearer akin to railway accidents than tones or attitudes anyhow – and accrete round them. "Si vous pattiez d'un fait bien exposé, l'idée viendrait l'habiter d'elle même." M.A. une idée. In concentrating as I must, on my sensations, I mustnt concentrate on them as not-new, but for their own value. Peace peace revolving brain

> The eyes that mock me sign the way
> Whereto I pass at eve of day,
>
> Grey way whose violet signals are
> The trysting and the twining star.
>
> Ah star of evil! star of pain!
> High hearted youth comes not again
>
> Nor old heart's wisdom yet to know
> The signs that mock me as I go.

Elusiveness Shut up always in the same carcase, one is puzzled by this charge, which is brought against me not only by an ill-bred-and-natured journalist Priestley in today's *D.N.* but by friendly and sensitive Leonard Woolf. Is it just that I am different to most people, or that, knowing the difference, I have developed to conceal it? Supposed an elf, I am actually a ——

Bunch of sensations. Listening in the late dusk to gramophone records I did not know; smoking; the 1/4 moon shone as the light faded and brought out sections of my books; motors coming down the Felday road shone through the window and flung the tulip tree-and pane-shadows on the wall paper near the fire place. When the music stopped I felt something had arrived in the room: the sense of a world that asks to be noticed rather than explained was again upon me, my restless and feeble brain was at peace for a tick or two. Then it started again, with lust and the sense of humour, its faithful companions.

Oscar Browning

Lost, lost!

I have been drawn to think rather of the tens who have failed than of the units who have succeeded, and of the ore that lies buried in our social strata rather than of the bright coins which circulate from hand to hand. If a field of coal or of some other mineral, lies unworked or unused, yet it is always there. It may be kept for some future age when its wealth will be more needed, and posterity will bless the prescience and parsimony of their ancestors who refrained from using it. But the human mind is born and lives and perishes. If it is unenlightened it passes away into its native darkness.

– O.B. in Wortham's admirable life of him: a passage recalling that elusive one of Carlyle.

Memory note. Yesterday I forgot two names, A, and B, and tried several times to get one through the other. Today I forgot a third name C, and when it came back I got A also, but not B.

A is L'annonce faite à Marie, a Claudel play which I haven't thought of sometime, but knew well. I could get '. . . . . Marie' and its alternative title La Jeune Fille Violaine, also names of characters.

12 years later I still can't remember Saxifrage 29–8–39

B is a small rockery plant which has troubled me for months. I grow it, know it well and for many years it has been in my mind [Saxifrage: come back at this point just as I was going to say: –] There is a large kind as well as a small; can the dissimilarity between them explain my forgetfulness? Very obstinate, quite a mental worry.

C is Hölderlin whom I knew an hour before, but forgot as I approached the book catalogue in the Union. Came back immediately, closely pursued by A.

Passion and Scholarship may enhance each other's effects. A. E. Housman.
Brahms, variations for orchestra upon a theme by Hayden.

Pensée 16–12–27

Just for a little while

The undigested, that which was not himself, lay within him,
And he felt sorrow or joy.

And he knew that out of them creative words could be spoken,
And tried: which trying softened the sorrow or the joy,
Accelerated the digestive process, assimilated the experience
    to the experiencer,

And he became the same as before, only a little older.

Nothing was added except age, no wisdom, no words differing
from the previously created words.
So he keeps the new thing within him now, hardly moving, in the
hope that it will keep new.
Insults, love given and received – they seem too precious now to
be used for character-building or creation; they came from
someone else or through someone else; they are not material,
but lumps of ice, sparks of fire, and a movement of the soul
that has received them will destroy them.

Proverbs

He that blesseth his friend with a loud voice, rising early in the morn-
ing, it shall be counted a curse to him. XXVII 14
As in water face answereth to face, so the heart of man to man.
XXVII 19
Now all is done, save what shall have no end.

> – Shakespeare, Sonnet 110, Tyrwhitt's emendation.

Where Thought hath thrilled and thrown his spears,
To hurt the heart that harmed him not

> – Lord Vaux, 1576, with the accidental
> profundity of his age.

Transit honor, transit fortuna, pecunia transit;
Mente deo similis, corpore transit homo.

> – On a fragment of stained glass in S.K. Museum.

Love is Enough?

Of course I'm as happy as ever can be, and of course doing no work.
Absolutely none. But what does that matter? Walking dancing, sight
seeing, loving. Everything else is nonsense.

The first time one hears such sentiments, they strike a responsive
chord, the second time thought is awakened; finally they are like
a bell which cannot be stopped tolling and from whose sounds
one flies in vain. At which moment does one listen to them justly?
I cannot decide, nor in consequence work out a philosophy of life.
The reasons for one's horror are (i) jealousy perhaps, but of this
I am doubtful, and think that modern critics often allege it to
forestall possible criticism of themselves.

(ii) irritation at the mechanical when it pretends to be spontane-
ous. Pretends? Not quite fair, for love always seems a new
experience, however often it recurs, and no one ever said of
himself during even his 1000th affair "Les amours qui suivent
sonts moins involuntaires". He said it afterwards, or of others.
Let us say "irritation at Jack because he thinks his box is opening
for the first time". His expression of permanent freshness grows
revolting.

(iii) Thou art the man. One has done unconsciously the same
thing, for an instant it emerges into consciousness through the
action of another, then plops back again as reprobation. And
here I touch a good and permanent guide to conduct. The brain
can educate the heart, and lead us through careful observation
and comparison into sympathy, although it is a draggled experienced sympathy, not that of the responsive chord.

[P.S. Why do I always find three reasons for everything?]

I love me, I love me, I'm wild about myself,
I love me, I love me, my picture's on the shelf,
You may not think I look so good but me thinks I'm just fine
It's grand when I look in my eye and knows that I'm all mine.

Oh I love me I love me and my love doesn't bore
Day by day in every way I love me more and more
I takes me to a quiet place I puts my arms around my waist
If me gets fresh I slap my face, I'm wild about myself.

                    – From a song book seen in a pub at Castle Acre.

Folklore (per C. Day). King Solomon had a valuable dog with a
    chocolate behind. He lost it, called all the dogs in the world
    together and promised the one who found it a handsome reward.
    That is why ———
    There was a leak in the ark. Noah's wife stood with her face to
    the hole. Noah applied his backside. That is why women stand
    with their faces to the fire men with their backs ever since –
    trying to get dry. Noah's wife stopped a small hole too by putting
    her elbow in it. That is why women's elbows are always cold and
    wet [didn't know they were] and men's dry.

Japanese include in their commercial school a course on English
    Humour.

Peer Gynt The main ideas of this great and bitter poem become
clearer at this last hasty reading (3–1–28), though my former
criticism stands [i.e. that it is a poem pretending to be a sermon –
there being something in Ibsen's character and method that
implied a message, though the message really rested on passing
irritabilities, not on any permanent view of conduct and the
universe]

No idea must be pressed, but the main one is that of *salvation by
being loved*, and rightly doubtful whether this would work Ibsen
gives a last word to the Button Moulder also. Peer Gynt can't be
himself, except by being outside himself (as he learnt in the mad-
house): he can only exist in the Faith Hope & Love of Solveig.
He never realises this, he cannot divine what God intended him
to be, and philosophically the poem depends on his having had
the luck to charm a steadfast girl: his character doesn't come in at
all, all that counts is her conception of it.

Solveig (always in the rays of poetry) becomes the mother-wife: she
assumes all that had been noble and devoted in silly Ase: there is
safety in the number of the cosmogonies that hurtle through
Act V: the climax of perfected drama and unanswered questions
throws additional splendour back into the past.

Troll, to thyself be enough
The Great Boyg

don't logically bear the weight put on them, though they are
effective and terrible as reminiscences [note I's knowledge of
how the past recurs as a half sentence during a moment of crisis,
or insinuates itself into an apparently straight line of thought. The
human equipment of the poem coheres] He who loses himself shall
find is latent, but the doctrines of self expression and abnegation
are not easily harmonised

Peer Gynt is always brave, but refuses to fight without a bridge
behind him, and one doesn't know whether I. disapproves of
this or not, though he serves his hero out over it – e.g. a lustful
glance rightly begets an Ugly Brat.

My book *is* poetry; and if it is not then it will be. The conception of
poetry in our country, in Norway, shall be made to conform to the
book.   I. to Björnson.

Lenin to Gorki:

> I know nothing more beautiful than the Appassionata, I could hear it
> every day. It is marvellous, unearthly music. Every time I hear these
> notes, I think with pride and perhaps childlike naïveté, that it is
> wonderful what man can accomplish. But I cannot listen to music
> often, it affects my nerves. I want to say aimiable stupidities and stroke
> the heads of the people who can create such beauty in a filthy hell.

Hedda Gabler fails because nothing of importance has been damaged.
Lövborg's book on the future of civilisation will be duly pieced
together by Tesman and Mrs Elvsted, so it doesn't matter the
author and the original M.S. being destroyed, and Hedda's
suicide is a positive convenience. If the notes couldn't be deciphered *or* were represented as mediocre we should be nearer
tragedy. Hedda has smashed nothing and is nothing herself once
the noise is out.

[Laura Cowie in the quite passable performance made her too
much in touch with reality. She ought to shoot herself in a vulgar
childish fashion and not attempt tragic pitches in her voice. People
don't do such things because they don't know what such things
are. Othello knew.]

However Ibsen may have known this as well as me and have
desired to stage absolute unimportance as his heroine. He certainly wishes to show her as cowardly, restless, and weak.

Sense of imprisonment in that awful interior – aunts over the way,
carpet slippers. Hedda in trying to escape her poverty has been
caught by something worse. Is she going to have a child?

Gerald Heard: from 'By any other Name':

> When you lose free will your compensation is fore-knowledge. We
> must keep a blind world from being burnt at, and so striking out a
> flame it cannot see.

Peace of Countryside too artificial to give me rest now. I used to think
a grass grown lane more real than a high road, but it is an economic anachronism, kept up by people like Lord Farrer who have
spare cash. Something in me still responds to it, and without
indulging in that response I should be shallow, wretched, yet oh

that I could hitch my waggon on to something less foolish.
Eddington's Stars & Atoms have beckoned, but only for a
moment.

The old crab tree near the second chalk pit on the downs has been
blown down this spring (1928) but is flowering as in other years.
Neither sad nor glad that this should be, yet my heart beats to its
importance. My head and deepest being said "We approve of
your heart – *it* is important – but why exercise it over nonsense?
Only those who want and work for a civilisation of grass-grown
lanes and fallen crab trees have the right to feel them so deeply".
Most people who feel as I do take refuge in the '*Nature
Reserve*' argument, so drearily and tastelessly championed by
H. G. Wells. The moment nature is reserved her spirit has
departed for me, she is an open air annex of the school room and
only the semi educated will be deceived by her. The sort of
poetry I seek only resides in objects Man *can't* touch – like
England's grass network of lanes 100 years ago, but today he can
destroy them and only Lord Farrer keeps him from doing it. The
sea is more intractable, but it too passes under human sway.
Peace has been lost on the earth and only lives outside it, in
places where my imagination has not been trained to follow. And
I am inclined to agree with G. Heard that those who do follow
will abandon literature, which has committed itself too deeply to
the worship of vegetation.

Re-reading my old short stories have forced the above into my
mind. It was much easier to write when I believed that Wessex
was waiting to return, and for the new belief I haven't been
properly trained.

To substitute the worship of motor pumps is unsatisfactory,
because it is mere assertiveness, and can never rise out of the
advertisement catalogue atmosphere. The man who says 'look
what I'm doing' is merely reassuring himself that he has done it.
Hence the quantity of empty noises in Walt Whitman.

Next day 8–4–28 I take a longer walk to Honeysuckle Bottom.
The path is blocked by trees that had fallen in the snow. Wild,
wild, wilder than the genuine forests that survive in the south of
Sweden. I excite myself by learning the names of the woods on
the Ordnance Map, by hearing a wryneck and by seeing a swallow
and a bat – all three phenomena early. Think I will learn the

names of all the fields in the parish, although the lease of the
house expires in a few years' time. Wish I had talked to old men.

Modern World Tenacity of literary outlook upon. Farewells and
returns belong to the past. Wireless etc. abolishes wavings of
handkerchiefs, etc. Death the only farewell surviving. We do not
get away from each other as we did. This isn't necessarily sad,
though the obvious literary reaction is a *lament* (safe stunt to
shake head and say 'things have changed'). But it is puzzling, new.
Most of my words and thoughts are about conditions and states
of mind that are past; and such of my fellow creatures as speak
and think are similarly out of date. Those in touch are practical &
uneducated. Specialists. Opposed to wireless etc. are passports
etc. – the desperate attempt of humanity to raise new barriers,
which, as far as it isn't due to commercial causes, is very
interesting.

François Mauriac

C'est notre douleur de voir l'être aimé composer sous nos yeux l'image
qu'il se fait de nous, abolir nos plus précieuses vertus, mettre en pleine
lumière cette faiblesse, ce ridicule, ce vice . . . . Et il nous impose sa
vision, il nous oblige de nous conformer tant qu'il nous regarde, à son
étroite idée. Et il ne saura jamais qu'aux yeux de tel autre, dont
l'affection ne nous est d'aucun prix, notre vertu éclate, notre talent
resplendit, notre force paraît surnaturelle, notre visage celui d'un dieu.
                          – François Mauriac, Le Desert de l'Amour.

La nuit était vouée au vent et à la lune
                          – F. M. La Pharisienne, 1942

Astronomy

Spatially the scale of man is about midway between the atom and the
star. I am tempted to make a similar comparison as regards time. The
span of the life of a man comes perhaps midway in scale between the
life of an excited atom and the life of a star. For those who insist on
greater accuracy – though I would not like to claim accuracy for
present estimates of the life of a star – I will modify this a little. As
regards mass, man is rather too near to the atom, and a stronger
claimant for the midway position would be the hippopotamus. As
regards time, three score years and ten is a little too near to the stars,
and it would be better to substitute a butterfly.
                          – A. S. Eddington, Stars & Atoms

[Of these two commonplaces, the second is at present more to my taste than the first. Love makes the lover unhappy and spoils the character of the beloved through excess of gifts and flattery. It needs must come, but I am against lending it any prestige. I am all for affection and lust, and for sending my mind, not my soul, out into the universe, which appears to be finite and to have an average temperature of 1,000,000° centigrade. See Eddington, op. cit;

Under ordinary conditions matter has rather simple properties. But there are in the universe exceptional regions with temperature not far removed from the absolute zero, where the physical properties of matter acquire great complexity; the ions surround themselves with complete electron systems and become the atoms of terrestrial experience. Our earth is one of these chilly places and here the strangest complications can arise. Perhaps strangest of all, some of these complications can meet together and speculate on the significance of the whole scheme.

If the jazziness of the heavens were recognized, would it react on our attitude towards love? Can this have been nourished by an external, an astronomical, mistake? Ever since men looked at the stars they have found in them a sanction for idealism in personal relationships, and so have been the readier to find friendliness petty and lust wrong. Is love, who still reigns and tyrannises, more than a compound of these two homely impulses, and if challenged as such will not his kingdom shrink? Shrink, not vanish, for there is probably a minority of men who are born to be lovers*, but I think of the majority and I think I belong to them, though too old to be certain.]

---

*Dante one of these, and wise, or helped to wisdom by Beatrice's early death. Disentangling from the beloved early, he made a good job of his idealism and star stuff. He could rest in the faith that he must grow worthier of her, and never experience the doubt that she might be unworthy of him, the doubt that torments all domestic idealists and often leads them into cruelty towards their passion's poor occasion.

Evening Walk 8.8.28 round by the yew wood on the Pilgrims Way that I have kidded myself into thinking terrifying. It isn't. The

junipers looked like men, the yew roots were silvery in the last
light, and resembled skeletons or snakes, a ghostly little plant or
two waved at the entrance of the great warm cave . . . Yet it isn't,
it isn't. And a rabbit moving suddenly in the dark as I came down
– it isn't either. The really terrifying things are microbes & bacteria or even the small trefoil that spoils my rockery. I have not
time to see or feel this, I am too old, I waddle on under a ruck-
sack of traditional nature-emotions and try to find something
important in the English countryside – man-made, easily altered
by man. The knowledge that I use statements that I've seen
through paralyses me. I am condemned to old-fashionedness and
insincerity. George Meredith, my predecessor on these downs,
could upset himself with a better conscience. What a pity the
poetry in me has got mixed up with Pan! Now, the other day,
from dining room, underneath little oak tree's boughs on lawn
there appeared on the down: yellow green strip below, purple
grey one above. They were in such perfect relationship to each
other and to the level boughs of the tree ruled above them, that I
feared my mother would speak. For two or three seconds I had
that rare pleasure an aesthetic emotion. It vanished or became
utilitarian as soon as I realised it had brought me peace, but for
several seconds I was content that the strips shouldn't recall
something else or even be fields. Is this the pleasure trained artists
can command? Their lives ought to be happy. Here, as with the
bacteria, I am at the frontiers of a kingdom but cannot get in.

Vulgarity of great men, if correctly reported in the Press, is staggering. The musician Gustav Mahler – he is, certainly, a German –
says "any one who has emotional capacity will be able to recognise
my development through my nine symphonies." I wasn't shocked
till I thought of myself saying "anyone . . . κ.τ.λ . . . five
novels."

Wherefore then doe you not marry (quoth Margaret)?

In my opinion it is the most pleasingst life that may be, when a woman
shall have her husband come home and speake in this sort unto her.
How now Wife? How dost my sweetheart? What wilt thou have? or
what dost' thou lacke? and therewithall kindly embracing her gives
her a gentle kisse, saying: speake my prettie mouse, wilt thou have a
cup of Claret wine, White wine, or Sacke to supper? and then perhaps

he carves unto her the leg of a Capon, or the wing of a Chicken, and
if there be one but better then other, shee hath the choise of it: And
if she chance to long for anything by and by it is sent for with all possible speed and nothing is thought too dear to do her good. At last
having well refresht themselves, she sets her silver whistle to her
mouth and calls her maid to clear the boord; then going to the fire, he
sets her on his knee, and wantonly stroking her cheeke, amorously he
chockes her under the chin, fetching many stealing toutches at her
rubie lips and as soon as he hears the Bell ring eight a clockes, he calls
her to go to bed with him. O how sweet doe these words sound in a
woman's eares? But when they are once close between a paire of
sheates, O Gillian, then, then,
Why what of that (quoth she)?
Nay nothing (saith Margaret) but they sleep soundly all night.

> – Thomas Deloney, The Gentle Craft (Pt. II)

Again he is but a dwarfe in respect of a man, a Wren, a hop of my
thumbe, such a one as a baby might hide in a crinkle of their buttocks

– comes from the same lively author.

Death an escape into the non-human. That, if consciousness survives,
will be an adventure worth attempting after roads full of cars,
skies full of aeroplanes, and the very heart of night throbbing
with little noises that man has made.

Unless the Pope is very well we each of us say we hope the Pope may
be as dead as a hostess – were the words on my lips when I woke
up the other morning (Oct. 1928).

Ibsen

When we Dead awaken
Which is worse, Life or Art? Life – Ulpheim's marrow bones for
dogs, and Maia's imbecile ditty. Art – Rubek's group which has
killed Irene's soul and his own. ['Some of the strings of your
nature have broken' – 'Does not that always happen when a
young warm-blooded woman dies?'] Ibsen probably does not
intend this question, just an old genius on the grumble, repeating
with good effect the 'kingdom' from the Master Builder and the
avalanche and Latin tag from Brand. But the question presents
itself owing to the pseudo-didacticism which runs through his

work from Peer Gynt onwards, always to the enhancement of its poetic effect. We are left with neither alternative, both are so grim, and the atmosphere steals in and fills up the void and consoles us.

N.B. Statue group. Like Lövborg's book and Solness' houses, must be accepted as a masterpiece and not as a top for an iced-cake.

The three acts are high, higher, highest, cf. P. Gynt and Brand and the subtler downstairs, upstairs, downstairs, outside, of Borkman, the play preceding.

A fine play – he called it a 'Dramatic Epilogue'. Resurrected without being transfigured, Rubek and Irene stand at the doors of their graves. She knows what has happened. He gathers it slowly.

Little Eyolf

A very beautiful one act play followed by two acts of talk, the last of which terminates in philanthropy. Recollections (Allmers & Asta) and hopes (Allmers & Rita) of healthy happiness are unsuitable material for Ibsen, and he has never seemed flatter, but I should like to see it on the stage, the silliness might vanish.

Tags: 'gnawing' in Act I, v. good. 'Law of change', II & III, unconvincing, for why should the brother-&-sister relationship be more exempt from it than any other?

This time sex is the villain.

The atmosphere: wateriness, cf. Lady from Sea.

Elderly possessiveness: cf. J. G. Borkman.

Lustful and chaste fishes

> The adultious Sargus doth not only change
> Wives every day, in the deep streams, but, strange!
> As if the honey of sea-love delight
> Could not suffice his ranging appetite,
> Goes courting she-goats on the grassy shore,
> Horning their husbands that had horns before.
>
> But, contrary, the constant Cantharus
> Is ever constant to his faithful spouse;

In nuptial duties, spending his chaste life;
Never loves any but his own dear wife

> – Du Bartas, quoted in I. Walton.

sent to S.S. as a joke and received by him seriously

The Vikings at Helgeland 5–10–28

The Master-Builder 6–10–28

acted bring out the *onrush* of Ibsen's dramatic method; leit motifs and reminiscences both forbidn to hold up the advance. When Hjordis and D   , Hilda and Mrs Solness sit down for a talk the action continues to stride, the past tickles the present up behind. Most playwrights are bothered when they have to hark back, he is helped.

Since neither wealth nor honour, arms nor arts

Kingdom nor empire pleases thee, nor ought
By me proposed, in life contemplative,
Or active, tended on by glory or fame,
What dost thou in this world?

> – Satan to Jesus, Par. Reg. IV 368

Also seen in Milton is: –

Alas too soon
After so short time of breath
To house with darkness and with death.

Four Precepts of Lord Bacon [Medical remains, 13]

To break off custom.
To shake off spirits ill disposed
To meditate on youth
To do nothing against a man's genius.

Ibsen

Ibsen's Plays. Dates

March 20th 1828 – b. Skien

1850 Catiline. The Hero's Grave ⎫
1852 St. John's Night   ⎪
1856 The Feast at Solhaug   ⎪ Theatre-work at Bergen
1857 Lady Inger. Olaf Liliekrans ⎬ 1852, and Christiania,
1858 The Vikings   ⎪ 1857.   m. 1858
1862 Love's Comedy   ⎪
1864 The Pretenders   ⎭
1866 Brand   ⎫ to Italy ⎫
1867 Peer Gynt   ⎬   ⎪
1869 The League of Youth ⎭   ⎬
1873 Emperor & Galilean – nine years work – finished at Dresden
1877 The Pillars of Society
1879 A Doll's House
1881 Ghosts
1882 An Enemy of the People
1884 The Wild Duck
1886 Rosmersholm
1888 The Lady from the Sea
1890 Hedda Gabler
1892 The Master Builder ⎫ Returns to Norway 1891 and
1894 Little Eyolf   ⎬ takes up residence as
1896 John Gabriel Borkman ⎪ national hero. d. 1900
1899 When we Dead awaken ⎭

Charlie Chaplin popular because recognisable like a satyr in Greek
drama or   in a *M* mystery play, or Punch. Jesus too
is supposed to be recognisable, and perhaps that is why Sassoon
and others have found religious feeling where I find sentimentality.

Rough and Ready Rules for character-reading

(i) Contemptuousness *may mean* mental-idleness; to reject everything as unworthy of consideration makes for a tranquil life *or*
self-defence – though I doubt this fashionable formula.

(ii) Words like 'fundamentally', 'absolutely' often just mean 'not';
unsure of himself or of his meaning, S.P.W. pads out his statement with metaphysical adverbs on the chance of making it
stronger or clearer.

(iii) 'Practically' often means 'not' too.

(iv) B. Russell pointed out to me once that people will say laughingly exactly what they mean, hoping thus to conceal it.

N.B. Probable that I am now better than most people and as good as I ever shall be at this game, and can therefore get to know anyone I wish, provided I am not physically repellent. And perhaps this is why personal relationships no longer seem to me a serious branch of study.

Horace Walpole

Funeral of George II

The real serious part was the figure of the Duke of Cumberland, heightened by a thousand melancholy circumstances. He had a dark brown adonis and a cloak of black cloth, with a train of five yards. Attending the funeral of a father could not be pleasant. His leg extremely bad, yet forced to stand upon it near two hours; his face bloated and distorted with his late paralytic stroke, which has affected, too, one of his eyes, and placed over the mouth of the vault, into which, in all probability, he must himself so soon descend; think how unpleasant a situation! He bore it all with a firm and unaffected countenance. This grave scene was fully contrasted by the burlesque Duke of Newcastle. He fell into a fit of crying the moment he came into the chapel, and flung himself back in a stall, the archbishop hovering over him with a smelling-bottle; but in two minutes his curiosity got the better of his hypocrisy, and he ran about the chapel with his glass to spy who was or was not there, spying with one hand and mopping his eyes with the other. Then returned the fear of catching cold; and the Duke of Cumberland, who was sinking with heat, felt himself weighed down, and turning round, found it was the Duke of Newcastle standing on his train, to avoid the chill of the marble.

– Horace Walpole to George Montagu

cf. Bloomsbury passim – funniness of King's death.

N.B. Gibbon at the Funeral too (Journal)

Eddington (5.1.29). After reading his *Nature of the Physical World* as carefully as I can, the new ideas become more possible to me and therefore less wonderful. They degenerate into mathematical symbols which we are content to use without understanding. That is why I would like to chronicle before they pass from me (like the extra sounds one catches immediately after one's ear is squirted out) the sensation I had on first realising that matter isn't solid, that we know everything through measurements only, that our spasmodic instincts and confusions about time have a value which 'Astronomer Royal' time hasn't, that one thing – the quantum – appears to have absolute existence in the physical world.

Because I understand the thought so little and find it so strange, it has helped me in human troubles during the past fortnight. I'm 50 and don't feel it. And don't need to feel it. I make mistakes, and so do others; in a world where so little is known, how shouldn't we, how should we happen to be friends? Such loose application is characteristic of the proselyte; the adept, who is nearer to knowing what relativity or entropy mean, knows they dont mean that, whatever they do mean. Significant, *E*'s bad taste in poetry and the decay in his style when he becomes edifying. He is approaching literary and moral ideas, which are comparatively familiar to me, and he respects them overmuch because they are fresh (unprofessional) to him. As long as he writes *for* the literary man he is brilliant and helpful, and leads up his subjects again and again. When he crosses *into* literature his vigour vanishes and he identifies it with God.

Coming at a moment when I felt literature and myself were played out, the book has convinced me that there is life in the latter-named yet, while it has

(i) increased my mistrust of thoughtful generalisations about poetry, philosophic by-the-ways, and all that, and even of the fancifulness which, in my own writing, may have justified such solemnities. The seriousness of a large housefly cant be taken very seriously. I don't think literature will be purged until its philosophic pretentiousness is extruded, and I shant live to see that purge, nor perhaps when it has happened will anything survive. I think if a new race could be born, unbothered by sunsets etc., a new literature *might* be born, but the spurious clouds of glory still trail round the writer and prevent his either accepting or rejecting the second law of thermo-dynamics. Writing has had too long a start on science, and consequently can only describe new discoveries, can't absorb them. Lucretius the last approach to a success. We might approach stability if discovery stopped; no use absorbing the molecule when it breaks into the atom, the electron, the quantum. Outlook so bad for literature, both here and else-where, that her reign and her sacred places may be passing. E's argument that since the surface of things and the depths of the mind are equally ignored by physics they have an equal claim to reality is not impressive.

(ii) My own gain of strength: the book coming when I saw I must be more self-reliant but did not see how. Without a moral effort [which I cannot ever make] I am steering through disappointment and betrayals. Thankful for my intellect and its power to retard ordinary emotional reactions until they have lost their power. – No doubt it would not function if I was cold or wretched. I have studied *E.* over excellent fires.

[Pee Shit. Of course all this went fut in a day or two]

Literature as Compensation "I shall make something out of this some day" must have occurred to many an unhappy man of letters, and to *have* made something is possible – Heine, A. E. Housman, Shakespeare avow it. But to cherish the hope implies a vulgarity of mind, the writing habit, the innate though unacknowledged faith that things in a book aren't so real, so that if anything agonising happens the first impulse is to regard it bookishly and blunt its edge. "The higher reality of art?" Yes, it exists, but the above is its counterfeit. – Literature, literature, literature, for the last fortnight I can't stick it, its (1) self-expression, (2) aesthetic, (3) deals with personal relationship, by-products all. I want expression, not self-expression. To add to the number of people who write down what they feel about a sunset or two imaginary characters in a bed together, is an ignoble profession, as soon as one sees its ignobility: all right as long as pursued naïvely.

Well one way and other, the writing down and printing of human words seems doomed to decay spiritually.

What I write down here is itself tainted by the hope of gaining relief from my pain.

Pain always includes insincerity

Sympathy
Self pity } brings the insincerity out.

After writing this commonplace I feel less pain. Anything does, even if trying to be truthful. By describing what has happened one gets away from what happened.

Guinea Worms. A note on these fascinating adjuncts has long been due. On a bitter day, in the upper story of the soulless university of Frankfort, Baber Mirza showed me his specimens and thesis. Entering a human being in a host (the cyclops), the G.W. is liberated by the gastric juices, becomes anything up to   feet long, and bores out through the muscles, extruding at last its modest snout. This must be wound round a match, and every day the match must be twisted, causing pain. If the worm snaps, consequences may be serious, but as a rule they stand the tug. They are not sexless but it seems doubtful how and when they experience love's ecstasy. Successive generations of German professors have alternately decided that they have and have not a nervous system, but Baber Mirza has discovered a ganglion, and upset his own professor. – I think, by the way, that the water of a great tank at Bijapur was shown to me as infected. – B.M.'s specimens were like transparent yellowish pieces of string.

Bloomsbury, hopes W. J. Turner, will not enjoy Schnabel, a pianist whom he enjoys himself. Why drag the place in, I wonder? I suppose because it is the only genuine *movement* in English civilization, though that civilisation contains far better and more genuine individuals. The other movements are anti-Bloomsbury and self-conscious/cheap, envious – wh. Bl. as a movement is not, being composed of people who hold similar opinions and dont quarrel violently with one another – But unkind, despite irritable protests to the contrary; Orlando regards the centuries of flesh and spirit as fresh fuel for her bonfire, and death can only be laughed at (I remember their laughter at Massingham's) or adorned with a tasteful garland like Lady Strachey's. – Its contempt of the outsider plays a very small part of its activity, and rests on inattention rather than arrogance. Once convinced that he is not a figure of fun, it welcomes and studies him, but the rest of humanity remains in a background of screaming farce as before. Meanwhile the intellect – thinking and talking things out – goes steadily ahead, 'things' looking rather like small Xmas trees when they come into the room, and trees minus their leaves and decorations when they are carried out. The final bareness isn't tragic, the horrors of the

universe being surveyed in physical comfort, and suffering apprehended only intellectually.

Essentially *gentlefolks*. Would open other people's letters, but
wouldn't steal, bully, slander, or blackmail like many of their
critics, and have acquired a culture in harmony with their social
position. Hence their stability. Contrast them with (a) gamindom
– Joyce, D. H. Lawrence, Wyndham Lewes (b) aristocracy who
regard culture as an adventure and may at any moment burn their
tapering fingers and drop it. Academic background, independent
income. Continental enthusiasms sex-talk, and all, they are in the
English tradition.

I dont belong automatically – from 1916 the gulf was bound to
widen. And I couldn't go there for any sort of comfort or sympathy.

G. Heard, the Ascent of Society, Ch. V, tho dealing with the
wider subject of intellectualism explains *Bloomsbury* without de-
nouncing it – never done before, I think. Why are intellectuals so
irritated at emotionalism? because they are not wholly intellectual.

Their intelligence permits them to see the future as the emotionalists
cannot but their own emotions will not let them give the true reason
of their fear at what they see. They will not face or at least give
expression to the fact that what lies before us is a revolution and that
the only choice before us is a metamorphosis so drastic as to the
individualist to be scarcely distinguishable from death.

The irritation is 'a by-product, a strain-symptom'.

cf. also in this connection a letter from Frances Marshall, a
Bloomsbury hanger on in which she complains of Miss MacMunn
as having a strong streak of the octopus in her, and making a bee
line for one's soul at the first opportunity. Fear of being interfered
with emotionally soon turns to hysteria.

G.H. argues that the intellectual always ascribes intellectual
motives to his opponents and argues that even if the emotionalist
rank and file don't know what they are up to, their leaders do.
26–2–29

Cambridge [in the above sense] attracts my heart more but depresses
me more because as soon as the train slackens at that eel-like platform it's settled who I can know, who not. The two universities

disintegrate and degrade their towns. Servile, extortionate manual workers and dons and undergraduates jigging in their midst.

Kindness and the Rules of the Game

Civis   'You oughtnt to treat me like this – I've been so considerate.'

Savage 'Have you? I forget.'

'Which, when I have picked myself up, had I better aim at? – Hold to my creed and be kind, or learn my lesson and be cautious?'

'You will do one or the other. Don't trouble to decide which, for that depends on things you can't control.'

'I love you. I couldn't love my own sort, who played properly. Did you ever love me?'

'I forget.'

Note Kindness' aggrieved and auntish tone – cattish if Lion gave her the chance.

Note my inclination and D.H.L.'s to sneer at her.

Difficult to grasp anything about the dialogue except that it will be repeated until one can rise no more.

Between two tamed creatures there can be no passion.

Until we are tamed we cannot be civilised, and as soon as we are civilised we revolt from civilisation.

'The soul of man is a dark vast forest, with wild life in it.' I hope it is vast. The rest is undeniable.

I'm a tough old bird if I get through this.

Not to repent.

Not to expect compensation.

Not to recognise the life-spirit, which is D.H.L.'s compensation dodge.

Self-pity? I see no moral objection to it, the smell drives people away, but that's a practical objection, and occasionally an advantage.

Pigmies (Schwartz, The Kalahari)

 1. Nicephorus [Hist. Eccl. XII. 37] states that in the time of Theodosius there was a pigmy in Egypt no higher than a partridge, who was very prudent, with a sweet clear voice and of a generous mind.

 2. The Ainu of Yezo slaughtered the little people with clubs, and they tell how these unfortunate victims raised their eyes to heaven as they were dying and cried: "Why were we made so small?"

Place (i) Bertie Russell points out in his A.B.C. of Relativity that it's only because the large objects on the earth happen not to move that we have the idea that we're in a definite *Place*. Yes. And:

if an object I knew (e.g. the covered bazaar at Alexandria) is destroyed, it remains vivid; but if it is transformed or rearranged (Stevenage Ry Sta or the paths on St George's Hills) I start wondering what it 'really' is, and get the same paralysis that I get with a change of clocks at a frontier. This bewilderment shows that our familiar notions are only local in their application.

cf. also this: a false idea of a place grows dim when we see that place. If I had never been to Aligarh I should still remember the impression Masood originally conveyed of it to me. And I once dreamt of a low-lying sallow city I called 'Perugia' which remained distinct till I saw the geographical Perugia. If I had happened to call it Capua which I haven't yet seen, it would be clear today. – This leads us more into psychology than physics, and further still is: Our desire to remember a dead or ailing friend 'as he really is.'

'Give me Permanency!' says Man. And limits his intelligence by the request.

(ii) Baby-leg-land, leg-land, bike-land, car-land, train-land and night-train-land with which in practise is steamer-land are roughly speaking the five countries into which a man divides the world he has visited. The extremes are the distended lanes of childhood and the telescoped cities of a trans-continental express. Map-geography is a convention which is useful for practical purposes but has nothing to do with experience.

It does not matter what men say in words so long as their activities are controlled by settled instincts. The words may ultimately destroy the instincts. But until this has occurred, words do not count.

                [Whitehead, Science & the Modern World.]

Thought and Logic. I possess the latter faculty. The former, classed by
G. Heard as an emotion, has only been serviceable twice, once in
a paper on Dante, written over 20 years ago, and once, more
recently, in 'Anonymity.' Here there was a process, as of a living
thing developing, it was a pleasure to create, and a satisfaction
afterwards, and the detection of flaws in my argument left the
general cleanliness and beauty unaffected. Why has this noble
quality come so seldom to me? After 'pure creation', from which
it is separated by a boundary I can't yet define, it is the most
desirable quality for a writer, and, unlike pure creation, it ought
to strengthen as he grows older. It is impressive without being
pompous: that separates it from rhetoric. It isn't the same as
thinking things out, which only demands acuteness and pertina-
city. It is a single organic advance, not a series of isolated little
attacks. It may survive when there is nothing left in the universe
either to be fanciful over or to criticise. Since reading G.H.'s MS
(in parts a fine example of it) I've seen it more vividly than ever
before. Stranded last year for an hour in Raphèle sta, without a
book or possible human being I said to myself 'I will think', and
when nothing occurred except a sort of sweaty discomfort I tried
to *think out something*: it was whether I believed in education or
not. Again nothing occurred and I was reduced to gazing at
posters of French colonial enterprise, and noting their slight hints
at native women for settlers or troops. Charles Mauron said afterwards that all this was inevitable – and he can think in my present
sense of the word. I hoped to be left with the feeling my mind
had progressed, but see now that it can't progress without producing, which brings us back to Literature.

[Something slightly 'acceptable' and therefore suspicious in the
above. I don't feel sure it'll wear well except as regards *Dante* and
Anonymity which are genuine examples of something I haven't
otherwise achieved.]

Almost: When looking at scenes or remembering them I have almost
command of a crowd of images and comparisons which would
seize and fix them, I am next door to poetry.

Edward Carpenter [Dec. 1929, after conference with his Lit Exors]
Astonishing how he drains away. Poems I actually copied out for
myself a few years back now seem thin whistling rhetoric. I know

that the spirit is there but it has got into the wrong skin. Gerald
Heard summed him up the other day at my request, and most
devastatingly: 'An echo. Walt Whitman was the first who blew
through that hollow reed. Morris, J. A. Symonds – there you
have the whole. He knew nothing, he couldn't think. "Civilisation, its Cause and Cure" – how can you conceive such a book
having a huge circulation? He knew *nothing* about civilisation. He
was always a clergyman, you were *not* to wear boots but sandles,
you were *not* to go to church, and he was always finding mystic
reasons for doing what he wanted e.g.   I suppose there
was something there, but as soon as one touches it, it's gone. Slow
but steady decline of power'.

The verdict of history, I suppose, and our so called knowledge of
the past is made up of such verdicts.

Medium, not Personality; in which impressions and experiences combine in peculiar and unexpected ways; is to be looked for in a
great poem. "Impressions and experiences which are important
for the man may take no place in the poetry, and those which
become important in the poetry may play quite a negligible part
in the man, the personality." This [T. S. Eliot, Sacred Wood,
p 52] seems sound, but "emotions which he has never experienced
will serve his turn as well as those familiar to him" is surely nonsense. He recovers in "Poetry is not a turning loose of emotion,
but an escape from emotion; it is not the expression of personality,
but an escape from personality. But of course only those who
have personality and emotions know what it means to want to
escape from these things."

Eclecticism in doctrine doesn't imply moderation in action. The
English church of Elizabeth may have held to the via media, but
it set fire to the county on either side of it when it got the chance.

Sympathy declines after exercising it too much, and less and less exercise is required as we grow older and start 'saving ourselves.'
F. Vic's second child has nearly died too, yet all I can feel this
time is 'more expense for me.'

Young people keep me young unless they are the sons of my
contemporaries; then I regard them as spies.

My vitality goes more and more in keeping myself young. When I was young it went in creating.

Visit to Virginia, prospects of, not wholly pleasurable. I shall watch her curiosity and flattery exhaust themselves in turn. Nor does it do to rally the Pythoness.

Civilisation (i) Tchehov's view:

Not more than a yard from me lay a homeless wanderer; in the rooms of the hostels and by the carts in the courtyard among the pilgrims some hundreds of such homeless wanderers were waiting for the morning, and further away, if one could picture to oneself the whole of Russia, a vast multitude of such uprooted creatures was pacing at that moment along highroads and side-tracks, seeking something better, or were waiting for the dawn, asleep in wayside inns and little taverns, or on the grass under the open sky . . . . . As I fell asleep I imagined how amazed and perhaps even overjoyed all these people would have been if reasoning and words could be found to prove that their life was as little in need of justification as any other.

                                                                – Uprooted.

(ii) Walter S. Gifford, President, American Telephone & Telegraph Co.'s view:

Today practically anybody, anywhere, can talk at any time of the day or night with anybody anywhere else.

                              – Address to Chicago Chamber of Commerce

"Untake thy silly-willy with a vengeance." – dream after lunch, 19–1–30.

Sympathy attracted by having neither too few misfortunes nor too many. Up to a point, people's interest increase when one's in trouble, they feel it a shame that so radiant a being should be harrassed and put themselves out to preserve one's charms. But the point once past, they quickly chorus 'This is too much,' and feel that since there is a great deal of sorrow in the world it may as well be piled on a single victim. It is safer to sprain a wrist than break a leg, and to walk on the golf-links after convalescence and get a second leg broken by a stray ball – as was done by a friend of Joe's – is to become a permanent comic, for whom nothing can be too painful, and whose death-bed agonies raise a hearty laugh.

Those who find human relationships important ought to work out this one. S. Butler was too crude about it, for moderate misfortunes and ailments certainly add to one's popularity.

Mistakes The preceding commonplace, though written with slowness and care contains three at least, and I can't get through the simplest letter without erasions – many of them being attempts at a wrong word – e.g. earlier in this very sentence I started to write 'last' in place of least. Some would say it's a case for a doctor, and my changes in handwriting another – it always goes sprawly. However to carry on is best, especially as there is no agreement as to what old age ought to be like. Mine will be hazy and fumbly, bad people may get hold of me, either through startling me or pandaring to what survives of my emotions. My mother's old age consists in giving orders.

Idea of Mother and son. She dominates him in youth. Manhood brings him emancipation – perhaps through friendship or a happy marriage. But the mother is waiting. Her vitality depends on character, and asserts itself as the sap drains out of him. She gets her way and reestablishes his childhood, with the difference that his subjection is conscious now and causes him humiliation and pain. Is her tyranny conscious? I think not. Could the same relationship occur between father and daughter? No.

A ruthless and unpleasant writer might make something of this. But two people pulling each other into salvation is the only theme I find worthwhile. Not rescuer and rescued, not the alternating performances of good turns, but

It takes two to make a Hero.

That's the only serious theme worth treating, though if pressed beyond personal relationships we get either to patriotism or civic cooperation, those rival evils.

Mild February Afternoon 3–2–30: Bone raking moss out of lawn. Wonham with ferret and nets in the wood. Scott hacking a fallen elm. Damon and his sheep who start lambring.

I walked about, so quiet and peaceful among them, and they liked it too.

Raw February Afternoon 2–30: Walked a new way across the mouth
of Cold Kitchen, saw no one (except Policeman Evans), felt
sad and a little frightened all the time, noticed nothing, countryside seems down and out between civilisation and its own late
storms. The defences seem pierced at last.

Reading Vaughan:

> Thou art a moon-like toil: a blind
> > Self-posing state:
> A dark contest of waves and wind:
> A mere tempestuous debate:
>
> Thou art a toilsome mole, or less,
> > A moving mist.
> But life is, what none can express,
> A quickness, which my God hath kissed

But reading F. L. Lucas also:

> Your quiet altar after all was best,
> > Fair sisters. Louder faiths grow cold.
> Not you forged earth's foundations: but you blessed
> > What flowers her deserts hold.
> Not yours alone is power that does not perish;
> But yours is Youth. Only what your hands cherish
> > Grows not old.

Felt after night came that the drawing room was sheltering me
from something I called "the night" because my imagination
could not grasp the terror of it. No one minds the Surrey night or
even the world-night: they are only relics.

Thought, after reading little Cyril Conolly, of the new
generation knocking at the door, and wondered whether it is
more than a set of knuckle bones.

Fallen Elms – have seen so many of these in the past week that I
ought to be able to describe them in a few vivid words. All the
black outer twigs are crashed and stamped into the earth and
stain it like the ghost of a tree. The wood, where it splits, suggests
commonness, where it is sawn and shows ruddy-chocolate surrounded by white – distinction. R. Bray showed me the sawn top

of a great one used as a table, polished, the old fellow what walks
on two sticks says that they were put to many uses when he was
young, only coffins now. Three fell across our garden, 17(?) in
Hackhurst Lane, one a double elm or cuckold (Broyd) which
broke the steps, one of the pair by the drive gate has shown a
surround of cracks as if it will heel over into the field, one leans
across the public path into the wood, and rests on three ashes.

To mind the death of trees is a characteristic of old age. I hadnt it
3 years ago when I had the great oak in the wood, the oldest
living thing I have ever owned, cut for fuel. I began to regret it
as soon as it fell, and now am quite incredible to myself. 'Hide me
oh my Saviour, hide' but I gave Him up to death thirty years at
least before His time. He would have outlived me and should
have done. The tree planting I have done since is partly expiatory,
the crashes of the last two months drive my imbecillity home. Yet
my crime was a young man's; it's only when age threatens that
we start wanting to screen ourselves from the tempest. [N.B. age
and death are more distinct than they used to be, owing to the
war]

The flesh of *Fallen Ashes* is beautifully pink here and there when
sawn and smells different to the elms, though here again I cant
describe or even remember the difference.

L'Heroism consiste à ne pas permettre au corps de renier les
    imprudences de l'esprit

runs an epigram of Maurois which bowled me at the first reading;
then, as so often, I thought 'not really worth writing down.' He
is only saying that *Byron* acted up to his theories. But he has
written a very fine biography in which one always feels secure
over the facts and has not to depend on the flashes of intuition
cultivated by the Strachey school.

[My unkind anecdote of Maurois: When he was Clark Lecturer at
Cambridge a couple of years back, I told him the following
anecdote:

A former inmate of Goldie's rooms used to give a party once a year,
open the big room, which was full of valuable china, and, for the

further delight of his guests, arrange with the dairy man who grazed Scholars' Piece that the cows should be pretty colours.

Next day I met two of his disciples, Robert de something and Julien Green. He had introduced my anecdote into a lecture, but applied it to Oxford. 'He has such a wonderful sense of English life – that is of course a thing which would have happened at Oxford but never at Cambridge' said they.]

Evil to interest must triumph over something. Have been trying to read Solent Wolf again – duck-weed and spittle unrelieved. Perhaps Joyce is readable for his inwit of agenbite as T.E. suggested: his intensity of remorse. Only to dribble upon a dribbling universe is monotonous, nothing's destroyed even if it *is* the slime underlying all evil. No wonder that those Hardyesque fungi, the Powys, have never got anywhere. Patiently advertising their own decay and searching the hedgerows for simples. Can't go to bed with anyone, only talk and think it over, don't know that lust and tenderness bring relief. Tenacity without vitality. Semivirous sextons.

The difficulty of growing old is that one doesn't know what to do, through want of experience, helplessly watches the waves breaking and civilisation growing older at the same rate as oneself. In youth experience is unnecessary: in age we count on it and, generally speaking, only act successfully when it is to hand. Inverted adolescence. The decay of our powers more puzzling than their birth, because our consciousness was born with them, but here it lags behind, looking at the symptoms and unable to decide which is to be taken seriously. Apart from its discomfort, its so baffling.

Collapsing Countryside 27-3-30 Owing to shortage of keepers, rabbits multiply and when short of food eat the bark of twenty-foot trees and kill them, and flish! a grey squirrel plumps past me on the downs, and the S.P.G. and C.M.S., very naturally urging children to pick primroses to save the heather, are dropped on by the Bp. of Gloucester in the Times. Since the storm, there has seemed too little of Surrey to hide me, even at night, or to go round. While I sat in rooms or in foreign trains and steamers the England I loved has crumbled. I wish I did not regret her.

J. B. Priestley's coarse joyless face, into which he caught me looking. It took on a dreary expression; he knew from experience what I was seeing.

That Meredith doesnt sell at all and Conrad only a little and Arnold Bennett no longer well and Hardy as well as ever was the tenor of their talk, also how Mrs Belloc Lowndes returned all her luncheon bills to the Income Tax authorities and claimed rebate on the ground they were necessary expenses in her work. The authorities saw the justice of her argument; unless you entertain, you cannot sell. Walpole claims for his London flat only.

D. H. Lawrence's Frieda, seen last week after an interval of 15 years, still uttered the old war cries [that people didnt *live*, that England was done for, that she and her husband had their fights out, that they were trumpets calling to the elect] but her manner was nervous, almost propitiatory, and I realise that she, and perhaps he, were as afraid of me as I could have been of them. There was something both pretentious and rotten about her, as in his pictures. She would rebuke me for disobeying the Message and then stop and watch me with a shy smile. Very proud of having no friends, equally so of her apparatus for collecting and compelling them. – And the tripe without the poetry was not attractive, and I retired unashamed into my academic tower. He and she haven't had a bad life, but it seems vulgar when they proclaim it as an Ensample and a Mystery.

Altogether a week of ladies. Their insincerity and desire to please intrigue me and fascinate F.L.L., who now prefers their company to men's: it is possible to be wrong and say so without feeling humiliated.

[later note]

Women have got out of hand: is the burden of his Assorted Articles and I think they have. Twenty years ago I thought 'It's unpleasing to me but it won't go further' and spoke with false enthusiasm of women's rights. She shall have all she wants, I can still get away from her, I thought. I grudged her nothing except my company. But it has gone further, like the degradation of rural England: this afternoon (Sunday in April) all the young men had women with them in far-flung cameraderie. If women ever wanted to be by themselves all would be well. But I don't believe they ever want to be, except for reasons of advertisement, and their instinct is never to let men be by themselves. This, I begin to see, is sex-war, and D.H.L. has seen it, in spite of a durable marriage, and is far more on the facts than Bernard Shaw and his Life Force.

Read the D. H. Lawrence letters. Gosh what an ungenerous soul It's all very well to put instinct above intelligence . . . . but see to weather cockery it leads.   – T. E. S. to K. W. Marshall

[much later note]

Tennyson and Trees

> Old warder of these buried bones
>   And answering now my random stroke
>   With fruitful cloud and living smoke,
> Dark YEW, that graspest at the stones
>
> And dippest towards the dreamless head,
>   To thee too comes the golden hour
>   When flower is feeling after flower:
> But sorrow – fixt upon the dead,
>
> And darkening the dark graves of men –
>   What whisper'd from her lying lips?
>   Thy gloom is kindled at the tips,
> And passes into gloom again.

[not in first edition of I.M.]

SPINDLE TREE Wearing his wisdom lightly, like the fruit
Which in our winter woodland looks a flower.

> Flow down, cold rivulet, to the sea,
>   Thy tribute wave deliver:
> No more by thee my steps shall be
>   For ever and for ever.
>
> Flow, softly flow, by lawn and lea,
>   A rivulet then a river:
> No where by thee my steps shall be
>   For ever and for ever,

But here will sigh thine alder tree
And here thine aspen shiver:
And here by thee will hum the bee
For ever and for ever.

A thousand suns will stream on thee
A thousand moons will quiver:
But not by thee my steps shall be
For ever and for ever.

—

Far in a western brookland
That bred me long ago
The poplars stand and tremble
By pools I used to know.

There, in the windless night time,
The wanderer, marvelling why,
Halts on the bridge to hearken
How soft the poplars sigh.

He hears: long since forgotten
In fields where I was known,
Here I lie down in London
And turn to rest alone.

There, by the starlit fences,
The wanderer halts and hears
My soul that lingers sighing
About the glimmering weirs.

Le Cid 1636. Action: heroine's (Chimène) father (comte) gives a
'soufflet' to hero's (Rodrigue) father (Diège). Hero kills heroine's
father. She demands vengeance while confessing her love, but he
delivers Seville from the Moors before the king has decided to
grant it her. She faints on believing him dead, but explains it
away – excess of joy, or mortification because his death is a glorious one. Demands vengeance again. Believing he has been killed
in a duel, she reveals her love. The king advises them to wait.

Examen du Cid 1660, after the unities have been tightened up:
hero and heroine pursue duty without renouncing their love,
which elevates them above the antique. They are brought together
but do not marry, perhaps do not intend to, in spite of King's
advice (Il est historique et a plû en son temps: mais bien surement
il déplairaît au nôtre) [instances of an author's timidity and

dishonesty when taxed with impropriety, for that Rodrigue and Chimene *will* marry is plain] True, he visits her twice after the murder, but 'leur conversation est remplie de si beaux sentiments' that the audience isn't shocked, and can be justified by Aristotle. King acts feebly, but had not been on the throne long. Superfluity of Infanta admitted.

Unity of time (24 hours) 'presse trop les incidents' Although Moorish invasion may follow d. of Comte closely, Rodrigue might well expect 2 days rest after it before his duel with Sanche. Also Chimène's two demands for vengeance suggest disloyal impatience. 'C'est l'incommodité de la règle; passons à celle de l'*unité de lieu*.' Seville: not as in history, but a town on a river necessary because the Moors could invade quicker from the sea than by land. Does the tide rise so high on the Guadalquiver? Let us hope so: it does on the Seine. Although the scenes all are in Seville, they change – and here follows a very curious passage [quoted in Ker, Drydens Essays I xlvii] Act I, scenes 3 & 4 bother Corneille. If Diège gets his soufflet on the public place, and soliloquises there, will not a crowd collect? 'Il faut quelquefois aider au théatre', so please either suppose that his ears were boxed out side his own house and then he went in, or else ignore the crowd. Comte's funeral also embarrassing 'soit qu'elles se soient faites avant la fin de la pièce, soit que le corps aie demeuré en présence dans son hôtel, attendant qu'on y donnait ordre.' Silence as necessary here as over the locality of Act I, or the attention of the audience would have wandered. – The soufflet is exhibited, the murder hidden, because what is seen evokes sympathy, and we must not be too much against Rodrigue.

[Very interesting, cf. H. James preface. Corneille, both creative and critical, is answering the type of criticism made by men who have never created, and wield in addition the now disused weapon of the Unities. Now he argues that its just like life, history geography correct etc., now that its justified by the needs of the play. I think most sensitive creators must share his worries, though H. James with his pure artistry only needed the second. To what extent does he rationalise his intentions afterwards?]

Aristote blâme fort les episodes détachés et dit que les mauvais poètes en font par ignorance et les bons en faveur des comédiens pour leur donner l'emploi'. L'Infante est de ce nombre . . . . . Discours I

'Denouement of a Tragedy is not married bliss but escape from peril.'
– Discourse du Poesie Dramatique

Moors, C. remarks, break one of his own rules – that all the principal
actors should be announced in the last act – Discours I

Cinna 1640. Better than *Cid* because Auguste is interesting, and gives
reality to the rhetoric about duty plus or versus love which
surrounds him.

Après un long orage il faut trouver un port
Et je n'en vois que deux, le repos ou le mort.

Examen 1660 Scene 'dans le seul palais d'Auguste, pourvu que
vous y vouliez donner un appartement a Æmilie.' (We accom-
modate her gladly, yet continue to remark the 17th cents instance
on *vicinity*. To us, if a scene changes it changes, to them it changes
less if the distance is less geographically.) – A narrative – such as
Cinna's of the conspiracy to Aemilia – needs calmness on both
sides if it is to be consecutive & distinguished.

The action is simple, hence the play's popularity. Complex plays,
like Rodogune and Heraclius, ont sans doute besoin de plus de
l'esprit pour les imaginer, et de plus d'art pour les conduire, but
simple plays n'ayant pas le même du côte du sujet, demandent plus
de force de vers, de raisonnement et de sentiments pour les
soutenir.

Trois Discours 1660, date of examens. Modern examples from himself, since he knows his own plays best; he will not fear to blame
them. Aristotle followed on points that he has treated (Et comme
peut être je l'entends à ma mode, je ne suis point jaloux qu'un
autre entend à la sienne) but Le commentaire dont je m'y sers
le plus est l'expérience du théatre et les réflexions sur ce que j'ai
vu y plaire ou déplaire.

I *Sur le Poème Dramatique*

P.D. a pour but le seul plaisir des spectateurs; but it is impossible
to please without introducing l'utilité. This can be done (i) by
moral maxims: which should not be in the form of generalisations
– e.g. L'amour vous donne beaucoup d'inquiétude is a better
remark for an actor than 'L'amour donne beaucoup d'inquiétude

aux esprits qu'il possède.' [But C., naturally a preacher, did not avoid this defect in practice] (ii) by depicting virtues and vices so that they are *distinguishable* – they need not be rewarded or punished: that, (iii) is only un usage que nous avons embrassé, dont chacun peut se départir à ses périls. (iv) by Aristotelian catharsis. P.D. must exhibit Quelque passion plus noble et plus mâle que l'amour, telles que sont l'ambition ou la vengeance, et veut donner à craindre des malheurs plus grande que la perte d'une maîtresse. Il est à propos d'y meler l'amour . . . mais il faut qu'il se contente du second rang dans le poême et leur laisse le premier. Keeps to this even in Le Cid.

e.g. Berenice is excluded.

Other points: Cleopâtre, en Rodogune, est très méchante; mais tous ces crimes sont accompagnés d'une grandeur d'âme qui à quelque chose de si haut, qu'en même temps qu'on déteste ses actions, on admire la source dont elles partent. [quite true – a superb character] Les sentiments: ce n'est jamais le poète qui parle, et ceux qu'il fait parler ne sont pas des orateurs. La versification, ceux qu'il fait parler ne sont pas des poètes.

II *Sur la Tragedie*

Mostly occupied with Aristotle & purgation, πιθανον ἀδυνατον, and with philosophic statements of the obvious. As usual, frank admiration of his own plays and frank acknowledgement of such defects as he can discover in them – e.g. double action in *Horace*. Interesting comparison between plays and novels, marred by the usual literalism: La reduction de la tragédie au roman est la pierre de touche pour démêler les actions necessaires d'avec les vraisemblables. Nous sommes gênés au théâtre par le lieu, par le temps, et par les incommodités de la représentation – – – Le roman n'a aucune de ses contraintes . . . c'est pourquoi *il n'a jamais aucune liberté de se départir de la vraisemblance*. Voltaire, his commentator, gets irritated at times.

III *Sur les Trois Unités*

Action: in a comedy, unity of *intrigue*; in a tragedy, of peril (C. always insists on danger). Narrative of previous events to be minimised: that's why Cinna was so liked. Also two things in the denouements: le simple, changement de volonté, et la machine. (always insists on will-power).

Time. 12 hours or 24? If it increases the effect 'Je pousserais sans
scrupule jusqu' à 30,' (Voltaire comments: Si vous faites verser
plus de larme, prenez le jour et le nuit, mais n'allez plus loin: alors
l'illusion serait trop detruite.) but it is best when the actual and
representational time coincide.

Place. Here too to coincide is best, but some licence permissible.

Il est facile aux spéculatifs d'être sévères; mais s'ils voulaient
donner dix ou douze poemes de cette nature au public, ils elar-
geraient peut-être les règles plus que je ne fais, sitôt qu'ils
auraient reconnu par l'experience quelle contrainte apporte leur
exactitude, et combien de belles choses elle bannit de notre
théâtre.

The Conquest of Granada. 1669, prefaced by

An Essay of Heroic Plays. 1672 They must, or may, be in verse
because

If you once admit of a latitude that thoughts may be exalted and that
images and actions may be raised above the life . . . . . you are already
so far onward on your way, that you have forsaken the imitation of
ordinary converse. You are gone beyond it: and to continue where
you are is to lodge in the open fields, betwixt two inns. You have lost
that which you call natural, and have not acquired the last perfection
of art.

They must imitate the epic.
They may contain the supernatural for

It is enough that in all ages and religions, the greatest part of mankind
have believed the power of magic, and that there are spirits or spectres
which have appeared. This I say is foundation enough for poetry: and
I dare further affirm, that the whole doctrine of separated beings . . .
may be better explicated by poets than by philosophers or divines.
For their speculations on this subject are wholly poetical: they have
only their fancy for their guide: and that, being sharper in an excellent
poet that it is likely it should be in a phlegmatic heavy gownman, will
see further in its own empire, and produce more satisfactory notions
on those dark and doubtful problems.

Almanzor criticised for neglecting his honour, changing sides,
etc , but

I shall never subject my characters to the French standard, where love and honour are to be weighed by drachms and scruples

[and to the modern reader Alm. is the only interesting character]

Action of play described, Saintsbury, Dryden, p. 46–50
cf. Rehearsal Act IV, scene 2

Examples of its verses, good & bad:

Pt. I a None knows what fate is for himself designed:
The thought of human chance should make us kind.

I.1.

b No man has more contempt than I of breath,
But whence has thou the right to give me death?
Obeyed as sovereign by thy subjects be,
But know that I alone am king of me.
I am as free as nature first made man,
Ere the base laws of servitude began,
When wild in woods the noble savage ran.

Almanzor
speaks

I.1.

c She's gone: and now
Methinks there is less glory in a crown;
My boiling passions settle and go down.
Like amber chafed, when she is near, she acts:
When further off, inclines, but not attracts.

II.1

d I'm pleased & pained, since first her eyes I saw,
As I were stung with some tarantula

III.1.

e She 'This day
I gave my faith to him, he his to me.'
He 'Good heaven, thy book of faith before me lay,
But to tear out the journal of this day:
Or if the order of the world below
Will not the gap of one whole day allow,
Give me that minute when she made her vow!
That minute, ev'n the happy from their bliss might give;
And those, who live in grief, a shorter time would live.
So small a link, if broke, the eternal chain
Would, like divided water, join again. –
It wonnot be; the fugitive is gone,
Pressed by the crowd of following minutes on:

That precious moment's out of nature fled,
And in the heap of common rubbish laid,
Of things that once have been, and are decayed.'

III.1.

f How blessed was I before this fatal day,
When all I knew of love was to obey!
'T'was life becalmed, without a gentle breath;
Though not so cold, yet motionless as death.
A heavy quiet state; but love, all strife,
All rapid, is the hurricane of life.

V.2.

Pt II

g He 'Do you then think I can with patience see
That sovereign good possessed, and not by me?
No; I all day shall languish at the sight
And rave on what I did not see all night;
My quick imagination will present
The scenes and images of your content,
When to my envied rival you dispense
Joys too unruly and too fierce for sense.'
She 'These are the day-dreams which wild fancy yields,
Empty as shadows are, that fly o'er fields.
Oh, whither would this boundless fancy move!
'Tis but the raging calenture of love,
Like a distracted passenger you stand,
And see, in seas, imaginary land,
Cool groves, and flowery meads; and while you think
To walk, plunge in, and wonder that you sink.'
He 'Love's calenture too well I understand:
But sure your beauty is no fairy land!
Of your own form a judge your cannot be;
For, glow worm like, you shine and do not see.'

II.3.

h O how unequally in me were joined
A creeping fortune with a soaring mind!
O lottery of fate! Where still the wise
Draw blanks of fortune, and the fools the prize!
These cross ill-shuffled lots from heaven sent,
Yet dull Religion teaches us content;
But when we ask it where that blessing dwells,
It points to pedant colleges and cells,
There shows it rude, and in a homely dress,
And that proud want mistakes for happiness.

III 2. Lyndaraxa speaking: wordly and towny, she is enough to wreck any heroic play, and almost enough to make this one readable.

> *i* The minds of heroes their own measures are,
> They stand exempted from the rules of war.
> One loose one sally of the hero's soul,
> Does all the military art control:
> While timorous wit goes round, or fords the shore,
> He shoots the gulf and is already o'er;
> And when the enthusiastic fit is spent,
> Looks back amazed at what he underwent.
>
> IV. 2 Almanzor speaking

[He goes to the door; the *ghost* of his Mother meets him: He starts back: *The Ghost* stands in the door.]

> *j* Well mays't thou make thy boast whate'er thou art!
> Thou art the first e'er made Almanzor start.
> My legs
> Shall bear me to thee in their own despite;
> I'll rush into the covert of the night,
> And pull thee backward, by thy shroud, to light:
> Or else I'll squeeze thee, like a bladder, there,
> And make thee groan thyself away to air.
>
> [The *Ghost* retires] IV. 3.

D's theory of the supernatural now in practice! though Ghost talks fancifully enough about her home in the Mountains of the Moon later on. – undenominational fantasy.

j Ghost superfluous constructionally. As a critic, D. understands supernatural, as a creator, he has no feeling for it. Contrast Hamlet I. 1. 'Shall I strike at it with my partizan?'

Defence of the Epilogue: on the *Dramatic Poetry of the Last Age*. We are superior to Shakespeare Fletcher Jonson etc. not so much in genius, but because our age has better tendencies in

i Language: *a* rejects improper words or phrases. "We are the first to have observed them: and certainly to observe errors is a great step to the correcting of them." [and their plots were lame and improbable – e.g. Shakespeare's historical plays, Pericles, Winters Tale, L.L.L., M. for M. "which were either grounded on impossibilities, or at least so meanly written, that the comedy neither

caused your mirth, nor the serious part your concernment"]
Criticises extracts from Jonson's Catiline Very interesting. *b* adds
proper words – not D's business to collect them, deprecates fop-
pish borrowings from the French: fops "are not the men to
refine us: their talent is to prescribe fashions, not words."

ii Wit (*Wit* elsewhere defined as a propriety of thoughts and words)
(style?). Shakespeare often dull "Never did any author precipitate
himself from such height of thought to so low expressions as he
often does. He is the very Janus of poets; he wears almost everywhere two faces, and you have scarce begun to admire the one
ere you despise the other." Fletcher "does not well always; and
when he does he is a true Englishman – he knows not when to
give over." – Jonson "always writ properly and as the character
required": could portray folly – "there is fancy, as well as judgement in it, though not so much or noble: because all poetry being
imitation, that of folly is a lower exercise of fancy, though perhaps as difficult as the other: for it is a kind of looking downward
in a poet, and representing that part of mankind which is below
him." J's 'clenches' or puns deplored: the clergy even clench "for
they are commonly the first corrupters of eloquence, and the last
reformed from vicious oratory." Moreover predecessors couldn't
depict *gentlemen*. Jonson's True wit, Shakespeares Mercutio
[amusing], Fletcher's Don Juan, all inferior. Which brings us to

iii Conversation: early dramatists, except Jon. who didn't profit,
moved little in good society. "Greatness was not then so easy of
access, nor conversation so free, as now it is." And our comedies
benefit: only "some few old fellows" object, who "were unlucky
to have been bred into an unpolished age, and more unlucky to
live to a refined one". Charles II has mainly caused this improvement and "awakened the dull and heavy spirits of the English
from their natural reservedness: loosened them from their stiff
forms of conversation, and made them easy and pliant to each
other in discourse."

Peroration: let us admire our predecessors, but not imitate them
servilely, and realise we live in a more civilised age.

A very important Essay.

Now E.M.F. ought to start, but the knowledge that D's often a
hack discourages me, and that he's a willing hack, like Arnold
Bennett, only makes him the less attractive. He has an acute social

doubled price
of Prologues
after 1682.
Rochester
had him beaten.

and historical sense, he is tactful in his persistant way, but compare him with a real gent, like *St Évremond*, and his carpet-bag
appears.

Nous pensons plus fortement que nous ne nous exprimons, il y a
toujours une partie de notre pensée que nous demeure. Nous ne la
communiquons presque jamais pleinement: et c'est par l'esprit de
pénétration, plus que par l'intelligence des paroles, que nous entrons
tout a fait dans la conception des auteurs.

Did D. move from self defence to criticism?

No, I think he was a natural critic, and was interested in 'placing'
other writers even when they weren't related to his work.

Cependant, comme si nous appréhendions de bien entendre ce que
pensent les autres, ou de faire comprendre ce que nous pensons
nous mêmes, nous affaiblissons les termes, qui auraient la force de
l'exprimer

Quotation continues; here's a charmer.

All for Love 1678

Preface analysed

(i) A & C a popular because a moral subject – unlawful love
punished "That which is wanting to work up the Pity to a greater
Heighth was not afforded me by the Story: For the Crimes of Love
which they both committed were not occasioned by any Necessity
or fatal Ignorance but were wholly voluntary, since our Passions
are, or ought to be, within our Power." [Which? Like D. not to
decide, and to write his play as if they are *not*] Unities attempted.
Octavia the chief blemish [like Corneille, notes complacently any
defect that has escaped his critics]

(ii) Attack on French poets for their super-nicety: they would not
have confronted Cleopatra and Octavia, and deprave modesty
into a vice, and "are so careful not to exasperate a critic that they
never leave him any work." [All sound, but unfortunately the
selected example is *Phèdre*: Racine should have "given us the
picture of a rough young man, of the Amazonian strain" instead
of "Monsieur Hippolyte"]

(iii) Attack on "our little sonneteers, who follow them," and have
"too narrow souls to judge of poetry," particularly of tragedy.

"Poets themselves are the most proper though I conclude not the
only critics," and then comes the havering qualification – provided
they are not "bribed by interest or prejudiced by malice. The wit
is only the average man, who merely has 'a gross instinct' as to
what he likes, but no average man admits he is average, though
he realises it clearly enough for his fellows. [v.g.]

Half wits are fleas, so little and so light
We scarce would know they live but that they bite

– Prologue

(iv) Attack on rich men who rush into poetry through discontent
i.e. Rochester.

(v) Return to A. & C. Shakespeare followed, Scene between A,
and Ventidius (I.1.) good. [it is]

Play analysed in Verrall

Except his lyrics, it's written more from within than anything else
I've read. Idea of the faithful courtisan appeals to him – he was
surely a womanizer – and Octavia the thorough lady, Alexas the
disembowelled intellectual, who tries to apply logic to jealousy,
are *almost* characters. Pathos: why has this been denied D.?
Good construction – excellent not to bring Octavius on.

Cl. to Octavia:

> If you have suffered, I have suffered more.
> You bear the specious title of a wife
> To gild your cause and draw the pitying world
> To favour it: the world condemns poor me.
> For I have lost my honour, lost my fame,
> And stained the glory of my royal house,
> And all to bear the branded name of mistress
> There wants but life, and that too I would lose
> For him I love.   III.1.

Albion and Albanius 1685

Preface – (cf. passim Ste. Evremond, *Sur les Operas*, 1677–) opera
'a modern invention though built indeed on the foundation of
ethnic worship: follow Italy.

Language: Italian the best, manly and sonorous.

French now reformed and improved, but harsh and ill-accent.

English even less happy than French, tho' our genius is 'incomparably beyond their trifling':

the effeminacy of our pronunciation (a defect common to us and the Danes) and our scarcity of female rhymes have left the advantages of musical composition for songs, though not for recitative, to our neighbours.

D. makes no excuses for "meanness of thought" his aim being the choice of words wh. here implies not elegancy of expression but propriety of sound.

Libretto as silly as one expects:

une sottise chargée de musique, de danses, de machines, de decorations, est une sottise magnifique, mais toujours sottise. . . . . . un travail bizarre de poésie et de musique, où le poete et le musicien, également gênés l'un par l'autre, se donnent bien de la peine à faire un méchant ouvrage.

And Ste. E. then confesses:

J'ai vu des comédies, en Angleterre, où il y avait beaucoup de musique; mais, pour en parler discrètement, je n'ai pu m'accoutumer au chant des Anglais. Je suis venu trop tard en leur pays, pour pouvoir prendre un goût si different de tout autre. Il n'y a point de nation qui fasse voir plus de courage dans les hommes et plus de beauté dans les femmes; plus d'esprit dans l'un et dans l'autre sexe. On ne peut pas avoir toutes choses. Ou tant de bonnes qualités sont communes, ce n'est pas un si grand mal que le bon goût soit rare. –

the essay, addressed to the Duke of Buckingham, may glance at D. (Dates?) Its personal criticism – D's broadminded intelligent journalism, out to make the best of a bad job, wh. is in this case the death of Charles II: he died while Albion and Albanius was under rehearsal.

D. has no personal standpoint, nor yet is detached: a series of attachments is all he provides. If he regrets anything he has said he apologises in a rapid manly way and passes on. Good smoking room style.

Dryden: dates [b. 1631. d. 1700]
  1658. Heroic Stanzas on Cromwell

1660–1681

Astraea Redux – for K's return.
Plays – beginning with The Wild Gallant, 1663 : first great success
        Indian Emperor, 65
        (Great Plague and Annus Mirabilis)
        (Poet Laureate & Historiographer Royal, 70.)
        Conquest of Granada
        (Buckingham's Rehearsal, 71)
        Aurangzebe – 75. Last rhymed play
        All for Love – 78. Blank verse
        Spanish Friar – 81 – anti R.C.
        22 plays in this period

1681–1688 satires

Exclusion Bill

        ⎧ Absalom & Achitophel, Pt. I.
        ⎪ Monmouth & Shaftesbury
        ⎪ acquitted of High Treason, to celebrate which was struck
  81– ⎨ The Medal
  82 ⎪ Shadwell's Medal of John Bayes produces
        ⎪ MacFlecknoe
        ⎪ Abs. & Ach Pt. II
        ⎩ Religio Laici – Ch. of England creed.

1686 becomes R.C. to keep in with James II
Hind & Panther next year

1688–1700

Cant turn coat again after Revolution. Resigns his offices (Tate
Laureate) and takes to plays again. Don Sebastian – 1690

Translates Virgil – 97
Fables – 99
buried Westminster Abbey 13.5.00

'And so much for Mr Dryden; whose burial was the same as his life variety and not of a piece; the quality and mob, farce and heroics; the sublime and ridiculous mixed in a piece: great Cleopatra in a hackney coach.'   Farquhar.

Rodogune 1646. Despite indistinct and I believe undistinguished diction, this is the most moving and exciting play of Corneille I've struck. Perhaps because the least Cornelian. Antiochus and Seleucus are devoted to each other, and there it is; their love for Rod. and the commands of Cléopâtre doesn't contend with their devotion – they keep steady from start to finish. Cleo. asks them to murder Rod., Rod. ditto Cleo.: their refusals not only make them lovable and consistent, but produce a splendid 5th Act. Sel., found dying at the moment of Ant's marriage dies without pro-nouncing the murderer's name – so that Ant. suspects both women. [Modern dramatist would have missed out V. 1. – we prefer not to be told first that Cleo. is the murderess, and intends to kill A. & R. but to begin Viennent-ils, nos amants?] Some years later read in Voltaire that this was Corneille's favourite play.

Examen?

Lessing?

Tinkerers: Tasso, Yeats, George Moore, Fitzgerald, H. James, De la Mare
feel their work remains theirs after the barrier of publication has fallen. Fiddling, masturbational.

Preface to The Maiden Queen 1667 [omitted in Ker]

Can a writer judge his own work?

Yes, 'as to the fabric and contrivance of them certainly he may . . . . as a master-builder he may determine whether the work be according to the exactness of the model . . .' But for the ornament of writing which is greater, more various and *bizarre* in poesy than in any other kind, as it properly the child of fancy [cannot be judged, self love operates]: and fancy judging of itself can be no more certain or demonstrative of its own effects, than two crooked lines can be the adequate measure of each other.'

[Interesting but not sound. It's true that a writer knows whether he has carried out his aims, but he may be biassed in favour of his model, all the same, & no fundamental distinction here between it and ornament.]

Rasselas on Poetry ch. 10, 11. 1759

Imlac begins by reading, but "soon found that no man was ever great by imitation. My desire of excellence impelled me to transfer my attention to nature and to life . . . . . I could never describe what I had not seen: I could not hope to move those with delight & terrour whose opinions I did not understand." So he "saw everything with a new purpose . . ranged mountains & deserts for images & resemblances, & pictured upon my mind every tree of the forest & flower of the valley." Rasselas remarks he must have missed a good deal, but "The business of a poet is to examine not the individual but the species; to remark general properties & large appearances: he does not number the streaks of the tulip, or describe the different shades in the verdure of the forest," but records "only those characteristics which are alike obvious to vigilance and carelessness." However, he must also know all modes of life, be a detached moralist, know many languages & sciences, and [finally] "by incessant practice, familiarise to himself every delicacy of speech and grace of harmony . . . To be a poet" he adds, "is indeed very difficult," – "So difficult, returned Rasselas, that I will at present hear no more of his labours."

Rasselas a charming and important (why decried as dull?) composition, though the characters are lifeless and their quest (choice of a mode of life) unsustained. Moral appears to be that there is a certain amount of sorrow in the world, but not the organised horror of Candide, and that thanks to our certainty of Heaven we can endure it: "Human life is everywhere a state in which much is to be endured and little to be enjoyed." Haunted, like Irene (1737) (a youthful discretion. Emotion in last act, but effect painful), with J's horror of sloth. As for the young: "Their mirth was without images, their laughter without motive: their pleasures were gross and sensual, in which the mind had no part, their conduct was at once wild & mean; they laughed at order and at law, but the frown of power dejected and the eye of wisdom abashed them."

For humour 'A glimpse of pastoral life,' ch. 19: while marriage can be wrecked by 'the rude collision of contrary desire, and the obstinate contests of disagreeable virtues' – ch 28

Interest increases towards the close. there is an analysis of waning sorrow, ch. 36, (drawn, like all J's reflections, from his own life), and another, ch. 44, of the danger of indulging the imagination – v. fine indeed – occasioned by an astromer who has persuaded himself he controls the weather and the stars.

No disease of the imagination is so difficult of cure, as that which is complicated with the dread of guilt: fancy and conscience then act interchangeably upon us, and so often shift their places, that the illusions of one are not distinguished from the dictates of the other.

46

In time, some particular train of ideas fixes the attention; all other intellectual gratifications are rejected; the mind, in weariness or leisure, recurs constantly to the favourite conception and feasts on the luscious falsehood, whenever she is offended with the bitterness of truth. By degrees the reign of fancy is confirmed; she grows first imperious and in time despotick. Then fictions begin to operate as realities, false opinions fasten on the mind, and life passes in dreams of rapture or of anguish.

Life of Savage 1743. Good tempered account of a trying friend. No literary criticism in it. Welcome remarks like:

– The liberty of the press is a blessing when we are inclined to write against others and a calamity when we find ourselves overborne by the multitude of our assailants.

– The whole range of his mind was from obscenity to politics and from politics to obscenity. [S. on a statesman]

– He was an indefatigable opposer of all the claims of ecclesiastical power, though he did not know on what they were founded; and was therefore no friend to the Bishop of London.

Unpunctual, unscrupulous, vicious, entertaining, in with all the literary sets – S. reminds me of what I've just heard of Cyril Conolly. Lord Tyrconnel = Logan Pearsall Smith.

Through most of this note-taking, I feel not to be using my mind. Or isn't it here to use?

Preface to the English Dictionary 1755. *Plan,* addressed to Chesterfield,
   1747.

N.B. – self conscious touches: desirous to show he has wit, a good
heart, and bad health – none of which are to be expected in a
lexicographer.

cf. final note on Othello: "I am glad I have ended my revisal
of this dreadful scene. It is not to be endured'. If he did this often,
he would anticipate Sterne.

Recommends uniform spelling, though not 'from an opinion that
particular combinations of letters have much influence on human
happiness . . . . . I am not yet so lost in lexicography as to forget
that *words are the daughters of earth, and that things are the sons of
heaven.* Language is only the instrument of science, and words use
but the signs of ideas: I wish, however, that the instrument might
be less apt to decay, and that signs might be permanent, like the
things they denote.'

Originally intended that 'every quotation should be useful to
some other end than the illustration of a word; I therefore extracted from philosophers principles of science: from historians remarkable facts; from chymists complete processes; from divines
striking extortations; and from poets beautiful descriptions.' But
too long! Also 'to show likewise my attention to things . . . that
my book might be in place of all other dictionaries, whether
appellative or technical. But these were the dreams of a poet
doomed to wake a lexicographer.' Against academies as unEnglish.
But also against colloquialism and technicalities: 'I could not
visit caverns to learn the miner's language nor take a voyage to
perfect my skill in the dialect of navigation . . . . . it had been a
hopeless labour to glean up words by courting living information
and contesting with the sullenness of one and the roughness of
another.

Generalities in Johnson are the result of experience, so never seem
   second hand or dull, and if he does particularise he *amuses* or
   touches us. But he loves them too much to criticise characters in
   Shakespeare soundly, and praises him for being not merely
   universal but abstract.

   Nothing can please many, and please long, but just representations of
   general nature . . . . S's persons act and speak by the influence of those

general passions and principles by which all minds are agitated, and
the whole system of life is continued in motion. In the writings of
other poets a character is too often an individual: in those of S. it is
commonly a species.

[In the last sentence J. goes off the rails (i) he confuses personality
with local characteristics or ideosyncrasy (ii) not true of S. in any
case]

N.B. Generalities/Universal: note the subtle divergencies between
these two words towards Typical/Mystical respectively. Perhaps
it is I, and not Doctor J. going off the rails. Now that my
intuitions are weaker I find critical work v. difficult. Often fall
asleep over sentence that entails argument.

Criticism is the most agreeable of all amusements [Lord Kames], and
not uninteresting or unprofitable, but a malicious imp always
tries to divert the critics from their subject to their colleagues.
cf. seaweed and corks left on the beach by the tide; once they
registered the motion of the sea, and they do not realise that it has
ebbed and that they are now concentrating on one another and
beginning to smell. The critics who has consciously developed
his apparatus is likely to resist the imp best.

Try to distinguish between

(i) Appreciation – inert acceptance of provender with grace after:
'lit. v. wonderful, v. kind of genius to write.'

(ii) Co-creation – where the reader enters into the writer's *achievement*, and is "carried away" – though in a wakeful state rather
than a dream, so that he retains words afterwards to describe his
rape.

(iii) Reader enters into writer's *intention*, but then becomes detached and notes whether he achieves it or not. Goethe's 'creative
or constructive criticism.'

(iv) Reader arrives with apparatus which he has *a* thought out
b borrowed from Aristotle or Mr Richards *c* constructed out of
his earlier reading; this he applies, and is apt to be more interested
in its working than in what it tells him of the author. Goethe's
'destructive criticism.'

August 19th, 1930, 11.0. P.M; aged 51 years, 8 months
   Hard little chatterer in the darkness,
   Chirping away chip cheek, little metal bird –
   Once you had feathers and a song.
   Slowly they fell from you, never came the moment
   When death twisted your neck and silenced you, and your lovers
   and subscribers knew it was time (to go home) for supper
   Always a few feathers remained, fewer than yesterdays more
   than tomorrow's,
   Always melody's outline, for your quack or caw to fill up,
   Always a little light left.
   No one can say you aren't cheerie, dearie, even cheerier than
   you used to be
   No one can say you don't still cock your clever head on one
   side and size things up and institute comparisons
   No one – even if detecting the little metal bird –
   Can advise you to behave differently.
   You benefit no one by dying, so you had better keep on
   Quack caw chip cheek.

   Fancy – shall I get wet? when the rain caught me on the downs.
   I had had diarrhoea in the chalk pit on the way up to Blind Oak
   Gate.

Johnson on Othello Consulted original ed. to see if Raleigh misses out
   much. Naturally J. is stupider than he suggests: but was not
   stupid. Cannot follow:

   Therefore my hopes, not surfeited to death,
   Stand in bold cure [suggests stand in bold cure/stand bold not
   sure]

   thinks chaos = mental perturbation in

             When I love thee not
       Chaos is come again.

   Steevens gets both these right. Gradual recovery of Elizabethan
   idiom thro' 18th cent., in which J. took his share.

Johnson on Macbeth Consulted original ed. to see if Raleigh misses out
   much. 'The second blunderer was the present editor' J. pleasantly
   comments on a note of Warburton's.

'Time and the hour runs through the roughest day.' Emends to:
Time! on!

'The author of the *Revisal* cannot admit the measure (of 'Mark Antony's
was by Caesar' – wh. J. had earlier rejected as an interpolation, but
now admits) to be faulty. There is only one foot, he says, put for
another. This is one of the effects of literature, in minds not naturally
perspicacious. Every boy or girl finds the metre imperfect, but the
pedant comes to its rescue with a tribrachys or an anapaest . . . . . If
we are allowed to change feet, it will not be easy to write a line not
metrical. To hint this once is sufficient.' (Is it!).

Battle of the Books 1704 (written 1697)

How I dislike Swift, and how is it possible to take this ill tempered ill informed stuff (where Boileau appears fighting for the
moderns and Dryden – he had said 'Cousin Swift you will never
be a poet' – is traduced) seriously as criticism, even as destructive
criticism? On a piece with his other works – Jerries emptied with
the same conscientiousness, same elaborate presentation of blame
as praise. I feel, (as usual except perhaps in Laputa) a void behind
the much advertised bitterness. I feel he never grows up.

Best are the fantasies of the Spider & Bee, – where we do escape
the pamphleteer's rasping tones, and have a little visual pleasure,
so that the satire proceeds on its own, cf. Erewhon – and the
ingenious evocation of *Criticism* "Tis I" (said she) "who give
wisdom to infants & idiots: by me children grew wiser than their
parents: by me beaux become politicians and school boys judges
of philosophy" Turns into a book (Bentley) and visits Wootton
her son, and snatching from spleen a monster throws it into his
mouth.

cf. *Tale of a Tub*, ch 3 – *A digression concerning critics* where S.
approves (i) critics who provide rules which help us to divide the
good from the bad in a book 'with the caution of a man that
walks through Edinborough Streets in a morning' (ii) archaeo-
logists & scholars; but devotes the ch. to finding fault with (iii)
fault finders, who don't help authors to improve although "The
Nauplians in Argos learnt the art of pruning their vines by
observing that when an ass had browsed upon one of them it
thrived the better" – : special reference to critics who pick out
faults in a play.

Ridicules instinct in criticism.

Had he any conception of his own character?

J's life Nice Dr J. can't of course discover "by what depravity of
   intellect he took pleasure in revolving ideas from which almost
   every other mind shrinks in disgust. The ideas of pleasure, even
   when criminal, may solicit the imagination: but what has disease,
   deformity and filth upon which the thoughts can be allowed to
   dwell?" Sex pigeon hole. – "If it be said that S. should have
   checked a passion [Vanessa's] which he never meant to gratify,
   recourse must be had to that extenuation he so much despised –
   men are but men."

No fountain on earth can compare with the clearness of Helicon,
yet there lies at bottom a thick sediment of slime and mud.
                                                    B. of B.

Boileau, L'Art Poetique 1669–74

Assumes an educated public: good work will be successful, and
vice versa. Confuses selection and generalisation: 'qui ne sait se
borner ne sut jamais écrire' means 'give *no* detail.'

Again. 'Avant donc que d'écrire apprenez à penser' is applicable
only to an examination paper as *he* says it.

Again: he realises that experience is valuable to a writer and that
the heart of the reader must be touched: but his conceptions of
experience and the heart are jejune.

Poem a series of precepts: follow the ancients and common sense.
No form – except when it considers, often in water tight compart-
ments, the different types of composition.

> Dans un roman frivole aisément tout s'excuse;
> C'est assez qu'en courant la fiction amuse;
> Trop de rigueur alors serait hors de saison;
> Mais la scène demande une exacte raison

is an example.
Under the yoke of the appropriate. Hecuba oughtnt

> sans raison décrire, en quel affreux pays
> Par sept bouches l'Euxin reçoit le Tanais

nor Othello presumably say to Iago

> Like to the Pontic sea
> Whose icy current and compulsive course
> Ne're feels returning ebb, but keeps due on
> To the Propontic and the Hellespont
> Even so my bloody thoughts, with violent pace
> Shall ne'er look back

Machinery of an epic mustnt be Christian: Tasso managed because of his human interest (What of Milton?). [However, Boileau is congenial when he pleads for pagan deities because of the pleasure they give, and no doubt, to an age which had to take Xtianity literally, they were a relief and stimulated aesthetic feelings.]

Two dreary remarks: (i) Big writers are above jealousy: 'C'est un vice qui suit la mediocrité' Cf. Coleridge B. Lit. II who also pretends that geniuses are 'of calm & tranquil temper in all that related to themselves.' [What's the evidence? I believe nearly all writers are jealous and all sensitive to praise or blame, though their reactions arent obvious: e.g. jealousy may emerge as nervous altruism.]

(ii) Don't be just a poet – be a gentleman too!

Important to translate B. from imperative to indicative. Sums up the practice of his age.

Dante, De Vulgari Eloquentia 1309 (?) which I'd never read and now only have in translation, must have been written excitedly, and while Div. Com was forming in his mind. What a pity it only deals with Canzone! ['Fictio rhetorica in musica posita.']

Subjects for Poetry, since Man is
- vegetable – seeking the useful
- animal – „ „ pleasant
- rational – „ „ right

are
- Safety – i.e. War, which
- Love ensures it!
- Virtue

or – as I would put it, though with hesitation, for its dangerous to read modern schemes into

Scholasticism:
- The social fabric
- Personal relationships
- Our place in the Universe

and Dante's come quite right. These are the three subjects for serious literature.

Style. Useless without knowledge and genius, for 'adornment is the addition of some suitable thing', and if the theme's poor, it will appear poorer in fine words, like an ugly woman dressed in silk.' Though if the blend is chemical 'as when we mix gold & silver' the superior and the inferior may produce perfection (II 1).

cf. his advice on *Vocabulary* (II. 7): *shaggy words* (hirsuta – monosyllabic, otherwise rough or very long) should be mixed with *combed words* (pexa – such trisyllables as 'amore' or 'salute'), and a harmony will result.

In both these cases D. seeks a living union in which higher and lower attain a perfection beyond the former's solitary scope. He trembles all through on the edge of other problems.

Why does he always incline us to follow him, and, whether he preaches or not, seem to be walking excitedly ahead?

Notes on the Coleridge – Wordsworth bother – bothering me for a fortnight and to little purpose.

1798 Lyrical Ballads
C's Ancient Mariner [he already takes drugs]
W's Alice Fell, the Thorn etc.
and Tintern Abbey

1800 – second edition, with W's preface

1803 – third   ,,   ,,   another preface

C. takes to metaphysics also. Lectures on Shakespeare, 1811–14
W's Excursion 1814 disappoints and stimulates him towards
1817 Biographia Literaria

C. after 20 years wakes up to the fact he has been labelled incorrectly. An intelligent and unwieldy bee, demonstrating to another of equal girth that they do not come from the same hive. Now and then he gets into a flower bed, more often against a window pane.

Did W. apply his theory of poetic diction to his own poems only or to poetry generally? I don't care, but he and C. did. And what was that theory? W. varies between

1. Language of the lower & middle classes.

2. Selection of language of men in state of *excitement.**

– C. commenting 'The property of passion is not to create but to set in increased activity' – i.e. all depends on the previous experiences of the excited person.

3. Selection of language really spoken by men. – C. objects that 'really' should be 'ordinarily'.

4. Language of Nature. (?)

But he never employs or discusses dialect [C. says he does in the Sailor's Mother, but no] nor slang. His country folk have taken emetics, and only a standardised dulness survives, as cf school teachers, school children and their parents established in the Lakes by some central authority [Contrast A. E. Housman, eclectic, who, usually with erotic intent, puts fragments of low speech into his academic robes. – And Dante, who also abstracted, but from educated speech, and thus produced the Noble Vulgar Tongue instead of the Ignoble. – I sympathise with W., but in depriving lower class speech of its spunk and sweat he has robbed it of graciousness & colour.]

C. pertinacious and considerate of his fellow insect, comes out very well, but B.L. not a great book. It contains (i) a just appreciation of W. – touched by self consciousness, but never spoiled by jealousy (ii) various valuable dicta (iii) much extraneous matter, largely philosophic, which one is excused from reading: but (iv) very little to my present purpose; I can trace scarcely any connection between it and the poems – an occasional fanciful metaphor is the most. The theory that his genius was aroused, as it was destroyed, by drugs is attractive; only when he was cured did he take to appreciating.

*important, though; his arguement that the very act of composition produces excitement and therefore a change in language: here he describes the process through which he once went himself, though his conscious aim is to correct W. (CLXVIII)

Ode to Dejection should be remembered while at the B.L.: rare instance of a failure described imaginatively – i.e. he had just not failed. A minute later, the sky shut, and he was left to resignation or regret. In the B.L. the horror at what feeling *would be* sometimes pierces through: 'Indignation to literary wrongs I leave to men born under happier stars: I cannot afford it.' [cf. Housman's preface to Last Poems 'I can no longer expect to be revisited by the continuous excitement under which I wrote the greater part of my other book, nor indeed could I well sustain it if it came']

Recollect the partition-scheme of L.B. – C. was to make the unfamiliar credible 'to produce that willing suspension of belief for the moment which constitutes poetic faith': W. to make the familiar attractive.

Recollect the two points at issue in B.L. – W's theory of Poetic Diction and his theory that language of poetry and of prose were the same.

And hope for the best.

> This breathing house not built with hands
> This body that does me grievous wrong . . . .

but to W. old age was a pulpit from which to harangue. He never saw through himself, and so continued fertile. [Koteliansky]

I am like C. in many ways, though heading for a different kind of crash. I have his idleness, diffidence, self-consciousness, gentleness, and am a gentleman. Consequently find it difficult to look at his work apart from the agencies that produced or curtailed it. I see him too much under the rule of Time.

> And I the while the sole unbusy thing,
> Nor honey make, nor pair, nor build, nor sing.

i *Ancient Mariner (1798): Lecture on Tempest (1811 etc)*

Convenient to find connections between the shipwrecks, but Coleridge, when he gets on Shakespeare, has *width of sympathy*, and his own narrow passion for the supernatural no longer appears. Ariel is indeed 'one of the invisible inhabitants of this planet, neither departed souls or angels' but his actions are not tragic. Never

> 'Under the keel nine fathom deep
> From the land of mist and snow
> The spirit slid . . .

He keeps to fantasy

He is neither born of heaven nor of earth; but, as it were, between both, like a May-blossom kept suspended in air by the fanning breeze, which prevents it from falling to the ground and only finally, and by compulsion, touching earth.   (p. 141)

All quite right: but it seems to me that C. wasn't even *tempted* to read his own creations into Shakespeare's: for the reason that they no longer lived in him. Good as a critic because dead as a poet. I had thought to connect the two faculties up not far below his surface, but facts forbid, the wedding guests pass on unmolested.

ii *Love (poem): Lectures on Romeo & Juliet, etc.*

Any connection between

> All thoughts, all passions, all delights
> Whatever stirs this mortal frame,
> All are but ministers of Love
>   And feed his sacred flame

and

Love is a desire of the whole being to be united to something or some being, felt necessary to its completeness, by the most perfect means that nature permits, and reason dictates

except a connection of opinions? Here again his past doesnt fetter him and "incomparably his best lecture" (H.C.R.) results.

Shakespeare makes it not only a violent but a permanent love – a point for which he has been ridiculed by the ignorant and unthinking.

[No – I'm starting to falsify in the other direction; all I mean is that when writing of Juliet he did not remember Genevieve, or feel as he had once felt.

iii *Hamlet's hesitation*, however, comes not from cowardice, un-practicality or stupidity but "from that aversion to action which prevails among such as have a world in themselves" (159) – Coleridge himself, who elsewhere pleads: "it seems to me a pardonable enthusiasm to steal away from sober likelihood, and share in so rich a feast in the faery world of possibility". 217 ..

[cf. *Ode to Dejection* – but here the 'shaping spirit of Imagination' is assumed to function]

e.g. flea on Bardolph's nose "which Falstaff compares to a soul
suffering in purgatory. The images themselves, in cases like this,
afford a great part of the pleasure." Points out that S's wit comes
from a combination of images rather than words, though his puns
too are defended "almost as if the first openings of the mouth of
nature."

cf. too C's ready admission that 'pure morals' lead to bad criticism:
no one would read the Spectator aloud to his daughters, and "the
effect is bad, however good the cause." Theatrical performances
take "a sort of domestic turn," and while they "improve the heart
there is no doubt that they vitiate the taste."

C's idea that Sh had high reasons for everything he wrote is
absurd, yet it led him into very little absurdity and many valuable
discoveries, because his instinct directed it to the right passages.

Ode to Dejection

Is not this the watershed I seek? Here he describes the death of
creative power, not knowing that his description means the birth
of critical: an inferior infant, yet it lived and made remarks
beyond the powers of its inspired predecessor. Turning over of
the genius in sleep, so that criticism comes uppermost.

Shaw's St Joan and Joyce's Ulysses into which I looked today (8–11–30)
made me ashamed of my own writing. They have something to
say, but I am only paring away insincerities. I cannot attend to my
stupid lectures as much as to the trees I am planting in Piney
Copse. They too are stupid but I do not think so while at work.

I wonder what morality is, whether eternal justice exists, immutable right
& wrong, or whether law and custom rule the world of humanity,
evolved for social convenience from primal savagery. I am led in my
actions by impulse, admiration, regard for the opinion of my fellows,
fear of consequences desire for what in moments of happiness I have
recognised as beautiful, dislike of what is vile, but never by fixed
principles. I do not know what these are, and I very much doubt
whether anyone is guided by them.

– J. A. Symonds: but whence? copied into this book off an odd
scrap of paper, and into an odd space in the book.

Whichelo Family Tree

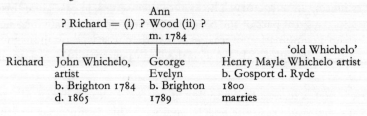

```
                               Ann
          ? Richard = (i) ? Wood (ii) ?
                          m. 1784
          ┌──────────────┬──────────────┐
                                                    'old Whichelo'
Richard  John Whichelo,  George          Henry Mayle Whichelo artist
         artist          Evelyn          b. Gosport d. Ryde
         b. Brighton 1784 b. Brighton    1800
         d. 1865          1789           marries
```

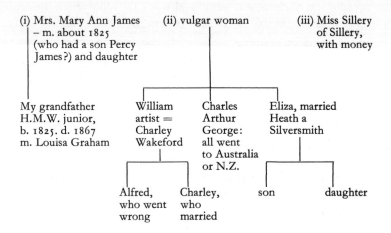

```
(i) Mrs. Mary Ann James   (ii) vulgar woman     (iii) Miss Sillery
    – m. about 1825                                  of Sillery,
    (who had a son Percy                             with money
    James?) and daughter

My grandfather       William    Charles    Eliza, married
H.M.W. junior,       artist =   Arthur     Heath a
b. 1825. d. 1867     Charley    George:    Silversmith
m. Louisa Graham     Wakeford   all went
                                to Australia
                                or N.Z.

                Alfred,     Charley,    son      daughter
                who went    who
                wrong       married
```

The descent from Richard W. and Ann Wood seems, from my cousin Percy W's researches almost certain, but there is no family tradition about it, or of the existence of George Evelyn W.; and there *is* a tradition, not here supported, that John W. and H.M.W. senior were half-brothers.

Mrs James. Her maiden name unknown. There is a Tasso inscribed Henry Mayle Whichelo Junr from his affect sister, and with 'Miss James' on the fly leaf too which must have belonged to her daughter.

"Richard Mayle Whichelo – Paymaster at Trafalgar: his brother T.J.M.W., master painter to Prince Regent" – ?

Dulness! whose good old cause I yet defend,
      With whom my Muse began, with whom shall end,
      O thou! of Bus'ness the directing soul! (J. B. Priestley)
      To this our head like bias to the bowl,

Which, as more pond'rous, made its aim more true,
Obliquely waddling to the mark in view:
O! ever gracious to perplexed mankind,
Still spread a healing mist before the mind;
And, lest we err by Wit's wild dancing light
Secure us kindly in our native night.

Dunciad I 165

Henry James on

(i) Faint pale embarrassed exquisite *Pater!* He reminds me, in the disturbed midnight of our actual literature, of one of those lucent matchboxes which you place, on going to bed, near the candle, to show you, in the darkness, where you can strike a light: he shines in the uneasy gloom – vaguely, and has a phosphorescence, not a flame. But I quite agree with you (Gosse) that he is not of the little day – but of the longer time.

(ii) My view (1897) of *Kipling's* prose future has much shrunken in the light of one's increasingly observing how little of life he can make use of. Almost nothing civilised save steam and patriotism – and the latter only in verse, where I *hate* it so, especially mixed up with God and goodness, that that half spoils my enjoyment of his great talent. Almost nothing of the complicated soul, or of the female form or of any question of *shades* – which latter constitute, to my sense, the real formative literary discipline. In his earliest time, I thought he perhaps contained the seeds of an English Balzac; but I have quite given that up in proportion as he has come steadily from the less simple in subject to the more simple – from the Anglo Indians to the natives, from the natives to the Tommies, from the Tommies to the quadrupeds, from the quadrupeds to the fish, and from the fish to the engines and screws.   Letters, I 278

(iii) I grant you *Hardy* with all my heart. . . . I am meek and ashamed where the public clatter is deafening – so I bowed my head, and let "Tess of the D's" pass. But oh yes, dear Louis, she is vile. The pretence of "sexuality" is only equalled by the absence of it, and the abomination of the language by the author's reputation for style. There are indeed some pretty smells and sights and sounds. But you have better ones in Polynesia.   Letters, I 204

Aubrey in young John Collier's book of selections has reminded me
of the value of the quaint and the charming: they may bring the

past when properly juxtaposed. How many anecdotes and conversations I've let die – half a civilisation already, and from Nixon
to Bob Trevelyan in the province of Cambridge alone.

'Oh of course Julian's *enjoying* Paris all right, that's not the difficulty,
in fact it is his spiritual home, but we told Julian what would happen,
he left Cambridge because he knew so many people there and of
course that has happened at Paris too now and he's so tall, people
crowd around him in the street, and a man who comes from the Gold
Coast and only saw him once recognised him and said 'Hullo Julian.'
And Julian's very nice, he doesn't feel he ought to be alarming like
some of the young, and he's working, or at least he says he is, and I
think Julian speaks the truth though I can't be sure. And he isn't dissolute – that is to say if his friends said to him come to a party at one
o'clock in the morning he'd come, because he is so friendly and fond
of everything, still I don't think he himself is dissolute. Clifford &
Joan Allen said to me 'But why do you worry about Julian? He'll
come through all right whatever happens.' That's an extraordinarily
nice thing to have said to you, still I can't feel always altogether easy.'

Thousands of streams like this run away and are forgotten.
Aubrey saved a few drops. I thought too of a visit to an old
gentleman called Frankie Schuster at Bray where Siegfried
Sassoon took me some years ago and of the weak-winged wren
that wobbled from my side of the river to the other in the dusk
when everything was quiet. It did not clash with Frankie
Schuster.

Love of Animals flaunts so unashamedly, unlike other forms of affection, which are never quite sure of themselves in the presence of
the public, and derive delicacy from the diffidence. Renier's 'The
English: Are they Human?' is sound on this point and has duly
distressed Vita Sackville-West.

Il parait bien difficile surtout que les organes de la generation ne soient
pas destinés à perpétuer les espèces. Ce mécanisme est bien admirable;
mais la sensation que la nature a jointe à ce mécanisme est plus
admirable encore. Épicure dévait avouer que le plaisir est divin, et que
ce plaisir est une cause finale par laquelle sont produits sans cesse ces
êtres sensibles qui n'ont pu se donner la sensation.

Voltaire, Des Singularités de la Nature, CLX

It may be added that Poe stands supreme, even in the only morally pure national literature the world has ever seen, in the absolute chastity of his every word.

> Charles F. Richardson, Introduction to P.

Ah No Ah No   2.2.32

> The world will yet be saved, Be saved,
>
> *Ah no Ah no*
>
> The world will yet be saved, be saved,

sang the second theme of the march movement of the Schumann Quintet the other morning. Lovely liar – working on my unexpressed hopes of the disarmament conference, now failing at Geneva. The thought of salvation, of a clean sweep of troubles and sins, has been too long with me, it is a sort of sleep. I cannot face eternal imperfection.

Money plays a much larger part than it should in your conversation – said BoB to me. It is true, but how to cure myself at 53? The ugly habit has crept on me. I bring myself to the front by saying jokingly that I am rich, poor, have made good terms in America, paid a lot at a restaurant; and a man who has had real worries over money rebukes me. 'A thing to use if one's got it' – I have always preached that, yet I am letting it use me, and take hold of me when I feel safest: through my sense of humour. Florence's accusation that I know no unemployed hit me in the same way, though not so hard. Both are reminders of another civilisation, not based on cash. Russia nudges the blind.

Money blurs everything now, takes the edge off every character, 'I can't afford' alternating with 'I'm in balance' or 'reckless' (generous). The produce of the world has become dimmer than the channel down which it slides to us. I wish I had not fallen so stupidly here. No one has ever tried to take my money away from me to my knowledge. Above all, I wish I didn't think my references to my own income amused people: nothing will cure me of that unlovely illusion.

How seldom one takes notice of a remark, as I have here! Usually they either please or annoy, and, once in either state, one forgets them. How wonderful conversation must be when the speaker means what he says and the listener attends! Now one only gets afterwards a general sense of its direction. The living words are missed.

'Money is simply a form of power, of energy rendered preservable' – G. Heard. He condemns the Hebrew prophets and the ⋒ church for opposing, rather than regularising, usury, but he does not account for the strange effect money has had on the character. We brood on it instead of on the things it buys

Letter to Goldie, 26–2–32, copied before posting, because it is now only in letters I write what I feel: not in literature any more, and I seldom say it, because I keep trying to be amusing.

"I am well and personally happy, though personal happiness has little meaning in these tragic days. I rather envy Dick Sheppard and Miss Royden in their wonderful offer today – they are doing something direct – offering to throw away their lives, which is the only thing they are sure of. How everyone – even people like you & me – will be tempted to laugh at them and be clever, but I fancy that the blood of the martyrs is always the seal of something – provided that the martyrdom is given publicity. It got it in the Roman Empire, it gets it today in the Daily News, – not in the Times nor will it be mentioned on the Wireless. I would like to write to them, but cannot do so without saying I will follow them and this I cannot do.

"I didn't mean to start on this. But what a civilisation! All one's goods are private and depend on one's meeting the right people. As soon as one looks into the general world, which one's emotions should enrich and be enriched by, there is nothing but negation & destruction. Meanwhile the Recorder of London sends a young poet for six months to Wormwood Scrubbs because he tried to print a poem with improper words in it for distribution as a joke among his private friends."

Well it's hardly a patent fang for the hob-dig-a-dig or hold-gum   : said I: and awoke from my dream. Nor was it. It was sprays of St John's wort which I think may exist botanically – each about two feet high and with one large yellow flower on the summit. Teeth and a dream are natural, for Joe showed me a nice story about a dream and teeth.

One can run away from women, turn them out, or give in to them. No fourth course.

Men sometimes want to be without women. Ah why is the converse not equally true? ["Yes – it is – don't you be so conceited" – even as I write the above I hear the insincere unfriendly shriek.] Destruction of Club Life – women will not rest till it is complete.

Birkenhead on Sir Herbert Samuel:

When they circumcised that Jew they threw away the wrong bit.

is what I call a good man's joke, and young John Collier makes them too.

Marjory Napier, a daredevil whom no one follows, was here today (11–3–32), also I read:

> And so with women, since some little care
> Of pretty custom causes them forbear
> Flesh teeth upon our carcases, they find
> Means to devour the spirit and the mind.

Indeed this note need never end. I must set against it the occasional beauty of their voices in singing. The male, even at his best, has a fruity complacency. A woman can forget herself here.

Is their triumph as complete as either combatant affirms? Sometimes I think men are clever too, and give out they are defeated for the sake of peace. This – unless we explain it by Masochism – would account for the large man-made and man-read literature on the subject of the humiliated male.

When one takes someone one loves to pay a call, one assumes that a great impression will be made for good or bad. It is surprising to learn from a fourth party that the visit was scarcely noticed.

I have to read a book at a certain rate and cannot look backwards or on. One of the pages turns out to be gold. I come to it with surprise joy and terror, and know it must be turned over like the others. How lovely if the next page could be The End.

Yes – I wish I could have died. To kill myself – no, frightening, also selfish. A minute's thought, for which there will always be time, will remind one of the upset it would cause – people rushing up to the corpse, hiding it from others, feeling self reproach or horror – and all the corpse's fault! Like those shits the Japanese to commit hari kari on their enemy's front door step. But to have died when happiness was at its height would be wonderful.

Happiness

I have been happy for two years. It mayn't be over yet, but I want
to write it down before it gets spoiled by pain – which is the chief
thing pain can do in the inside life: spoil the lovely things that
had got in there first.

Happiness can come in one's natural growth and not queerly, as
religious people think. From 51 to 53 I have been happy, and
would like to remind others that their turns can come too. It is
the only message worth giving.

Invocation of Poetry by Rhetoric. A mass of dead words is set spinning,
   then kindles. *Or*: one's taste and critical faculties, thoroughly
   roused at first, are lulled unaccountably, and one heaves
   'gorgeous!' er 'splendid'.

Instances in Romeo & Juliet [Yet now I cannot find them, though
they suggested this note and I have been looking at the play most
of the evening]

When this succeeds, it is unmistakable. The zest for the rhetoric
must be genuine. The poet mustn't start ranting in the hope it will
lead him home – the method of Humbert Wolfe, where the head
and throat are thrown back in the hope of kidding on the Pythoness. Shakespeare & his lot enjoyed using words insincerely,
and the sudden occupation of their sentences by some other
authority is uncanny.

This is not to the point, but: –

So frowned he once when in an angry parle
He smote the sledded Polack on the ice

occurred to me in the train through Poland this summer, and I
experimented changing a single word or vowel sound anywhere.
'Frowned' and 'once' belong to one series, 'angry' and 'parle' to
another, opening on to the terrific 'O' and the meaning of
'smote.' 'Sledded Polack' is visual. Having gained our ears and
minds Shakespeare now assails our eyes. But his last effect is the
greatest – 'ice', a sound not employed before, and a substance
unexpected, and suggesting a Baltic civilisation.

These clashes and alliances of sound, sense, and imagery certainly are common in Shakespeare, and – bearing in mind that he dashed them all off – could be much discussed.

I have also noted the second rate hysterical laments over the supposed death of Juliet (IV.5). Sh., knowing she is all right himself, has failed to dramatise the mourners properly. Lady Macbeth upon Duncan is not a parallel; there the second rateness arises from a bad conscience, and the need to over-act.

Death – what a grand easy proprietor! Romeo & Juliet, Hamlet were his banqueting halls, Macbeth his dormitory, and nobody either ignored or belittled him. Thus they strutted around grandly themselves, and attained *Poetry through Rhetoric* in a way we can't. If I died like Romeo I should do so in irritability.   18–11–32

Malcolm Darling on his younger son.

This streak of mulishness combined with an extreme hypersensitiveness is his most serious handicap, for it both alienates and exasperates. It hardens in him, too, what is already hard enough. But even with this handicap he should do great things: for he has an unusually firm, though slow, intelligence, with great powers of thought, and, where his intelligence is allowed free say, a noble sense of value. There is much spiritual yeast in him, and if only it will make his heart ferment, a remarkably fine man should in time emerge; for his resolution and energy are boundless.

– From a Diary of their Kashmir Holiday (nearly 40,000 words) which Malcolm wrote for his wife for the anniversary of their wedding. I can scarcely imagine happiness such as they must have had, my own however intense being scraps, and it's no wonder, since matrimony does offer such prizes, nearly everyone should enter, and ignore the deplorable average.

Beethoven G. Major Piano Concerto, 2nd movement, which is a
    dialogue between an angry orchestra and a soothing soloist,
    = scene between the Furies & Orpheus, Gluck.

Today 29–9–34 in the garden, rockery side, looking up to the house
    where Bone was working, sky bluish, light gentle, I looked without theories or self consciousness. This happens very seldom, though I can prolong the delight if I prevent my engines from restarting. This time they were restarted by Bone, who glanced at

me. I felt I had to look pleasant and amused, and was lost at once, walked about admiring the garden in a duty-doing way.

Is this rare sensation what the artist feels all the time? And is it less exquisite when constant?

Pip Pip!

In an age of violent change we have no time for evolutionary process.

– Sir Oswald Mosley.

Gordon Stansfield made a great beginning in Burma, set a standard and began a tradition. But on a dark day in December, after nine months, he pursued a runaway boy to the Irrawaddy, took to the water in the chase, was caught in a fishing net and was drowned. He died on duty, as he had lived.

– The Times. [G.S. was at B $\begin{cases} \text{ermonsey} \\ \text{orstal} \\ \text{urma} \end{cases}$]
(leader)

Dostoevsky is a phenomenon which has lately burst upon our astonished minds, one towards which an attitude must be determined quickly, almost at the peril of our souls.   – J. Middleton Murray.

. . . some passages of such singular beauty that you are almost impelled to read them twice   – Ralph Straus on L. A. G. Strong

She herself was forced to flee before the oncoming German armies, and for a fortnight had no other home than the royal train. Nevertheless her courage did not fail her in this darkest hour

– The Times on Queen Marie of Rumania.

Masculine ann Feminine Beauties

Among the subjects being treated now-a-days whether in Indian or Western style or in the style which does not claim to be of any school, the representation of the feminine is too very frequent. Raphealle's 'Madonna,' the Greek image 'Venus-de-Mello or the 'Mother and Child' of Ajanta are the outcomes of noble and aesthetic souls, while the repeated appearance of a lady, as once she is proceeding towards the toilet-door with a soap-case in her hand, only signifies the poorness of the creator's mind.

–Indu Rakshit, writing in the Calcutta School of Art Magazine. He speaks also of *Other Animate Objects*: 'Even there are the

insects to be treated in picture if only a ray of light form the   from(?)
retina of the soul reflects on them.'

Charles XII oubliant que Patkul etait ambassadeur du czar, et se souve-
nant seulement qu'il était né son sujet, ordonna au conseil de guerre
de le juger avec le dernier rigueur. Il fut condamné à être rompu vif et
à être mis en quartiers. Un chapelain vint lui annoncer qu'il fallait
mourir, sans lui apprendre le genre du supplice. Alors cet homme qui
avait bravé la mort dans tant de batailles, se trouvant seul avec un
prêtre, et *son courage n'etant plus soutenu par la gloire ni par la colère, sources
de l'intrépidité des hommes,* repandit amèrement des larmes dans le sein du
chapelain. Il était fiancé avec une dame saxonne nommée Mme
d'Einstedel qui avait de la naissance, du merite et de la beaute, et *qu'il
avait compté d'épouser à peu près dans le temps même qu'on le livra au supplice.*
Il recommenda au chapelain d'aller la trouver pour la consoler, et de
l'assurer qu'il mourait plein de tendresse pour elle. Quand on l'eut
conduit au lieu de supplice, et qu'il vit les roues et les pieux dresses, il
tomba dans des convulsions de frayeurs et se rejeta dans les bras du
ministre, *qui l'embrassa en le couvrant de son manteau et en pleurant.* Alors,
un officier suédois lut a haute voix un papier dans lequel étaient ces
paroles : –

On fait savoir que l'ordre très de sa majeste, notre *seigneur très-clément,*
est que cet homme, qui est *traître à la patrie,* soit roué et écartelé pour
reparation de ses crimes et pour l'example des autres. Que chacun se
donne de garde à la trahison, et sauve son roi fidèlement!

A ces mots de 'prince très-clément': Quelle clemence dit Patkul; et à
cause de 'traître à la patrie', Hélas! dit il, je l'ai trop bien servi.

Il recut seize coups, et souffrit le supplice le plus long et le plus affreux
qu'on puisse imaginé. Ainsi périt l'infortuné Jean Reginold Patkul,
ambassadeur et général de l'empereur de Russie.

> – Voltaire
> Charles XII Bk. 3

Each time I read the magnificent paragraph above – at last
transcribed – I am struck by the economy of the *irony* and even of
the *pathos.* Yet the whole passage vibrates with both. There is a
sort of religious grandeur – cruelty and cowardice are both noted
without contempt.

When will there be such writing again, or even the leisure to
transcribe it? Voltaire and I do speak the same language, vast
though be the difference in our vocabularies, we are both civilised,

he in a way Charles XII wasnt and I in the way George Arliss
isnt. We belong to the cultured interlude which came between the
fall of barbarism and the rise of universal 'education'. We understand, for instance, that a good prose style doesn't have to make
its point straight away, and that it's difficult to say where it does
make its point. We believe in reason, in pity, and in not always
coming out right – that is to say I hope to be logical and compas-
sionate (V. thought he always could be), and I know that Patkul's
wheel may be waiting for me too.

> The life of Man is but the imperfect story
> Of his adventure towards endless glory.

Imperial Items. (1) Complaints at the Colonial Office that the natives
of Tanganyika wear the Union Jack as a loincloth. (2) The King
says to the tallest guardsman in the Bn.: 'Whats your height?
Six foot six?' – 'No your majesty, six foot three', and is punished
afterwards for contradicting royalty.

Sandy Field, between Deer Leap and the Ry. Here, a few years ago,
three black cinerary urns of the 1st cent. A.D. were found, the
most perfect of which was given to the B.M. by Mrs. Evelyn,
now herself dead. I saw it there, proferred by a polite colonel, and
today went to the field. There is a pond, large but difficult to find,
and no doubt of the Silent Pool type, for its under the down.
This was crammed with carp, and when it was cleared out some
of them stocked Paddington. Ernest Read told me all this. Up in
Deer Leap is a tumulus, spiky with trees, and the field called
'Great Slaughter Field' is on the other side. Peaceful feeling after
turning out this tiny pocket of history. Pond lies on watershed
and drains towards Mole.

Letter to Stephen Tennant, 14–3–35, copied before posting.

Last weekend – very odd, at Eastbourne, with Hilton Hutchinson, son
of my former preparatory school master. Hilton now a widower himself, did a conversational rubbish slide from Saturday night to Sunday
morning. He lives in a small house with three absent sons, all the floors
are covered with oil cloth, all the walls with snap shots of glaciers, enlarged and all the doors stand ajar. You will never meet Hilton. He
was once a consul at Livorno, he did secret service during the war,
then he became continental manager to a marble merchant. Such is a

life (une vie); no meaning in it at all as far as I can see, and somewhere during it his wife died, he does not know how, and most of his money went, that is to say it is in some marble quarry and they will not let him get at it, and he has been to South America too and to Czecho-Slovakia, and now he lives at Eastbourne, close to his widowed mother and to the shelled preparatory school – where I was once a little boy and he an even smaller one and he talks and talks and talks and makes everything sound the same. There is Hilton – more clearly seen than anyone has ever seen him, I do believe, and yet I have missed out his long melancholy face, and sad little eyes, and heavy brown moustache and the constant twitter of two budgerigars which hang in the window, and the garden which rises so steeply that the chestnut fence at the end of it seems pasted on the upper window pane.

How I like 'Camilla'? I do not care to say how little. Alas! she has reversed experience, which I have long thought reverses its utility by coming at the wrong end of our life when we do not want it. This author knew the world and penetrated characters before she had stepped over the threshold; and, now she has seen so much of it, she has little or no insight at all.

> – Horace Walpole to Hannah More, Aug. 29, 1796.

Remorse is not for the elderly. When it comes to them it is not purging or uplifting, but merely degrading and wretched, like a bladder disease.

> – Christopher Isherwood.

There were many words that you could not stand to hear and finally only the names of places had dignity. Certain numbers were the same way and certain dates and certain dates and these with the names of the places were all you could say and have them mean anything. Abstract words such as glory, honour, courage, or hallow were obscene beside the concrete names of villages, the numbers of roads, the names of rivers, the numbers of regiments and the dates.

also

The world breaks every one and afterward many are strong in the broken places. But those that will not break it kills. It kills the very good and the very gentle and the very brave impartially. If you are none of these you can be sure it will kill you too, but there will be no special hurry.   – Ernest Hemingway.

Employé at Golders Green crematorium can't stand roast beef for his Sunday dinner any more. Smell just the same.

Prostate gland now wakes me every night, sometimes to cold wet pyjamas and a patch on the sheet which oozes through to the mattress. Feeling of desolation as I try to get tidy. The night started so cosy and safe, and now ——— One of those little devils who hid in the saint's robe and travelled where he did. My troubles are increased by thirst, which tempts me to drink before I go to bed. "Oh my god, my god?" Not yet. It is so far nothing compared to the emotional misery from which I am now free, and but for the fear of war I should be cheerful. How lucky that urine smells so little. Dabbing and stuffing in towels are bearable.

Lines composed by myself for Robert Bridges, when he declined to be a pall-bearer at the funeral of Thomas Hardy.

> Twas breakfast at Boar's Hill one January morn;
> Woe wimples the housewife, awake to the menace
> Of burial bell from far Peter's monastery,
> Where with undue pomp and excessive attendance
> Of Jack and his apes rhymster Hodge is enterrèd.
> All windows she hath shut, all newspapers witheld,
> Blaming this icy weather or postman's laggardness.
> Surl husband sits silent still, ah but for how long?

But not sent to him. In a letter to Roger, recently returned by Margery.

As he laye unravelling in the agonie of death the Standers-by could hear him say softly, I have seen the glories of the world.
— John Aubrey on Isaac Barrow

I will not add, I will diminish; I will train myself down to the standard of what is unchangeably true.   H. Melville, Mardi.

Love is sad: and heaven is love   – idem –

I stand for the heart. To the dogs with the head! The reason the mass of men fear God and at bottom dislike Him, is because they rather distrust His heart, and fancy him all brain like a watch
— idem. Letter to Hawthorne.

How many avenues of delight are closed to the mere moralist or immoralist who knows nothing of things extra-human; who remains absorbed in mankind and its half-dozen motives of conduct, so unstable yet forever the same, which we all fathomed before we were twenty! Well,

their permutations and combinations afford a little material for playwrights and others, and there is no harm in going to the theatre now
and then, or reading a novel, provided you have not anything better to
do.   – Norman Douglas: Together

We cease to grieve, cease to be fortune's slaves
   Nay cease to die by dying.   – Webster, The White Devil

All very well and courage is the goods, but my snag is that I try
to be plucky in order to gain peace of mind and have no use for
bravery for its own sake.

The proud treacherous night has almost puzzled me

(One of my dream sentences, rescued from oblivion).

Nice-nice as candles, ev-ry-fing you want (is another).

Do you reason yourself with a beast? Hushed and hushed it goes
to the terrible. – (Another)

Machiavelli, in a passage which I cannot find, and the Chinese sages
   agree that certain formalities are necessary before reading or
   writing can be properly pursued. M. dressed himself after his
   work in the country, and lit wax candles. The Chinese "sit down
   before a bright window, at a clean table, burning a stick of incense
   to dispel anxiety, in order that the fine verses and excellent con-
   cepts should take shape." How amused and contemptuous I
   should once have been of this! I thought I could read or write
   properly anywhere; yet "if one does not act in this way inspiration
   will soon be restrained, distracted, dulled or hindered; and how
   would one then represent the appearances of things and emotions?" Lust, fun, kindness, and fear are my own restraints and
   distractions: fear the strongest of the four, for the collapse of
   civilisation seems to eat up from below into anything I do. A
   clean table and proper lighting make me solider, I find. Tonight I
   have swept all the rubbish off my board and read some of Oedipus
   Tyrannus with only the lamp and two vases in sight. One vase
   has four roses, the other a spray of oak leaves: the acorns when
   the sun falls on them, have a blue bloom.   [Midnight 5–9–36]

Osbert Burdett's death has its usual effect on me. That is to say here is
a man whom I do not respect or care for or know well, and suppose that I shall see from time to time at a committee meeting. He
slips on a moving staircase and dies of the injuries. His unimportance reminds me that he might be anyone. He went to my preparatory school after I left it, followed me to Kings ditto, wrote
some faint and fretful essays, tried to get off with Forrest Reid in
the lavatory of the Savile Club, became an R.C., feebly denigrated
Goldie, had to marry the housemaid, worried Mrs Hardy about
blue vinney cheese, and God knows why he was elected to the
committee of the L.L. to represent literature alongside of Desmond & myself. I have not a charitable thought about him, nor
a vehement one, yet his absence frightens me, I keep on hoping
he didn't suffer.

Dreamt last night I pissed. Urine became sticky and difficult to
brush away, and then the jet solidified into a thick scarlet strip
which lay along the ground like a worm, straight. Adhered to
fingers etc., but was lifted away and returned to me, flattened out.
Now it was two inches broad and dark brown, like a razorstrop.
I could see webbing across it. I was not the least disgusted or
perturbed by this dream, which is so horrible to describe, and
awoke quite calmly. One of the strange things in the dream-state
is the lack of correspondence between the visions and the emotions. Literature has made the mistake of rationalising too much –
unless indeed the experience of other writers has differed here
from mine. – What happened before my piss? A faint revelation
of my character I was sitting with other people, there was an
animal which had to be rescued, then came the shock on my
cowardice that I ought to rescue it, and, next in sequence, the
piss. A good deal to be got out of this dream-world if one can
remember it unconventionally and not with the traditional apparatus of the oneiromant. It appeals to me now that my waking
thoughts are all saddened by world-affairs. Here is freshness and
richness, and even when war gets in it is changed.   – 26–12–36.

About a month later than the above: dreamt I was slicing the
bared tip of a penis – memory of underdone kidney at lunch –
mixed with some book-opinion of Bertrand Russell. Again had
no feeling of disgust. Almost my first war-dream came last night
(14–2–37): the Italians had directed a poison-ray from an aero-

plane upon their own villages, and it had turned one jar of
preserved cherries whitish and half another whitish.

In the War would be necessary not only to fight the enemy but one's
own side. The sgt.-major C.I.D. and profiteering types would
come to the top, bully & plunder the civilised. Soft by nature &
decent by habit, I shall sink after a few peevish cries. So would
most of my friends, for they're the same type as myself. Two or
three small figures will block one's horizon, pretending to protect
one perhaps. When the war ended (if it did) one would be left
drained and mocked. The people who depended on one would
probably have perished utterly.

So upon Trinity Sunday at night King Arthur

dreamed a wonderful dream, and that was this, that him seemed he sat
upon a chaflet in a chair, and the chair was fast to a wheel, and there-
upon sat King Arthur in the richest cloth of gold that might be made.
And the King thought there was under him far from him an hideous
deep black water, and therein were all manner of serpents, and every
beast took him by a limb. And then the King cried as he laid in his
bed and slept, Help! And then knights squires and yeomen awaked the
King, and then he was so amazed that he wist not where he was, and
then he fell on slumbering again not sleeping nor thoroughly waking.

Le Morte Darthur. XX. 3.

Copied, with modernised spelling, just as King George VI
returned from his coronation to his palace. Chaflet = platform

Art should be an expression of life in all its aspects, and so should include
an escape from what officials call life and artists call officialism.

Correct this shallow Sovietism into:

Art should be etc. and so should include an escape from what officials
call life and artists call officialism.

'Escape from life' – what slip slop! Who first used the phrase?

Shakespeare and Milton share an England for which this page shall be
reserved.

> And the yellow-skirted Fayes
> Fly after the night-steeds, leaving their moon-loved maze,

belongs to them both, though the night steeds, noctis equi, make it M's. His too:

> Under the shady roof
> Of branching-elm star-proof
> Follow me.

because the elm is slightly the ulmus, and scholarly; but his might have been

> you demi-puppets that
> By moonshine do the green sour ringlets make
> Whereof the ewe not bites.

No words are delicate enough to define this England. Kipling, trying to make it do something, got it all wrong. As Prospero says, the demi puppets etc. are 'weak masters'; they do not belong to a hierarchy or form a mythology. They are best understood when misunderstood – as by Verdi, in the last act of his Falstaff. Goldie knew of it. It can be reasoned away:

> well you know
> The superstitious idle-headed eld
> Received and did deliver to our age
> This tale of Herne the Hunter for a truth.

[Through Herne may be the Cerne Giant, a very solid one, and the syllabubs mushrooms and pinchings of the 17th century must have derived from primaeval rites and faiths.]

Ezechiel opens like a Wagnerian act: the creatures and the wheels.

xxi. 10. The sharpened furbished sword repeated until the glitter & blood became physical.

xxiv The orgy turns from gore to filth: horrible cookery.

xxviii A lovely eulogy of Tyre.

xxvii The valley of dry bones.

Except for these, no sustained poetry. Storms of temper with occasional gleams of forgiveness.

Zechariah I. 11

And they answered the Angel of the Lord that stood among the myrtle trees and said: 'We have walked to and fro through the earth, and, behold, all the earth sitteth still and is at rest."

Accidental poetry. The spurt begins v.8 with "I saw by night" and is magic and meaningless.

This morning at about 8.30. when the sun was already high, its rays entered Stisted on a level and threw the shadows of the casements on to the mantelpiece. *Explanation* The rays struck a glass frame in the village and were reflected up from it.   June 9 1937

Subjects: (i) *The Gentleman*, esp. v. the artistocrat (Desmond on W. Blunt – 'We must never forget that Blunt led the Cads' Chorus': Belloc –) and v. the Catholic Saint: Newman in an admirable and infinitely malicious passage which Hilton read out from the Idea of a University, eluding most of his hearers. For the gent. as someone nice, see Norman Douglas. Also read, while at Hilton's, The Lanchester Tradition by Bradby, a deplorable and revealing tale of a school. Recommend it to foreign students. Then went to Brussels and read Christopher's North West Passage: about the volunteers at the general strike.

(ii) *The English and their Birds*. Lord Grey. The over-praising of Bewick and Peter Scott. Attempt to be-bird Neville Chamberlain. Much subtler and sillier than the hunting tradition. You look through field glasses and so become good and wise.

(iii) *Civilisation*. 'Ils ne donnent rien et ne reçoient' said Charles of a Manchester Guardian couple who did not possess it. We agreed that the scenery near St. Rémy might be a test. T.E. used to say I was civilised. Max certainly is, also Desmond, but no great cont. English writer whom I at present recall: though many of them are cultivated and enlightened, and some of the younger ones are adult. – Not Housman nor Virginia though they are educated.

(iv) *Siva or Vishnu*: never Brahma.

Ibsen's Letters

I am conscious in personal intercourse of only being able to give incorrect expression to what lies deepest in me and constitutes my real self: there I prefer to lock it up.   – to Bjornson, 1864.

An aesthete in Copenhagen once said to me: "Christ is really the most interesting phenomenon in the world's history." The aesthete enjoyed him as a glutton enjoyed the sight of an oyster.   – to Bj. /64.

My little boy shall never with my consent belong to a people [Nor-
wegians] whose aim it is to become Englishmen rather than human
beings.   – to Bj. /64.

[Modern Rome] All that is delightful – the unconsciousness the dirt –
will now disappear: for every statesman that makes his appearance
there, an artist will be ruined – – – Yes, I must confess that the only
thing I love about Liberty is the struggle for it: I care nothing for the
possession of it.   – to Brandes, 1870.

The state has its roots in Time: it will have its admiration in Time.
Greater things than it will fall: all religion will fall. To how much are
we really obliged to pin our faith? Who will vouch for it that two and
two do not make five up in Jupiter?   – to Br. /70.

Copied from some notes made for lecturing on 1. (cf. p. 44)

Someone Else's Letter.

I wonder if you would tell us of a place near ———, not chalk, where
there is a very nice church. I hate party names, so won't use them, but
we require the H.E. every Sunday and Saints Days *early*, and if possible
once or twice in the week as well. As long as one has the teaching, we
would do without ritual.

Copied from a scrap of paper about twenty years old.

Copied from another scrap:

The first time I was in London I had a veal and ham pie at ——— is
there a Criterion? Well I thought it was good so I had it again yesterday.

– one lady to another in Gt. Russell Street.

Cowley to Evelyn

I never had any other Desire so strong, and so like to Covetousness as
that one which I have had always. That I might be Master at last of a
small House and a large Garden, with very modern Conveniencies
joined to them, and there dedicate the remainder of my Life to the Culture of them and the study of Nature.

But several accidents of my ill Fortune have disappointed me hitherto,
and do still of that Felicity: for though I have made the first and hardest
step to it, by abandoning all Ambitions and Hopes in this World, and
by retiring from the noise of all Business and almost Company: yet I
stick still in the Inn of a hired House and Garden, among Weeds and

Rubbish: and without that pleasantest Work of Human Industry, the
Improvement of something which we call (not very properly, but yet
we call) our own. I am gone out from Sodom but I am not yet arrived
at my little Zoar: O let me escape thither (is it not a little one?) and my
soul shall live.   Aug. 16, 1666.

Bunyan: Death of Mr Badman's wife

Now, said she. I am going to rest for my sorrows, my sighs, my tears,
my mournings, and complaints: I have heretofore longed to be among
the saints, but might by no means be suffered to go, but now I am
going, and no man can stop me, to the great meeting, to the general
assembly and church of the first born which are written in heaven.
Then I shall have my heart's desire; there I shall worship without
temptation or other impediment; there I shall see the face of my Jesus,
whom I have loved, whom I have served, and who now I know will
save my soul. I have prayed often for my husband, that he might be
converted, but there has been no answer of God in that matter. Are
my prayers lost? are they forgotten? are they thrown over the bar?
No: they are hanged upon the horns of the golden altar, and I must
have the benefit of them myself, that moment that I shall enter into
the gates, in at which the righteous nation that keepeth truth shall
enter: I say I shall have the benefit of them . . . . My prayers are
not lost, my tears are yet in God's bottle: I would have had a crown,
and glory for my husband, and for those of his children that follow in
his steps; but so far as I can see yet I must rest in the hope of having
all myself.   – 'Mr Badman', ch. XVI

La Bruyère

On ouvre un livre de devotion, et il touche; on en ouvre un autre qui
est galant, et il fait son impression. Oserai-je dire que le coeur seul con-
cilie les choses contraires, et admet les incompatibles?

Les Caractères IV

Bunyan: Death of John Cox.

There was about twelve years since a man that lived at Brafield by
Northampton, named John Cox, that murdered himself; the manner
of his doing it was thus. He was a poor man and had for some time
been sick, and the time of his sickness was about the beginning of hay-
time, and taking too many thoughts how he should live afterwards, if
he lost his present season of work, he fell into a deep despair about the
world, and cried out to his wife the morning before he killed himself,
saying, We are undone. But quickly after, he desired his wife to depart

the room, because, said he, I will see if I can get any rest; so she went out; but he, instead of sleeping, quickly took his razor, and therewith cut a great hole in his side, out of which he pulled and cut off some of his guts, and threw them, with the blood, up and down the chamber. But this not speeding him so soon as he desired, he took the same razor and therewith cut his own throat. His wife, then hearing of him sigh and fetch his wind short, came again into the room with him, and seeing what he had done she ran out and called in some neighbours, who came to him where he lay in a bloody manner, frightful to behold. Then one of them said to him, Ah! John, what have you done? Are you not sorry for what you have done? He answered roughly, It is too late to be sorry. Then said the same person to him again Ah, John, pray to God to forgive this bloody act of thine. At the hearing of which exhortation he seemed much offended, and in an angry manner said Pray! and with that flung himself away to the wall and after a few gasps died desperately. When he had turned him of his back to the wall the blood ran out of his belly as out of a bowl, and soaked quite through the bed to the boards, and through the chinks of the boards it ran pouring down to the ground. Some said that when the neighbours came in to see him, he lay groping with his hand in his bowels, reaching upward, as was thought, that he might have pulled or cut out his heart. It was said also that some of his liver had been by him torn out and cast upon the boards, and that many of his guts hung out of the bed on the side thereof; but I cannot confirm all particulars; but the general of the story, with these circumstances above mentioned, is true.   – 'Mr Badman', ch. XIX

Marx-cum-Engels from Les Grands Textes du Marxism, sur littérature et l'Art. – Jean Fréville.

Surprised at M's humanity culture and sensitiveness.

A man cannot become a child again without falling into childishness. But he can enjoy a child's naivety and he ought to reproduce its truth-fullness in his own (higher) conditions. So with the social childhood of Humanity, which gave us at its best the Greeks. They were normal healthy children. Their art, which keeps its power over us, proceeds from their imperfect social conditions, and like them cannot recur.

Renaissance. Artists entered public affairs and fought. Exceptions: 'savants de cabinet' who either were 2nd rate or afraid of burning their fingers like Erasmus.

Goethe failed because he was too universal. He wanted to *act* and the only action he could find was in a bourgeois German court. He sacrificed his *aesthetic* sense, which disgusted him with the misery of Germany, and produced Götz, Prometheus, Faust, to the doing of little jobs.

Shakespeare realises that money is (i) the transforming power which turns virtues into their contraries, confuses falsifies reconciles the un-reconcilable – Timon (ii) universal prostitution.

? Comedy (Lucian) the last phase of a historic cycle: "so that mankind may separate joyously from their past."

New masked by the old, Men make their own history but under con-ditions which they have inherited from the past. They evoke the dead when they are engaged on revolution – e.g. Luther, St Paul, Cromwell the O.T., the French Rev. ancient Rome, though its task was the establishment of the bourgeoisie: 'complètement absorbée par la pro-duction de la richesse et par la lutte pacifique de la concurrence, elle oubliait que les spectres de l'époche romaine avaient veillé sur son berceau.'

Marx's poems. The last of them made him see what Poetry *was*: an unattainable fairy palace, and at the sight of it his own creations fell to dust.

Carlyle sympathises with the Workers and especially in his early work attacks the bourgeoisie. But his solution is the bourgeois Hero who keeps the workers in order. He has no sense of historical development.

'New England' of Disraeli. Pretended alliance of nobles and workers against bourgeoisie. The nobles may lead for a little, waving a crutch but the workers will soon see their crests emblazoned on their behinds.

The more the political opinions of the author are concealed, the better the work of art – Engels.

The Materialist Method must be used as a thread to guide us through our historical studies, not as a model against which facts must be measured.

– He is speaking here of Ibsen and the Norwegian Bourgeoisie, who he suspects are superior to the German bourgeoisie who came up after the 30 years' war.

I read this anthology to find material for The Ivory Tower. No luck – unless Communism condemns Individualism in condemn-ing the middle classes with their idealism and romanticism.
M. and E. evidently respect the individual artist – and don't set him to work for the state. They seem to admire him most when,

like Balzac, he upholds the system whose ruin he records. Pity for the down-trodden disgusts them.

Hitler: Die Kunst ist in den Volkern begrundet: his address at Munich, 1937, read by me for the reason stated above, and with equal luck.   He says:

Jews, with their so-called artistic criticism, muddled the public mind, and asserted that art is international and that it expresses the spirit of the age. Putting it on the level of fashions which change yearly. Nat.-Soc. Germany demands not modern art but German art, which will be, like the national spirit, eternal. Those whose achievements are not destined to be eternal do not care to talk about eternities. [I read this sentence missing out its first 'not', and agreed with it] No doubt the nation (Volk) will pass, but so long as it exists it constitutes a stable pole in the whirling flight of time. We Germans are made up of more or less different races, moulded by one predominant racial nucleus [for which read 'set of gangsters']: What does 'to be German' mean? The best answer to this question does not define but lays down a law [!!!]: To be German is to be clear (klar), and therefore logical [!] and true, and this must inspire our act. The artist must set up a monument to his people and not to himself. Our 'romantics' tried sincerely to express this 'inwardly defined law of life': both their subjects and treatment were German, and it is terrible that their masterpieces have perished in the Crystal Palace fire of 1931.

As for degenerate artists, I forbid them to force their 'experiences' on the people. If they do see fields blue etc. they are deranged and should go to an asylum, if they only pretend to see them blue, they are criminals and should go to prison. I will purge the nation of them, and let no one take part in their corruption – his day of punishment will come [He will only allow Germans to see what he knows they ought to like] and the Haus der Deutscher Kunst is declared open.

cf. passim Julian Huxley We Europeans.

Lenin-cum-Stalin on literature. Being a 2nd instalment of Les Grands Textes du Marxism.

Lenin on its organisation [1905]: Literature ought to be 9/10ths Party Literature. Not only shouldn't the individual get rich on it, but it shouldn't be an individual affair. Down with non-party writers! Down with the literary superman. Hysterical intellectuals will complain that this turns literature into a bureaucratic machine, but it only means that it can't be organised just like other Party-activities; inside the *Party* it does admit personal tendencies, imagination etc.

Thus we shall have a free press – free not only from police-supervision and Capitalism, but from bourgeois individualism.

Call this Freedom! the intellectual exclaims [as well he may]. Yes, for (i) there's no necessity to be inside the Party. (ii) all talk of absolute Freedom is pure hypocrisy. To live in a society and not depend on it is impossible. The bourgeois writer's Freedom is a pretence because he's covertly connected with Capitalism: the Soc. writer's Freedom will be a reality because he is openly connected with the Proleteriat [No. The contrast is between lit. which pretends to be free and lit. which doesn't pretend to be, and there is an advantage in pretending – the writer may snatch a victory from under the nose of the authorities.] Paper and the printing press will one day be free to all [To print what?].

Lenin on the Cultural Heritage [1919].

Impossible to build communism except upon the knowledge, science and art which Capitalism has left behind. Bourgeois specialists, under proletarian supervision, must be used. But they are wrong when they think they will always be indispensable. He is against too rapid an assertion as to the nature of Proletarian Culture, and snubs the 'Prolet-cult' partly for this partly for presuming to work independently of the Commissar for Public Instruction. The communist mustn't just learn the past, he must assimilate it, and assimilate it *critically* [i.e. he could never have disinterested enjoyment of a work of art, he must always be considering how far it will be suitable for Communism. cf. Lenin's own dislike of enjoying Beethoven – p. 36 of this commonplace book.]

Leninism less cultured than Marxism – i.e. less interested in the creation and enjoyment of works of art. But it does not openly denounce individualism or recommend corporate emotion, as the Nazis do. There seems no reason why Communism, if left in peace, should not become civilised.

Stalin says as little as possible.

Coriolanus Ouverture, says Tovey the ever tiresome, *means something* and Wagner has analysed it: opening bars = decision to destroy the Volscii, then a sweet tune for the ladies, then the dotted-quaver restlessness of indecision. This seems right, and I am distressed that it should be so, and feel that a masterpiece has been spoiled for me. Which shows that non-programme music moves

me more deeply. I did not know this. I have lost my Coriolanus
in the sense that I have lost an old building which has been restored, or Hackhurst Lane which has been tarred for traffic. It
remains, but the sounds have been vulgarised and hardened. Not
to comment is the best – i.e. the only road to the best.

God and the Aristocracy have perished and nothing has taken their
place. Hence the architecture of 20th cent. London. Money-
making everywhere. Query: Why should money-making produce
meaness and ugliness? Carlton House Terrace, says Robert
Byron, was nearly pulled down: "not even allowing the King a
decent drive to his own front door."

Train Talk – 'There's a companion volume to this, I'm pretty sure:
Rossini' said an old man in the train who had taken down Hall
Caine's Life of Rossetti from the rack, when I had hoped to lose
it for ever. 'I don't know whether Hall Caine wrote it. A bit too
dry for me, though mind you I like some poetry very much:
Macaulay's Essays. Now who *was* the name of that writer who
died the other day and knew so much about horses: not Sherlock
Holmes . . .'

I broadcast about books and deplored the absence of freedom on
the Continent: Mrs Jeffrey said she quite agreed – it was a great
mistake to stop men from reading – kept them from going to the
Public House. Another lady writes to ask me who wrote the
Bible. Its seldom one can test the effect of one's remarks.

Dream-Tags 1938 – all written down on waking.

"Philip of Fisham" [English history name]
"The other man made a noise as if he'd been pickling potatoes."
"It's my fault – depending entirely on its weight, – The door's
open –"
"How country-simple the white mice! How very young –"
"A pretty face. An eager pleasure to become the bride of either
snoozling soldier."
"I merely told you the intelligent talk of an important husband."
"What is the name of the grand villa he [Victor Hugo] occupied?"
– "Arouille-Marine."
"What's that but a pog mind?"

"It will be hard on road sense. What a pity? Road sense lives on Rôtairs of road sense."
"I'm sure he has been well fed in between. I have often said so, and in these surroundings." [woman speaking]
He says he's never had a cremant – a wicked wife.
"To get well known, one builds a road like Benjamin Terrace, or failing that one can go abroad."

> – on an old scrap of paper.

Oh I always do admire the royal family of your foolery.

Claude and the Poussins were weak men, and have had no serious influence on the general mind. There is little harm in their work being purchased at high prices: their real influence is very slight, and they may be left without grave indignation to their poor mission of furnishing drawing rooms and assisting stranded conversation.   J. Ruskin

A work of art must be treated like a prince. It must speak to you first.

> – Schopenhauer

At the Alexandria camp five sailors clubbed and bought a woman brought by the Arabs to market for seven dollars: she cried much during the auction, but when her lot was decided quietly submitted to be led by a cord to the lake where she was stripped naked, scrubbed well, then embarked on a boat and carried off to their ship.
General Sir R. T. Wilson: History of the British Expedition to Egypt.

I should think no sacrifice on my part too great, if I could but convince the grovelling editors of our old dramatists that the filth and obscenity which they so sedulously toil to explain is better understood by ninety nine out of every hundred readers than by themselves, and that the turpitude of corrupting the remaining one is a crime for which their ignorance offers no adequate excuse.   – Wm. Gifford, Memoir of Ben Jonson. Lord Macaulay has written 'Very Good' in the margin of the copy at Wallington –

Tu mihi curarum requies, tu nocte vel atra
Lumen, et in solis tu mihi turba locis
Propertius

There can be no timidity when there is only one life to be lived.
> – Kenneth Searight in an old letter to me

Early Greek Science. – And Lucretius. –

Farington (Science and Politics in the Ancient World) thinks that Ionia observed and experimented freely; that Science became conditioned by politics, esp. by the oligarchies of mainland Greece, who did not want the common people to benefit by it; that Plato, the arch-villain, advocated the Royal Lie; that Epicurus took up the tradition of Ionia and claimed that Science belonged not to govts but to all; and that Lucretius, carrying on Epicurus, tried to free men not so much from superstition as from the state-cult. An exciting and rather noble left-winger.

Now I am reading Cornford (From Religion to Philosophy). I doubt whether Farington has. For Cornford proves that Ionian Science was conditioned by religion. This, though less exciting, is probable.

I find these early speculations useful in clearing my own mind, and helping it to see how it has been twisted. And Farington recalls me to my proper job. Now that I feel better I ought to think a little more, and not to slop about being diffident or charming. Perhaps I may find in some classical writers (Sophocles, Lucretius) what Goldie found in Plato. Farington shows up Plato very well: and shows that *The Laws* were his natural conclusion. He makes, however, the mistake of dividing men into deceivers, deceived, and truth-seekers, and visualises the first class inventing suitable gods for the second. If Plato had been consistently on the side of the State and the Golden Lie, he would not have starred the martyrdom of Socrates.

> Denique avarities et honorum caeca cupido
> Quae miseros homines cogunt transcendere fines
> Juris et interdum socios scelerum atque ministros
> Noctes atque dies niti proestante labore
> Ad summas emergere opes: – hoec vulnera vitae
> Non minimam partem mortis formidine aluntur.   Luc. III. 59.

Farington put me on to the above: but he misapplies 'vulnera vitae' to colour his own picture: calls it 'the false doctrines of the state cults'. I dont think he is impeccable.

The Rev. John Newton on the Messiah

They are entirely regardless of their danger, and wholly taken up with contriving methods of amusing themselves, that they may pass away the term of their imprisonment with as much cheerfulness as possible. Among other resources they call in the assistance of music. And, amidst a great variety of subjects in this way, they are particularly pleased with this one: they choose to make the solemnities of their impending trial, the character of their Judge, the methods of his procedure, and the awful sentence to which they are exposed the groundwork of a musical entertainment: and as if they were quite unconcerned in the event, their attention is chiefly fixed upon the skill of the composer, in adapting the style of his music to the very solemn language and subject with which they are trifling. The King, however, out of his great clemency and compassion towards those who have no pity for themselves, prevents them with his goodness: undesired by them, he sends them a gracious message: he assures them that he is unwilling they should suffer: he requires, nay he entreats them to submit: he points out a way in which their confession and submission shall be certainly accepted: and in this way, which he condescends to prescribe, he offers them a free and full pardon. But instead of taking a single step towards a compliance with his goodness, they set this message likewise to music: and this, together with a description of their present state, and of the fearful doom awaiting them if they continue obstinate, is sung for their diversion; accompanied with the sound of cornet, flute, harp, sackbut, psaltery, dulcimer, and all kinds of instruments.

From a Sermon preached at St Mary's Woolnoth in 1784.

The Rev. John Newton's Familiar Conversation

I endeavour to walk through the world as a physician goes through Bedlam: the patients make a noise, pester him with impertinences, and hinder him in his business: but he does the best he can and so gets through.

A man and a beast may stand upon the same mountain and even touch one another: yet they are in two different worlds: the beast perceives nothing but the grass: but the man contemplates the prospect, and thinks of a thousand remote things.

[J.N. began life as a sailor and a hard case: after conversion, he became the friend of Cowper and of my gt. gt. grandfather John Thornton]

Argument on the Immortality of the Soul, between miners and fishermen:

1st miner: If you can answer me this bloody question I will believe that Man's bloody soul is immortal. If a man gets drowned at sea and a shark eats the man (bloody soul and all, mind) and another fish eats the shark and another fish eats that fish, and fish keeps on eating fish, where does the bloody soul of Man go to, eh?

2nd miner: Yes, tell us that, old cock.

Chorus of fishermen: What do you know about the bible?

2nd miner: I was brought up with the bugger, had the bugger for breakfast lunch and tea, and sometimes for bloody supper too.

This ended the argument. I find it in an old letter of Frank Vicary. Swearing apart, subject matter apart, it could not be broadcast. It is real talk, not entertainment talk.

(i)

Mon ami, il faut avoir des –––– pour faire une bonne tragedie: or a quatre vingtquatre ans, on n'a plus de ––––
                    – Voltaire, but on Madame du Bocage not on himself.

(ii)

Malheur à qui ne corrige pas soi et ses oeuvres: il faut se corriger, eût-on quatre vingt ans! Je n'aime pas les viellards qui disent: "J'ai pris mon pli." Eh! vieux fou, prends-en un autre   – Voltaire

(iii)

Son dessein, apparemment, était d'être pendu; c'est un homme qui cherche toute sorte d'élevation.   – Voltaire on Rousseau

Dulness: quotations from the Dunciad.

> Daughter of Chaos and Eternal Night:
> Fate in their dotage this fair Ideot gave,
> Gross as her Sire and as her mother grave,
> Laborious, heavy, busy, bold, and blind
> She rul'd, in native Anarchy, the mind   I. 12.

> O when shall rise a Monarch all our own,
> And I, a nursing Mother, rock the throne;
> 'Twixt Prince and People close the Curtain draw,
> Shade him from Light and shelter him from Law;
> Fatten the Courtier, starve the learned band,
> And suckle armies and dry nurse the land:
> Till Senates nod to Lullabies divine,
> And all be sleep, as in an Ode of thine.
>   [– D. is addressing Cibber] – I. 311.

And gentle Dulness ever loves a joke.   II. 34.

A place there is, betwixt earth, air, and seas,
Where, from Ambrosia, Jove retires for ease,
There in his seat two spacious vents appear,
On this he sits, to that he lends his ear,
To hear the various vows of fond mankind:
Some beg an eastern, some a western wind:
All vain petitions, mounting to the sky,
With reams abundant this abode supply;
Amused he reads, and then returns the bills,
Signed with that Ichor which from Gods distils.   II. 83.

[How undull! And how gay are Pope's ordures beside Swifts!
This dusky pearl is the finest of the string: Publishers in pursuit
of an Author who evaporates: Bk II is taken up by it and other
games; it is grand and frolicsome, and belongs to that happy
moment when aristocracy catches hold of ordinary experiences
and common life, and plunges, retaining its own proper form.
Earlier, it ignores it or despises from a distance; later, it sympathises and tries to be matey. Pope lived at the right instant, and it
takes a 19th century critic, and a British one, to deplore his
persecution of small fry.

Dipsychus – read after many hesitations – is not clear what world it
    opposes to the spirit: the world of action or the world of ambition
    greed & snobbery. So its effect is fumbly.

> I am a man of peace
> And the old Adam of the gentleman
> Dares seldom in my bosom stir against
> The mild plebeian Christian seated there.

> To do anything
> Distinct on any one thing to decide,
> To leave the habitual and the old, and quit
> The easy chair of use and wont, seems crime
> To the weak soul, forgetful how at first
> Sitting down seemed so too

Don't expect to pursue Clough beyond the anthology-pieces.
Goldie must have studied him.

A speech of Antigone, a single sentence of Socrates, a few lines that were
    inscribed on an Indian rock before the Second Punic War, the foot-

steps of a silent yet prophetic people who dwelt by the Dead Sea, and perished in the fall of Jerusalem, come nearer to our lives than the ancestral wisdom of barbarians who fed their swine on the Hercynian acorns.

Finely put, O Lord Acton, but nearer to whose lives? This afternoon (29–2–40) I was at Bishops Cross, where new born lambs were dying in the cold, and Hughie Waterston, a Nazi by temperament, was trying to save them. He had put one of them in a bucket over a valor-perfection lamp. Him the ancestral wisdom inspired. Lord Acton is right, but by a much narrower margin than he supposed. He forgot that most people do not respond to culture or intellectual honesty. He forgot that there was something irresponsive to them even in himself. Ignoring social variety, neglectful of psychology, he appears to this generation as an old man lecturing in a cap and gown. What he said was true yet it can be written the other way round, and not make nonsense, and it is always so written in Germany, I will so write it myself: he would not disapprove of the exercise: –

The ancestral wisdom of barbarians who fed their swine on the Hercynian acorns comes nearer to our lives than a speech of Antigone, a single sentence of Socrates, a few lines that were inscribed on an Indian rock before the Second Punic War, the footsteps of a silent yet prophetic people who dwelt by the Dead Sea and perished in the fall of Jerusalem.

This is the first time I have used my mind today; day of inertia and of waiting for the end. Yet my duty is plain enough: to talk this late nineteen century stuff with a twenty century voice, and not to be shoved out of believing in intellectual honesty and in the individual. – How paltry, beside Acton, is Middleton Murry's 'A Christian looks at the World'. How he whimpers and looks at the imaginary stigmata on his own feet and hands. What a drop, even in religious standards! What an abysmal drop in behaviour!

Also from Acton ("The Study of History"): –

We cannot afford wantonly to lose sight of great men and memorable lives, and are bound to store up objects for admiration as well as may be; for the effect of implacable research is constantly to reduce their number,† . . . .

A historian has to be treated as a witness, and not believed unless his
    sincerity is ascertained. The maxim that a man must be assumed to be
    honest until the contrary is proved, was not made for him.

† c.f. Prelude, Bk. XII:

> I could no more
> Trust the elevation which had made me one
> With the great family that still survives
> To illuminate the abyss of ages past,
> Sage, warrior, patriot, hero; for it seemed
> That their best virtues were not free from taint
> Of something false and weak, that could not stand
> The open eye of Reason.

and Sonnet on Napoleon (1803):

> The great events with which old story rings
> Seem vain and hollow; I find nothing great
> Nothing is left which I can venerate.

However this is getting away from Implacable Research; nor
does that enter into Stephen Spender's Vienna, where the emotion
of the present debunks the events of the past.

I glanced at these two books of the Prelude to see whether
Wordsworth's Imagination and Taste had been impaired in the
same way as my own. The result was interesting enough to
branch into another note. He was upset like myself by a European
crash, and "inwardly oppressed

> with sorrow, disappointment, vexing thoughts
> Confusion of the judgement, zeal decayed,
> And lastly, utter loss of hope itself,
> And things to hope for!

But this was not the root of the trouble. *That* had started when he
began to compare one piece of scenery with another,

> even in pleasure pleased
> Unworthily, disliking here, and there
> Liking

– comparison being even more destructive than analysis. There
is sense in this, though some of us think the price worth paying
and we cannot in any case restore imagination and taste by the
means open to Wordsworth; when *he* was tired of Europe and
the Revolution he could return to the Lakes and find them un-

changed by speed boats and aeroplanes. To become again a
"creative soul" is in these days not easy: the world of our infancy
has altered too drastically.

Human felicity is produced not so much by great pieces of good fortune
that seldom happen, as by little advantages that occur every day. Thus
if you teach a poor young man to shave himself, and keep his razor in
order, you may contribute more to the happiness of his life than in
giving him a thousand guineas. The money may be soon spent, the
regret only remaining of having foolishly consumed it; but in the
other case he escapes the frequent vexation of waiting for barbers, and
of their sometimes dirty fingers, offensive breaths, and dull razors; he
shaves when most convenient to him, and enjoys daily the pleasure of
its being done with a good instrument.   – Benjamin Franklin

Middle-sized, sturdy, snuff-coloured Doctor Franklin, one of the
soundest citizens that ever trod or "used venery" I do not like him.
                                                    – D. H. Lawrence.

The Church has given to Christ a lot of things which never did belong to
him and has taken away things that did belong to him. To my mind
they have stripped him of his manhood and wrapped about him oriental rags of mistery and immagination which makes it almost impossible
to get to his real self. There is small credit due to any person who is
good simply because its impossible to be bad . . . . . I do not think that
his intellect was deep or keen. Outside his moral inclinations he appears to be quite indifferent to the things that are interesting to the
average thinking man.   – Letter from F. Vicary, 23-8-16

Vous me demandez, ma chère fille, si j'aime toujours bien la vie: je vous
avoue que j'y trouve des chagrins cuisans, mais je suis encore plus
dégoûtée de la mort; je me trouve si malheureuse d'avoir à finir tout
ceci par elle, que si je pouvois retourner en arrière, je ne demanderois
pas mieux. Je me trouve dans un engagement qui m'embarrasse; je
suis embarquée dans la vie sans mon consentement; il faut que j'en
sorte, cela m'assomme; et comment en sortirai-je, par où, par quelle
porte? quand sera-ce? en quelle disposition? Souffirai-je mille et mille
douleurs, qui me feront mourir désesperée? aurai-je un transport au
cerveau? mourai-je d'un accident? Comment ferai-je avec Dieu?
qu'aurai-je à lui presenter? la crainte, la nécessité, seront-elles mon
retour vers lui? n'aurai-je aucun autre sentiment que celui de la peur?
que puis-je esperer? suis-je digne du Paradis? suis-je digne de l'Enfer?
Quelle alternative! Quel embarras! Rien n'est si fou que de mettre son
salut dans l'incertitude; mais rien n'est si naturel, et la sotte vie que je

mene est la chose du monde la plus aisée à comprendre. Je m'abîme
dans ces pensées, et je trouve la mort si terrible que je hais plus la vie,
parce qu'elle m'y mène, que par les épines qui s'y rencontrent. Vous ne
direz que je veux vivre eternellement, point du tout; mais si on m'avait
demandé mon avis, j'aurois bien aimé à mourir entre les bras de ma
nourrice, cela m'auroit ôté bien des ennuis, et m'auroit donné le Ciel
bien sûrement et bien aisement; mais parlons d'autre chose.

The above quotation from Madame de Sevigné (16–3–72) is not
the one I wanted to copy out. Her orthodox, gaiety, and caution
are better combined in the following (10–6–71): –

Je me suis ni à Dieu ni au diable: cet état m'ennuie, quoiqu'entre nous je le
trouve le plus naturel au monde. On n'est point au Diable, parce qu'on
craint Dieu, et qu'au fond on a un principe de religion: on n'est point
a Dieu aussi, parce que sa loi paroit dure, et qu'on n'aime pas à se
détruire soi-même. Cela compose les tièdes, dont le grand nombre ne
m'étonne pas du tout; j'entre dans leur raisons; cependant Dieu les
hait, il faut donc en sortir, et voilà la difficulté.

And still better – gaiety dominating – in this quotation (24–4–71)

J'ai acheté pour me faire une robe de chambre une étoffe comme votre dernière jupe; elle est admirable, il y a un peu de verd, mais le violet
domine; en un mot, j'ai succombé. On voulait me la faire doubler de
couleur de feu, mais j'ai trouvé que cela avoit l'air d'une impénitence
finale; le dessus est la pure fragilité, mais le dessous eût été une volante
déterminée, qui m'a paru contre les bonnes moeurs, je me suis jetée
dans le taffetas blanc.

Ibsen from old note book: for pp. 35 seq. of this book, and now
transcribed (1–12–40) because they sometimes hit at this world
and its war.

Undermine the idea of the State: make willingless and spiritual kin-
ship the only essentials in the case of a union – and you have the begin-
nings of a liberty that is of some value.

4   I must confess that the only thing I love about Liberty is the struggle
for it: I care nothing for the possession of it. – Letter to Brandes, 1870
The state has its roots in Time: it will have to culminate in Time.

5   Greater things than it will fall: all religion will fall. Neither the conceptions of morality nor those of art are eternal. To how much are we

obliged to pin our faith? Who will vouch for it that two and two do not make five in Jupiter? – ditto.

1   I am conscious in personal intercourse of only being able to give incorrect expression to what lies deepest in me and constitutes my real self: therefore I prefer to lock it up.   – letter to Bjornson, 1864.

2   An aesthete in Copenhagen once said to me 'Christ is really the most interesting phenomenon in the world's history.' The aesthete enjoyed him as the glutton does the sight of an oyster.   – ditto.

3   My little boy shall never with my consent belong to a people whose aim it is to become Englishmen rather than human beings.   – ditto.

The costliness of keeping friends does not lie in what one does for them, but in what one, out of consideration for them, refrains from doing.   – Letter to Brandes, 1870.

Eighteenth Centuriana

Sir Robert Walpole dying:
Tis impossible not to be a little disturbed at going out of the world, but you see I am not afraid.   1745

Sir Thomas Mann dying:
Though I am not vehemently attached to this world, I must do it the justice to own that I have no right to complain of my lot in it, during a very decent course of time and with more comforts than I had any pretensions to, at the beginning of it, upon the whole therefore I am perfectly well satisfied and look forward with a total indifference as to myself, though to the last hour of my existence I shall be anxious to hear of your welfare.   1786

Horace Walpole:
I almost think there is no wisdom comparable to that of exchanging what is called the realities of life for dreams. Old castles, old pictures, old histories, and the babble of old people, make one live back into centuries that cannot disappoint one. One holds fast and surely what is past. The dead have exhausted their power of deceiving – one can trust Catherine of Medici now.   Jan 5, 1766

Squabbles and speeches, and virtue, and prostitution amuse one sometimes; less and less indeed every day. But measures from which you must advance and cannot retreat, is a game too deep; one neither knows who may be involved nor where will be the end. It is not pleasant.   Nov. 1. 1762

Mr Doddington entertained these Fuenteses at Hammersmith; and to the shame of our nation, while they were drinking tea in the summer house, some gentlemen, aye, my lord, gentlemen, went into the river and showed the ambassadress and her daughter more than they had ever expected to see of England.   June 7, 1760

Voltaire's Zaire. The warmth of feeling between Z. and Orasmane, the easiness of the action (except in the frigid double-recognition scene) surprised me, and as I cannot appreciate the badness of the French as Lytton could; I enjoyed the play and should like to see it acted.   1732

Bigotry is an odd thing. To be bigoted you have to be absolutely sure that you are right, and nothing makes that surety and righteousness like continence. Continence is the foe of heresy.   – Hemingway

Wordsworth on Machinery ("Motions and Means" he calls it)

> Nor shall your presence, howsoe'er it mar
> The loveliness of Nature, prove a bar
> To the Mind's gaining a prophetic sense
> Of future change, that point of vision, whence
> May be discovered what in soul you are.

> [Sonnets of the Imagination XLII]

Right! The problem of 1941 has never been better put. And it could be so well put only by someone who had not all the facts. "Steamboats, Viaducts and Railways" were all that W. was coping with. His imagination was not distorted by Tanks & Dive-Bombers, like ours, they have put the wind up us, and we cannot see past their barrier, seek undistorted imagination in the past,

> Salimmo su, ei primo ed io secondo
> Tanto chi'io vidi delle cose belle
> Che porta'l ciel per un pertugio tondo
> E quindi uscimmo . . . .

Instances of Broadcast English

A Naval Spokesman has looked forward to fewer Atlantic sinkings.

– Allan Howland, 9.0. P.M. news, 6–10–41

The defences of the Dutch East Indies are very far from being able to be ignored.

– Postscript, 21–11–41

Malherbe on the Death of Abel: –

Ne voilà t-il pas un beau début!

on his own Death, when the priest described the Joys of Heaven:

Ne m'en parlez plus; votre mauvais style m'en dégoûte.

Dolly Winthrop (in Silas Marner) *on Christmas.*

But now, upo' Christmas-day, this blessed Christmas as is ever coming, if you was to take your dinner to the bakehus, and go to church, and see the holly and the yew and hear the anthim, and then take the sacramen; you'd be a deal the better, and you'd know which end you stood on, and you could put your trust i' Them as knows better nor we do, seein' you'd ha' done what it lies on us all to do.

G.E. shows her greatness in this minor interview. Who else in her century or in any could present simplicity and goodness without patronage *and* without self-abasement? Atmosphere all through both thick and unforced; buried buried are we in the depths of a deeper England than Hardy's. Extravagant young men in need of money are here, as in Middlemarch, as in Ralph the Heir, as endlessly, a bore; it is Victorian economics, not Victorian prudery, that has to be stomached before we can enjoy their fiction. When did this preoccupation with cash and with the horrors of losing it, come in? It did not obsess Jane Austen. It connects with Trade, and Family Life. (It and the Family both denounced by Christ) – But to go back to Dolly Winthrop, how poised she is, and G.E. through her, and how falsely would she be described in any words but their own.

Discovery of corpse a well-kept surprise. But why does it make Godfrey confess to his wife? And is not the riding whip found with the body a relick of an earlier draft, in which *he* should be suspected of stealing Silas' gold? Eppie – oh that Victorian hair – dubious as Esther Summerson until her big scene, when she hardens.

Quoi! je ne vous ai point parlé de Saint Marceau, en vous parlant de Sainte
   Geneviève! je ne sçai pas où j avais l'esprit. Saint Marceau vint prendre
   Sainte Geneviève jusques chez elle; sans cela on ne l'eût pas fait aller.
   C'étoient les Orfévres qui portoient la Châsse du Saint: il y avoit pour
   deux millions de pierreries. C'étoit la plus belle chose du monde. La
   Sainte alloit après, portée pas ses enfans, nuds pieds, avec une devotion
   extrême. Au sortir de Notre-Dame le bon Saint alla reconduire la
   bonne Sainte jusques à un endroit marqué, où ils se séparent toujours;
   mais sçavez-vous avec quelle violence? Il faut dix hommes de plus pour
   les porter, à cause de l'effort qu'ils font pour se rejoindre, et si par
   hazard ils s'étoient approchés, puissance humaine ni force humaine ne
   les pourroit séparer. Demandez aux meilleurs Bourgeois et au peuple;
   mais on les empeche, et ils font seulemont l'un à l'autre un douce
   inclination, et puis chacun s'en va chez soi.
                                          – Madame de Sévigné, 7-8-75

>   . . . aussitot que la Parque
>   Ote l'âme du corps
>   L'âge s'evanouit au deça de la barque
>   Et ne suit point les morts. – Malherbe
>
>   Toutes les autres morts n'ont mérite ni marque
>   Celle-ci porte seul éclat radieux
>   Qui fait revivre l'homme, et le met de la barque
>   A la table des Dieux.   – Malherbe

Donner un sens plus pur aux mots de la tribu.   Mallarmé

If I admire this, do I like French poetry? I do admire it. And,
mythology lost, what will become of poetry? Mythology gave a
stiffening to the fabric.

[*Christ*] *was the Son of Man*, because, though greater than any of his generation, he was their junior, he was younger, he belonged, by the creative
   power which he allowed to keep flowing in renewal through him, to
   a generation of men, who even now after two thousand years, have
   yet to be born.

Thus does Gerald Heard spice up his urge to prayer in *The Creed
of Christ*. Have written (20-9-41) a letter to him which I ought to
have transcribed. Like other priests, he so emphasises the perils
of mis-prayer that one feels it was wise never to have started. He
identifies the mentality of this war with the last's: otherwise he
makes a case and points out *how* a change of heart can be started,
and 'the idea of keeping ones religion just to oneself so that no
one need ever notice one had any, is just no use.' and that 'We

face an actual world which produces at its lower end men who can claim with some right and record to be diabolic, and at its upper end – ourselves. But nothing can start unless we can realise the existence of God; and the Lords Prayer is written from G.'s point of view, our daily bread being the Eucharist.

Servants – Friends – Sons: this hierarchy.

Like H. R. Williamson A.D. 33 and all this neo-Gospel stuff, the selections from the Gospels are quite arbitrary, and their interpretation often based on a pun. But G.H. puts himself in a strong position by asserting it doesnt matter what he selects.

And what do I believe? That sainthood is ineffective against diabolism but that diabolism will lead to exhaustion, and a tired harmless generation will arise and begin to look around them. Date? 1980 at the earliest. This will give time for babies at present unborn to mature.

Written when Kief had fallen and Leningrad, Odessa and Sebastopol may have fallen.

Written in peace, after playing the first movement of Op. 101 and before going to evacuate in the next room.

Written on a bared oak slab, by a window through which I see heavy green trees and a pale grey sky.

Written with a sense of Charles Mauron near me, and of *his* far greater wisdom: Charles now blind and composing his work on Aesthetics and Mysticism on the typewriter and with Marie's help.

E. K. Bennett's letter to me:

What you say about Christ is what I feel about the Church. It is always telling one it knows everything and is everything, and I think it ought to wait for me to say that. When they preach I feel that it is as if I should give a lecture saying the whole time how good my lectures were, and nothing else.

The Disappointment of God.

The Times, in an article with this title, announced that though God is certainly disappointed by the state of the world we must not go so far as to suppose that he is surprised. – Very funny effect, especially in its paginal context. Deducing Gods personality must be a fascinating game. But the world has disappointed *me* so much that I scarcely smiled.

The Vision of the Cross (from a 10th c. MS.): –

Then the young man who was God Almighty stripped himself strong and steadfast. Bold in the sight of many he mounted the high cross when he would redeem mankind. I trembled when he clasped me, yet I durst not bow to the ground or fall to the lap of earth.

This magnificent and male vision is quoted in Trevelyan's History of England, and foreshadowed in the Runes round the Ruthwell Cross (A.D. 700). But the poem, when looked at, will probably prove to be turgid maunder.

Religion is nearly always for women and priests, and literature is mostly composed by the latter for the former: certainly my novels have been, and it is only lately, through Bob and perhaps through old age, that I have got freer.

> Our tough redeemer, ere he breathed
>   His husky last farewell
> To us a heavy weight bequeathed
>   On earth to dwell –

as opposed to the usual feathery flame. Disentangle this from the commonplace Christ the Warrior. The Anglo Saxon poem keeps the idea of redemption: the powerful lad decides that it is worth doing and that he can do it, and gets up on the cross and starts. And he has no arrière pensée: he will not come again to judge the quick and the dead.

Bob on Blessed are the Meek: = those who realise the smallness of man's position in the universe, he thought, and will consequently come to own this planet.

Written when the Russians were hoping to retake Mojaisk.

Sylvia's Lovers 1863, though I have not finished it, has been an eye-opener after the twitterings of Cranford. The sensuousness of the sailor, the characterisation, without fuss, of S's parents, the amusing deterioration of S's friends after marriage. And the wisdom in this account of old fashioned country-mentality:

Taken as a general rule, it may be said that few knew what manner of men they were, compared to the numbers now who are fully conscious of their virtues, qualities, failings, and weaknesses, and who go about comparing others with themselves – not in a spirit of Pharisaism and arrogance, but with a vivid self-consciousness that more than anything else deprives characters of freshness and originality.

May the faith in self-sacrifice and atonement give an extra polish to the sensuousness above noted? Mrs Gaskell is anyhow not fully conscious of *her* qualities, anyhow. I wonder what she will do with Philip Hepburn in the long run, and must pull myself away from the resonances of French poets to find out. [Later: after the sailor's smashingly true return, atonement takes charge and Mrs G. works away like a housekeeper to clean the repulsive Philip, whom her genius has effectively befouled.]

Revelations are the aberrations of faith; they are a distraction that spoils simplicity in relation to God, and that embarrasses the soul, making it swerve from its directness towards God, and occupying the mind with other things than God. Special illuminations, auditions, prophecies and the rest are marks of weakness in a soul that cannot suffer the assaults of temptation, or bear anxiety about the future and God's judgement upon it. Prophecies are also marks of creaturely curiosity in a being towards whom God is indulgent and to whom, as a father towards his importunate child, he gives a few trifling sweetmeats to satisfy his appetite. – Jean-Jacques Olier, quoted by Aldous Huxley.

I do not know, never shall know, whether passages such as the above – and it is one of the best of them – are to be classed as examples of good taste or of canniness or as statements of the truth. The reluctance of the mystic to remove mountains, coupled with his reiterations that they are movable, takes a good deal of explaining.

Liberty, morality, and the human dignity of man consist precisely in this, that he does good, not because it is commanded but because he conceives it, wills it, and loves it.   Bakunin

It is possible to have a proletarian art, but will it ever do more than amuse or inspire? Will it extend sensitiveness, and so evolve new forms?

Can the sensitive man be happy in the coming state, or useful to it?

Will not everything combine to crush him out, and the evolution of humanity, which hitherto he has stimulated, slow down?

Function of the writer in wartime? Same as in peace time.

We are fighting for self-preservation, and can't know what we shall be like until we have won. When we have won we shall arrange this planet in accordance with our characters. Planning now is merely a game.

Disgusting Death.

Fortunately History and Life are not the same thing, as Gerry well and unexpectedly remarks, and Great Events and Great Movements are paralysing one's views in the same way as did once the dates and reigns of Kings. The 1066 Fallacy is difficult to eradicate.

Men wiser and more learned than I have discerned in history a plot, a rhythm, a predetermined pattern. These harmonies are concealed from me. I can only see one emergency following on another as wave follows waves, only one great fact with respect to which, since it is unique, there can be no generalisations, only one safe rule for the historian – that he should recognise in the development of human destinies the play of the contingent and unseen.
H. A. L. Fisher: preface to History of Europe:
infuriating communists.

Every mutiny every danger every terror and every crime occurring under or paralysing our Indian legislation, arises directly out of our national desire to live out of the loot of India.
Ruskin: Slade Lecture on The Pleasures of England.
The Pleasure of Deeds.

Les gendarmes se sont multipliés en France bien plus encore que les violons quoique moins nécessaires pour la danse.
Le peuple est sage, quoiqu'en disent les notres secrètes.
Courier. Petition à la Chambre des Députés, 1820.

Hegel was right when he said that we learn from history that men never learn anything from history. – Shaw: preface to Heartbreak
House.   Where did Hegel say it?

L'Histoire est le produit le plus dangereux que la chimie de l'intellect ait élaboré. Ses propriétés sont bien connues. Il fait rever, il enivre les peuples, leur engendre de faux souvenirs, exagère leurs réflexes, entretient leurs vieilles plaies les tourmente dans leur repos, les con-duit au délire des grandeurs ou à celui de la persecution, et rends les nations amères, superbes, insupportables et vaines.   Paul Valéry.

Easter, 1942. The Four Accounts

Mark	Matthew	Luke	John
Mary Magdalene & Mary the mother of Jesus see where body is laid	M. Magdalene & the other Mary sit by the tomb A watch is set	The women see where the body is laid.	——
Easter Mary Magdalene Mary the mother of James & Salome bring spices, find stone rolled away and young man sitting on the right inside: he tells them that Jesus is risen and tells them to tell Peter etc: they fly in terror and tell no one (in appendix) Jesus appears to Mary Magdalene: she tells the others and they disbelieve her.	Easter Mary Magdalene & the other Mary come to look. There is an earthquake (While they are there?) an angel in white descends, rolls back the stone and sits on it. The watch is frightened: The angel tells the women to look at the empty tomb and tell the others. Afraid but happy, they run to do this, and are met by Jesus and take hold of his feet.	Easter They (i.e. Mary Magdalene) & Mary the mother of Jesus & others) bring spices, find the stone rolled away and the tomb empty, and two men in white stand by them and tell them that Christ is risen. They tell the others and are not believed. Peter goes by himself, finds tomb empty & linen wrapped up: no mention of angels.	Easter Mary Magdalene goes and sees stone has been taken away. Runs and tells Peter & John. They go. John arrives first, looks in and sees the linen folded, but does not enter. Peter goes in, followed by John. They both go home. Mary Magdalene, who has been weeping now looks in and sees two angels in white at the head & foot of the bier. They ask her why she weeps, but do not enlighten her. Going away, she meets Jesus ('Noli me Tangere') and proceeds to tell the others.

The Titian show at the N.G. led me to formulate the above. It is a melting morbid highly sexed picture *I* should have thought, and the change from the early draft, where Christ is striding manfully away in a hat, is startling. But Bob found only compassion in the evasion: 'will these human beings *never* understand me?' I thought of Bapu Sahib's 'Morgan, I am so very sorry, I am holy today, you mustnt come near me.'

The accounts prove nothing except an early diffused story in which the Magdalene was prominent. Were I a judge, I should think St John's evidence the best. Aimlessness is always convincing.

You can't understand life or live properly without the help of God, you can't believe in God unless you believe in Christ, you will find what Christ taught and was in the Bible, you can't read

the Bible properly without the help of God, but you can't believe
in God unless you believe in Christ, you will find what ——

So spins the 24 hour record on the B.B.C. 194 .

Penetrabis ad Urbem (i)

: thus to entitle a few notes on late 3rd and early 4th cent.
events, for which I will leave the next few pages free. I have (May
1942) been seeking in that period *not* an explanation of our
disaster, but wisdom with which to bear them. The situation is
queered by the existence of Christianity, and the attendant
denunciation of sex. St Augustine, my main hope, is at any
moment free to shrug his shoulders and say 'What else can you
expect in such a world?' To him, the collapse of Rome seemed a
natural enough incident, though he does admit that some govts
may be worse than others. I am impressed by his psychology: his
references to babies in the Confession are sound[2], and his belief in
original sin is only an unsound way of saying that characters are
conditioned in the womb and indeed at the instant of conception.
But I cannot make out whether he minded the crash, or thought
anything could have been done to avoid it, or learnt from it anything he couldn't have learnt anywhere. If you deny sex, you
diminish your investments.

> Haec quidem gaudebat, sed tota terra gemebat.[2]
> Vir tamen advenit illia retributio digna.
> Luget in aeternum quae se jactabat aeterna. – Commodian, Carmen
> Apologeticum, denouncing the Roman Empire in hexameters
> rightly called rough, but terribly apt to the mouth of an Indian
> today.

again: –

The intrepid city endeavours to communicate her language to all the
lands she has subdued to procure a fuller society and a greater abund-
ance of interpreters on both sides. It is true, but how many lives has
this cost? and suppose that done the worst is not past, for —— the
wider extension of her empire produces still greater wars ——
—— Wherefore he that does but remember with compassion all these
extremes of sorrow *and* bloodshed must needs say that this is a mystery.
But he that endures them without a sorrowful emotion or thought
thereof, is far more wretched to imagine he has the bliss of a god when
he has lost the natural feelings of a man.
                              – Augustine, de Civ. Dei, XXI. 7.

Is the translation correct? If it is, note how the generosity and tenderness fails to carry through, and gives place to censorious rhetorick. I think I note often in him this failure in warmth:

(1) Rumpe omnes, Alarice, moras; hoc impiger annO
Alpibus Italiae ruptis, penetrabis ad urbeM

Claudian: de Bello Getico

(2) The innocency of infancy depends on the weaknesses of its limbs, not on its character   Confessions I. 8.

again: –

That detestable father *St Jerome*, thus reacts to the Fall of Rome: –

'To quote a common proverb, I well nigh forgot my own name.' When the refugees, many of whom had been in good position (cf. Bath) began to reach Palestine: 'I was long silent, knowing that it was the time for tears. Since to relieve them all was impossible, we joined our lamentations with theirs, and in this state of mind I had no heart for explaining Ezechiel.' – 'Quid salvum est si Roma perit' – adapted from Lucan. Virgil's 'Urbas antiqua ruit, multos domi-nata per annos' quoted, which I myself was to read 1500 later, after seeing the Docks on fire from my roof in Chiswick. – Writing to a friend about the friend's baby: 'Into such times as these our little Pacatula has been born; these are the toys by which her infancy is surrounded; she is learning tears before laughter, sorrow sooner than joy. Oh let her think that the world has ever been like this let her be ignorant of the past, avoid the present, yearn only of the future.' – And going still further off his rocker on learning that a certain Demetrias intends to remain a Virgin, he exclaims 'Italy changed her garments of mourning and the ruined walls of Rome almost resumed their former glory.'

[Extracted from Hodgkin. Jerome has to leave Rome for the desert because he found the ladies too charming there. On return-ing to it as secretary to Pope Damasus, he collected a pious cohort of matrons and virgins, to the annoyance of the regular clergy.

Demetrias was congratulated by many other saints.

St Jerome (c. 340–420) b. in Dalmatia. Greek & Hebrew scholar, Christian antiquarian. The Vulgate etc. What did he & St Augustine squabble about?

He was accused before the Throne of being a Ciceronian rather than Christian, was severely flagellated by the angels, and awoke with bruised shoulders. – Delighted by the sorrow St Paula caused her family by abandoning them, pietatem in filios pietate in Deum superans, and at the poverty in which she left them at her death. – 'In this matter cruelty is the only piety' he tells Heliodorus, about to become a hermit.

Extracted from ch. iv of Lecky's 'Morals from Augustus to Charlemagne', interesting, ill-indexed, strong on the Egyptian anchorites.

Must read Jerome, Ep. iii which details the holy endearments applicable to females. A sublimated womaniser. But I find myself, through Gerald Heard, less contemptuous of asceticism and the anti-family stunt than were the Victorians. (i) new faculties are developed by abnegation (ii) I have lost faith in the orderly progress of Society [I cannot however trace any *connection* between anti-sex and the Fall of Rome]

Pope Damasus his pal, 'Auriscalpius Matronarum' or the Ladies' Earscratcher, fought his way into the episcopate at the head of his own clergy and gladiators.

again: –

St Augustine. Some scattered notes.

Have glanced at his work *On Marriage & Concupiscence*, part of his attack on the Pelagians. What he thinks wrong in copulation is not the semen but the pleasure attending its emission, and he thinks the pleasure wrong because people are ashamed to be seen doing it. (The 'post coitum tristitia' argument, which is more impressive, doesn't seem to be used.) Before the Fall: 'it was quite possible to effect the function of the wedded pair . . . just as many a laborious work is accomplished by the compliant operation of our other limbs, without lascivious heat.' [Bk II ch. 26]. Elsewhere, he says that the time for giving in marriage was B.C., and the time for abstaining from it A.D., but he does not urge the extinction of the human race, and hopes that husbands and wives will continue to go ahead, with as little pleasure as possible, until the establishment of the City of God. I find it difficult to follow, in any one so intelligent, such opinions, and think they may have been induced by the unintelligent asceticism of his age; by the knowledge that thousands of stupid men were sitting in the desert all along Africa. *Not* a hypocrite.

Pelagius says that whether you're saved or whether in Hell you burn
Its nothing to do with the Church, my boy, but purely your own
concern.

Pelagius = Morgan, I am glad to say:

b. in England. Condemned at Carthage in 412 for the following
errors: –

(i) Adam created mortal
(ii) His sin personal, and not transmitted to his descendants
(iii) Babies are as Adam was before he sinned
(iv) His sin is not the cause of our death
(v) The Law of Moses, like the Gospel, leads to the Kingdom of
Heaven
(vi) There were sinless men even before Christ
(vii) Children dying unbaptised will be saved.

– thus bye-passing a good deal of nonsense, and winning over
Pope Zosimus for a time, but crushed by the superior genius of
Augustine, who warns every one, virgin, Demetrias, against him,
and in 424 he is driven, my namesake, from the Holy Places, and I
hear of him no more.
                    – From a good article in the Biographie Universelle.

St Perpetua, the sister of Dinocrates the good thief, dreamt that she was
changed into a man and wrestled with an Egyptian. St Augustine
[On the Soul, & its origin, ch. 30] does not say with what intentions
or results.

The home-thrust of sin plays the King in the foul indulgences of adultery,
etc. . . . . . . whilst in the indispensible duties of the marriage state it
exhibits the docility of the slave.   [Bk I, ch. 13]

They felt their shame when, after their own disobedience to their
Maker they felt their members disobedient to themselves. [Bk. II ch. 14]

again: –

St Augustine Some questions raised rather than solved in Figges'
'Political Aspects of the City of God'.

Had he a Philosophy of History? Yes – in as much as 'no one who
takes the Incarnation seriously' can avoid having one, God did
historically become Man, and a philosophy follows, postulating
the unity of the human race and its sociability.

Did he approve of the State? It was too useful for him to condemn: he had to call it in against the Donatists, to persecute them.
But I must look up De Civ. Dei II 21, where he says Christ is
King, and III 10, IV 3. 15, where he condemns imperialism and
wants 'as many states in the world as there are families in a city.'

What did he think of the Fall of Rome? That the Pagans were
wrong about it – and no doubt they were. Not concerned to
explain it, as Salvian was, and not as much upset as St. Jerome.

> Ut magnum esset imperium, cur esse deberet
> inquietum?   III. 10

> An latitudo imperii, quae non nisi bellis requiritur, in
> bonis sive sapientium habenda sit, sive felicium.   IV. 3

> Remotu itaque justitia, quid sunt regna nisi magna
> latrocinia? quia et latrocinia quid sunt nisi parva
> regna?   IV. 4

> An congruat bonis latius velle regnare   IV. 15

[He feels he ought to say something on such subjects, but has no
intention of opening out.]

Is *The Confessions* the first introspective book? As the *Vita Nuova*
is the first examination by an author of his own writings?

again: –

St Jerome's Letters (Loeb).

(i) *Sex*. Violent and continuous irritation about women.

"Where my only companions were wild beasts and scorpions, I
found myself surrounded by dancing girls . . . The fires of lust
kept bubbling up before me when my flesh was as good as dead".
Letter 22. And later on – it is his most famous letter and to a woman:
"I praise wedlock, I praise marriage, but because they produce
virgins for me". They must be Christian: heretical virgins are of
the devil.

Indignant (letter 45) about the scandals which had sprung up
around him in Rome "Was I ever attracted by silk dresses, flashing
jewels, painted faces. No matron could dominate my mind . . .
unless squalid with dirt, almost blinded with weeping' . . . . You
belch after wild duck and sturgeon . . . I fill my belly with beans" –
elsewhere connecting indignation with lust, and realising one can
even eat too many vegetables. Wine naturally dangerous.

"Frequent gifts of handkerchiefs & ties, pressing a woman's dress to your lips, tasting her food beforehand . . . of all this a holy love knows nothing." 'Mel meum lumen meum, meumque desiderium.' (52)

Single standard for men and women indicated in (77): both sexes serve God equally.

Letter 117 is the most remarkable: to a mother and daughter in Gaul whom he has never seen. Inflamed by the anxiety of the girl's brother, a monk, he details to her all the sins she *might* commit with her young major-domo. "Some boy with a little beard will give you his arm and hold you up if you are tired, and as your fingers squeeze he will either be tempted himself or will tempt you . . . . To induce you to visit the baths they will speak of dirt with disgust . . . . Desire in virgins is the sharper set because anything of which nothing is known seems specially delightful . . . . . your vest slit to let something be seen within . . . . your shiny black shoes by their creaking give an invitation to young men . . . your hair comes down over your forehead or over your ears . . . your shawl drops so as to leave your white shoulders bare . . . . . then hastily hides what it intentionally revealed . . . ," and so on, till one can hear him swallowing in his throat. Angrily rebuts suggestion that he is malignant and suspicious; how can he be when he has never known the young lady? – Dictated letter in haste through the night, "my volubility baffled the tricks of my secretaries' shorthand"; "wished to show my detractors that I too can say the first thing that comes into my head." Really a terrifying letter for its blindness and vigour; unlike St Augustine, he has never sized himself up. Date – 405; he was 60.

(ii) *Politics*. Letter 60, written 396 touches on the frail fortunes of human life and the downfall of our age. "For twenty years the blood of Romans has every day been shed." Matrons & virgins raped of course, horses in church, relics dug up.

Romanus orbis ruitet tamen cervix nostra erecta non flectitur. Only last year the Huns irrupted. "It is because of our sins that the barbarians are strong."

Letter 77 – date 399 – refers to same invasion "We had to think not so much of our own lives as of the chastity of our virgins" of course, and so to find ships. The Origenian controversy which he was holding with a former friend "seemed more important than fighting with the barbarians."

In letter 107 on the other hand, Christianity seems to be triumphing – the shrines of paganism in Rome are deserted, and "Getarum rutulus et flaxus exercitus" carry tent-churches about, and perhaps fight with us on equal terms because they believe in the same religion.

Letter 127 (A.D. 412) deals with the life of Marcella, who had had a palace on the Aventine, and with the sack of Rome, where she was haled through the streets by Goths, but to the church of St Paul.

Now farewell St Jerome for ever, but I must not ignore some similarities between us: we both decline to concentrate on the political catastrophe. Your obsession with virginity helps you, for it is in danger whether there's peace or war. I avoid concentration by trying to find a place where the catastrophe becomes a problem. I try to understand, not quite sincerely for I know I shall fail.

Your dates: b. 345, first went to the East 373, at Rome with Damasus 382–385 then to Bethlehem, d. there 420.

again: –

Apollinaris Sidonius, introduced by Hodgkin, is of Lyons and the Auvergne, and over-responsive through nostalgia, I read into his descriptions that South of sittings down, of easy walks, which I shall never see again. For my period he is too late (c. 430–480), swaying in the Châlons afterwash. He saw the universe as still Roman, it seems, and the Goths as a poor joke; I believe that he and they thought they would pass: so do we – not he – think Hitler will pass and cannot imagine a new barbarism. Sidonius – a bishop and connected with emperors – felt secure. Patronises the smelly giants. Details, as though he was a boar, King Theodoric of Toulouse. Hodgkin blames his superficiality and squeamishness: why didn't he find out about Ulfilas, Runes, etc.? I find him soothing. Few of us can think long at a time or often about tragic changes. We keep on pretending that the past continues – Rome unpillaged for him, Lyons attainable for me – It *can't* be that so much has been withdrawn, or that I have never even seen the English Channel since the war started. Little untragic men do happen to be born into great events – and in great numbers. As I write, Egypt may be lost to me also. *30-6-42*

(N.B. Smith's Dictionary finds S. subtle forceful intelligent)

Remember story of the woman who was sold into slavery and lost. It may happen to us. It will happen to us.

No. I generalised too quickly. Sidonius at the end of his life was scared by Euric a cid of Toulouse, brother and murderer of Theodoric, who got hold of Berry & Auvergne, leaving only Provence to the Empire, and he writes some sharp truths to his fellow bishop of Marseilles, who had negotiated an anti-Roman peace.

Sidonius probably a wiser and finer man than Hodgkin allows.

Art Peirce et Tyler 'L'Art Byzantine', seeking order where perhaps it is not, distinguish periods, passing from the vigour of the Tetrarch style (Diocletian: the knights outside St Mark's) through the feminine delicacy of the Constantinians to the recrudescence of vigour which suits the character of Valentinian I. From their beautiful illustrations I select

Bronze statue at Barletta, Valentinian I? The profile certainly expresses his attempt to stop the rot.

Enormous and badly executed gold medal of Valens.

Marble relief from S. Agnese, Rome: draped, coy, plump, extended hands.

Silver disk of Theodosius, Spain: the emperor, with Arcadius & Honorius (?) is already hieratic: supported by Frankish guards. 394 – just before he had his fit.

Base of T's obelisk, Constinople: between his brats again.

Silver disk of Valentinian II at Geneva. Decorative.

Diptych from Monza, Stilicho, Serena & their son (?)

The Traprain treasure, the Woodchester pavement; the paintings in the catacombs of S. Priscilla, the mysterious Patène de St Denis in the Louvre, all dated about 400.

Mosaics of Galla Placidia dismissed as over-restored.

Wilpert: Die römische Mosaiken: (a superb work; published in the other war at Freiburg, for the G. Emperor.)

St Costanza – Mausoleum of the unsuitably sainted d. of Constantine, 310

Sta. Maria Maggiore – Old Testament scenes (Liberius, 360)

Baptistery, St Giovanni, Naples. 375

St Pudenziana: Apse: Christ between Apostles and Saints and below the Cross and the Evangelistic Signs. Masterpiece. Innocent I, 410

Sta Maria Maggiore: Childhood of Christ (Sixtus III, 440)

Milan: St Ambrogio. St Ambrose. c. 425

Ravenna: Galla Placidia: esp. Deer Drinking, 450

„ Bapt. of Orthodox: St Batholomew etc. (Neon, 450)

Lateran: St Giov. Ev's chapel. The Lamb (Hilarus, 460)

St John of the Studium, 463, the only Constantinople remain of my period?

Why did Rome fall?

A quaker banker's view.

"Because it had completed its work," naturally, "and the time has come for it to be cut down" and to make way for the Teuton.

Subsidiary causes were

i. *The foundation of Constantinople*, due to fear of Persia: danger from the north never realised. "It was the diffusion of her vital force over several nerve centres, Carthage, Antioch, Alexandria, but above all Constantinople that ruined her. Some of the suckers lived on but the old tree perished."

ii. *Christianity* – despite St Augustine's view. For it opposed the deification of the Emperor which consecrated the state. And a strange jumble resulted from their alliance – e.g. all emperors until Gratian keep the title Pontifex Maximus, and Claudian turns Theodosius into a star. Intolerance: those who keep away from the Hippodrome will have the far more delightful spectacle of prefects and philosophers burning in hell, Tertullian had said. Theodosius quietly persecutes heretics & pagans to uphold a religion which did *not* uphold the state, or interest the intellectuals (Amnianus Marcellinus, Zosimas, Priscus).

Ecclesiastics, like St Ambrose & St John Chrysostom, also weaken the state by their criticism, and the Monks by their abstention from public service.

iii. *Slavery* 40,000 fled to Alaric between the sieges of Rome. Stiff resistance to invaders impossible cf U.S. Civil War, also Singapore.

And effeminacy luxury, all that, promoted among the citizens.

iv. *Bread-dole* Injures Italian small-holder and leads to large grazing estates and agricultural Concentration camps. Theodosian Code much worried. Palace-servants, soldiers, and people *as householders* eligible for 'Panis gradilis' which they get by sitting on steps and presenting a relief-ticket personally [registration, coupons, food office snobbery, penalties, British Restaurants interfering with private trade – all the familiar administrative mess: e.g. the children of a Guardsman mightn't inherit his ticket.]

v. *Municipal Govt* (curia) once an honour becomes a horror: middle classes throughout the empire clamped into it by the central authority, bled white and destroyed.

vi. *Bad finance.* Rome had no genius for it, though the Empire stopped the Republic's straightforward plundering. Customs duties and death duties existed, but negligibly. Chief source – a crushing land-tax, reassessed every 150 years. Banking highly developed, "but a banker's true business is to act as a broker between lenders and borrowers". Would a National Debt have checked decay?

vii. *General* Autocracy not harmful to the Empire, but the Imperial household – freedmen & eunuchs – often interfered disastrously in state affairs. Decay of army follows that of the Italian agricultivatist – once its backbone – until soldiers complain that armour is too heavy.

> The ruin of such a mighty fabric as the world empire
> of Rome can hardly be contemplated by the citizen
> of any state such as our own, which has ex-
> tended its dominion over alien people
> and far distant lands without stir-
> ring some foreboding fears that
> of our country too it may
> one day be said: –

> How art thou fallen from Heaven
> Oh Lucifer, Son of the Morning.

Thus, as philosophically as he can, does our quaker banker end (1880), and thus far have I transcribed with a heavy heart (1942). My original impulse in this excursion was the discovery of parallels, then I was diverted into interest in the past, now that too is flagging, and I have driven myself with difficulty to finish this analysis. My ignorance and the powerless of knowledge weigh on me. After Tobruk Sebastopol and the search for something small enough to do, such as the arranging of a vase of flowers.

St. Basil (329–379) (i.e. died just after Adrianople and the first smash) is a Father easily disposed of, and a glance at the second volume of letters in Loeb shall suffice. Interested in the Arian controversy, though tactful even with Valens, and in coenobatic life; not in chastity. Of Caesaria, in that comic place Cappadocia which he takes very seriously. Promotes local life, redresses local grievances, and stands up – on one occasion – to the governor. Well educated at Athens, decent; when crossed fretful rather than virulent; shows up well as a critic of literary prose in a letter (No 135) written in 373 to a Presbyter of Antioch; he doesn't like "the continuity of the thought" interrupted by aimless accusations or counter-accusations, or by character-sketches.

A perfect society is that which excludes all private property. Such was the primitive well-being which was overturned by the sin of our first fathers. – quoted by H. Read, 'The Philosophy of Anarchism'.

Literary and topographical description of summer retreat at Pontus   – Letter 14

Mother, brothers (Gregory of Nyssa one of them) and sister all saints. Orthodoxy. Alliance with St Athanasius, his Senior – Friend of Greg. of Nazianzen. Funny that he should be tempted to patron-ise St Basil; who was at all events threatened with death and could answer back. Out of what a curling sea of bishops does he rise? Where did they get their money from?

The humble and abject spirit is attended by a gloomy and downcast eye, neglected appearance, unkempt hair and dirty clothes; con-sequently the characteristics which mourners affect designedly are found in us as a matter of course. The tunic should be drawn close to the body by a girdle; but let the belt not be above the flank, for that is effeminate, nor loose so as to let the tunic slip through, for that is slovenly, and the stride should neither be sluggish, which would argue

a laxity of mind, nor on the other hand brisk and swaggering, which
would indicate that its impulses were rash

– Letter 11 : on Monastic Rule

St Gregory of Nyssa (331–396 or so), brother to the above; married,
compelled to the Bishopric of N. After the deaths of St Basil and
Valens, becomes important organiser of orthodoxy. He too has
left many works, into which I shall not look.

St Gregory of Nazianzen (328–329) also a Father and a Cappadocian;
the most interesting of the three. Same culture as St Basil who spoilt
their friendship by giving him a bad bishopric. Rode in under
Theodosius and was a b. of Constantinople for *two exciting years*
(379–81) which are described by Gibbon and show sensitiveness as
well as enthusiasm. Establishes orthodoxy, gets hated, and retires.
Poem *De Vita Sua* and *peroration to last oration* [farewell to men &
angels, city & Emperor, east & west) are praised. He can describe
his own victorious party at the Council of Constantinople as wasps,
magpies, flight of cranes, flock of geese – not bad. [The other
Gregory of Nyssa says of the city at this time: 'If you desire a man
to change a piece of silver, he informs you where the Son differs
from the Father; if you ask the price of a loaf you are told that the
Son is inferior to the Father; and if you enquire whether the bath is
ready the answer is that the Son was made out of nothing.']

St Cyril Damned if there are'nt two of him too, and more were I to
go outside the period.

i. *Him of Jerusalem* (315–386). Troubled career. Suspected of
Arianism, but gets straight; calm end under Theodosius. For
pilgrimage-morality and manufacture of relics, see Gibbon.
St Jerome shocked at Bethlehem.

ii. *Him of Alexandria* (3 . .–444) whom I have too imperfectly considered in my Guide. He was one of the worst, and I should like
some day to go deeper into him. Became bishop after uncle
Theophilus' death, with the help of the troops, robbed the Nova-
tians, expelled the Jews, tried to canonise the monk Ammonius,
who hit Orestes the Prefect in the eye; and Hypatia was killed. All
during 412–415. Outside Alex, attacks St John Chrysostom, and,
when headed off from him, Nestorius. They were both arrested for
their violence at Council of Ephesus – where C. brought a body-
guard of Egyptian sailors, 431. But triumphs.

When I have made a note on St John Chrysostom I should be through with these saints. I don't think I need bother with St. Ambrose.

St John Chrysostom (344–407)

Synesius (370–403) b. Cyrene, stands between Greek Xtianity and Paganism. ed. at Alex by Theon & Hypatia. Baptized by Thophilus and became a bp. straightway. Moderate, civilised, against 'men in white' – pedants – and 'men in black' – monks. Letter 105 gives prose and cons for his episcopacy. To Arcadius he could say:

> The fear that you emperors may become men if you are often seen keeps you close prisoners besieged by yourselves. You never see or hear anything which could give you knowledge of realities. You have no pleasures but those of the body, and of them only the most sensual, such as taste and touch give. You live the life of a mollusc, and disdaining manhood you can never reach manhoods perfection
>
> – Oration on Kingship. (Poem?)

Emperors

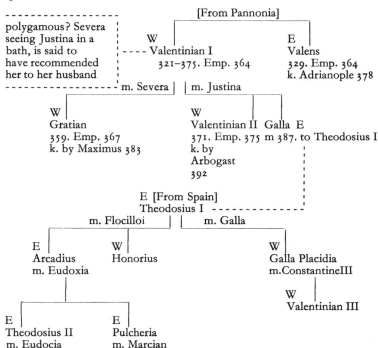

Sophists:

Himerius (310–393). Bithynian. At Athens.

Themistius: ["A Love Speech concerning the beauty of the Emperor", addressed Gratian as 'Boy Emperor, Boy Father, Boy who surpassest hoary virtue.'] (320–388). [addresses Jovian on Toleration ".... allowing each man's soul in matters of religion to follow that path which it thinks best ... You can break and kill the body if you will, but the soul will escape, taking with her the law and the freedom of her thought." Important imperial official. Tutor of Arcadius.

Libanius (314–393) Chief literary Greek of century. Of Antioch. Friendly with Fathers. Complains to Theodosius "For the defence of Temples" of monks who destroy temples: "these men in black, more voracious than elephants, never satisfied with the cups which they drink to the sound of hymns, but concealing all that beneath an artificial pallor" (384). Panegyric on the water supply and public lighting of Antioch, evidently a civilised unstrenuous spot, and on the Daphne Gardens, 10 miles in circuit. – Would I had visited Antioch! May I remember it amongst dulness and death!

The three foregoing hung on to the Emperor Julian (331–363) and were chronicled by Eunapius (346–415), though he was keener on the neo Platonists.

Proclus (410–485) b. Constantinople. Head of neoplatonic school wh. had been moved from Alex. after the murder of Hypatia to Athens. It survived Christian opposition until Justinian closed it. cf. Oxford & Cambridge. P. 'a great thinker' unmarried, ascetic, charming – according to F. A. Wright, History of Later Gk Literature, my unsubstantial guide. – Culture & carnality seem to have held their head up better in the east.

Greek Poets: Quintus Smyrnaeus fl. 400 Posthomerica – epic. fills gap between Iliad & Odyssey. *Nonnus* from the Thebaid, fl. 420. Christian, but his epic, the Dionysiaca, is warm pagan stuff. Bks 10–12: Ampelos Bk 48 Pallena & Aura. Must look up these timely indecencies but they have not been translated. – *Palladas*, fl. 400, about Alexandria. A secondary schoolmaster. Look up him too in the Gk. Anthology. X. 45 78.

Three Western Cities

Trèves [founded by Augustus]

> To guard the Rhine. Esp. under Constantine and Gratian. Its monuments – never seen by me –

> Amphitheatre and pieces of Bridge over Moselle (1st cent). 'Barbara' Baths, and Porta Nigra – c. 270.

> Basilica – b. by Constantine? now Prot. church.

> Basilica forming nucleus of Cathedral.

> Imperial Baths – intended for the Palace, but converted into a forum etc. by Gratian as trouble started.

> And a few miles away at Igel, 4th cent. column of the Secundinii, rich cloth-workers: must see photo of this.

[Many years after inscribing the above (June 1960) I paid a hasty and ill informed call on the city, Bobs car, Where park, where lunch, where the antiques?

Porta Nigra disappointing because merely large, and the days are over when antiques could impress by largeness. We could build a Porta Negrissima ten times its size.

Amphitheatre – Provincial – Viewed from its rim.

Igal monument or Denkmal. Yes – curious and amusing.

Battered, repaired clumsily, sculptures almost indecipherable but brought back a peaceable Roman past on the edges of Empire. It is almost plumb with the street, so that we passed it, and a church-yard, into which its enclosure is cut, rises steeply behind it. I let down a tiny anchor on Igel. Not on the other antiques, which we did not visit, nor on the deadish old cathedral, nor on its gracious Gothic neighbour. Nor did I visualise the Mosel flowing N.E. towards the gracious lower reaches where we had stayed a fort-night earlier. It was a typical motorist's call. But its dry bones serve today for a kind of soup which is not unpalatable and may send me back to Ausonius. It was I remember a sunny day, not particularly charming. We had come from Pirmasens in the Saar, sleeping very pleasantly in a Gasthaus there, and were making for Aachen which indeed we confusedly surpassed, and slept near the Dutch frontier. – Written on July 20th, 1960.]

The other two cities would have been Milan and Ravenna.

Socrates of Constantinople. I have run through his Ecclesiastical
History with amusement and without contempt. Possibly a Nova-
tian and certainly no fool. Bk V ch. 18 on the purity campaign of
Theodosius is very funny. There was a machine which lowered
visitors to a brothel into a bakehouse, where they worked for the
rest of their lives. And there was another which rang bells when an
adultress was copulated with. Funny too is the bishop who trod
on another bishop's foot, with the result that it festered and had to
be amputated. Bk VI ch 19.

Prudentius. see B. Farrington, Science & Politics in the Ancient World.
ch IV. b. Spain. c. 450.

"The Battle for Britain in the Fifth Century", by T. D. Reed argues
tendentiously that the Roman withdrawal (410) and the arrival of
Hengist at the invitation of Vortigern (443) did *not* lead to the
steady Saxon occupation of England. Ambrosius, a Brito-Roman,
becomes over-king, 460, builds Wansdyke and his general (and
nephew ?) Arthur wins a victory at Badon (Liddington in Wilt-
shire) in 497 and started a half-century of peace. It was a second
Saxon invasion which was continuous, and produced the Hept-
archy. Chief witnesses Gildas (vi c.) and Nennius (viii c.)

> Once Gildas knew, but now
> Death only knows!
> Night has received them all.

St Germain d' Auxerre : his two visits to the above mentioned island
to root out Pelagianism. 429 he wins the Alleluia victory. b. 390?
d. 448. Curious anecdotes of the tree of hunting trophies and the
compulsory consecration. His church in Paris, idly glanced at by me
in the irrevocable days; ornate entrance.

British Gods : Sul, goddess, Bath; Nodens, hunter, Lydney; Brig-
antia, north; Maponus, the Youth, Hero, whose name may not be
spoken?, north; Cocidius, Roman Wall; Matunus, the kindly,
Northumberland; Condates, Watersmeet, river Wear; Contrebis,
god of a fair open place dwelling among us.

Bakunin (1814–1876) shall bring me to my own times from St Aug's.
Reading Carr's pitiless and ungenerous account of him, I am often
carried outside it to contemplate the endless senseless torturing
of Europe; the same places occur in the 18th cent, as in the 5th,

and people are still being killed and thwarted, and beautiful and useful objects being destroyed. The 19th cent was, in comparison, peaceful, but what misery awaited anyone who did not fit in, and how difficult it was to fit in! The Liberal – Herzen: reform – the Communist – Marx: reorganisation – and the Anarchist – Bakunin when he had developed: individualism & destruction – all go into exile and quarrel with one another in London.

'States cannot be made to change their nature since it is in virtue of that nature that they are States . . . There cannot be a good just and moral State. Only a weak State can be virtuous, and even it is wicked in its thoughts and desires.'

The seven degrees of happiness: 'to die fighting for liberty; love and friendship; art and science; smoking; drinking; eating; sleeping.'

'The passion for destruction is also a creative passion.'

'All exercise of authority perverts, and all submission to authority humiliates.'

'Every State, like every theology, assumes man to be wicked.'

So that the Marxian state could never 'wither', and must remain 'a herd of animals driven together by force, pursuing exclusively material aims, and knowing nothing of the spiritual side of life.'

'Everything will pass and the world will perish, but the Ninth Symphony will remain.'

The biography pursues him from Romanticism and Premakhino to exile; belief in democracy and nationalism; 1848; Siberia; escape via Japan to London; belief in the proletariat; the quarrel with Marx and the International; swinging full circle, the aristocrat dies as a rentier in Switzerland, though not paying his rent; the Romantic, soon sexually impotent, has an old man's passion for Nechaev, the Tiger-Boy.[1] All presented by Carr as sordid

---

(1) We recognise no activity but the work of extermination, but we admit that the forms in which this activity will show itself will be extremely varied – poison, the knife, the rope, etc. – Nechaev

---

and absurd, and best so presented, leaving the reader to strike the match and make Bakunin a light in the darkness. For he is that. And it is the artists, not as he hoped the common people, who will follow him; they know however that it is not for them to destroy, but to be destroyed.

The perfect society has no govt. but only an administration, no laws, but only obligations, no punishment but means of correction.

– Weitling: influencing B.

Quotations

> music heard so deeply
> That it is not heard at all, but you are the music
> While the music lasts.   – T. S. Eliot The Dry Salvages

The human body is like a temple marching. Like a temple it has a central point round which volume is placed. When one understands that one knows all.   – Rodin

Les aberrations sont comme des amours où la tare a tout recouvert, tout gagné. Même dans la plus folle, l'amour se reconnaît encore.

– Proust. Le T.R.

Une oeuvre où il y a des théories est comme un objet sur lequel on laisse la marque du prix.   – id.

Théories . . . reprises pendant la guerre . . . qui tendaient à faire sortir l'artiste de sa tour d'ivoire a traiter de sujets non frivoles ni sentimentaux, à peindre de grands mouvements ouvriers, et a defaut de foules a tout le moins non plus d'insignificants oisifs . . . mais de nobles intellectuels ou des héros.   – id.

Les chagrins sont des serviteurs obscurs, détestés, contre lesquels on lutte, sous l'empire de qui on tombe de plus en plus, des serviteurs atroces, impossible à remplacer et qui par des voies souterraines nous menent à la vérité et à la mort. Heureux ceux qui ont rencontré la première avant la seconde, et pour qui si proches qu'elles doivent être l'une de l'autre, l'heure de la verité à sonner avant l'heure de la mort.

– id.

Il en est de la vieillesse comme de la mort, quelques uns les affrontent avec indifference, non parce qu'ils ont plus de courage que les autres, mais parce qu'ils ont plus d'imagination.   – id.

Nos plus grandes craintes, comme nos plus grandes espérances, ne sont pas au dessus de nos forces et nous pouvons finir par dominer les unes et réaliser les autres.   – id.

I sit under a tree, and feel alone: I think of certain insects around me as magnified by the microscope: creatures like elephants, flying dragons, etc. And I feel I am by no means alone.

– Thomas Hardy, Diary, 28–11–75

A man who is not interested in his stomach can be but indifferently interested in anything else.

– Dr Johnson; but where? and what nonsense!

The number of men in the world is as nothing compared with that of all other sentient beings, and they often suffer greatly without any moral improvement.   – C. Darwin: where?

Farewell, Australia! You are a rising child, and doubtless some day will reign a great Princess in the South: but you are too great and ambitious for affection, yet not great enough for respect. I leave your shores without sorrow or regret.
        – C. Darwin, Voyage of the Beagle 7–2–36

By the spirit are things overcome, they are stark and the spirit hath
    breath
It hath speech, and their   are dumb: it is living and things
    are of death.
But they know not the spirit for master, they feel not force from
    above
While man makes love to disaster and woos desolation with love.
        – Swinburne: Hymn to Man.

It was a bitterly cold night, and the subaltern on duty found in the early morning that the Boer prisoners and the Inniskilling troopers of their guard were sleeping together in comradeship under the same blankets. Somewhat scandalised at this fraternisation with the enemy, he hurried to Allenby and woke him. "Let them be" said Allenby; "that will do more to end this stupid war than anything else."
        – Wavell, Life of Allenby

No sensuousness in contemporary novels. If lust is described it is with contempt or scientifically. No effect to involve reader in toils. Contrast Silvia's Lovers (p. 127): how attractive, and to each other, are Silvia & Charlie.

Women and War. Mrs Nicholson wishes that she could be in Berlin for an hour in an invisible cloak, and hopes she could see all the women looking starved and ill. Mrs King suggests that strikes could be stopped by exchanging strikers for our P.O.W. in Germany: she did not think that Hitler need be consulted. Listening to these two village fools, I told myself that they talked in order to be thought clever, and that Mrs N. in particular inhabits a cocoon of self-esteem. Yet it is difficult to grasp that they meant nothing (Ap. 43)

Commando Troops. Trained killers – steal up behind a man and kill. How will they settle into anything else? Merry policemen two

years back: now grim chinned fascists, thinking themselves the
cream of the army. What process will detrain them? – This
through Bob. – (Ap. 43)

The war has lasted too long and the peace will last even longer.
July 43

Cocteau

J'admirai l'insuccès de Dieu: c'est insuccès des chefs-d'oeuvre. Ce qui
n'empêche pas qu'ils sont illustres et qu'on les craint.

Les experiences dangereuses, le monde les accepte dans le domaine de
l'art parce qu'il ne prend pas l'art au sérieux, mais il les condamne dans
la vie.

Corps parfaits gréé de muscles comme un navire de cordages et dont
les membres paraissent s'épanouir en étoile autour d'une toison où se
soulève, alors que la femme est construite pour feindre, la seule chose
qui ne sache pas mentir chez l'homme.

Je suppose que beaucoup de journalistes ne veulent pas mentir mais
qu'ils mentent par ce mecanisme de la poésie et de l'Histoire qui
déforment lentement pour obtenir le style.

Il est amusant et significatif que Bergson ne parle jamais du rire
injuste, du rire rire officiel en face de la beauté.

Victor Hugo était un fou qui se croyait Victor Hugo.

What a wildness south of St Paul's! I stood (Feb. 43) by St Augustine's
– a tiny Wren – and saw the tower of St Nicholas Cole rising from
the plain. Two dirty little boys had discovered an echo born in the
desolation (as in the Coliseum's) and were inclined to exploit it
commercially: "The old man doesn't know where it comes from."
The sun had set, coldish. A few birds whirled. In the portico of
the Cathedral hundreds squeaked. Full of my own desolation, I
thought "It will never get straightened out", also 'Here is
beauty.' Oh I long for public mourning in the sense of recognition
of what has happened.

One more novel? Bob's plea for one (8–3–43) shall start this page,
though fitter for a diary. Yes – I am drawn into trivialities (home
life) and diverted to unimportancies (Civil Liberties, B.B.C.) yet
I can still write well and I am wise. 'Repeat yourself' he said: 'it

does not matter, so changed are the conditions.' 'Say again that you believe in human relationships and disbelieve in power.' I consider my age 64, my family record of idleness, inability to start, and three years of war which have weighed down my spirits, like everyones, so that I no longer hit out vivid similes or make big jokes. And my mind would slip off into cynicism, or – more readily – into affection for Bob for bothering to attack me. But his voice: 'Leave all that out and start a new novel at once' cuts at me. So easy to reflect that he is crude and was a bit alcoholic. The plea remains, something which cannot be whittled away or stated in any other words. And my fear that – in spite of success far beyond my hopes and of a gratification far beyond most men's – I haven't fully come off, would be laid. Rather tired – for it is 11.30 P.M. 10–3–43 and I have interrupted this prayer, or vow, to listen to the shallowness of Shostakovitch – I seem to see a bier carried past on which, veiled, is the human being to which I couldn't give life. I make no resolution. But I have seen my obstacles: trivialities, learning and poetry. This last needs explaining: the old artist's readiness to dissolve characters into a haze. Characters cannot come alive and fight and guide the world unless the novelist wants them to remain characters.

One More Novel?

Agriculture. Perhaps (17–3–43) it is well to write here a bit in the morning, for myself, before the world of worries and kindnesses gathers strength, and here I think of my two days driving with Hughie Waterston in Northants, whose beauty he is ploughing up. District Officer of the War Agricultural Committee, which supervises farmers and has also acquired a 600 acre estate. This is run by officials, Irish indentured labourers, and W.L.A. girls in hostels and is a high lying bald cheerless contour from which hedges have been removed. A derelict farm is being repaired for a supervisor. Not an animal in sight. Only crops, or what will be crops, and drains, and holes dug at a dowser's suggestion, for there is no water. This was 'Rockingham Forest' once. Seen in bright sun, it glowed as the English countryside of the future – one huge food-tub from which the lorries will proceed to the mills. Shall here the drama of human life – Crabbe – be set? Yes – I can just see it but not the gods who will control it. Produce produce produce produce produce. Punish the non-consumers.

Yes – this writing after breakfast for a little has something to it, and makes me more my own during the day. Write difficultly! Write carelessly! Be alone! [But alone with your tools. Dassera!] Don't topple into prayer.

Yes – just this added, 22–3–43, before going to shop in Dorking. Thank the sun – can again use my room.

Charles Mauron's Letters: -

Raphèle – 2 janvier

SNOW. Ecrivez moi mon cher ami. Et faites que le printemps vienne vite. Il ne parait pas se presser – nous sommes dans la neige la glace et les frimas. Les prés sont immaculés les coups de l'horloge sont tout assourdés – un timbre d'horloge enrhumée, vielle, cassée, ridicule – Hier soir je suis sorti sur le chemin pour voir les flocons voler autour de la lampe electrique. J'avais les pieds gelés, mais j'étais bien heureux: j'ai pour la neige un amour absurde, depouillé de toute la sentimentalité ordinaire, mais bien profond Le contact des flocons sur le visage me fait toujours un immense plaisir. Ecrivez.

[Raphèle]

WINTER. L'hiver va recommencer. Ma grande pièce vide est toujours telle que vous l'avez connue, et dejà j'y passe de grandes heures a ecrire, fumer, et me promener de long en large. Seulement le soir, de temps a autre, comme il pleut beaucoup au dehors, un souris vient Dieu sait d'où gratter a la porte. Nous avons recueilli un chat des voisins, mais dedaigneux des souris il s'est contenté d'aller deposer un incongruité dans le tub de cautchouc. Les cordes de la harpe cassent. Nos deux pigeons – nous avons deux pigeons – ne veulent pas s'aimer d'un amour tendre. Quelquefois un parent arrive avec un panier plein de raisins de salades et d'anecdotes: les derniers morts de St Remy, les derniers cocus. Le soir Marie me lit La Guerre et La Paix. Ici, c'est la paix, la paix complete.

Raphèle 10 Février 1930

SPRING Il faisait assez beau jusqu' a hier: les amandiers sont en fleur; le poele chauffe: la paix, la bonne humeur et le desordre regnent incontestés: Marie joue de la harpe et moi du très cher piano.

[Mas Blanc] Vendredi, Avril 1927

CIVILISATION. Quant à ce qui attend notre civilisation, voici: elle deviendra la civilisation d'autres hommes, et elle leur paraîtra tres jeune: en verité elle sera toujours tres vieille: à la fin de tout elle se gelera, en virtu du principe de Carnot. A cette époque, il y aura longtemps, vous et moi que nous serons traités de barbares ou de décadents, ou de barbares décadents, ou de rien: mais tout cela nous sera parfaitement égal. J'aimerais bien vous voir pour ne pas vous parler de notre civilisation.

Angirany

T. E. LAWRENCE Ce Lawrence m'épuise et il faut en finir – dans quinze jours je suppose. Voilà cinq mois que je vis enclusivement en tête a tête avec lui et comme il y a peu de style aussi révelateurs que le sien, je crois commencer à le connaître. Je ne dis pas que je le comprends – il a toujours de difficultés avec lui même alors que je n'en ai jamais – mais je sais comment il a souffert et triomphé et souffert davantage. Au fond il a été dupe, de lui même des autres et des circonstances – et il a payé cher un livre beaucoup trop "viande crue" par certains cotés et "coucher de soleil" par d'autres pour satisfaire vraiment. Et pourtant l'on sent une carrure, une maitrise. Mais cette duperie est trop cruelle: pauvre homme! adorer les 'jolis mouvements du menton" d'Allenby! adorer, detester, adorer, detester, sans trop savoir pourquoi et pour recueillir en echange beaucoup d'amertumes, très peu de joie, et un infini d'indifference. Car les Arabes, n'est ce pas, pouvaient être, quoique insupportables, gentils quelquefois; mais les généraux s'en foutaient, le laissaient choir quand il avait servi; et en fin de compte il travaillait pour les généraux ou leurs frères; et il le savait; et il les adorait les detestait *vraiment*, sans pouvoir s'en empècher, je pense. Triste vie, qui n'aurait été rachetée que par de belles oeuvres; les souffrances de Beethoven, vues de près, devaient être idiotes.

Raphèle 14 Juin 1930

CLIVE BELL J'ai eu toute une soirée sous les yeux la vanité de Clive Bell. Il parait qu'il était dans un mauvais jour: mais vraiment c'était un spectacle superbe d'infatuation creuse, de fausse intelligence, d'esprit en 'sham'; tout Bloomsbury autour de moi, tressaillait devant cette image de son propre idéal – en simili.

Raphèle, 6–11–29

POEM J'étudie la poesie moderne francaise ou plutot quelques tentatives. J'explique d'abord ce qu'est pour moi la poesie, en m'appuyant sur un poème de Baudelaire – Un poème, sachez le, Morgan, est un être qui aime à se souvenir, qui prend plaisir aux ressemblances et aux échos. – J'etudie les surrealistes et je vois que leurs poèmes oublient tout, tout. Une phrase ne se souvient pas même de la precedente. – Je salue Proust en passant et je m'aperçois que s'il se souvient souvent d'une façon magnifique, il a aussi d'étranges defauts de memoir. – J'envient à Valery et je montre qu'il se souvient très bien, mais que souvent il n'a pas de plaisir – ces souvenirs la ne comptent pas en art. Enfin, je parle du groupe Duhamel, Romains, Vildrac, qui sont émus souvent par

tout autre chose que des échos. – Ma conclusion est que maintenant
comme toujours beaucoup de grandes choses, le chaos, l'intelligence,
le sentiment cherchent a etouffer le tout petit poème et à l'empêcher
de jouer avec ses souvenirs. Mais le petit poème se defend – Il n'est
jamais etouffé. Et ainsi le monde continue.
Moi je continu a vous croire mon ami. Marie vous envoie her love.

Raphael, 16 Janvier 1928

MRS. ZANGWILL Cependant un jeune éditeur, M. Hazan, ayant
remarqué une très belle traduction parue chez Plon au mois d'Octobre
m'a offert de faire pour lui la traduction de Ghetto Tragedies de
Zangwill. Je n'aime pas Zangwill mais je n'ai pas d'argent. J'ai
accepté. Mme Zangwill a fait la sourde oreille: elle ne connaissait pas
M. Charles Mauron et craignait qu'il n' honorât pas assez la memoire
de son Juif d'epoux. Le jeune editeur a declaré tout net que la traduction serait faite par M. Mauron ou qu'il n'editerait pas le livre. (Ciel!
pourquoi tous les evenements de la vie deviennent-ils heroiques autour
de moi qui suis si pacifique?) Mme Zangwill s'est inclinée. Mais
ecoutez, my dear dear Morgan, le bruit qu'elle fait quand elle s'incline:

Dear. M. Hazan,

. . . . . You mention that Mr. Mauron has translated Forster's Passage
to India, but, of course, this work in no way compares with Ghetto
Tragedies, which most people consider will be a classic.
Yours etc.

Marie Mauron's Great Uncle His birth. Christmas, about 1820, his
mother was returning from Mass and fell into labour by a row of
cypresses in a valley. We looked down on them [in the 1930's]
while she remembered the story. Delivered of a boy, she put in a
fold of her petticoat and walked on to the Mas (Mas du Gros),
where her mother in law, preparing the Christmas dinner, was
thrown into some agitation. There were many children afterwards.
The baby grew up to fight through the Crimea, Solferino,
Magenta, and all Nap. III's wars, and to lose his leg. He had many
medals and a pension, for which his wife avowedly married him;
but it wasn't a large one. – They went to live in St Remy when
Marie knew them – ate mostly potatoes as the aunt was an idle
cook, but rabbit on Sundays. The uncle was handsome and
charming. He was good company for himself and would talk
aloud while preparing vegetables or "They say the earth is round,
but how do they know? ––– Anyhow a little piece of it must be
flat – one can see there are corners" – He knew many French and

Provençal songs. His wife used him every spring to hatch out the
silkworms, which have to be kept at an even temperature: she
made him stop in bed and had them in a box at his feet. Obliged
him to have his café au lait there. He was going over his songs to
sing them at Charles & Marie's wedding, but died before it happened [i.e. he must have lived till nearly 100] – The cypresses are
now old, one of them dead. The farm is only used by the shepherds. The valley is better watered and its sides more wooded
than the vallée de cinq sous to its west. – Nightingales sing in it. –
Many petrified sea-urchins on the ridge.

Carent quia vatice sacro.

Le Silence de la Mer by 'Vercors' (Schlumberger?) was given me by
Raymond Mortimer yesterday and read without much admiration
though with plenty of sympathy: published secretly under the
Nazis in France. Read also too slow a story by Giono of the
coming of Pan: it quickens at the end where human beings and
animals dance together, with regrettable results. Écrivains!
écrivains! Read too in Illusions Perdues, to which this criticism
cannot apply, and in Gide's Journal, which is partly responsible
for this note. Gide aroused my envy by reading, reading, but if I
kept a journal too I should appear to have read, read a lot.

Receuillement. Resolution, which will sometimes be kept – the best
part of resolutions – to sit at an empty table with this book or
another before me as early as possible in the morn, and collect
my pieces which have been lent out to worries and kindnesses.
N.B. this book and pensées not important and the temptation to
mistake them for Creation must be resisted. – It is so still and to
heighten that rarity and approach silence I have stopped the
Clock.

Listen out for silence! The mind so accustomed to noise that it
goes on imagining it even when there is no message from the ear.

The eye even in darkness and blindness (Charles) sees something.
The ear *can* hear nothing, can register the last vibration of a note
and enter a state of negation, of absence, which should please the
mystics. But the state is best reached when there is something to
listen *for*, when the window is open as now and the vast landscape
might pop and seethe but does not. Silence would be unsatisfactory in a cell.

Has any creature, except a man had such thoughts as above, or attempted to record them?

Yes writing down the above strengthens me. Reading entails docility. And writing to others insincerity, putting things. With some thankfulness I will return to the ins and outs of the day, and restart the Clock.

Sunday, July 25, about 11.0 A.M. In my sitting room at West Hackhurst.

Silence again.

Rec. cont. next day. It is 11.0. again. Musso has resigned and disturbed me by superficial hopes. I *know* that there will be no betterment in my lifetime – or that betterment like worsement is something too deep to be observed at any particular moment. What I do see and this morning hear is machinery used for evil. And machinery will be used increasingly. That is the knockout first intercepted by Ruskin and Baudelaire, & S. Butler, now by Gandhi and by punies like Barbe Baker, Lionel Fielden, William Plomer & myself. I cannot rid myself of the theory that one day men will stop making & using machines, and revert with a tired sigh to the woods. But who will start the stopping? The Managerial Class? My dears, is it likely? Bombless anarchy? Honester in my thinking than most people, I fake the remoter future instead of the present, to help myself to bear the present. If I pursued my conclusions, I should let down my friends. I *do* love several people and want to help them. Don't know why and am incapable of asking why and bored by the answers pasted on me by psychoanalysis. I may read Burnham's Managerial Revolution disingenuously, but can't read Freud at all. This then is the falsity in my outlook: 'I say chaps – don't let us develop machinery any more – let's be less organised?' Is it likely that the decay of human energy, which may come about, will take this congenial form:

> What would the world be, once bereft
> Of wet and of wildness? Let them be left
> O let them be left, wildness and wet:
> Long live the weeds and the wilderness yet.

Wildness and Wet are being removed, and if they do return we shall be too degraded & feeble to appreciate them.

This receuillement has proceeded too long.

And by 10.0 P.M. I have done no work. Have just heard a helpful sincere and untrue talk from Priestley: man the master of his future (isn't); young wouldn't have fought as they have without believing in a better future (they fought to save their skins and their homes).

I simply dont mind is the last word in human wisdom, but I recoil from saying it. It would deliver me from fear, wastage of strength, entanglements with the unworthy or the perishable. It offers an inviolable sanctuary. My reluctance to enter implies some form of faith. It *is* my goal, but I would rather be dragged to it protesting. When I seek it and shed things or people, guilt mixes with my relief, and when I see anyone going further than myself, like Joe, I feel horror. *Not to mind* is to present a retreating back. "Which is bad form?" – An insufficient answer, because it reduces the problem to personal pride; it's greater.

To *forget* people or things because more interested in something else would be excellent. Up with Art therefore. Up even with work. The negative is all right while it is accepted as a negative. But when 'I simply don't mind' presents itself as something positive, I get scared.

Maugham has lost that scrap of innocence which prevents most men from becoming a bore.

> Du schlank und rein wie eine flamme,
> Du wie der morgen zart und licht,
> Du blühend reis vom edlen stamme,
> Du wie einquell geheim und schlict,
>
> Begleitest mich auf sonnigen matten,
> Umschauerst mich in abendrauch,
> Erleuchtest meimen weg in schatten,
> Du kühler wind du heisser hauch.
>
> Du bist mein wünsch und mein gedanke,
> Ich atme dich mit jeder luft,
> Ich schlürfe dich mit jedem tranke,
> Ich küsse dich mit jedem duft.
>
> Du blühend reis vom edlen stamme,
> Du wie einquell geheim und schlict,
> Du schlank und rein wie eine flamme
> Du wie der morgen zart und licht

A la très-chère, à la très-belle,
Qui remplit mon coeur de clarté,
A l'ange, à l'idole immortelle,
Salut en immortalité!

Elle se répand dans ma vie
Comme un air impregné de sel,
Et dans mon âme inassouvie
Verse le goût de l'eternel

Sachet toujours frais qui parfume
L'atmosphere d'un cher reduit,
Encensoir oublié qui fume
En secret à travers la nuit.

Comment, amour incorruptible,
T'exprimer avec vérité?
Grain de musc qui gis, invisible,
Au fond de mon éternité?

A la très-bonne, à la très belle
Qui fait ma joie et ma santé,
A l'ange à l'idole immortelle
Salut en immortalité!

The *George* and the *Baudelaire* above express, the one with studied
starkness, the other with studied affectation, the masculine and
feminine of the same idealism. I encounter this, in life, as a disaster
(Joe, Goldie), as bad temper or bad-spirits on a physical groundwork of indigestion: and have come to reject it furiously. Yet how
else could these two poems or most of Beethoven's music have
been composed? Hedonism would not do it. The passionate pursuit of the non existent is consummated. Excursions into nothing
(Capetanakis on Rimbaud), which may be dangerously prolonged
until the traveller can't live again on earth.

Given over to habits of comfort, I feel insincere when I enjoy
these poems. They are not for me or for anyone who is not
'prepared' to sacrifice comfort.

'Prepared' itself a habit-word: for how should one know beforehand whether one is going to be brave?

The Ordeal of Mark Twain by a bothered and bothering American of
the psychoanalysing 20s has succeeded in bothering me a bit.
M.T. nearly found himself as a Mississippi Pilot, but sacrificed

his creative genius to kindness, his mother, his wife, the pioneer spirit, mateyness, humour. His constant unconventionality was a futile attempt to escape – he never did or could escape, but having shocked his wife came back to her, and when in old age he determined to blaze out there was nothing to ignite. Much of this hits me, but I am not bitter against the human race, as M.T. became, and never read my failures into it. His "Anybody that knows anything knows that there was not a single life that was ever lived that was worth living" is just boring, and an unrealised Englishman better than an unrealised American because more civilised. How my life has been cumbered with rubbish, all the same. By how much am I surrounded which I never summoned and can't manage to throw away! There are moments when this house seems an evil genius. By the time I am free of it I shall be too old to do anything with my freedom. I am humanity-sogged. Down in the river Huck Finn sits, watching the light come. It is a lovely fresh passage in a book I enjoy less than *Tom Sawyer*. How foolish it seems to put the writer through an ordeal while one is in contact with such a passage.

12–10–43

Floating above the depths of myself and unable to sink into them. All the opinions I can arrive at, arrived at. Sense of my own smallness, and I must preserve it or lose touch with reality. Sense of my own greatness and I must preserve it or cease to act.

What was the thought I was nosing after the other week about 'other people'? To the effect that the more I understand others the more am I removed from them [unlike to them], for the reason that they do not understand one another. Sympathy from the human race means detachment from it. – This paradox needs shaking. Some falsity in it arising from careless use of the word 'understanding.' –

Wisdom, when acquired, proves incommunicable and useless and goes with our learning into the grave. The edges of it occasionally impinge on people, though and strike a little awe into them.

Impression made on me about 1901 by Lord Acton's lectures at Cambridge on the French Revolution. I knew that something was passing me, and copied into a note book: 'Every villain is followed by a sophist with a sponge', and 'Equality means government by the poor and payment by the rich.' The first quotation still makes sense. The sense of the latter died with its times.

So this page runs out and the delicious sense of *being collected* has been induced by writing it, as I hoped. I belong to myself for a moment, not to my three nibblers – kindness, lust, and fun. My enemies they are not, there is no enemy but cruelty. But they waste me and diminish me – especially kindness.

October 27th 1943

cont

Shall I not continue though? Shall any note end because the page ends? Shall anything but its own tuggings restrain the human spirit?

Human spirit: hypnotic phrase: to be examined like 'deeds which will be remembered for ever,' and to be rejected as implacably if necessary.

Thoughts, ideas, keep starting in me; when followed up they yield little, and Bessie Trevelyan tells me that this, a symptom of old age, is troubling Bob. I am so far only concerned to note the symptom, and the spinning down in the darkness of Catherine Wheels. Absolute absence, inanition unqualified, do not repel me but are never to be striven for. We must all be dragged into Death backwards. [27–10–43 as before.]

Two Events have made me *feel* lately (i) the sight of Neil Stuart, aged 60 now, running round in the low sunshine after mushrooms at Chesfield and untouched by time (ii) the slim oak which nearly hit me as it was felled yesterday. Neil seemed holy, part of my childhood. Though frightened by men he moved towards us rapidly as if going to speak, then swerved. I am glad I did not speak to him. The tree might have killed me. Bone's stupidity. He was not penitent or upset, and gave a short gruff laugh. So, this way and that, we are beckoned out of the life where we keep engagements, make points, do kindnesses, etc., into regions of emotions where we do not feel at home. My wisdom seemed loss for an instant when I saw Neil; he had been preserved from experience – which is not necessarily either good or bad, but which always makes a general modification in the same direction, and causes men of 60 to meet in their 60s. The tree means that great pain or death are always close in terrible freshness. All this in connection with Trilling's book on me as an important writer is welcome. Will play piano a little. (Played 1st B. sonata)

The Neil Stuart emotion was strictly poetic and of the depth which de la Mare used to reach: no deeper. The right words for it are unfindable, for the particular contours of the path, the particular slant of the sun, Ralph Poston's superciliousness have to come in.

Balzac: Illusions Perdues

En disant ces paroles avec une aigreur qui brisa le coeur de Camusot, Coralie trouvait la jambe de Lucien et la pressait entre les siennes, elle lui prit la main et la lui serra. Elle se tut alors et parut concentrée dans une de ces jouissances infinies qui récompensent ces pauvres créatures de tous leurs chagrins passés, de leurs malheurs, et qui développent dans leur âme une poésie inconnue aux autres femmes, à qui ces violents contrastes manquent, heureusement.

The bad taste of Balzac, his unpolished yet journalistic style, his formlessness, his unevenness, his obsession with money – which blinds him to everything in a work of art except its price – take some getting over; but a passage such as the above does him credit, and there is a lovely scene later on where Lucien is sick on Coralie's dress and she preserves it as a relic. His zest for life is recognisable.

It is some months since I finished this book, and Splendeurs et Misères des Courtisanes remains unbegun. Here is a great author very much not to my liking: the greatest not at all to my liking if I may exclude the still untried Cervantes. I read him over a fence – leaning against a parapet which is my own France sometimes, my own barrier not against vulgarity but against the acceptance of vulgarity with gusto.

His characters are so ambitious that they blunt their intelligence, and come to resemble each other monotonously; even Madame de Bargeton, so poignantly human at Angoulême, and at Paris so long as she is under the influence of fear, becomes uninteresting before her transmigrations close. And Lucien becomes indistinguishable from Rastignac. No: Balzac is not a great character-drawer: he is a great motive-hunter, and more of a specialist than Proust over the motives he hunts. Having never had to earn my living, I pick faults in him where I can.

Gide : Journal

Cette torpeur est parfois insupportable. Mais je crois que rien ne m'a mieux permis de sympathiser avec des etres d'intelligence inférieur que ces dépressions, ces diminutions de valeur. Quelque chose manque à Valery, pour ne pas s'être reveillé quasi idiot certains matins.

Certains pourrisent et d'autres s'ossifient; tous vieillissent. Seule une grande ferveur intellectuelle triomphe de la fatigue et de la flétrissure du corps.

L'indignation certes, mais point la haine. Je suis et je resterai incapable d'haïr. Même au temps le plus affreux de la guerre. Et sans doute c'est une grande faiblesse, ou ça le devient lorsqu'il s'agirait d'agir; mais rien à faire.

Cette méprisable comédie que nous jouons tous plus ou moins; à laquelle je voudrais me prêter moins que tant d'autres, et sorte que mes écrits trouvent dans ce refus même leur principale valeur.

Quoting from Baudelaire

Quand notre coeur a fait une fois sa vendage
Vivre est un mal. C'est un secret de tous connu.

J. S. Mill's "How can great minds be produced in a country where the test of a great mind is agreeing in the opinions of small minds" is not as good as I thought at the first reading, but a convenient reinforcement to Kenneth Clark.

Lord Acton Some 'shining precepts' for the historical student: –

Keep men and things apart; guard against the prestige of great names; be more severe to ideas than to actions; do not overlook the strength of the bad cause or the weakness of the good; never be surprised by the crumbling of an idol or the disclosure of a skeleton; judge talent at its best and character at its worst; suspect power more than vice, and study problems in preference to periods.

And 'The critic is one who, when he lights on an interesting statement, begins by suspecting it.'

The above are from his lecture 'The Study of History' (see also p. 118 supra). Transcribing them while the planes whirr, I wonder how far Liberalism would have progressed if the world had kept calm. Suppose Acton tested as Erasmus was. He would have behaved as badly, or worse, to Ulrich von Hatten.

Thought shall be the harder ⎫
Heart the keener   ⎬   The Lay of the Battle of Malden
Mood shall be the more   ⎪   (date –) quoted by Arnold Toynbee
As our might lessens   ⎭   on the title page of his History.
                                Again the bombers whirr (14–3–44)
                                as I transcribe it.

> On Hydon's top there is a cup
> And in that cup there is a drop
> Take up the cup and drink the drop
> And place the cup on Hydon's top.

– Local rhyme quoted in Murrays Guide to Surrey.

I always feel more and more how hard it is for the rich man (or those born in that state of life) to enter into the kingdom. It is so very easy to drift, instead.

– Extract from letter from E. Carpenter to Goldie written early in the century about Roger Fry. Today for the rich man supply 'the properly insured man.'

Carlyle on Wordsworth: A genuine but a small diluted man: and Newman had no more mind than a rabbit. cf. D. H. Lawrence passim. The uneasy social origins. Hatred of democracy. Ungenerosity to others – as T.E. pointed out. Lady Ashburton and Lady Ottoline. The shriek of the declassé. Sexual impotence. Froude, a civilised fellow = Aldous Huxley. Sterling = me? All that is intimidating and (hateful) detestable in him is (in the last resort) pitiful, but too much to pity; there wasn't in D.H. because in him was a larger proportion of poetry. Measure of Carlyle's in the following: –

. . . running about amongst people and things, looking even of a bright sunset on Hyde Park and its glory; I sitting on the stump of an oak, it rolling and curvetting past me on the Serpentine drive, really very superb and given gratis. Unspeakable thoughts rise out of it. This, then, is the last efflorescence of the Tree of Being. Hengst and Horsa were bearded, but ye gentlemen have got razors and breeches; and oh, my fair ones, how are ye changed since Boadicea wore her own hair unfrizzled hanging down as low as her hips! The Queen Anne hats and heads have dissolved into air, and behold you here and me, prismatic light-streaks on the bosom of the sacred night. And so it goes on. (1875)

Bede v. 13

Two most wicked spirits rising with forks in their hands, one of them struck me on the head, the other on the foot. These strokes are now with great torture penetrating through my bowels to the inward parts of my body, and as soon as they meet I shall die.

Amiel

S'en aller tout d'une fois est un privilege; tu périras par morceux.

I encounter these two mournful small fry on the same day. Boo hoo down the ages.

H. Melville

> But where is his blazon?
> Must merited fame endure times' wrong –
> Glory's ripe grape wizen up to a raisin?
> Yes! for Nature teems, and the years are strong,
> And who can keep the tally o' the names that fleet along!

from John Marr.

Waterton

Amongst us the needy man works from light to dark for a maintenance. Should this man chance to acquire a fortune, he soon changes his habits. No longer under "strong necessity's supreme command," he contrives to get out of bed betwixt nine and ten in the morning. His servant helps him to dress, he walks on a soft carpet to his breakfast table, his wife pours out his tea, and his servant hands him his toast. After breakfast, the doctor advises a little gentle exercise in the carriage for an hour or so. At dinner time he sits down to a table groaning beneath the weight of heterogeneous luxury: there he rests upon a chair for three or four hours, eats, drinks, and talks (often unmeaningly) till tea is announced. He proceeds slowly to the drawing-room, and there spends best of time in sitting, till his wife tempts him with something warm for supper. After supper, he still remains on his chair at rest till he retires to rest for the night. He mounts leisurely up stairs upon a carpet, and enters his bedroom: there, one would hope, that at least he mutters a prayer or two, though perhaps not on bended knee: he then lets himself drop into a soft and downy bed, over which has just passed the comely Jenny's warming-pan.

– Wanderings in South America, from the 3rd Journey (1820). But his stupid obscene cruelty to the reptiles out there displeases me.

Seeing this house [West Hackhurst] as if for the first time, as I have twice done today (20–8–44), once outside from the wood, and again as I came up the stairs, made me feel that I should soon lose it, perhaps by my own death.

The properly insured man, as well as the rich one, will find it difficult to get into the Kingdom of Heaven.

'*One's wretched little Self*' But the individual important because there are so many other individuals; bats for his side; let him try not to be wretched and he will not be little. It is for the ant to say 'Nothing matters but the heap.'

Lover of Danger : enviable but disgusting; coprophagist.

Semi-dream Withered man dying. Stretches out arms like matches. But the right arm, where it thrusts into darkness, thickens, and the wrist and hand are large and muscular, and the hand grasps another, athletic as itself, and belonging to a body invisible [And proportionate.]

I do not trust my reporting, for as I wake up I catch myself modifying dreams into ideas.   Oct. 1944

Areopagitica. Having to broadcast on the mysteriously uncongenial Milton, I will tot down points here: refs. to pp. of Temple Classics Edition.

36 'What advantage is it to be a man over it is to be a boy at school .... if serious and elaborate writings, as if they were the theme of a grammar-lad under his pedagogue, must not be uttered without the cursory eyes of a temporising and
37 extemporising licenser?' ...... an unleisured Licenser, perhaps much his younger, perhaps far his inferior in judgement, perhaps one who never knew the labour of book writing ...... The printer dares not to go beyond his licensed copy; so often then must the author trudge to his leave-giver
38 I hate a pupil teacher, I endure not an instructor that comes to me under the wardship of an overseeing fist. I know nothing of the licenser, but that I have his own hand here for his arrogance; who shall warrant me his judgement? The State sir, replies the stationer, but he has a quick return: the State shall be my governors, but not my critics.

Unwise to resent maliciousness: you play into its power.

Abdollatiph, likewise, after relating that the dead of antient Egypt were interred, some in thick coffins of sycamore; some in sarcophagi of white marble, basaltes, or granite; and others in troughs full of honey; adds, upon the authority of a credible voucher, an account of a party, which, in search of treasure near the Pyramids, having met with an oblong vessel carefully closed, opened it; and on finding that it contained honey, began to eat, till some hairs which clung about the finger of one of them, being drawn forth, a young boy was discovered, his limbs entire and flesh soft, decked with an ornament and a jewel.
Samuel Henley.

From an appendix contributed by S.H. to 'The Tomb of Alexander,' a dissertation by Edward Daniel Clarke, Cambridge, 1805. The reference given to Abdul Latif is Histor. Aegypt. Compendium c. iv. p. 146 This is the first entry I have made since the death of my mother, today three months in her grave.

Morning breaks as I write, along those Coniston Fells, and the level mists, motionless and grey beneath the rose of the moorlands, veil the lower woods and the sleeping village, and the long lawns by the lake-shore.

Oh that someone had but told me, in my youth, when all my heart seemed to be set on these colours and clouds, that appear for a little and then vanish away, how little my love of them would serve me, when the silence of lawn and wood in the dews of morning should be completed; and all my thoughts should be of those whom, by neither, I was to meet more!

Written by Ruskin at Brantwood, 12–2–78 he says, in the introduction to his note on his Turner drawings. What good would it have done him, at that date, if he had been more attentive to   40 years previously? He would only have found something else to regret. All the same, but for remorse, the two magnificent sentences would not have been written. '*Oh that someone* . . .'' He made something out of the weakening whining emotion.

The Walls of the little room in which we are sitting are crammed with photographs. Every branch of the family is represented; it is like a cross section of the Indian empire . . . . . There is something so fantastic, so incongruous about this gallery that one is reminded inevitably of the great spawn of temples which stretch from the Himalayas to the tip of Ceylon, a vast jumble of architecture, staggering in beauty and at the same time monstrous, hideously monstrous because the fecundity that seethes and ferments in the myriad ramifications of design seems to have exhausted the very soil of India itself. Looking at the seething hive of figures which swarm the façades of the temples, one is overwhelmed by the potency of these dark handsome peoples who mingled their mysterious streams in a sexual embrace that has lasted thirty centuries or more. These frail men and women with piercing eyes who stare out of the photographs seem like the emaciated shadows of those virile massive figures who incarnated themselves in stone and fresco from one end of India to the other in order that the heroic myths of the races who have intermingled should remain for ever entwined in the hearts of their countrymen. When I look at only a fragment of these spacious dreams of stone, those toppling sluggish edifices studded with gems, coagulated with human sperm, I am overwhelmed by the dazzling splendour of those imaginative flights which enabled a half billion people of diverse origins to thus incarnate the most fugitive expressions of their longing.

This modern attempt at the grand manner is by Henry Miller (Tropic of Cancer, p 97). There are many weaknesses and insincerities in it, beginning with 'one is reminded inevitably' in the fourth line. There are also vivid pictures, and the stature of Khajraho does manage to emerge.

Gently and happily relate the evening. In some sort of poetry if it is was mine after the vexatious little prosaic day. I go down to Paddington old Edwards fishing there, and chubb dace bream pike perch gudgeon are all mentioned as being in the pond, seldom caught because they find so much in the mud and their fins break the surface like tiny sea-serpents or float like sticks. There was a woman once nearly drowned bathing – she had been making a film of the Clock House and bathed. The rope flayed her arms. The fish moved, the trees regrouped, the lovely summer night came on, I did not want fun or wit or lust, sat on a rail by a young couple and heard old Edwards talk. Did not want anything else or think of my wrongs and approaching expulsion from unexplored paradises. One gentle fact after another hit me – as that a pigeon's nest is close. Teeth of the pike, dorsal fin of the perch, they hurt, the fin is poison. Old Edwards and I are old and moderate friends, he regrets I am going but did not say, he wanted to talk about fish. The loveliness of indifference! the restfulness! The happiness not mystic or intense. Nothing hanging on it. – Now it is 1.0. A.M. I lie down on my pond, but first will read what I have written.

Have done so. My hour at Paddington has not come through. I have not the vocabulary, my mind is not sufficiently equable. Yet I still see the fishes' backs breaking the water, and the small white float which they never approached.

I am sleepy. I should like the kindly meaninglessness in my dreams.

I must go to my pond, to its depths which are not deep only a couple of feet but out of sight.

Monday, July 2nd 1946

Plan of Kitchen Garden, West Hackhurst, the year I was driven out and after it had been cultivated for 70 years.

S.

| | | | Herbs | Horse Radish |
| Rhubarb Broad Beans Cabbages Chives | Spinach | | | |

Three Apple Trees

		Potatoes	
Tomatoes	Potatoes		
Seven rows of peas		Lettuce	

Potatoes

Flowers Fraxinella etc.

Apple Tree

E.

3 B. Currants	Gooseberries	Scarlet Runners
Cabbages	Red Currants	2 rows
Sprouts		F. Beans
Peas		Lettuces
F. Beans		Turnips
Turnips	Fruit Cage	
Carrots		
Beets		
Turnips	Red Currants	
Carrots		
Onions		
Shallots		

Raspberries

Logan Berries

The Cabbage Tribe

2 Pear Trees or Fresh Flowers

F l o w e r s W

Lavender

Pond

| cu | cu | mbers |

Dahlias

Bushes

N.

The world is too much with us; late and soon
    Getting and spending, we lay waste our powers;
    Little we see in Nature that is ours;
    We have given our hearts away ––––

I thought of these lines today as the last word on the subject, and was surprised at the defectiveness of the sonnet when I reread it. 'A sordid boon' is to rhyme with moon, and what does it mean? An unsatisfactory or degrading transaction? '*This* sea,' which I had always read as 'The,' particularises the scene, yet weakens it, for 'pleasant lea' is a daylight phrase, and it is unacceptable that W. should be standing on one in the moonlight. 'Great God' is another flop. The classical close is fine literature, and 'the sea' can be read more lightly when one realises the preceding this; thus allowing all the weight for the Nereids. But the passionate wisdom he passed before the fourth line is finished. Verbal incompetence has helped to expel it, for in the first line what is 'soon'? early?

World much with me before I could write the above. Lost this book. Also the key of the cupboard which contained the Blake.

Am therefore sleepy. 2ce dozed off. 10.70 p.m. 16–9–46.

The sneering and hardness, the scorn of retreat today, are un-answerable, because they are connected with genuine and even generous indignation: the world can't be too much with us, we are urged, because we have to alter it, and make it bearable for others. I am thus condemned to enjoy myself and, indeed, to touch reality at the price of a bad conscience. I will pay the price, I will be less forlorn.

THE LAST ENTRY

There you may wither, and an autumn bring
Upon yourself, but not call back his spring.

Suppose this done, or were it possible
I could rise higher still, I am a man,
And all these glories, Empires heaped upon me,
Confirmed by constant friends and faithful Guards,
Cannot defend me from a shaking Feaver

Or bribe the uncorrupted Dart of Death
To spare me one short minute.

> – Beaumont & Fletcher, The Prophetess, iv. 6.

Talk not of comfort: I have broke my faith,
And the gods fight against me; and proud man,
However magnified, is but as dust
Before the raging whirlwind of their justice.

> – id. iv. 1.

Tis a monstrous thing to marry at all, especially as now 'tis made:
methinks a man, an understanding man, is more wife to me, and of a
nobler tie, than all these trinkets; what do we get by women, but our
senses, which are the rankest part of us, satisfied, and when that is
done what are we? Crest-fallen cowards. What benefit can children be,
but charges and disobedience? What's the love they render at one and
twenty years? I pray die Father: when they are young they are like
bells rung backwards, nothing but noise and giddiness; and come to
years once, there drops a son by th' sword in his Mistresses quarrel, a
great joy to his parents.

> – id. Wit without Money, iv. 1.

Will your Lordship please to taste a fine Potato?
T' will advance your witherèd state
Fill your honour full of most noble itches
And make Jack dance in your Lordships breeches.

> – id. The Loyal Subject iii. v.

Was I three or older when I fell and knocked out a front upper tooth
(on the right)? The new tooth was doubtful in coming and ill
nourished when it came. It was small, and half way up it on each
side was a nick of decay. There was a cavity at the root at which
I sucked. Periodically a 'gumboil' formed above it, and when this
burst the liquor ran down through the cavity on to my tongue.
The ill conditioned little thing gave me some satisfaction. I liked
sucking at it, and the slight pain which accompanied the emission
of pus, also the taste. It was removed – when? and my first false
took its place, clasping its neighbours with gold.

The last month or so – all my upper teeth now being false – I have felt very precisely the situation of my vanished playmate, and suck at his ghost. Second childhood? The physical result of much brooding on the past? For half a century that tooth has been out of my mouth and my mind.

I have always wanted to share my advantages with others. But I am asked to give up my advantages so that others may have things I don't want; to help build a world I should find uninhabitable. It is a severe demand. The generous-minded of the past century – Shelley and the Liberals – have not appreciated its irony. They have assumed that, once the chains had fallen, art, scenery, passionate personal love, would become popular. One is placed in the equivocal position of the aristocrat who believes in the real goods – for they are real – and is tempted to defend them against democracy. The town here (Cambridge) is bitter against the university for preserving their joint amenities and preventing industrial development.

Shelley's *Defence of Poetry* merits more respect than I supposed. It is free of the vagueness, the boats, and the cars which invalidate his poems, and, written with intense sincerity, it contains some salutary truths. But there are too many hopes in it. The above one, for instance. Also the Platonic hope that the stuff's percolating from God. Also – strangest of all – the belief that if men had not been sharpened by poetry they would not have taken to mechanical inventions. The real defence – that art is important in itself, even if it does no good – is shirked by him. His mysticism is utilitarian.

Let me quote though:

Poetry lifts the veil from the hidden beauty of the world, and makes familiar objects be as if they were not familiar; it reproduces all that it represents.

This accurately describes a sensation.

Clare

> I left the little birds
> And sweet lowing of the herds
> And couldn't find out words,
>   Do you see,

To say to them good bye
Where the yellow cup do lie
So heaving a deep sigh
Took to sea ———

Dream Sentences 'Now Caesar which was rather nice as you remember was taking the east end of the climate of Shakespeare.' – 27–11–47. Flat.

"Roughly speaking 92% of the earning population come out of the Straits of Gibraltar."
"I will pull down Hastings, you shall see
Companion to India as a boat gnawed . . . ."

(my first modern blank verse).

Joseph Conrad loses virtue when he touches a woman. Silliness and flatness invade the scenery: the decor, the operatics, [seem not   ? worthwhile,] true accounts have been given neither of Karain nor Kurtz, who were so heroic and genuine when we first sighted them. Is this intense and inferior chivalry part of his Polish legacy? Poetry and common sense throw up the sponge together when she of the high white forehead looms. Feminism is not all pervading: were it that, it might be acceptable. Grand rhetoric pervades and we are required to believe, late on in the tale, that a Woman was the cause of all that is said, as of all that was done, even when we are allowed to see her limitations. Neither in Karain nor in Heart of Darkness can Her Name be mentioned. – 21–12–47, after reading the latter tale in Zabel's edition.

Dream Sentences "The names – those are the names of people who have apologised for making mistakes on the way back."

"I like this light & Children – either [pron. eether] pet children or children.' 27–2–48, Oxford.

"I must tell mistress that I don't think it right to be bothered and uncoated with unskilful labour." – Agnes and from West Hack-hurst.

"I sat down yesterday to pay a call with a coloured voice and no other coloured voices" 12–10–49, Cambridge.

'You don't want to lose your everyday importance, do you?"
1956. Cambridge.

The Conduct of something beautiful seen or heard a few days ago is
baffling. It fidgets at the back of the mind, asking to be preserved.
One can write it down, when it hardens into a form which was
not the original. Or one can let it melt. I have had two experiences
this month.

(i) The evening sky behind Fellows' Buildings. A cone of cloud
forming the very obtuse angle of Etna seen from Taormina, and
mottled with pink and gold – both faint, and the word mottled is
too strong. Immensely large aesthetically speaking. I have no
idea of its linear measurement.

(ii) The Kangra Miniature (No   ) in the Indian exhibition of
Krishna holding an umbrella over Radha. Grey-black, yellow
dresses, green. I had seen it two years ago at Lahore, and the
excitement of recognition sharpened me.

The experiences are not the same, because the cloud has gone for
ever, whereas the miniature can be revisited. The recognition of
the miniature cannot be repeated though, and perhaps I am
securer with the cloud, thanks to the droll reaction of my scientific
colleague, Mr Shire. I pointed it out to him as he hurried by, and
he remarked "a cold front" and would have proceeded. Asked,
he explained that the phenomena was caused by hot air rising and
contacting cold air. I was glad to know this. I said, 'Isn't it
beautiful.' He looked at it politely. He had not expected to find
beauty in a cold front. I think he was trying to see beauty to please
me. To please him, I made the comparison with a volcano. He
civilly moved on. Comedy can be a preservative, and I see my
cloud today better than I could have hoped, thanks to our mutual
bewilderment.   Dec. 47

"Isn't it wonderful the beautiful things that exist out of sight
mostly." I found this lovely remark of Maimie's on a stray sheet of
paper. It must have been there for 40 years. How much else of her
has been lost? – Here's its home for a little longer.   Sept. 52

Lord Chartley is a very effeminate young man – sometimes He wore pink ribbons to His Shoes – & having married a young Lady only a few months ago He is said to be upon the point of separation from her. – In Italy, while on his travels, some circumstances were observed in Him that gave an unfavourable opinion of Him –

This quotation – perhaps from Faringdon's Diary – has been hanging about for years on half a sheet of Reform Club paper, and scarcely is worth inscribing here. It belongs to my litter period.

On Christmas Day six young policemen, ex-service men, went off duty at 10.0 P.M. and returned to the Section House where they lived. They had some beers at the canteen, and, three hours later, the young married woman who had been serving them rushed nearly mad into the street. They had all raped her or tried to. There is enquiry from a high level (the D.D.I.), whatever happens they will be fired, and they will probably go for trial.

I wonder what did happen. My imagination won't work enough. The man-rape of an unwilling object is so difficult to conceive. Did she want it with one of them, and did the others fall in love with his action? At what point – for they seem to have begun with friendly drinks – did she recoil? What did she say to her husband, or he to him? Does each policeman now look back on himself with amazement? Will he ever lose control of himself again? These questions are outside my range. Knowledge of Lord Chartley does not help, nor does the theory of abysses in human nature satisfy. It is something stronger and wilder than anything I have experienced, and perhaps can only be understood physically, through similar violence. The Law, though acting rightly in the community's interest, will not understand it either. What do I or Lord Chartley or even the college servants guess about Mass Rape? Even   , with his knowledge of crime, was lost. It is what is superficially called Primitive – orgies, tribal sacrifices . . . Being occasional, it can't do much harm.

Alain-Fournier, according to an article by David Paul in the 'Cornhill,' (Autumn 1947) refers to: ––––– human experience, pushing itself into a new dimension, where the old scale of measurements no longer applied, where heroism and suffering became so intense as to lose meaning. He saw that scientific expansion could mean little but contraction to the spirit at least for a time.

Elle est toute assertion, mais quand on demande la preuve, c'est son secret.

> – Talleyrand on Lady Holland.

Give me birds flying about free in the beautiful woods. Keeping a bird in a cage looks as if you were brought up in St Giles.

This exclamation of my grandmother's must have been made at the beginning of the century, and must refer back to the 1840's or 50's, when St Giles was a slum, a 'rookery.' What a way I have travelled! How many phrases have lost their meaning! For instance 'it doesn't matter. I can have an egg' or 'There was literally nothing in the house but bread and cheese.'

The years seem to fly now I am older. I had a dream of Mrs Forster last week. I thought we was in the kitchen at West Hackhurst and talking of what we could have for lunch. But I woke up before we settled anything – it did seem so real.

– Letter 2–4–48 from my dear Ruth; in the actuality she opposed every obstinacy and disagreeableness. Mother would return worn out.

The Victorians moved out of man's ancestral home, with its temples, palaces, cottages, cathedrals, golden with age, tenderly formed by the hands of the masters, into the fine new city of science – so convenient, so hygienic, so reasonably planned, but devoid of human tenderness and human beauty. The loss has never been repaired and man today is still a displaced person in a land that he has yet to make his home.

– Final sentences of a broadcast on Victorian geology by Sherwood Taylor.

Everything depends on the things you want to make happen. They must be good things –––– And if you make them good things always, the time will come when there won't be any others.

From my dear Forrest Reid's *Uncle Stephen*; I have been re-reading it and *The Retreat* and shall reread *Young Tom*. He grasps his essentials – his 'moral fragrance' – and yet he muffs his books. Floppiness and freshness. I keep longing for him to click, as he did when one talked to him. He pays for rejecting so much experience.

The Deverell appearances in *U.S.* are more exciting, and more acceptable than I remember.

The supernatural in *The R.* does not cohere imaginatively. A cat is too feeble a link.

Roderick Hudson }
Princess Casamassima }
The Bostonians } read recently
Washington Square }
The American }

Princess Casamassima: and the people.

I haven't the least objection to his feeling badly. If a few more people felt badly in this sodden stolid stupid race of ours, it would wake up to an idea or two, and we should see the beginning of the dance.

'The people – the people? That's a silly term. Whom do you mean?'

'Those you used to care for, to plead for: those who are underneath everything, and have the whole social mass crushing them.'

'I see you think I'm a renegade. The way certain classes arrogate to themselves the title of the people has never pleased me. Why are some beings the people, the people only, and others not? I'm of the people myself.

'He changes constantly and his impressions change. The misery of the people is by no means always in his heart. You tell me what he has told you: well he has told me that the people may perish over and over rather than the conquests of civilisation shall be sacrificed to them. He declares at such moments that they'll be sacrificed – sacrificed utterly – if the ignorant masses get the upper hand.'

'He needn't be afraid. That will never happen.'

'I don't know. We can but try.'

Paul was looking off towards London with a face that expressed all the healthy singleness of his vision. Suddenly he remarked ———.

'Yes, I don't believe in the millenium, but I do believe in the democracy with a *chance*.'

He struck Hyacinth while he spoke these words as such a firm embodiment of the spirit of the people: he stood there in his sturdy newness with such an air of having learnt what he had learnt and of good nature that had purpose in it, that ————.

I have let myself go to Trilling on the subject of this startling and attractive novel. I wish that I had kept a copy of my letter to him, but his wrong-headed article in Horizon will remind me of my points. It is an avenue which H.J. ought to have pursued. It would have done him no harm to develop the journalist in him, and to get up scenes and characters from the life. Imitating Balzac, disastrous to most authors, would have benefited him.

I thank your Ladyship for the information concerning the Methodist preachers: their doctrines are most repulsive and strongly tinctured with impertinence and disrespect towards their superiors in perpetually endeavouring to level all ranks and do away with all distinctions. It is monstrous to be told that you have a heart as sinful as the worst wretches that crawl on the earth. This is highly offensive and insulting, and I cannot but wonder that your Ladyship should relish any sentiments so much at variance with high rank and good breeding

– The Duchess of Buckingham to the Countess of Huntingdon –

My Mouth keeps dropping open today, and reminds me of the long-intended note on my physical decay. Age: 69 years, 6 months.

Toenails misshapen through idleness. Quite difficult to cut them through large belly. Sometimes get at them with scissors from underneath. Between two of the toes of the left foot there is a slight long established infection. Right big toe came off last year, no harm done.

Left ankle. Red mark caused by falling last year in York Minster. Poisoning started, checked by May & Bob bandaging with penicillin (?)

Left shin. Skin trouble – to be hoped no worse: cancer even leprosy have crossed my mind. No pain, scarcely ever any sensation, doesn't get bigger. Valderma had no effect. Noticeable if I bathed?

Farts With and without smell. Seem to pass by some blockage. I always know when it is safe to release them, and when they will blow some moisture down to the opening. This is sometimes pure liquid, sometimes shit.

Arsehole Tickles badly at night, especially during the past week. As far as symptoms go, what is worse with me. Partly due to uncleanliness? Piles? Constipation? Worse? Often signalled to in an unknown medium before the tickling starts. I put cotton-woolf or bumph up the hole or lay a cool finger to prevent friction. One or two nights I have been kept awake for several hours, or have been woken up. – Scratch a lot. Shit-stained vest & drawers.

Piss. More than normal, tuffet sometimes full by morning. Sometimes wet pyjamas, as in Prostate Days. In day, suddenly taken, but can usually control myself, and it passes off. *See* fart above. Little piss and great fart.

Belly Much bigger this year, and makes me miscalculate my weight and poise. Gates a trouble. Cannot stoop, sometimes slumped in bath. To see Eric Fletcher at Hinchinbrooke jump straight off the asphalt on to a high brick post amazed me.

Ears assumed as good as ever, but are not: telephone often heard by others when I can't.

Eyes Getting worse. Cannot see either to live or read without spectacles, and get sick of them.

Moustache going grey. Hair also, and rather prettily.

Teeth No upper. Six in lower jaw and one stump [just wrote 'tower jump' for this sentence, am so sleepy, and have been all day] loose and held in place by masses of tartar, which, suicidally I try to chip off with scissors. – Too sleepy to proceed but glad to have got this unimportant record down.   8–7–48

When Thomas Gray writes

I know what it is to lose a person that one's eyes and heart have long been used to, and I never desire to part with the remembrance of that loss, nor wish you should – 21–9–53

and

. . . . . to inform you that I had discovered a thing very little known, which is, that in one's whole life one can never have any more than a single Mother. You may think this is obvious, and (what you call) a trite observation. You are a green Gossling! I was at the same age (very near) as wise as you, and yet I never discovered this (with full evidence and conviction I mean) till it was too late, it is 13 years ago, and seems but yesterday, and every day I live it sinks deeper into my heart – 26–8–66

I reckognize an affinity. Laziness and loyalty have a connection. And sexuality? E. Fitzgerald. How this academic gentle gentlemanly type has survived! 3 Trumpington Street, where I write, is in a straight line with Gray's rooms in Pembroke and Fitzgerald's in King's Parade. We have our place in history – the small enclosure reserved for old dears – and if noticed will awake some affection. Coleridge and Goldie have left us to follow large visions.

I think though, to be honest, that I am a more important writer than either Fitzgerald or Gray. I have taken more trouble to connect my inner life with the world's, even though I have not been strong enough to stick.

Ruskin:

With me the great obstacle is not so much Unbelief of Heaven as the want of desire of Heaven. I find no promise in the Bible that excites my longing.   Letter written 1847

I think *in general* that not to give up a thing because we "will not be beaten" has more of bull dog-ism in it than of sense. There are times when we "Must not be beaten" as the Duke said at Waterloo, but there are other times when we ought to be beaten, when the victory is useless.   id.

From Admiral James Order of Release which attempts to rehabilitate his own grand parents, and denigrate R but has the opposite effect.

Notes on a talk with Bob

Life, so far as we know, is a freak in the universe and even in the solar system, it does not even persist through this globe, but is confined to its surface. Of living forms, only a small proportion utilise sex to continue themselves, and of that fraction only a fraction is monogamous. Yet we are invited to regard marriage as natural! If anything is 'natural' it is the entire universe. What an aberration are we all in relation to it!

Consciousness the unique experiment. I consider that you are romantic about the Life Force, whereas I with better reason am romantic about what can be made out of it. They are the aberration of an aberration.

Goldie and the Platonists, going further than I can and much further than you, regard them as premonitions of reality.

Unfortunately I did not copy out these notes at once and they are confused and weakened.

Ruskin's Praeterita vol 1 ch VI ends with an excellent apology for the non-human tourist "I dont say that our isolation was meritorious, or that people in general should know no language but their own. Yet the meek ignorance has these advantages. We did not travel for adventures, nor for company but to see with our eyes and to measure with our hearts". He rejects, without condemning, the festive desire to see something of the natives which has meant so much to myself. "Virtually you are thinking of yourself all the time; you necessarily talk to the cheerful people, not to the sad ones; and your heart is for the most part vividly taken up with very little things." With people of sensitiveness, like Ruskin and his parents, the British morgue was a protection to the spirit. Thousands of tourists have stalked like them since, with nothing to protect. Thousands and thousands have rushed around like me, affable and conciliatory and anxious to get into touch, and uncritical of the poorness of the human quality which they touched.

The epoch of pleasure-observation has closed now. We travel to Europe in gangs or on a mission.

Understand better why Proust admires Ruskin. Skip him when he is noble pathetic or indignant; his sensitiveness to scenery and to *some sides* of human conduct is remarkable. Like him, I have mooned before objects without getting any forrader.

Two dreams, last night [13–11–48. Bob in same room]

In a small victoria with my mother and another lady, and a dear tabby purring in my arms. "Not a safe carriage to carry a cat in," and it turned and settled itself more securely, to my happiness. But there was a jolt, and it jumped or was jerked out into water – a dyke. I leapt to rescue it in blue serge trousers, caught at it and it dissolved into brown filmy weed. I awoke in misery, then had a second and more benignant dream. Goldie and his three sisters were standing to be introduced by prearrangement to Reg Palmer. I came along with him, he lagged behind, a little suspicious because he knew most of them to be dead, and I woke. He was younger and slighter than usual, with a pinkish shirt open at the throat. I knew, when I was awake, that there had been an attempt of humanity to meet and to ignore the grave, and this pleased me. The first dream agonised because of Toma and Tinka and their connection with West Hackhurst and my lost stability.

Jane Austen: Emma: its deterioration after – indeed during – the Box Hill party. To a reader not hypnotised by its previous achievement, the final chapters are most disappointing. The *dreadful* Churchill letter.

Keynes:

We were at an age when our beliefs influenced our behaviour, a characteristic of the young which it is easy for the middle aged to forget.   [from his early memories]

Cocteau

La poésie se forme à la surface du monde comme les irisations à la surface d'une marécage. Que le monde ne s'en plaigne pas. Elle résulte de ses profondeurs.   [Preface to El Greco]

Wm Plomer

She came of a race whose ethic is supposed to have been to 'play the game', and of a family that had played it for generations – the deck-game of dying at sea, for a flag, the game of skill called sporting with danger, the game of chance called saving souls, the indoor game of laying down the law.   [Sado]

Mercury and Lethe speaking of dead Lovers

"Nay, faint not now, so near the fields of rest.
  Here no more Furies, no more torments dwell
Than each hath felt already in his breast;
  Who hath been once in love, hath proved his hell.

Up then, and follow this my golden rod,
   That points you next to agéd Lethe's shore,
Who pours his waters from his urn abroad,
   Of which but tasting, you shall faint no more." –

"Stay; who or what fantastic shades are these
   That Hermes leads?" – "They are the gentle forms
Of lovers, tost upon those frantic seas
   Whence Venus sprung." – "And have rid out her storms?" –

"No." – "Did they perish?" – "Yes" – "How?" – "Drowned by Love,
   That drew them forth with hopes as smooth as were
The unfaithful waters he desired them prove." –
   "And turned a tempest when he had them there?" –

"He did, and on the billow would he roll,
   And laugh to see one throw his heart away;
Another, sighing, vapour forth his soul:
   A third, to melt himself in tears and say,

O Love, I now to salter water turn
   Than that I die in; then a fourth, to cry
Amid the surges, *Oh! I burn, I burn*
   A fifth laughs out, *It is my ghost, not I.*

And thus in pains I found them. Only one
   There is, that walks, and stops and shakes his head,
And shuns the rest, as glad to be alone,
   And whispers to himself, *he is not dead.*"

I am always discovering new merits in Ben Jonson's Masques.
The above is from the Masque of Lethe, restored by me to its
stanza form. Yesterday, in his Panegyric to the King's First
Parliament, my eye fell

> Into those dark and deep concealéd vaults
> Where men commit black incest with their faults.

I am unable to understand the reluctance with which Ben Jonson
is approached. I find him such an accessible writer.

Ruskin

I find nothing in myself whatsoever *changed.* Some of me is dead, more
of me stronger. I have learned a few things, forgotten many; in the
total of me I am the same youth, disappointed and rheumatic.

> Praeterita. 11. xii (looking back from 1886 to 1837).

Ordinance passed in Norphelt, Arkansas, 1925

> Hereafter it shall be unlawful for any man and woman, male or female, to be guilty of committing the act of sexual intercourse between themselves within the corporate limits of said town.

> This ordinance shall not apply to married persons as between themselves and their husband and wife, unless of a grossly improper and lascivious nature.

Purcell set the following bawdy catch and others to music: they are omitted from all standard editions of his work, so that of him, as of other famous artists, a fake reputation has been transmitted; and artists of the present work in unnecessary loneliness.

> Young Collin cleaving of a Beam
> At every thumping blow
> Cried Hem hem and told his wife who the cause would know
> That hem made the wedge much further go
> Plump Joan when at night to bed they came
> And both were playing at the game
> Cried Hem Hem prithee Collin do
> If ever thou lovest me dear Hem now
> He laughing answered No No No
> Some work will split at half a blow
> Besides now I bore, now I bore, now now now I bore
> I hem when I cleave but now I love.

From 'The Catch Club or Merry Companions,' London. Printed for and sold by Walsh, Musick Printer and Instrument Maker to his Majesty at the Harp and Hoboy in Catherine St. in the Strand.

[Two books bound into one, seen at Bens]

Terence Rattigan: Who is Sylvia?' world première here. Camb. Oct. 1950.

> *Act I* Nobleman in fuck-flat with comic butler who reads solid books (so original!), military pal, and girl who reminds him of girl he's lost.

> *Act II* N. in f.f. with c.b., m.p., and 2nd g., also n's son wants to be a great actor.

Act III N. in f.f. with c.b., m.p. and 3rd g, also n's wife who *has known about it all along*, (so original, such deep humanity). N's son a gta.

This took over three hours. Some years pass between each act and sometimes during it.

Il donne aux fleurs leur aimable peinture.

> – Racine on the Almighty, in Esther.

Recent evening train, Liverpool Street to Cambridge. Lay in a 1st Class carriage, looking towards corridor and tried to enumerate the levels I saw. Difficult, and the notes I jotted down are partly incomprehensible by now

   1 Objects in carriage
   2 Their reflection in the corridor glass
   3 Objects seen through corridor glass

no it is idle to go on, for I did not observe properly or distinguish the categories – there were at least six of them. The point is that when I flattened the levels, and did not arrange them according to my preconceptions, they bewildered me, I was staring at a new world. No wonder that painters, post impressionist and others, have tried to get at it. Sneers at them prove our own inability to see. I scarcely ever see. Nor does the scientist, for as soon as he has explained *why* the various reflections appear as they do, he ceases to see them. I only see what I am used to, and I behave to it as if it were used to me.

Mowbray Morris, editor of Macmillan's Magazine, to an under-graduate friend at Cambridge, January, 1886:

I still keep and always shall keep to my theory that it is not fair to lump all the Greeks together under one hideous ban. Nothing will ever per-suade me that the best Greeks of the best time deserved such an impu-tation. There are of course some desperate passages in Plato, which it is impossible to get over. But then, Plato was not quite of the best time. The decadence had begun when he wrote; and moreover he always wrote impersonally, dramatically. But men such as Aeschylus, Sophocles, Phidias: they could not have done the work they did had they used a vice which must degrade a man all over, intellectually as well as morally:

> Not from a vain or shallow thought
> His awful Jove young Phidias brought.

Still less from a bestial one. "Oh that my lot may lead me in the path of holy innocence ——" Sophocles wrote that . . . a Pagan. You cannot tell me that the man who wrote those words was – well, what we need not name.

Quoted in Hector Bolitho's A Biographer's Note Book.

When a man becomes infirm and weary of the world he is said to invite his own children to eat him. In the season when salt and limes are cheapest he ascends a tree, around which his offspring and friends assemble; and, shaking the tree, they join in a dirge, the burthen of which is this. – "The season is come; – the fruit is ripe, and it must descend." The victim descends, and those that are nearest and dearest to him deprive him of life, and devour his remains in a solemn banquet.

Dr Leyden in his dissertation on the language and literature of the Indo-Chinese nations, vol x of the Asiatic Researches as quoted in Edward Moor, Hindu Infanticide.

Munificentissimum Deus: Pope Pius XII's Bull, proclaiming the bodily Assumption of the Virgin Mary: extracted from the full text in the Tablet of 23–12–50

"A kind of inner coherence" in the gifts and graces bestowed on the B.V., which the Church has been studying; we have been able to see her bodily Assumption more clearly. Connected with her Immaculate Conception, defined by Pius IX: "contained in the *deposit of faith* entrusted to the Church", and emphasised by campaigns of prayer. "It was remarkable how many of the Bishops sent petitions to the Throne of Peter in the same sense [2 vols of them in Vatican Polyglot Press, 1942]. Logical outcome of Virgin Birth and Immaculate Conception. Logical too that a woman as well as a man should be exempted from natural laws, and that a son should wish his mother to enter Heaven undecayed. Nor have any relics of the Dormition ever been shown.

[The Church of Ireland has however protested against the dogma, as lacking scriptural warranty]

I am now on the Bridge which Mr Addison discribes, arriv'd to the middle
of it and have escaped those thousand trapdoors which have let so
many others slip into the Ocean of Eternity, perhaps my next tread
will be upon one, and then where am I? Living perhaps in the memory
of a few kind relatives who may now and then say thus she did, who
may kindly excuse my follies and overrate my Virtues, but in a few
years even this imaginary liveing is also over, and perhaps it will never
be known but upon old parchment or on a register that Lucy Thornton
ever liv'd.

Written by my gt. gt. grandmother at Clapham on April 23rd
1757 and transcribed by me at Cambridge, April 8th 1951.

If Science declines, there will be more work, not less, on the comparatively
easy problems of destruction. It will be the real science, where the
adversary is not man but the Universe itself, that will suffer.

– From Fred Hoyle's broadcasts, 'The Nature of the Universe,'
which rightly made such a stir.

Reading it, I note that the earth is not hot at the centre, that the
rocks containing radioactive, lie near the surface, that the earth
and planets are *not* from the sun, but from the explosion of a
companion-star, a supernova, whose core has been thrown out
into the Galaxy, and is now unknown. I learn too of the Expand-
ing Universe, and of new Galaxies forming out of the Inter
Stellar Gas, but I do not share Hoyle's hope that there maybe life
and possibly "human" life elsewhere. I learn that the observable
universe is half covered by the Mount Palomar telescope; a telescope twice as strong could observe the rest, beyond which
nothing can be observed. I learn that the galaxies fly from us, and
that in the gaps between them, creation goes on, so that the over-
all picture is the same. Hydrogen underlies all. I long to see the
stars, and get the sense of the moving earth. For months the
weather and I have been wrapped-up invalids. The nonsense of
Korea against such a background. Sparring of politicians. The
Daily Express boycotts the Festival of Britain. Everyone's mind
beckoned to killing or to nonsense. Here and there someone like
myself, who has money, leisure, and a streak of noble obstinacy,
cuts free for a few hours, but we have not sufficient staying
power, and no importance. I feel new courage and fierceness in
me, but they may come from old age.

Notes on the day; (May 26th 1951)

> Perhaps what Keats called "death in life" has only a sexual meaning.
> Many poets, when they speak of death, mean something quite
> different.

> – Demetrios Capetanakis, who combines imagination with
> common sense, and has just quoted Troilus' announcement of
> the death of Hector, in contrast.

His memorial volume has stirred me to day, as has so much else,
even the proofs of my own book here and there. If I can forget the
horror of Korea, Persia, U.S. intolerance etc. – and I often can
for they are uninspiring as well as alarming – I find "us" striving
towards something important and, in failing to grasp it, achieving
something important. "We" are the poets, to whom I do belong.
Wordsworth on Londoners was read by me to day

> Living amid the same perpetual whirl
> Of trivial objects, melted and reduced
> To one identity, by differences
> That have no law, no meaning and no end –

a true description of them, but displaying another truth: the
power of poetry. For note how the fourth line, though its words
are prosaic, annuls the prosiness of the previous three and makes
them retrospectively profound.

There is so much to absorb all day – except when I am tired; and
of course at my age the blotting paper dries quickly. Only recent
experiences remain vivid; yesterday was equally interesting, but
I can't remember much about it. [To the young, the creative
mind, it is not important *when* an experience happens – it sinks
down into storage. I can't store.]

This same day I spent ten minutes with a case of Eg. predynastic
stuff in the Fitzwilliam. Lovely design on a pot of an ear of corn (?)
coming out of a whirligig (?). Three ivory tusks, length from
about 4 inches to 8, and tipped with a delicately carved bearded
head. "Use unknown." I fancy I know it, and think of the
pleasure and pain women might have received from them. For
there was already sophistication: palettes for mixing cosmetics.

So all the time objects are calling to me, whether I answer them
or not.

The world is inexhaustible for those who are fairly free. If however the Soviets or the United States get going, the world will shut up, minds will be darkened by bullying or fear. Those of us who want to understand what has been made (and through it something else), and those of who want to make will be equally checked. – Yes, also today I read an account in the New Yorker of a man who was detained for ten months on Ellis Island. He left France with his papers in order. He was trapped.

Always the narrow margin, the thin ice. Korea etc. explodes and we can't apprehend Capetanakis or Wordsworth or look at Egyptian stuff any more.

Denton Welch: extracts from his unpublished journal.

I think really that I get worse all the time, so that I have the picture of myself draining away. The only thing that can withstand is the will, in its own weak shabby obstinate joyless way.

In my heart are hung two extraordinary pictures. One is called 'Accident and Illness' and the other, exactly opposite and tilted forward as if to meet it, is called Love and Freindship

The [nudist] booklet is uncomfortable. I am fond of naked people but not of a great to do and business over nakedness. To read this magazine is to be told that if everyone would suddenly strip off their clothes, the world might be made quite wonderful. The articles are a little like the tracts Evie's sister brought me from the Bible and Tract Society. God and Jesus are replaced by Sun and the Naked Body.

It becomes more right and acceptable to believe that the other things in the world were made for us to enjoy if we think that we were made to be enjoyed.

Our hearts, into which something has eaten once when we were ill or weak, must be mended or patched so that that terrible pettiness and fear of being overlooked may be wiped out for ever.

Herman Melville

> But where is his blazon?
> Must merited fame endure time's wrong?
> Glory's ripe grape wizen up to a raisin?
> Yes! for Nature teems and the years are strong
> And who can keep the tally o' the names that fleet along

Flying induces a mood of religious scepticism. One realises the fallacy of supposing that God can be 'up above' and can 'look down' on us. For the view of the observer up above is necessarily one of indifference. One sees a man bicycling, one sees a little farm with its stream and bridge, and they have nothing human about them. One does not wish to help the man on his road or to drop a blessing on the little house. To feel well or ill disposed towards them one must see them horizontally, on the human level. Man can only be man to those who walk on the earth beside him.

I imagine the world as a ship sailing through space: it is likely that the ship has a captain, but I don't know him.   – Spanish Guide

The feeling of affection that can grow up for a house and its corner of land is surely one of the more valuable kinds of piety that civilisation has produced. When we pour scorn on the human spirit, we forget the frigid nomadism, the camping ground in the desert of flats and villas with which we are replacing it. How is it that every step we take in the intellectual mastery of Nature leaves the world more uncongenial and unassimilable to our other faculties?

– Gerald Brenan: The Face of Spain.

How decorative can be Beards, how some male faces may thereby alone attain their natural fulfilment or new special beauty is perhaps not realised until they are closely lived among. Their variety, if let fulfil their natural bent, astonishes. Some grow broad or bushy, spade like; others bifurcate; yet others concentrate on length, or sideways to the moustaches. Some are of wavy, wiry or tangled texture, smooth of surface, compact, others straggly or lank. Some sprout from high on the cheek bones, obliterating the countenance almost utterly, others flourish only lower down, others again are sparse throughout, the facial contours being hazily discernible. Some are not black but brown or even ruddy, and above may peer a pair of blue eyes. There are fascinating diversities in methods of dressing and tending *beards*, by strings and nets, pins and clips, combings, and tight pressing cloths. The best are the exquisitely fine-spun snowy *beards* of age, and the soft delightful budding ones of boys in the teens or twenties. All true *beards* young and old, have the same distinctive virginal silkiness, unroughened for ever by ravaging razor.

– Ian Stephens, in the course of recommending the Sikhs. A comparison of other growths would interest me more. Beards usually depress me: illogically, for I believe people ought to look natural.

To the Supt.
Atlantic City Railroad, New Jersey.   Sept. 1896

Dear Sir,
    On the 15th yore trane that was going to Atlanta ran over mi bull at
30 mile post

> He was in my Pastur
> You orter seen him

    Yore ruddy trane took a peece of hyde outer his belly between his
nable and his poker at least fute square and took his bag most off and
he lost his seeds – I don't believe he is going to be any more use as a
bull
    I wish you would tell the President he is ded, for he is as good as
ded ever since he was hit by yore trane.

> Your respectfully
> A. T. Harris

    P.S. – Be sure and report him as ded as he has nothing left but his
poker. He was a red bull but he stand around in these days looking
dam blue.

In 1851 Alington thought it would be instructive for his men to attend
    the Great Exhibition; and as most of them were strangers to London,
    and were fearful of being lost in that 'den of wickedness', he directed
    them to lay out baulks of timber in the Park, and arranged these him-
    self so as to represent the principal streets between King's Cross and
    Hyde Park. Then, for a whole week, he drilled his men in the way that
    they should go; those walking to the Exhibition being distinguished
    with hay bands tied about their right knees; those returning from the
    exhibition with straw bands tied around their right knees. In the end,
    he decided that they were all of them too stupid, and would not let
    them go.

    – Hine – a boring buffer –: 'Hitchin Worthies': Have just visited
    the odd ruined town. Aug. 52

Imagination may consecrate the world to a man, or it may merely be a
    visualizing faculty which sees that as already perfect which is still
    lying in the raw material. The Scot has the lower faculty in full degree

        George Douglas: The House with the Green Shutters.

Writers ought to write and I take up my pen in the hope it may loosen my spirit. I am in my Cambridge room, recovering from shock of extracted teeth, though I felt no shock, and from Bob's rebuke for life-long idleness – no assistance to industry so far. It is 6.45. Feb. 26th, tic-tac the old clock, fire has gone out, electric stove functions. Tony Hyndman has been in, recovering from shock also, administered electrically at the Fulbourne mental. He has been bothering Patrick & Sydney in my absence, and now bothers me, but Natasha Spender has come out well. I did not suspect such generosity and responsibility. I saw only the climber, who is always with the most interesting people. Hyndman *says* he has reported to the Cambridge probation officer, says he gave himself up over a cheque, says when he finishes with Fulbourne he is assured of a work and a home at Norwich. We shall see. Says the Franciscans (Anglican) are his friends here but they do not feel like that at all. He is disintegrated and unreliable. Why? Conditions from which I am sheltered have shattered him. I was not very friendly to him, I did not want to be bothered, and was not warm-hearted. He was friendly and unresentful and rather charming, and I now recall a short-story of Don Windham's about a negro who cheated a white in little ways until the white went sour on him. Hyndman is a mess-up – always liquescent. I am an artificial shape, √

Then Nick Furbank came and we lunched at the Arts and talked about Our Mutual Friend and elsewhere in Dickens. No artificial shape he, but a mess-around who was beginning by that time (its a late book) to suspect good heartedness, and therefore more ready to make Boffin pretend bad heartedness. We discussed that preposterous act which was so well done that it couldn't have been written as acting. It has made me recoil from Dickens – When I got back after a short work, Norman Routledge returned with me and made me scream over his Girton hostess who had illegitimate triplets and fed them in the bath because they were so dirty – thus washing them and the dinner things up at the same time. – As soon as their grandmother died they were legitimised and baptised. She had been the impediment. It is 7.30. Cannot writers write quicker? I have been "thinking".

Saint Peter's Chapel in the Tower

Within four years the pavement of the chancel was again disturbed,

and hard by the remains of Monmouth were laid the remains of
Jeffreys. In truth there is no sadder spot on earth than that little
cemetery. Death is there associated, not, as in Westminster Abbey and
St Paul's, with genius and virtue, with public veneration and imperishable renown; not, as in our humblest churches and churchyards, with
everything that is most endearing in social and domestic charities; but
with whatever is darkest in human nature and in human destiny, with
the savage triumph of implacable enemies, with the inconstancy, the
ingratitude, the cowardice of friends, with all the miseries of fallen
greatness and of blighted fame. Thither have been carried, through
successive ages, by the rude hands of gaolers, without one mourner
following, the bleeding relics of men who had been the captains of
armies, the leaders of parties, the oracles of senates, and the ornaments
of courts. Thither was borne, before the window where Jane Grey
was praying, the mangled corpse of Guilford Dudley. Edward
Seymour, Duke of Somerset, and Protector of the Realm, reposes
there by the brother whom he murdered. There has mouldered away
the headless trunk of John Fisher, Bishop of Rochester and Cardinal
of Saint Vitalis, a man worthy to have lived in a better age, and to have
died in a better cause. There are laid John Dudley, Duke of Northumberland, Lord High Admiral, and Thomas Cromwell, Earl of Essex,
Lord High Treasurer. There, too, is another Essex, on whom nature
and fortune had lavished all their bounties in vain, and whom valour,
grace, genius, royal favour, popular applause, conducted to an early
and ignominious doom. Not far off sleep the chiefs of the great house
of Howard, Thomas, fourth Duke of Norfolk, and Philip, eleventh
Earl of Arundel. Here and there, among the thick graves of unquiet
and aspiring statesmen, lie more delicate sufferers; Margaret of
Salisbury, the last of the proud name of Plantagenet, and those two
fair queens who perished by the jealous rage of Henry. Such was the
dust with which the dust of Monmouth mingled.

– Macaulay, History of England Ch V

'Have been carried', 'was borne', 'reposes' 'mouldered away',
'laid', 'conducted to doom' 'sleep' 'lie' 'dust mingled'–

all oratorical variants, with whose help the noble paragraph is
constructed. The only touches of genius in it are in the first sentence and at the conclusion, its genius not being dependent on
touches.

You must not think me necessarily foolish because I am facetious, nor
will I consider you necessarily wise because you are grave.

– Sydney Smith (whom I might echo) to Bishop Blomfield: –
Provided one does not apply the facetiousness automatically.
See p. 200 of this Commonplace Book.

The Cult of the Superman. By Eric Bentley

No man ever wanted more vehemently to be a mystic, but the heavenly
powers seem to have been unresponsive.   – On Carlyle.

D. H. Lawrence is to be understood as an artist, but the artist's function in modern times has been a peculiar one.

The modesty of the modern intellectual would be commendable were
it not based more on cowardice than upon genuine incapacity.

Many such readable remarks are in the book, which has the more
solid merit of an intelligible account of Nietzsche. The section
on Wagner also v. good Carlyle and Stefan George less so. The
author has turned from academic life to small-scale play-
producing.

George Crabbe: note book:

> –––. "Turn, stranger, turn!"
> "Not so!" replied a voice: "I mean
> The candle of the Lord to burn
> With mine own flock on Save-all-Green."

The meaning of the last phrase is ambiguous but anyhow
acceptable.

Although the naked body is no more than the point of departure for a work
of art, it is a pretext of great importance. . . . . . It is ourselves and
arouses memories of all the things we wish to do with ourselves: and
first of all we wish to perpetuate ourselves. This is an aspect of the
subject so obvious that I need hardly dwell on it; and yet some wise
men have tried to close their eyes to it. "If the nude" says Professor
Alexander, "is so treated that it raises in the spectator ideas or desires
appropriate to the material subject, it is false art and bad morals." . . . .

And since these words of a famous philosopher are often quoted, it is
necessary to labour the obvious and say that no nude, however
abstract, should fail to arouse in the spectator some vestige of erotic

feeling, even although it be only the faintest shadow, – and if it does not do so, it is bad art and false morals.

Kenneth Clark.

Chapter from a forthcoming work, perhaps. Later on he remarks of the Greeks: –

Nothing which related to the whole man could be isolated or evaded; and this serious awareness of how much was implied in physical beauty saved them from the two evils of sensuality and aestheticism.

Lydia Keynes, every whose word should be recorded, said to me as I was leaving her flat the other night: "You know I once tumbled from the stairs and believe me I paid the price." I took the sentence down before I forgot it. One word in it changed, and all vanishes.

Disorderly conduct sharpens the mind and falsifies the judgement.

– Bonald. (Who is he and where anyhow did I pick up this little teaser?)

Advice from Eric Fletcher to the Fighting Forces: –

1. Keep a copy   2 Pass the Buck   3 Volunteer for F——— All.

Scrap overheard:

Shirley Cook who's just as Bolshie and naughty
as he used to be, but I can't help liking Shirley . . .

suggested to me a low level of enlightenment which would never become either lower or higher.

All are as busy as Georges, straightening out the problems of the Matisse estate. The shadow of that old gentleman indeed hangs as heavy upon the household as the canvases of his early works hang upon the walls of this flat: influential still, he burst in his coffin last week, which is

still in a mortuary chapel awaiting ceremonious interment, blew out
the expensive wooden sides and dripped upon the floor. – Parisian
letter from Joe Ackerley. 1955

Religion is World Loyalty – Whitehead.

Casual reading today Oct 17 1955 produces:

Is it not most important to explore especially what has been long for-
bidden, and to do this not only "with the highest moral purpose", like
the followers of Ibsen, but gaily out of sheer mischief, or sheer delight
in that play of the mind.

– Yeats' "Autobiographies" of all places: had not thought it of
him. Quoted by Patrick Wilkinson in his Ovid.

In that Ovid:

> Jamque quiescebant voces hominum que canumque
>   Lunaque nocturnos alta regebat equos.
> Hanc ego suspiciens et ad hanc Capitolia cernans,
>   Quae nostra frustra juncta fuere Lari.
>
> 'Numina vicinis habitantia sedibus' inquam.
>   Jamque oculis nunquam templa videnda meis,
> Diqui reliquendi, quos urbs habet alta Quirini –
>   Este salutati tempus in omne mihi ––– Tristia I. 3

No Ovid I expected – though Goethe quoted it –

Then I've read:

La vieillesse nous rend d'abord incapable d'entreprendre mais non de
désirer. Ce n'est que dans une troisième periode que ceux qui vivent
très vieux ont renoncé au desir, comme ils ont dû abandonner l'action.

                              in Proust. Albertine Disparue

All this in an ostensibly wasted day, when I have not been feeling
very well, have been losing my papers, have not wanted to meet
people

'L'art n'est pas rêves mais possession des rêves.'

Read again it arouses the suspicion of swank.

Tom Coley's impression of British Adverts

Use Bile Beans	Have a Bile Bean	Say Hovis
Be Healthy	Bubbly	and Bile Beans
Be Vital	—	for Tea
Use Bile Beans	Make your	—
—	Baby Bubbly	Say, Hovis
Have a Baby	with Bile Beans	Did you
Bubbly		Maclean
		Your teeth
		Today?
		Huh?

Dream Rubbish

Have you escaped, sir, the Locked Door policy?

Isolation, though in poor yield, of 3:5 dimethylphloracetophenone
(LXXXVIa) during nuclear methetion of phloracetophenone 64, 67
therefore indicates the possibility of dialkylation before pyrone ring-
closure in the evolution of 6:8 dimethylchromone derivatives.

being the last sentence of an article by Jain and Seshadri of the
Department of Chemistry in the University of Delhi; printed in
the Quarterly Review of the Chemical Society, London, 1956,
Vol x. No 2: and reminding me of the extent of the English
language.

Affection made vulgar by undemonstrativeness

I have just come across this acute remark in a letter of Goldie's,
and since he says it is Mrs Meynell's I suppose it is.

Robert G. Brehmer, Jr., Probation & Parole Agent, State Department
of Public Welfare, Division of Corrections, writes to me from
405 Hutter Bldg, 20 Forest Avenue, Fond du Lac, Wis, or it may
be from 214, S. Hickory St, Fond du Lac, Wis., as follows:

Dear Mr Forster – Would you be interested in exchanging a copy of
"Marianne Thornton" for a copy of "Bulwark against Communism –
Social Doctrines of the Catholic Church"? Justice Wicktham of the
Wisconsin Supreme Court, endorses the book. Kindly advise.

His address reminds me that as a boy I was romantic about Fond du Lac. The name suggested the limit of my world and the frontier of the unknown one. Even on a map – where it now appears as one or two places – it was exciting. – Mr Brehmer resides inland.

Depuis si longtemps il avait renoncé a appliquer sa vie a un but ideal et la bornait à la poursuite de satisfactions quotidiennes, qu'il croyait, sans jamais se le dire formellement, que cela ne changerait plus jusqu'à sa mort: bien plus, ne se sentant plus d'idées elevées dans l'esprit, il avait cessé de croire à leur realité, sans pouvoir non plus la nier tout à fait. Aussi avait-il pris l'habitude de se refugier dans des pensées sans importance qui lui permettaient de laisser de côté le fond des choses.

From Du Coté de chez Swann, p. 195.

No thoú are cóme too láte, Empédoclés!
And the wórld hath the dáy, and must bréak thee,
Not thóu the wórld.

Coming across the above as a quotation, I thought it was modern and stressed the second line as indicated. It was much more poignant than it is now, when it has to follow Arnold's composed hammerings.

Shield of Aeneas. Have just rushed through it (Aeneid VIII) with unexpected ease and little pleasure. How seldom it reverberates:

rerumque ignarus imagine gaudet,
Attolens humero famamque et fata nepotum

is certainly a final magnificent boon and I remember how Mr. Floyd, a form-master in faraway & forgotten Tonbridge laid his head on one side when it finished and squeaked 'Marvellous, but you cant see it, wretched boys, cant see it ---' We couldn't, and I was puzzled by his enthusiasm, which I realised was genuine, and he helped me by puzzling me and making me realise that I might see more in Virgil and elsewhere, when I was mature. His squeak survives as a fruitful sound, and I remember his fat intelligent screwed up face. Mr Floyd was said to be frightening, but he was never unkind to me, and I pay him this faint far away tribute. The lines that moved him are magnificent, the stretching forward in time, the epigrammatic flavouring. But what of the poem they conclude? the conception of a large circular

metal object is constantly stated and instantly lost, and the pictorial
takes charge, or rather the cinematic, for the pictures are full of
motion. The incidents are dull and some of the lines – secretosque
pios, his dentem jura Catonem – read ludicrous. Will see what
Homer is up to.

Lord Brooke

From A Treatie of Warres:

> And when the reines of humane hopes and fears
> Are thus laid on your neckes, and order chang'd
> Pride will no long the yoke of heaven beare
> Nor our desires in any bounds be rang'd
>
>> The world must take new forms of wrong and right
>> For warre did never love things definite.
>
> Here bookes are burnt, faire monuments of mindes,
> Here ignorance doth on all arts tyrannise
> Vertue no other mould but courage findes,
> All other beings in her being dies.
>
>> Wisdome of times grows infancy againe
>> Beasts rule in man, and men do beare thy raigne.

———— . ————

> Audit the end: how can humanity
> Preserved be in ruin of mankinde?

From A Treatise of Monarchie:

> There was a time before the times of story
> When Nature raign'd instead of laws or arts,
> And mortal gods with men made up the glory
> Of one republick of united hearts.
> Earth was the common seat, their conversation
> In saving love, and ours in adoration

[The above hanging about on a piece of paper from the 2nd
World War]

Copulation – Topulation

Sexual acts divide into (i) congress in the hope of producing a
child (ii) everything else. – Which is on reflection the R.C. point

of view, though they further limit theirs by insisting on a solemn-ised marriage. For me (ii) – i.e. all toppings and bottomings – can only be estimated in terms of response. Human beings could be mutual and so respond best, human being and animal less well, human being and hair brush not at all.

As for Living novelists I suppose E. M. Forster is the best, not knowing what there is, but at least he's a semi-finalist, wouldn't you think? Somerset Maugham once said to me, "We have a novelist here, E. M. Forster, though I dont expect he's familiar to you." Well I could have kicked him. Did he think I carried a papoose on my back? Why I'd go on my hands and knees to get to Forster. He wrote once something I've always remembered: "It has never happened to me that I've had to choose between betraying a friend and betraying my country, but if it ever does so happen I hope to have the guts to betray my country." Now doesnt that make the Fifth Amendment look like a bum.

Dorothy Parker, interviewed in the Paris Review gave the above agreeable surprise. Has she not dusted over and failed? I have not read her lately and she sounds to be out at elbows.

Sydney Smith. Full text of the passage to Bishop Blomfield: –

You call me in the speech your facetious friend, and I hasten with gratitude in this letter to designate you my solemn friend; but you and I must not run into commonplace errors; you must not think me necessarily foolish because I am facetious; nor will I consider you necessarily wise because you are grave.   The Times, 5 Sept., 1840

"Short views, for God's sake short views." – S.S.

Bacon? Where?

And this dear freedom hath begotten me this peace, that I mourn not that end which must be, nor spend one wish to have one minute added to the uncertain date of my years.

Hippocratic Oath. I have at last read this, having intended to do so for many years and more particularly since my visit to Cos. It has the expected gravity, nobility and rationality. Beginning by affirming the cameraderie of Doctors, it goes on to their duty to their

patients: not to give poison, or to cause abortion; or to castrate –
if this is the meaning of the text; not to do harm in the houses
they visit or to seduce anyone, female or male, free or slave; and
not to gossip, where ever the subject matter for gossip may have
been acquired.

No one knows when, where or by whom the Oath was written.
With the rest of the Hippocratic writings – 4 vols in Loeb – it may
have formed part of a Med. Library in Cos.

Proust to Paul Morand:

Ce qui me désole, c'est de voir des gens d'intelligence mettre le goût
avant tout, ou du moins ce qu'ils nomment tel, et nier d'avance tout
que produirons les âges qui vont venir.

How right and how courageous he was – assuming that the ages
to come will produce Art. And it did not occur to him, writing
in 1921, to make any other assumption.

Darwin's Fairwell

Farewell Australia! You are a rising child, and doubtless some day will
reign a great princess in the South: but you are too great and
ambitious for affection, yet not great enough for respect.
Feb. 7th 1836.

Love in St John's Gospel is a two-way merry go-round or rather
sadly-go-round. God loves Christ who loves man who loves God,
and conversely God loves man who loves Christ who loves God.
Sadly: because no guide is given as to the nature of love. In the
cases of God and Christ, silence is understandable; but can nothing be said about man? All we get is the arid advice of obedience;
and the mystic circle splits. They that love me obey my commandments. Follow the know-betters.

Honour. Loss of Honour. There are such things, though I admit them
reluctantly, and Honour is easily if gradually lost by dons. And I
have been a don for over ten years now, strange though it looks.
There are two preservatives, or rather props: action and silence:
and if one has failed to act it is more dignified not to cadge for
sympathy afterwards. Stephen Spender loses honour constantly

through an interminable diarhoea composed not entirely of words. Tolerance, easiness, laughter, even sympathy have their leaky aspects, and while exercising them – which I do – something essential drains away. Where the honour-mongers go wrong is in supposing that Honour can be Asserted or Avenged. Its preservation or loss has nothing to do with other people. Bob is in un-interrupted possession of his Honour.

My failure to speak yesterday (16–11–57) on the Bursarial Business in Congregation has left me dissatisfied. Yet I should have been disappointed had I spoken. It was one of those situations where Honour had to drain away, and many of my colleagues appear to be in the same plight.

Inscription outside Chesterton Church, Cambs. Date. July 21st, 1797. Four lines above it, and the name, I could not decipher.

> Her father, born of Afric's sun-born race
> Torn from his native fields – ah foul disgrace
> Through various toils at length to Britain came
> Espoused, as Heaven ordained an English dame
> And followed Christ: their hope two infants dear
> But one, a hapless orphan, slumbers here,
> To bury her the village children came
> And dropped choice flowers and lisped her early fame
> And some that loved her most, as if unblest,
> Bedewed with tears the white wreathes on their breast
> But she is gone and dwells in that abode
> Where sons of every clime shall joy in God.

Did the conception of Peace and Rest as final goods for the Individual exist before Christianity? It assumes that life has been tiring.

It is tempting when you have something you think worth saying to seek publicity for it, but the search alters what is being said.

Shelley. Queen Mab. Who would have believed it? Though in its context its magic fades, and glows for me because the last two lines recall a poem of Cavafy's.

Those who had looked upon the sight,
Passing all human glory,
Saw not the yellow moon
Saw not the mortal scene
Heard not the night wind's rush
Heard not an earthly sound,
Saw but the fairy pageant
Heard but the heavenly strains
That filled the lonely dwelling.

"Dwelling" is an "enchanting" word. Cf. it in Housman.

I may read Shelley more than I expected to, so complete is the denial of *all* his hopes. He stands on an extremity behind which a whole mountain has 'crumbled'.

Let Freedom and Peace fly far
To a sunnier strand
And follow Love's folding star
To the Evening Land

– to the land of McCarthy and Nixon.

This absolute denial of despair, this complete misreading of the future have their attractions. I heard them yesterday at the close of the first movement of Vaughan Williams Sixth Symphony, and began to weep.   11–1–58

Three Inscriptions on a rock in Santorin:

Lacydidas nice
Eumelus nicer jumps
Crimon nicest jumps dirtily Simias

So I paraphrase and epigrammatise I. G. XII. 3, 540. The decipherer, Friedrich Hiller von Gaertringen, found it a difficult job, and only succeeded when he took a mould and examined it elsewhere. There are said to be more such inscriptions and more. This is a fruit of my sudden hunt for Greek oddments, including Beesley's study of vases at Cyprus, and Pindar in Bowra's The Greek Experiment.

Howards End my best novel and approaching a good novel. Very elaborate and all pervading plot that is seldom tiresome or forced, range of characters, social sense, wit, wisdom, colour. Have only just discovered why I don't care for it: not a single character in it for whom I care. In *Where Angels* Gino, in *L.J.* Stephen, in *R. with V.* Lucy, in *P. to I.* Aziz . . . and Maurice and Alec . . . . and Lionel and Cocoa . . . . Perhaps the house in *H.E.*, for which I once did care, took the place of people and now that I no longer care for it their barrenness has become evident. I feel pride in the achievement, but cannot love it, and occasionally the swish of the skirts and the non-sexual embraces irritate. Perhaps too I am more hedonistic than I was, and resent not being caused pleasure personally.   – May 1958

What goes on in the darker side of a boy's mind?

But what about the boy in the darker side of whose mind nothing much goes on at all?
What about the boy whose mind has not got much of a dark side?
In fact, what about the boy who has not got much of a mind?
[Amusingness from '*The Ever-interesting Topic*' by William Cooper a good novel that is almost a great deal better. Not sure what its trouble is – connected with the exploration of character rather than its presentation]

St Remy – notes made during a visit there, c. 1938

Serpent – A female got into the Mauron's garage. Should have departed through the drain, but realised that when her head was engaged the rest of her person would be exposed to attack. So she hissed and sent the dogs hysteric. Charles poured hot water from a pannikin on to her tail, but it cooled in transit so she did not mind that. Finally he poked her with stick.

Snakes here are harmless, yet a labourer was killed by one not long ago. He was mowing – it got entangled in his sickle, and then wound round both his hands, tying them together. He managed to cut in two, but died of fright.

How to get thin. A friend of Roger Fry's bought a glycerine capsule for this purpose. Falling ill, she did not take it, but found it some- what perished in a cupboard. Something moved in the glycerine: it was a 'ver solitaire' which she would have swallowed.

Les Soureilles Well to do peasants in the marsh land below St. Remy. Ardent atheists, they have a meat banquet every Good Friday, which Charles has to attend. The youngest, Gabriel, is 'not quite there' and of great beauty, and set to mind the family sheep while the others feasted. I met him alone – we sheltered in a meadow under a great ridge of rock from the Mistral. Piercing brown eyes, a broad forehead with wings of hair. An old crimson hanky round his throat, but no socks. Denounced capitalism without realising it had anything to do with the family sheep. 'Guillotine Hitler'! A well dressed gentleman, ribbon in button hole, asked to photo him. 'Vous êtes anglais?' – 'Mais non' he replied testily. 'Puisque mon camerade est anglais – – –'

Why has our Mistress gone away? asked little Laura. Her school-mate then drew a picture of the mistress with a huge belly and a little baby inside it.

Rogue Elephant [Jaipur, 1945]. Dribbling as from Prostate. Also Sexual [?] discharge of black flakes from temples. Hay on head. Expressed dignity, suffering malice. Fastened by 3 of his feet. Teased, he pulled out his hind ones, and one of the wooden pegs round a stone connected with his front foot. He was wily and thoughtful. Now and then he dashed his tusks against the wall and punched holes in it, or with difficulty raised a flat cake with his trunk, eating straw with it. [note made at time]

The Trial of Marshal Ney has been read through by me with interest, and it is one of the changes in my habits I hope to make in my life since E.K.B's death: i.e. to read book *through*. A book on Ney is the strangest of starts. For he did nothing but kill people all his life and be the Bravest of the Brave, and when he betrayed his employers and nearly defeated them at Waterloo, I cannot see w' they should not have killed him. He himself had never caught sight of any other standard, or of any spiritual choice other than the arid choice between loyalty and disloyalty. His able biographer – Harold Kurtz of whom I have never heard – builds him too much but makes him interesting by connecting him with subtler and more intelligent people. He never enjoyed what I should call a life of his own. "Je suis frog, je mourrai frog", et il meurt, having sent to death Austrians Russians Prussians Italians

Spaniards Portuguese English and other Frogs first. Quelle hecatombe magnifique! And how well Wellington comes out in comparison!   July 1958

The Artist must be partly male and partly female. Unfortunately the female part is nearly always intolerable.

> Cocteau: quoted in H. Acton, Memoirs of an aesthete

"*Kathleen is so optimistic* that she thinks the civilisation of India may one day reach the level of that of Australia" said Sir George Young of his sister in law, Lady Kennet. She made a moue. I also remember myself, in the uncongenial yet not ungenial house, making a poem to balance the much quoted "What is a Communist?"

> What is a Capitalist? One who hopes
> To gain Heaven through knowing the ropes

and Hilton's entertained and grumpy "So he will". They were pleasant visits on the whole – the Broads and Cornwall – and once they lent Fritton to E. V. Thompson and myself so that I might convalesce there from something.

Letter from me to Ben B., which I have just written and find good enough to transcribe: I have only once done this with a letter:

> K.C.C. Aug 27. 1958

I was very glad dearest Ben to have a sight of you in your new surroundings. They look perfect for working in, and I do hope you are on something you like. It is the only satisfaction in these days – or rather in this trend of our days. Which are so depressing – not because one will die or even because one's friends will, but because the human race seems advancing to disaster via vulgarity. It is very difficult to see anything great in the general movement of the last ten years. Science might be wonderful, but it is applied so contemptibly that one is disgusted or bored; the mucky doings on the bed of the sea, the attempt to land on the moon in the hope of finding something there which might hurt another human being on the earth drive one back to the act of creation as the only possible escape. Unfortunately one doesnt create by being driven, but I do hope you will evolve something that will help you and others to see what we are moving into.

For it is very curious and unusual – no doubt of that – and sometimes
in trying to look at it I get the sort of pleasure that comes from taking
exercise.

Much love and much to Peter when you see him from

Morgan

Talleyrand's death extremely depressing and related by Duff Cooper
with undue complacency and unctuousness. He was cornered by
beautiful women who loved him and were anxious about him,
and by a sincere young priest, and by distant papal rumbles, and
badgered until he signed. The same has happened to many of my
own literary contemporaries – Siegfried, Edith Sitwell and others
– and I wish to add that I hope it may not happen to me and that
I may not be caught at a moment of terror and fear to deny my
unbelief and to become additional propaganda for the believists.
One would have supposed us, in our 70s or 80s, to be such negligible prey, but they appear to be the decades inviting assault.
Heaven knows what one's right mind is, but I wish to affirm this
13th of December, 1958, that I think I am in mine now.

But maybe not in my powerfullest mind, for I read the whole of
this book thinking it was Harold Nicolson and abusing him to
myself as a Master not of Letters but of Squitters. I must say
though that it is a very interesting book, which breeds and rami-
fies, and that Harold Kurz [see p. 205] is wrong in saying it wasn't
worth writing. The period, too, is so interesting – contrast that
arch bore the English Civil Wars. "A bad man but a good European" barked G. M. Trevelyan at me the other day. T. is certainly
bad even by my lax standards, and the goodness of Europeanism
is today doubtful. T. tricked people like Napoleon, who deserved
it, but others too. Detestable about Decazes. So far as he can be
praised, it is as a worldling against brutality. He was also a worldling against integrity – a virtue which except in the most chancery
sense of the word – he despised.

Reading about Tilsit in these pages, I turned to Hardy's:

It is the day after midsummer, about one o'clock. A multitude of
soldiery and spectators line each bank of the broad river which, stealing slowly north west, bears almost exactly in its midst a moored raft
of bonded timber. On this as a floor stands a gorgeous pavilion of
draped wood-work, having at each side, facing the respective banks of

the stream, a round headed doorway richly festooned. The cumbersome erection acquires from the current a rhythmical movement, as if it were breathing, and the breeze now and then produces a shiver on the face of the stream

Edith is said to have become a Catholic because she was frightened at the violence of her own hatred for David Horner.

Siegfried Sassoon: 30–12–58

> In bygone days I sometimes sauced a
> Confederate crony – Morgan Forster.
> Query: do I now dare accost a
> Figure as famed as E. M. Foster?
> I do. In bed with glum lumbago
> Watch I my words upon their way go,
> And wafted by affectionate wings,
> Join the glad 'goings on' at King's.
>
> With Morgan I can still be 'matey'
> Though grown so eminent at eighty.
> I, ever most unintellectual,
> And, as a thinker, ineffectual,
> I, a believer in believing,
> Can hail his genius for perceiving
> Reasoned humanities which led
> Where angels have not feared to tread,
> And thus, forbearing further fuss,
> Award my friend an Alpha Plus.

Written on the other side of a pic. or photo, of the exterior of the chapel, with a collage of my head in the west window. Lovely skilful sincere stuff and illustrating that "I love you though I never trouble to see you" attitude which is also characteristic of Ben and Peter, and which I do not share.

Wystan Auden's wish to me, Jan 11, 1959 [I read it at the lunch]

Dear Morgan wish I could be with you in more than spirit stop may you long continue what you already are stop old famous loved yet not a sacred cow stop love and gratitude Wystan Auden

Inert, influenza-ed, gouted, awaiting acquaintances whom I was not anxious to see, I dared myself and W. B. Yeats to find a poem by him I thought good. Here it is, after many petulant rejections:

The Magi
Now as at all times I can see in the mind's eye,
In their stiff, painted clothes, the pale unsatisfied ones
Appear and disappear in the blue depths of the sky
With all their ancient faces like rain-beaten stones
And all their helms of silver hovering side by side,
And all their eyes still fixed, hoping to find, once more,
Being by Calvary's turbulence unsatisfied,
The uncontrollable mystery on the bestial floor.

This is superior to the famous vision of the New Birth which it
reminds me of, yet how difficult I am to please over Yeats. His
faults always do damage whereas those of Wordsworth and
Hardy . . . His poetic pedestal wobbles if it encounters the minut-
est pebble. There is not *much* literary padding in 'minds eye',
'stiff painted clothes', 'blue depths' 'rain-beaten stones' etc., yet
one is inclined to detect it, and to fear that one scrap more will
falsify the whole effect.

This insecurity, this fear of the sudden apparition of a noble lady
with her breasts far apart or of a tense and uncompanionable
Irishman striding up Ben Bulben haunts me when I peruse Yeats.
The poem cannot be spoilt: the last line is the most deep and
terrible yet written on the Nativity. I had never expected to be
discovered by anything new in these days. And the cleverness of
making the Magi hang about to find out what happened.

Unexpected end to a half-hearted quest.
St Valentine's Eve
1959

The great poem stumbled on accidently by me above has had
a little pendant this evening. Annoyed with myself and with
my hearing – for I am deafer and distort worse this week – I put
on without expectation a *Boccherini* Quintet (C minor 29.1) to be
ravished by it as far as its apparatus allowed. A quiet largo sliding
into a slightly less quiet trio in the same key – ! what competence!
what grace! It cheers me that all this must be lying around me,
even if I don't happen to touch it. Boccherini, too, seems to have
had a good character, and I think that Hamburger who does him
into sausages on the disk-"sleeve" must have another, for his
touch is homely and quiet.

St Valentine's day

Half mast was the flag for Pigou's death – he faded out last Saturday, March 7th I think, at Addenbrookes, bored and feeble ('Poor soul. But never mind.' – Mrs Blackwell, his bedmaker –); he rather charmed me of late years, I respected him and tried to please him as I passed him lolled back in his deck chair. Well, Sunday the flag was half mast for him and a group of cadets came over from Sandhurst and stole it off the top of Gibbs. Reactions are interesting particularly my own, for I am furious and seized with blasphemy-rage. Let them be punished! So say the porters, but dons cling to "Its a rag and rags are larks," as they did over the Reading professor who was such a joker over diamonds. It was a reprisal for a gun stolen from Sandhurst by Caius, but an interesting one for never before, say experts, has a flag at half mast been stolen. I record this silliness because the army and the university may combine to keep it out of the papers. The flag was recovered or located this morning.   Monday, March 9/59

Henry IV, 2

An odious play, on the whole odiously served by the overpraised Marlowe Society which banged the tavern-scenes to the death they probably deserved and robbed the country-scenes of the charm and nostalgia that make them unique in S. I had forgotten the infamous betrayal of the rebels: preceding the betrayal of Falstaff, it spreads the unpleasing taste widely. We were asked to accept a plump and tartish little Prince Hal, whose nose my neighbour behind me said was artificial, as were other noses: but he certainly spoke his lines well, as did other characters.

The whole performance, including the shouty bits, was so *feeble*; what a contrast to the tense and terrible Edward II last year.

I was feeble too: fell into a matinée sleep.

I ought to have described Grey Walter's Lecture last night on Is the Brain a Machine? But its brilliancy and profundity are beyond me.   12–3–59

Pagan Minimum

Inscription on Stele in B.M., c. 350 B.C., representing middle aged man on horse whose tail a slave holds:

After many pleasant sports with my companions, I who sprang from earth am earth once more. I am Aristocles of Piraeus son of Menon.

Not quite enough. Perhaps undertranslated.

Pigou's Funeral

Noel read: from Donne:

No man is an island, entire of itself; every man is a piece of the continent, a part of the main; if a clod be washed away by the sea, Europe is the less, as well as if a promontory were, as well as if a manor of thy friends or of thine own were; any man's death diminishes me, because I am involved in mankind; and therefore never send to know for whom the bell tolls; it tolls for thee.

Sebastian Halliday read: from the Wisdom of Solomon, ch. 3.

Eastern Sunset, and where is the diary which I got to chronicle such prodigies? 6.15, 28–3–59. I stand in the Jumbo House. Westward the sky clear and uninspired. Eastward, over the Screen, skeins of orange and red clouds, semi-circling; over them bright soft blue sky, as of an undisturbed summer's day. The prospect exciting and gratuitously presenting itself to an absent audience, and I felt 'How much goes on unnoticed' and hope that it will be noticed when I am not here. I have had very strongly of late the wish that others may be as sensitive as myself and the fear that they will not be. Colleague Sir Frank Adcock stumped by the sunset-portent unheeding. And I can't argue that I gain, or that others would gain, anything for humanity by observing and recording what went on for a few moments in the sky on Boat Race evening. I sometimes pretend to myself that I am public-spirited. I am not. I am a hedonist who wants pleasant sensations. On the other hand I am not the usual type of hedonist, for I want sensations *to be had* – if not by myself, then by someone else. The show shouldn't end with my death, which becomes a minor boo-hoo.

I seem in a strong and superior position here, and must look further into it. The flaw I anticipate is the unexpected one of idleness: I am so ready to delegate things and they may include sensations. "Here, feel that for me" do I say to posterity.

Western Radiance A month after the overleaf entry I find myself in the same mood wanting to record the same sort of thing: this time the view from the Combination Room towards the Backs – tender green, sunlight, blue and black sky, all in themselves agreeable but pulled out of themselves by the bright orange brown of an advancing jersey. The effect only endured for the half of a second, for the jersey advanced out of sight and was lost, and whether it was on a man or a woman and what even was its exact colour I forgot. But there was a definite statement. I called my colleague Jasper Rose to enjoy the sight with me, but he was too late. He paints, and might have liked it. But the incident drew us together and bred warmth. I spoke of the tiny cherries on the Michael Schweetz in the National Gallery years ago, and could have mentioned Arthur Snatchfold's canary-coloured shirt which brought its wearer to prison; J.R. of the match box etc. which a painter introduces to set the figure alight (they dont his, the poor lad.) We agreed that we are inobservant because we have too many ideas. What indeed have I secured from that split second beyond the *idea* of its importance? It dissolved into nothing as soon as the jersey passed behind the stone work to my right, and is now nowhere – leaving me back in the world of boredom and laughter, which it cancelled during its passage.   27–4–59

?

And now behold me in the tepidarium of the Turkish bath. Enter an Arab youth – Oculis nigris, capillis crispis et concinnis, ore jucundo. He takes this arm which has been paining me for the last four days, extends it gently across his naked body, and bids me lay hold of his foot – "Attrape!", and shields it somehow without giving it additional pain; he bids me recline my head on his breast. "Couche!" while he draws the same arm upward, to its fullest extent, also without pain. He puts his lips to my ears, sucks the dust of travel from them, and then blows a clear breath (without a drop of spittle) into the ringed cavities. And then, for I had been too tired to think of any things at all up to that point, the fancy struck me that Apuleius himself – who was reputed a great magician as well as a Platonic philosopher – had sent one of his slaves to cleanse, and look after me before I stood in his native forum the next day – but it was more than a fancy, for with that breath in my ears I could imagine that, as to those who couched in the porticos of Aesculapius or Osiris, a spiritual change had come to me, and I was purged not only of material but incorporeal dross, and was in fact to become a clean, fresh, resilient being, as the Lusius of the last book of the *Golden Ass*

Transcribed from the otherwise bad-tempered and ungrateful
letters of *E. H. W. Meyerstein.* – Mohammed el Adl, over 40 years
ago, spoke to me of the same thing in Egypt, though there the
operation was less elaborate, and the operator was a policeman.

I have looked in Apuleius, but found no parallel.

I recall

After this day of sunshine and youthful joy, sitting on the river bank
in the morning, scrap-lunch with Christopher Bacon, sitting near
Robert Alexander and girl in Fellows Gardens in afternoon,
leaving my spectacles on the lawn to be graciously retrieved by
Ashok Desai and offering Cavafy to Mark Elvin –

I have very nearly been run over by a car in the backs. My second
escape. At 9.0. P.M. the lamps hadn't burnt up, the car had not
turned its lights on, my clothes were of the prevalent duskiness, it
suddenly existed and nearly hit me. I was more angry than
frightened by this

end to a perfect day.   May 1959

nearly got again, motor bike Peas Hill, Aug.

Jumping Spider. Lively slightly sinister insect, bigger than an ant but
too small for a wasp, was espied by me about midday on the
woodwork of the Orangery window-sill. Summoned John Raven
(naturalist) who was alarmed, but Donald Parry (zoologist)
greeted it heartily as the male of the most common of the (14?)
species of *Jumping Spiders* inhabiting this country. Its muscles being
weak, it is believed to jump by altering its blood-pressure! It has
four large eyes and it utilises its thread in unexpected ways. It
hopes to fall upon a fly. After much skipping and slipping it was
assisted on to the warm sill outside where I saw it half an hour
afterwards, though not an hour afterwards, still very content, and
abounding in cheerful and disconnected little movements. –
– July 20 1959.

Knowledge is power they say. Knowledge is not only power it is good fun
Norman Douglas

Fear that the Companions will not continue, that the dogs cats will
follow the rabbits whom the horses are already following, that the
little common birds will follow the rare and large ones, that the barley
will follow the silphium and the rose the musk, that Man will suppose
himself the only form of life, that armed and capsuled imbeciles will
penetrate the new regions accessible above and beneath us to murder
whatever is stirring: the regions beneath us from which we came. This
distant cousinhood! There was a time when we – i.e. what we came
from – communicated. This is clumsily recognised in the so called
crime of Bestiality. The man-modified earth on the way to being man-
destroyed. After which the man-modified sea ———

Here the entry, written about 1955 on two little bits of paper,
breaks off. I like it and copy it in here, while I am conscious of
"failing powers" but not of failing interest

and having been to all this trouble find I have already copied it
out later on [under Book]

Failing memory!

Smells

No locker room could have more pungent air than Devon's; sweat
predominated, but it was richly mixed with smells of paraffin and
singed rubber, of soaked wool and liniment, and for those who could
interpret it, of exhaustion, lost hope and triumph and bodies battling
against each other. I thought it anything but a bad smell. It was pre-
eminently the smell of the human body after it had been used to the
limit, such a smell as has meaning and poignance for any athlete, just
as it has for any lover.

> – 'A Separate Peace'. By John Knowles.
> Good novel, scene American.

Here is recognisably a school story, yet into it get large adult issues.
It set me off thinking of the Philoctetes of Sophocles, not that the
scope or even the intention of the two works is the same, but they both
deal with physical prowess and pain, and with betrayal.

Wrote this to the author who will use it as a blurb in the States.

The Kind Ghosts

> She sleeps on soft, last breaths; but no ghost looms
> Out of the stillness of her palace wall,
> Her wall of boys on boys and dooms on dooms.

She dreams of golden gardens and sweet glooms
Not marvelling why her roses never fall.
Nor what red mouths were torn to make their blooms.

The shades keep down which well might roam her hall,
Quiet their blood lies in her crimson rooms,
And she is not afraid of their footfall.

They move not from her tapestries, their pall
Nor pace her terraces, their hecatombs,
Lest aught she be disturbed or grieved at all.

I have long realised the greatness of this, but only this evening its clarity.

Yeats Scraps:

For meditation upon unknown thoughts
Makes human intercourse grow less and less.

Repentance keeps my heart impure.

Oct 19, 1959 an enjoyable day during which I neither thought of anyone else or thought I was not thinking of them.

Morning: sun-browning in the Fellows' gardens, reading Il Gattopardo.

Afternoon: listening to Goldberg Variations.

Unremarkable tea with undergraduate.

The Human Spirit will survive until it becomes non-human: that is to say until the discoveries and inventions we are increasingly making react upon us so strongly that they change our characters. We could no more understand that evolved human race than the monkeys can understand us.

This and other ideas have been coming unhappily to the surface all the day. I had meant to catalogue my three days' London season, which I devoted to the meeting and recapturing of friends. But on returning to Cambridge I heard from Elizabeth Poston that Rooksnest, so long protected by me, is to be destroyed and this has reminded me of the impending destruction of the country-side, the home, and perhaps of the family. Their withdrawals,

and the universality of mechanisation is sure to alter people
whether there is an international show-down or not. Perhaps if I
lived to see the dear little Clive a young man, we should not be
able to communicate. He is bound to a swifter maturing than
mine.

But things have turned out so extraordinarily that I cannot tell
where they next turn. The Conquest of Space – to use that boast-
ful and silly phrase – has not yet begun to hit back. America in
the 16th cent. took a little time to hit back after she had been
discovered by Europe.

The above flow has been partly generated by an invitation to give
the Henry Sidgwick Lecture at Newnham. I should have liked
to give it, but it demands a *sustainment* that I cannot provide

I will write another night about my success as a writer and an
individual. They surprise me   March 17 1960

SLOWLY

Slowly ————

Slowly our ghosts drag home: glimpsing the sunk fires glozed
With crusted dark-red jewels; crickets jingle there;
For hours the innocent mice rejoice; the house is theirs;
Shutters and doors all closed; on us the doors are closed –

We turn back to our dying.

Refusal to deliver the Henry Sidgwick lecture at Newnham

April 10 1960

Dear Miss Cohen

I have thought over that gratifying invitation to give the Sidgwick
Lecture, and have decided regretfully to decline. The Lectureship has
a serious tradition, and I cannot talk seriously about the world to day
– which is what I would like to do – without coming to conclusions
that are both depressing and unhelpful. Thanks partly to technical
discoveries, all the things I care for are on the decline. The arts –
especially the art of Letters – are weakening, the countryside is being
destroyed, personal contacts are being impaired, and we witness
instead the triumph – by shock-methods of advertisement and psychological attacks – of what used to be called Mammon and is now called

British Trade. I don't see any way of getting round the lions at present in the human path – the lion of commercialism particularly – and it isnt fair to an audience just to moan without offering a remedy . . . . .*

*Letter was more effective when I drowsed through it in bed and in my bath. Most of my good stuff is created and forgotten in the morning   10–4–60

To *abolish* a *status* which in all ages GOD has sanctioned, and man has continued, would not only be *robbery* to an innumerable class of our fellow-subjects, but it would be extreme cruelty to the African savages.   – Boswell on Slavery (where?)

Tesserete, August of 1911, which I spent with S.R.M. greatly involved. I have just torn up letters to my mother and Aunt Laura. They convey nothing at all. Tesserete, like most of everyone's past, is lost. It was in Italian Switzerland, and Pino Ithen, a commercial youth known to Masood, got us rooms there. I recall no scenery but faintly some scenes, for we were at the stage – so familiar to me – where the other person has ceased to be interested. It was a honeymoon slightly off colour, and perhaps that is why the letters are so dull. With difficulty do I recall an expedition up the mountains where Signor Ithen bit ants in two to refresh himself with formic acid, while his daughters shrieked 'Papa'. And Masood having an ugliesh waitress, or visitor; for I think he had her, but thought me too much of a muff to be told. – There's a photograph of us there somewhere, I starry eyed with a huge moustache looking very odd indeed. – But why, having already published 3 novels, did I write such wet letters?   – 1960

Edwin Muir, whose poems followed by his Biography have moved me so much lately, especially when lying in bed in the morning, eyes filling with tears, planning to write down about him. As soon as I got up, the plan scattered, he would have understood this. Now, 8.30 A.M. with a morning too bright to last – he understood that too – I will anyhow copy out a few sentences I dog-eared in the Biog. I am *not* conscious of a sense of sin, I *don't* expect or desire immortality, and here are two differences in our temperaments, and I have had better health, more money and more fun.

I had acquired in Scotland a deference towards ideas which made my entrance into poetry difficult.

I do not know what value such experiences have [i.e. that distinction had fallen away like a burden, that substance had been transmuted: the familiar and transient mystic experience]; I feel they should 'go into' life; yet there seems no technique by which one can accomplish the work of their inclusion.

I had reached the stage [   ] when boys stick together to hide the shame of their inexperience, and turn without knowing it against their parents and the laws of the house.

The age which felt the connection between men and animals was so much longer than the brief historical period known to us that we cannot conceive it, but our unconscious life goes back into it. . . . . They were protagonists in the first sylvan war, half human and half felted and feathered, from which rose the hearth, the community and the arts.

[here he is on something v. important though he goes on into guilt feelings because we won the war]

I do not much admire personalities . . . A personality is too obviously the result of a collaboration between its owner and time, too clearly *made* and no matter how fascinating or skilful the workmanship may be, it ultimately bores us.

The gentleness and dignity of that family in that lonely place [near Carrara], the veil of flies hanging from the walls, bemused us as we walked on, and I became dimly aware of a good life which had existed for many centuries before medicine and hygiene identified goodness with cleanliness.

Drowned in Cam at 6.0. this morning – hideous little disaster – Lindsay Heather, woken by the cries when half awake, saw the hands disappear of a boy from Queens', West Indian theologian according to the C.D.N. Our matron had already told me, adding "But never mind" when she saw I was upset. Walking out wretchedly I met an old lady – Hal Dixon's mother-in-law – wheeling a baby. She asked me who had died at Queen's – for their sumptuous flag was at half-mast. I told her. She was about to reply when a tickling cough seized her. When she could speak she said 'I've a tickling cough.' Then she said to the baby "Granny's got a tickling cough. Have you got a tickling cough?"

Thus was the news assimilated. – That dirty little prettified river!
To think that it could kill! And over the lawn from it is the chapel
from which Ivor Ramsay leapt. But that was suicide – some
sense. This boy was murdered when, after his exams, he put on
his trunks for a dip. (For one may be sure he wore them.)

June 7th 1960

Dies Irae

Peacefulness to be found in writing. *Why* do I not write every day?
  Partly because I feel I ought to write well and know I can't. But
  that is not a good enough reason for not writing, if it gains me
  poise & peace.

Back on p 145 I have written in a scrap about our German tour.
It fell into shape as I rambled forward.   July 20 1960

And now, the following day, I adopt the same technique and
assure myself it is better to dribble than dry up. On either side
doors threaten, for I do not feel my peace important enough to
be locked in, steps sound on the stairs, there's a faint car, a fainter
plane, a doubtful bird, the weather, odious since my return, has
again clouded over after the thunderousness, and my own hand,
not writing so badly, moves over this paper which is 159 years
old and presses this book whose covers have come loose. The
Chapel Bell rings not agressively, and I like it.

Have just remembered that I don't like peace for its own sake,
only because it may be a road to mastery. Requiem Aeternam – a
natural goal for the underprivileged but for me No, who has been
given so much. I want to own, or rather use, what I have been
given and make something out of it. The whirring of what the
world is making may disturb. Unity with the Godhead or God-
tail? No, less than ever. The conception of a fluid universe and
the absence of universal laws makes Pantheism feebler than ever.
It is rather a little local silence that enfolds me, a rug for a bug.

Still the bird sings, our companion about to leave us, though it
does not know this and though most men do not know it. It has
sung in human earshot for millions of years.

I am afraid that by now I am tired again, the mortal drowsiness is

upon me with so many little things undone. My British Cough –
three weeks of it now – may be weakening me. Trying to keep
brisk I have had no alcohol.

Yes – thunder.

Christians and Pantheists may insist that the soul is separate from the body,
but this is not true. There is a live body, that is all.

Gaudier-Brzeska – gets there in one.
 Remarks of Picasso, read recently, do the
 same, and suggest that the dicta of painters
 should be noted and culled. The
 verbalists are too likely to know
 beforehand that they have
 something to say.

Little Clive [aged   ]. Touching yesterday to see him entering the
world. Hitherto he has always rushed to show me a toy. Now he
hovered about, claiming attention, or asking what people were
saying. He had lost confidence and gained self-consciousness.
Charm had gone because he felt insecure. Realisation that his little
brother Paul had come to stay and was beginning to walk had
precipitated this. He couldn't have *all* of everybody's love any
more. He had lost the state of innocence in which grown ups so
selfishly wish babies to remain. God furious because he could no
longer enjoy the innocence of Adam and Eve in Eden. He had
hoped all through time to amuse himself by visiting a nursery
untouched by time. Viewed from this point of view – and from no
other – the Fall makes sense. Here is dear little Clive falling into
the world, and not liking it, and the utmost grown-ups can do is
to conceal their annoyance and regret. Bob talks cheerfully of
readjustment, which no doubt will occur both for Clive and Paul,
but not without bruising their freshness and disappointing their
elders. Fortunately we're none of us as old as God. Nor do we
think – as he is credited with thinking – that it is possible to
create a changeless enclave.

I have only lately cared for or thought about children, and no
doubt my fondness for folly has attracted me. Much displeased if
when I jump in the air they look grave.

[Mem. My best hours for writing seem to be in the morning, after 5.0, and after 9.0. Always sleepy in the afternoon even if I dont drink sherry for lunch]

Next day learn that Rob's jaundice has taken him to hospital.

A Week in Rome – transcribed from a loose page

Nov 10th, 1959: Palazzo Doria, S. Ignazio, Gesu. S. Maria in Via Lati, S. Maria sopra Minervan

Nov 11th: Farnesina, Bosio Parrhasio, S. Sabina

Nov 12th: S. Maria in Trastevere, S. Cecilia in same, S. Maria in Cosmedin, Isola Tiburina, S. Andrea el Quirinale

Nov 13th. Ss Giovanni e Paolo, S. Nereo e Achilleo, S. Cesario, S. Giovanni a Porta Latina, S. Clemente

Nov 14th Villa Celimontana. Palestrina.

Nov 15th Sperlunga, S. Agnese P.a Navona, S. Maria della Paie

Nov 16th Palazzo Mattei, Palazzo Grillo

All the above, except Sperlunga which was British Conciliar, were seen with Enzo Crea.

Recommended to anyone who is through with the Heavies.

One Light Year = 5,880,000,000,000 miles

Distance of nearest star = *4 light years*
Distance of Galaxy in Bootes – farthest measurable – is

500,000,000 Light years.

I have at last got hold of these distances, if that is their name. They mean more to me than they seem to mean to most people, who are indeed faintly offended when they are alluded to. The measurable extent of the physical universe which has produced me is a personal concern. I have been also looking, with still more concern at large scale maps of Russia – in the big Times Atlas, where no name of town, river, or mountain was known to me, and I could not guess which frontier was nearest. Such an area if competently organised, and it is reported to be, should control all other areas in an incalculably small fraction of a Light Year.

Boredom short note on unimportant subject
        whom I like, and he is pleasant, friendly, sympathetic and

intelligent, has left me ironed out by a three hours visit which a thunderstorm prolonged. I minded it less when he couldn't go because of the rain then when he might have gone but didnt. He has had this effect on me before, and I cannot find out why. He ironed me out, I was mad to be alone and now that I am can make no better use of it than this note.

My dictum that being bored doesn't matter remains true.

an explanation – a partial one – has occurred to me a few days later: I feared he was inviting me to what I could not accept. Hence my malais.

The Nude, by K. Clark. Quotations, 1936 edition.

The small full manageable body which has always appealed to the average sensualist 130

. . . . . that balance between intense participation and absolute detachment which distinguishes art from other forms of human activity. 124

. . . . that kind of animal earnestness with which antique art treated everything to do with sexual intercourse. 127

[I wish I was more intelligent and more energetic. This would not make me more helpful or competent, but – as a small increase of light will greatly increase the area of the circle illuminated – it would extend my knowledge and my joy. In the last two days, I have seen The Wild Duck, heard a Brandenburg Concerto and a Beethoven cello sonata, and read and looked at this Nude book further: I have annexed more than I can govern, carried home from the shops more than I can unpack, I feel a bit annoyed over this, but neither envious *or* contemptuous of others who can comprehend more *or* less than myself. Competition doesnt intrude, which is part of my strength. I see so many people glancing sideways at a rival as they run, and falling down in consequence.]

The vast crowds which attend a motor race or an air rally are there to witness a display of power of a different order to anything they could see in an athletic stadium. The poor human body has been put back where it was in the stone age; or lower, for it was at least on the same plane of activity as the sabre-toothed tiger and ruled by the same natural laws: yet perhaps it will be a long time before we renounce our old symbol which, for almost three thousand years, has provided the invigorating joys of self-identification. 213

Chronologically the contents of pp. 227, 228, should follow here. They dont.

"You're getting rather more ruthless at excluding sensitive feelings about yourself." – Dream sentence, 13.12.60, agreeably uttered by a companion of C.D. ty[pe]

Hansard. House of Lords 14–12–60. Lady Chatterley expressions of opinion.

Lord Teviot – What are we coming too? It is all very well for one noble Lord to laugh. This is not a laughing matter . . . . They say there should be physical recreation for the young, is this sort of thing going to help towards that? . . . Today I am an old man. In my earlier days of my life as a miner I mixed with rough fellows on the frontiers of the Empire . . . : but there has been nothing that has been said during my life . . which touches the horrible situation which I see in this situation today. We must do something about it ––– I cannot believe that the Obscene Publications Act can permit it to be called a Classic or that it is a thing of literary merit. It cannot possibly have anything of that sort in it.

The Earl of Craven My Lords I am no plaster saint. Neither am I a plaster philosopher – I hope! But all things considered I have the greatest understanding for youth . . . . Purity is sacrificed on the altar of promiscuity as woolly headed intellectuals pour their vociferous sewage into the ears of the public. The god of progress takes up the cloak of a shabby but sensuous Bacchus washed by science and narcotics while things of the spirit are relegated to the inferior position of discredited fairy tales. I added this in the train coming up. If Omo adds brightness to material whiteness, we surely need a spiritual detergent for the mind.

[reading from a letter] "Much to my regret I am an authority on pornographic literature – " – That is not me; I am only quoting the letter [continuing] "Most of the pornographic books are written by the best authors in England and France under a *nom de plume*" [invited either to confirm or withdraw this statement.] Certainly not. I am quoting from a letter. [from Basil Black- well?]

Lord Amwell My Lords I am sorry to interrupt

Several Noble Lords: Oh!

Lord Amwell Why not? You interrupt enough, and it is an important point here – The question has now gone from my mind and I shall have to leave it now . . . I am sorry

Going to Bits. This phrase describes me to day and is indeed the one I have been looking for; not tragic, not mortal disintegration; only a central weakness which prevents me from concentrating or settling down. I have so wanted to write and write ahead. The phrase "obligatory creation" has haunted me. I have so wanted to get out of my morning bath promptly: have decided to do so beforehand, and have then lain in it as usual and watched myself not getting out. It looks as if there is a physical as well as a moral break in the orders I send out. I have plenty of interesting thoughts but keep losing them like the post cards I have written, or like my cap. I can't clear anything up yet interrupt a 'good read' in order to clear up. I hope tomorrow to copy out a piece of someone else's prose: it is the best device known to me for taking one out of oneself. Plunge into anothers minutiae.' 31–1–61

Remark of my own, aged c. 6:

I should like to be a flower, a primrose that nobody picks.

R. A. Furness wrote half a century ago:

> A splinter from the bathroom door
> Pricked Everards posterior:
> Think how my human feelings stood
> For one who raised a piece of wood

– a place for which must be found somewhere.

John Addington Symonds travelled from Whitby to Clifton & back at the age of 19 in order to denounce his headmaster's homosexual practices to his father. He himself had the tendencies confusedly, saw them gratified around him brutally, and was horrified when another boy, out of conceit, showed him the headmaster's love-letters. "Disgust mitigated by a dumb persistent sympathy", and ending in "fatigued cynicism'. He took mature counsel before sneaking. (Had just left the school). His father orders the h.m. to

resign and to accept no further preferment in the church, nor did
he relent when the h.m's wife – and she a Stanley – fell on her
knees before him, and assured him that her husband's lapses did
not injure his work. The h.m. bowed before the threat and resigned, and then accepted the see of Worcester. After three days
he cancelled his acceptance, for Dr Symonds had threatened
again, also Soapy Sam had smelt something. The career of this
'sphinx-masked sham' was scotched, not destroyed, and reads well
in the D.N.B.

The above, and all that follows, is in J.A.S' unpublished
autobiography in the L.L. which may not at present be quoted
from, nor I think referred to. *Will any one who reads this remember
that?* Publication possible in 1976. About 150,000 in typescript.
A complete life, the many 'literary' bits of which S. has published
elsewhere. – He gave up all work to complete it.

Early dreams and dreamfulnesses: a little finger – nothing else –
becoming, coming nearer, terrifying. – Half dream: couched on
the floor amongst naked sailors at the age of 9. – "What my own
self contained was a terror to me. Things of flesh and blood,
brutal and murderous though they might be, could always be
taken by the hand and fraternised with. They were men and from
men I did not shrink. I always felt a man might be my comrade."
– Reads Venus and Adonis as Venus. – Reads of Apollo among
the sheep cotes of Admetus "clasped with the sturdy shepherd
folk, drinking life and love more naturally than on the peaks of
Parnassus, surrounded by the Muses." – Unerring choice of
myths appropriate to his own development. – Sailor fantasy
idealised through Greece.

Early affairs – semi-if not semi-demi; a warm imagination and
excitable body checked at the last moment by delicacy. A choir
boy at Clifton – tenor or bass by the description of him – was
provocative, and "Would to God that I had fraternized with
him and that he had suffered that union which the world calls
sin, but which leads as I know well in frequent cases to brother-
hood and mature good services through life." Sins of the body
are less pernicious than those of the imagination, the inevitable
alternative, which entangle us "in the close unwholesome labyrinth of tyrannous desires and morbid thoughts." Surprisingly
enlightened for c. 1860, partly because after the h.m. affair he had

the confidence though not the support of his father, partly because
he had knowledgeable if high-minded friends at Oxford – e.g.
Conington the Virgilian scholar.

Married Katherine North of his own world on Nov. 10, 1864.
Trained for it carefully: "it is much to feel that a woman is my
ideal" in his diary, and he flirts not unsuccessfully with a superior
Swiss housemaid abroad and had feelings for her that could be
called sexual. When he returns he has a breakdown, his father,
friends, and a specialist recommend marriage. His feelings for
Katherine seem harmonious, "but I missed something in the
music, the coarse and hard vibration of sex, those exquisite contacts." Off they go after the ceremony to a dreary double bedroom
in Brighton there to perform what neither was keen on. For K
was undersexed.

She told me afterwards that such manifest proofs of my virginity were
agreeable to her. Truly we civilised people of the 19th cent are more
backward than African savages in all that concerns this most important
part of human life. I found my way by accident having teased and hurt
both my wife and myself. Nature refused to show me how the act
should be accomplished. I was born with slowly matured sexual ap-
petites, and these were incapable of finding their satisfaction with a
woman. Nuptual intercourse developed them by the exercise of the
reproductive organs. It did not and could not divert them from their
natural bias towards the male.

Three daughters are born, the third by accident, the parents are
endlessly ill, and more poignant than anything he can write are
the extracts from *her* diary:

My God, grant me strength and faith, that I may look forward to the
time when my children shall be a pleasure to me. And Johnnie is so
good and patient to me, and I am no comfort to him, only a trouble.

The lust, or lusty-love that appeared in his early dreams grows
up: a grenadier speaks to him in a narrow passage that once connected Trafalgar Square and Leicester Square, a graffito "leapt
like a wolf" near Clifton, and "defined his sensuality" for him, his
dull marital exercises had their use, and he has a pleasant time
with a well-made and obliging soldier in a brothel near Albany
Street. They meet afterwards "as friends" and he is sincere in
wanting this, and lucky in frequently getting it. A superior Swiss
peasant and Venetian gondoliers crown his life physically, shortly

before it closes. Died of tuberculosis, aged 53. And how much
did his wife know? She was aware, that much is certain, and they
had a row about 'Norman', an educated English boy of whom she
had reason to be jealous. But they seem to get through their lives
in the way that happens in life and not in poetry and fiction. They
actually agreed that their marriage was not a failure.

[see p. 228 for addenda]

Death-Dream, 30–31/10/60, did not scare or disgust me, which has
    happened to me before with dreams gruesome in their subject-
    matter. It was not very vivid and the items arrived without shock.
    I was told that the Dead were upstairs, and found them in a couple
    of attics, lying in seedling boxes or other shallow trays, and mostly
    in small pieces. There was no liquefaction, and the bones darkled
    rather than glittered. Skulls like pickled cabbages. They seemed
    to know I was there, and I heard myself saying "I like the Dead,"
    to a pleased murmur. This was as I was going out where there
    was one of them not all that dead, with a huge clipped tooth-brush
    moustache, and on the parchment of the right-cheek was still a
    splosh of colour. We shook hands. Going out of the house, I was
    in a field I had known before which was now improved by the
    growth of bushes. Walking away through them left was a man in
    a red tarboosh who might be Mohammed, but just couldnt be,
    too long an interval had passed since we parted

    I woke up from this into pitch darkness and absolute silence. I
    have always liked these extremities, and seldom experience either
    of them in the world I have lived on into. Lay enjoying them and
    glad I failed to locate any of the light that usually leaks in from
    Chetwynd Court. I then knew much more of the dream.
    Mohammed was reasonable, since I have been copying out his
    letters, but I can't think where the harmless charnel-house came
    from. I like it better than other peoples' visions, which have to
    end either in God or a scare.

    After writing this I thought I had done so on All Souls, and that
    the Propaganda of Revelation had scored. But no I did not even
    write it on All Saints. Today (Nov 2nd) is All Souls and later in
    the evening I hope to think again of the Dead. Not of "I miei
    Morti" as d'Annunzio so possessively put it. One vanished person

is the Dead of many Living if he has been well known and Loved.

The night is again dark, unbothered by stars or thoughts of light years. The earth and all that lives and has lived on it is enclosed in a capsule of clouds. Man, excellent man, unpuny man, sees a few yards around himself and tries to think.

John Addington Symonds; addenda from p 227

What is human life other than successive states of untruth and conformity to custom?

I knew that my right hand was useless – firmly clenched in the grip of an unconquerable Love – the love of comrades. But they [academic friends] stung me into using my left hand for work.

The progress of a lad of 17 has to be measured not by years but by months.

Some sorts of self-deceit are crimes. They are signs of the soul's willingness to accept the second best.

Desire awoke like a neuralgic spasm.

Henry Sidgwick criticised "the thread of etherialised sensuality in my diary," and might well have criticised: –

> . . . short sheltering velvet,
> Short clustering down luxuriously wanton
> Round the trim marble man-spheres shyly circling,
> Round the firm rondure of love's root of joy,
> The smooth nude muscle, calm and slow and tender,
> The alabaster shaft, the pale pink shrine,
> The crimson glory of the lustrous gland . . .

There are one or two poems or fragments of this type in the 150,000 words of the autobiography: this one describes a young Sorrento cab-driver whom he saw asleep – saw only, for many years he was inhibited from touching even when invited to do so, and he is anxious to emphasise that he never did anything "unworthy." It is preceded by a poem called "Phallus Impudicus" – a fungus, trodden on by him in a musty shed, explodes:

> . . . with a leap the life that lurked within
> Sprang skyward: forth it shot a curving trunk
> And on the trunk an egg-shaped cone that stunk.

Further nightmares: that his wife beside him, whom he has promised not to touch, is male; that he was clasped from his cradle by a serpent which followed him into the waters of oblivion and found him there when they dried up.

A literary resolution: "I struggled long to conquer fluency."

Ludovico Sforza (1488)

The object of all art and learning is that we may know how to live.

Quoted in Burkhardt

When Tennyson writes: –

> I loved the woman: he, that doth not, lives
> A drowning life, besotted in sweet self,
> Or pines in sad experience, worse than death,
> Or keeps his wing'd affections clipt with crime

one has a smile ready. But if one translates his three alternatives into self absorbtion, melancolia and promiscuity they are seen to cover most of the ground.

And this in the Princess. And Maud with the garden-rose floating down the rivulet

> And lost in trouble and moving around
> Here at the head of a tinkling fall,
> And trying to pass to the sea.

The words shine, are adorable. They exemplify the discontinuous glory of Tennyson which must be continually watched for.

Bacilli: harmless ones only are allowed into the university. M. Yudkin, a research-student, took me to see his cultures the other day, and I saw the soups, clouded tubes, and writhing vermicelli that my studies had led me to expect. The individual bacillus has a tough outside, a tender inner rim about which not enough is yet known. Quiet sunlight, upstairs laboratory in the Tennis Court Road. Young biologists sit on the steps drinking their tea. His supervisor had heard of me and greeted me kindly – toughish, closely cut beard. My only other lab was nearly 15 years ago,

physics. Edward Shire. What severance from the main stream of
University work!   March, /61

> Reading a penguin on Virus has stirred me a little.

Bironic Entry Returned from Addenbrooks yesterday, an expensively
preserved octogenarian, to find that the boy in the room above
my bedroom, Du Vivier by name, had just gone into it with a
fractured femur and skull. He had given too drunken a party, slid
down the banisters after it, and over balanced. He had been a
great nuisance with his thumps and noise and his guests – largely
female – had removed objects from the staircase as they swept
away, and the little I had spoken to him suggested arrogance. But
others liked him; bedmakers chant "he was always the same --
always so gay ---" and the Pantry says "He was one of our best
customers." His pursuit of wine women golf, his open handedness
warmed their hearts, Mrs Tresaille, so stout, knelt by his head of
a morning, offering it a cup of tea. – the head that is now likely to
kill him. Gold hair, fair complexion, thin. A skinny Stephen
Wonham? Should I have liked him in one of my novels?

I think of Du Vivier compassionately and hope he may be restored to a life that he likes but I am not ashamed of living on
cossetted, while he vanishes or suffers. Elderly men have grown
an extra skin since the 19th century, even since Goldie

> April 19th 1961

N.B. – this best of papers will not take this vulgarest of pens.

Ackerley, Joe, sentence in letter from:

> The days potter by here much the same; sometimes the sad sound of
> their ticking feet gets into my ears as they disappear into history,
> carrying nothing in their delicate hands but a yawn.

Can the day that produced such a sentence be lost?

Illnesses. Dates of, many details of, already confused.

> *April 3rd* Easter Bank Holiday, fell, Collis' fracture, outside Joe's
>   flat.
> *Ap. 4th*   Evelyn Nursing Home, bathed by Barry

Ap	Left Evelyn. Taken drive by Frank Iredale to the American Cemetery, which having seen I puffed. Heart trouble diagnosed by cardiogram in my room by Dr Cole and Dr Fleming, resulting in
Ap 8th	Addenbrooke's. Private Ward
Ap 18th	Left Addenbrooke's [date taken from previous page]
Ap 25	Ill while trying to copy 'Surview' by Thomas Hardy, Sicked blood during night, rang bell for Drummond in the morning and
April 26	Wednesday, returned to Addenbrookes, Public Ward and nearly died.
April 28	Moved to Private Ward and stayed there till
June 3rd;	when I left – night in College with Bob to look after me, and drive me next day to Coventry.

Nearly Dying: meant to record this sooner. No pain, no fear, no thoughts of eternity, infinity, fate, love, sin, humanity, or any of the usuals. Only weakness, and too weak to be aware of anything but weakness. "I shant be here if I get weaker than this" was the nearest approach to a thought. I know that Bob and May were to my right and left – they had been summoned by the police and arrived about 4.0 – and was not surprised and liked touching them: Bob's little finger pressed mine and pursued it when it shifted. This I shall never forget. Blood – 3 pts ? of it – dripped from a high-suspended ampoule into the back of my right hand. I liked watching this later, or the white saline that sometimes took its place – bubbles ascended through this later and demonstrated that it was descending. – But this diverts me from the "nearly-dying" moment that I am trying to recapture; for then I had no awareness of anything except weakness. I may not have watched the ampoule until the next day. It was certainly then that I made Bob and May laugh by telling them an anecdote about Ben which I knew would amuse them. The Sister pounced outraged. "I must have my little joke" I said, conciliatory.

This experience has convinced me that death is nothing if one can approach it as such. I was just a tiny night-light, suffocated in its own wax, and on the point of expiring. I may feel differently when my death really succeeds, and others may feel different. I didn't find my mother different – she just stopped eating some nice stew which Agnes had made her and with which I was feeding her, and showed no perturbation although she had told me half an

hour before that I should not have her long. – And I find a close
parallel to myself in the Caliph Amr, who conquered Egypt in the
7th century. A friend said to him: –

You have often remarked that you would like to find an intelligent
man at the point of death and to ask him what his feelings were. Now
I ask *you* that question.

Amr replied: –

I feel as if the heaven lay close upon the earth, and I between the two,
breathing through the eye of a needle

His experience was more colourful than mine, and he was aware
of littleness whereas I was too weak to register anything but
weakness. Still there is a parallel here between two very different
types of human being.

If a person had been present, imploring to be clung to, things
might have hotted up, but I had fortunately remembered to give
my religion as none or Humanist, and the sister must have put one
or the other down. I feel now little hostility to the C. of E., for
atavistic reasons, but can't accept either it or its more pretentious
rivals, as a guide beyond death.

All this is written at Coventry, where I am convalescing – a convalescence not as complete as I hoped, for rheumatism has
developed in my wrist, and a slight and occasional flutter and
tightness round the heart. Disappointing, but disposing to serious
thoughts. For it is serious to have had one's life "practically"
ending and then to be given a little bit more. I try not to hurry up
and get another good deed or so in – a blunder which Lazarus fell
into, I imagine – but the remembrance of that *almost* everlasting
weakness and of Bob's finger seeking my own when I shifted is
intensified, and I hope I shan't have a lot of pain during this
addendum or cause a lot of extra trouble to those who love me and
have brought me back.

I have had a little more talk about the last illness – that of April
26th – since I began this wandering note: *either* the Hospital mis-
calculated the doses, which had to be readjusted daily in accordance with the blood tests, *or* – their explanation – I was the one in
a thousand who was allergic to it. Whichever is correct, I believe
that it is only hospital, and Leslie Cole the only specialist, who

could have brought me back from the weakness that passes perception.

Written at Coventry, mid June, 1961

Burning Words

Our thinking is not sufficiently national in intention, and our application is not sufficiently national in character.   – Carron, Pres. A.E.U.

I have always been having constantly to struggle to force myself to work, and constantly suffering from a more or less bad conscience for not succeeding better. This state of things seems to me so natural, that I find it difficult to believe that is not the same with everyone; and if it were the same with everyone, it would not be worth mentioning – it would go without saying. But I have met with facts which seem to me to suggest that, unintelligible though it may seem, there are some people who don't need to struggle so hard to make themselves work as I do, and are not so constantly or strongly tempted to do something else. Perhaps such people form only a small minority; but if there are any of them at all, it is perhaps worth mentioning that I have never, since I grew up, been one of them.

= 'I am idle'. [By G. E. Moore.]

Fun in Fitzwilliam

(i) Two bound books of Indian miniatures, priced at £500: each contains a man and woman drearily and variously cohabiting: the woman sometimes holds a fly whisk in her hand. The backgrounds of views, kiosks, long flowering sprays of trees are executed with their habitual charm

(ii) – [three photographs of] – A small silver cup, Roman, about 100 B.C. and found near of all places Jerusalem. Gentlemen penetrating slave-boys. One of the latter full grown and classically beautiful. Seen in profile, expressionless. The other, younger, sprawls uninterested, and the fact that he should be shown so emphasises the heartlessness of the outlook. A third boy, a child, looks through a window, amused. £6,000 is asked for this! But how can the museum or any other institution buy it? – I don't want it myself, though I have the money and like bits of it.

July 17, 1961

Dream Sentence "The 17000 smells of God."   Dec 1961

How peaceful it was here this quiet afternoon with a crescent moon
thickening, and terrors and duties rushing close to me and failing
to perturb, with my diarrhoea likely to improve under treatment.
I just don't know or care what ought to be done in Katanga, it is
part of a still distant storm. I thought of the imperfect but tear-
drawing poems of Yeats – no, greatness-drawing, though
between his utterances he is still the unreliable and even dishonest
bard who has always put me off. And I thought of the Rubens
which has come to spend its last days in our chapel and with our
chapel's. *It* is not dishonest, it does not try to take us in when its
inspiration flags; but it is an inadequate mystery compared to the
one surrounding us, and our pretty blunt sickle of a moon! How
can I tell or know what ought to be done about Katanga? Black
men are getting killed there, white men women children may soon
get killed

Enter ruddy-faced boy in American sea scouts knitted round
brown cap, says 'Dont get up Morgan' and hands me a copy of
the Christian Science Monitor. Not sure of *his* name, it may be
Bevan, but this is the sort of thing that delays my nose from the
approaching grindstone

My calm, idleness and good temper may irritate my colleagues
shortly, especially when they find I never do or say anything
helpful. I believe that the game is up, and the top shelf of the cupboard labelled Dangerous is being rifled now that the children's
arms have grown longer. I know of nothing I can do.

                                                        14–12–61

How peaceful it is here, with the West Hackhurst clock still
ticking, the Rooksnest fire irons still warm in the hearth, and
Little Master, his feet on Bob's rug, nodding towards the end of a
successful career.

From Letter of thanks from cousin Florrie, gladly received Dec. 18,
1961 : –

The rain seemed to be penetrating the roof etc. but have been afraid to
get them on it in case there was more trouble. Now with this behind
me I can go ahead when I wish

The Woodlanders – reading which Jan. 1962 I am constantly touched and tolerant. I should have started this entry two days earlier to record

> Any one can joke when one is well, even in old age; but in sickness one's gaiety falters; and that which seemed small looks large; and the far off seems near.

though on the lips of a regulation rustic. Or despite its obviousness

> The spot may have beauty, grandeur, salubrity, convenience; but if it lack memories it will ultimately pall upon him who settles there without opportunity of intercourse with his kind

A few days after beginning this note, more of Hardy comes my way

(i) A letter I wrote my mother, 19.7.22, from the Kings Arms, Dorchester

Simple almost dull tea at the Hardy's – nice food and straggling talk. I am to lunch there tomorrow, "but the cook only came today, I don't know what it will be like" says Mrs H. gloomily, and then we proceed to a performance of Midsummer Nights Dream in the Rectory garden, of which likewise little is expected. T.H. showed me the graves of his pets, all overgrown with ivy, their names on the head-stones. Such a dolorous muddle – "This is Snowball – she was run over by a train. . . . This is Pella, the same thing happened to her . . . . This is Kitkin, she was cut clean in two, clean in two . . ." "How is that so many of your cats have been run over, Mr Hardy? Is the railway near?" – "Not at all near, not at all near . . . I don't know how it is. – But of course we have only buried those pets whose bodies were recovered. Many were never seen again." I could scarcely keep grave, – it was so like a caricature of his own novels or poems. We stumbled about in the ivy and squeezed between the spindly trees over "graves of ancient Romans", he informed me. "Sometimes we are obliged to disturb one." He seemed cheerful, his main dread being interviews, American Ladies, and the charabancs that whizz past while the conductor shouts "Ome of Thomas Ardy, Novelist." He went in a charabanc once but "I didn't much like it – I was the last to mount and had to sit at the back, and was thrown up and down most uncomfortably." – Thus the visit wore away, though he talked away now and then about his books – A sign of favour I believe – I never pressed him to it.

They were both very pleasant and friendly.

(ii) Emma Hardy's recently published recollections. She comes out even worse than I expected – vain, vindictive, and vulgar. Her editor rightly claims that she inspired him as a poet and strengthened his nostalgic faculties. But it must also be conceded that she warped and vitiated his conception of the feminine, and enters into most of his exasperating and capricious heroines.

(iii) – And – a day or two later than the above – a letter from an earnest and decent Harvarder who fears that Florence H. will be forgotten, as she probably will be, and will I not write something on the next anniversary of her death, to postpone oblivion a little. I will not. Let it approach.

(iv) Two months later than the above comes Elliott Felkin's diary of 1919 in the current no. of *Encounter*. – E.F., pretentious and now living in the south of France, was a protege of Goldie's, who overestimated him. But he gives an unaffected and convincing account of Hardy and his generosity to Goldie warms my heart.

The Queer

> Tell me, o tell, who did thee bring
>   And here without my knowledge plac'd:
> Till thou didst grow and get a wing,
>   A wing with eyes and eyes that taste?
>
> Sure, holiness the magnet is,
>   And love the lure that woos thee down
> Which makes the high transcendent bliss
>   Of knowing thee, so rarely known.

The two previous verses were Oriental, perhaps of Eden, and Vaughan may here be seeing, or half seeing, a phoenix or some holy winged reptile, the sacred antithesis to the dragon in Uccello's Saint George. The period-silliness of "eyes that taste" is not only redeemed by the surrounding mysteriousness: it redeems, and exalts what might otherwise be unacceptable. These last-instant felicities are characteristic of V.: he is always arriving after threatening the fanciful or flat.

Heroic Nude The earlier work of Keith Vaughan is praised for this, so is Michelangelo. Who else? and what is it? I have been collecting my ideas, and as often wasted them in a letter. The H.N. is not

unclad for he (or she) never hid behind clothes, and is therefore
never defenceless. If any action were made it would be an aggres-
sive one – in my own K.V. the swimmers are threatening the
ice-dark sky and the sea. Secondly – for the above was one point
– the H.N. is neither sensuous nor sexless. The 'come to bed' call
is not there, not even there is the future and favoured occasion
when the powerful genitals will be used. But *they* are there,
because the whole human being is there. The nude is the only
human totality.

Kenneth Clark may have said this in his good book. The bathing
slip is worse than prudish. It segments.

I think I've got down what I want. I like orgies too but they
aren't and can't be heroic. – Can erotic Indian sculpture be?

> ————————; its rocks knew almost nothing
>   Nothing about the glum reptilian empire
>   Or the epic journey of the horse, had heard no tales
>   Of that pre-glacial Actium when the huge
>   Archaic shrubs went down before the scented flowers
>   And earth was won for colour —————

– from *Hammerfest* by W. H. Auden. How he can still bring it off!
How he sweeps pre-history into his passion! How falsify history
when necessary, for it was the scented flowers that actually went
down at Actium. The whole poem (March 1962) is very fine – rest-
ing though it does on a familiar theme: the power of modern man
to possess and ruin anything he wants on this globe.

[cf. myself on p 216 of this book.]

The unfortunate Ashton had been in a state of insanity since the receipt of
the awful warrant for his execution. He was the fifth who mounted
the scaffold and ran up the stairs with great rapidity: and having
gained the summit of the platform began to kick and dance, and often
exclaimed "I'm Lord Wellington." The Rev. Mr Cotton, who
officiated for the first time as Ordinary, enjoined him to prayer, to
which he paid little attention, and continued to clap his hands, so far
as he was permitted by the extent of the cord. When they released him
for the purpose of the Lord's Prayer being said, he turned round and
began to dance, and vociferated, "Look at me, I am Lord Wellington".
At 20 minutes past 8 o'clock the signal was given and the platform
fell. Scarcely however had the sufferers dropped, before, to the awe

and astonishment of every beholder, Ashton rebounded from the
rope, and was instantly seen dancing near the Ordinary, and crying
out very loudly and apparently unhurt "What do ye think of me, am
I not Lord Wellington now?"

– From the *Annual Register* for 1814, August.

Thomas Mann's "The Tables of the Law" is an idle and frivolous
paraphrase from the Pentateuch. But it contains ". . . the pliable
soul of the lonely spiritual man, the man who nods his head
thoughtfully at the cleverness of the world and understands that
the world may well be in the right." Do I see myself there? Does
he see himself?

Old Age – the idleness of mine! And I might achieve something if I
made more notes. Memory is so bad that it is impossible to enrich
oneself as formerly by going about and observing and feeling. In
a short walk, visual delicacies and splendours rush at me as frequently as, perhaps more frequently than, ever but the power to
retain them has gone. An amelioration, no doubt an imperfect
and deadening one, would be note-taking. The same applying to
what I listen to and read. – My friends are charitable to my idleness, others indifferent to it or unaware of it. It is of no public
importance for at 83 one hasn't much to give the world. [I have
still a little – that first class introduction by me to the American
edition of *Lord of the Flies*.]

Bertrand Russell's Birthday Dinner. Speech at it *not* delivered by me,
praising.

an irreverence which is the more impressive because it is a positive
quality and not the negative of reverence, and because it is devoid of
arrogance.

I find in myself the same indifference to prayer, but an interest in
thanksgiving which doesnt seem to tempt him. I have often wished to
find someone who was good enough to be thanked for what's good –
not a god, no deity could subsist on such meagre fare.

Like him, I have no sense of sin, and the comment you think you
havent but you have may be true but leaves me cold.

Je suis protestant, car je proteste contre toutes les religions.   – Bayle.

J. F. Millet whom I dismissed as sentimental and mawkish, is being rehabilitated in the Burlington (July 1962) and illustrated. A lovely eroticum, a drawing of 1850. He is seated squarely, his knees apart, she sits on his left knee, her left leg falling between his, her right stretched over his right thigh. There is a gap at her junction and his hand has discovered it, and her hand is discovering at his which cannot be seen. What of their heads? Hers is bowed on his breast, his rests on her shoulder behind. A moment more, and he will "take" her and they will become unsuitable for art.

Si vous voyiez comme la forêt est belle! J'y cours quelquefois à la fin du jour, après ma journée, et j'en reviens, à chaque fois, écrasé. C'est d'un calme, d'un grandeur épouvantables: au point que je me surprends ayant veritablement peur. Je ne sais pas ce que ces gueux d'arbres–là seclisent . . .   – From a letter or journal.

May this and the Giver/Be yours for ever./

– Inscription on a cracked little snuff box in the Pitts-River Museum, Dorset. To how few could one give such a box? To no one, for it would upset them extra when one died. – Michael P.R., the present hardy scion of the house, had not noticed the object, which is an unobtrusive one, and sub white.

[N.B.] From all future entries, try to exclude "I". That omission always strengthens. If "I" has to go in for reasons of clarity, let it only do so after thought. The above little entry would read weaker if spattered with "I saws"

In life and painting I can quite well dispense with God. But, suffering as I am, I cannot dispense with something greater than myself, some thing that is my whole life: the power of creating.

                       – Van Gogh per Malraux

The Coronation of Justin, Nov. 15, 576

During the last years of Justinian, his infirm mind was devoted to heavenly contemplation, and he neglected the business of the lower world. His subjects were impatient of the long continuance of his life and reign; yet all who were capable of reflection apprehended the moment of his death, which might involve the capital in tumult and the empire in civil war. Seven nephews of the childless monarch, the sons or grandsons of his brother and sister, had been educated in the splendour of a princely fortune; they had been shown in high commands to the provinces and armies; their characters were known, their followers were zealous; and, as the jealousy of age postponed the declaration of a successor, they might expect with equal hopes the inheritance of their uncle. He expired in his palace after a reign of thirty-eight years; and the decisive opportunity was embraced by the friends of JUSTIN, the son of Vigilantia. At the hour of midnight his domestics were awakened by an importunate crowd, who thundered at his door, and obtained admittance by revealing themselves to be the principal members of the senate. These welcome deputies announced the recent and momentous secret of the emperor's decease; reported, or perhaps invented, his dying choice of the best beloved and most deserving of his nephews; and conjured JUSTIN to prevent the disorders of the multitude, if they should perceive, with the return of light, that they were left without a master. After composing his countenance to surprise, sorrow, and a decent modesty, JUSTIN, by the advice of his wife Sophia, submitted to the authority of the senate. He was conducted with speed and silence to the palace; the guards saluted their new sovereign; and the martial and religious rites of his coronation were diligently acomplished. By the hands of the proper officers he was invested with the Imperial garments, the red buskins, white tunic, and purple robe. A fortunate soldier, whom he instantly promoted to the rank of tribune, encircled his neck with a military collar; four robust youths exalted him on a shield; he stood firm and erect to receive the adoration of his subjects; and their choice was sanctified by the benediction of the patriarch, who imposed the diadem on the head of an orthodox prince.

– Copied from Gibbon's Decline and Fall, ch 45 on August 17, 1962 for various reasons; partly stylistic; partly in homage; partly because I am just back from Lombardy and wanted to read something of the people who gave it its name. They will appear in the following pages; to JUSTIN's regret . . –

Since last September I have not held a pen, except perforce to sign my name . . . . We who have loved the motion of legs and the sweep of the winds, we come to this. But for myself, I will own that it is the Natural order. There is no irony in Nature.

– George Meredith to Leslie Stephen, shortly before the deaths of both.

Edwin Muir, opened casually, provides

> ... and while he lives content with child and wife
> a million leaves, a million destinies fall,
> and over and over again
> the red rose blooms and moulders by the wall

Is he the poet for casual openings? For when I read him continuously I don't get this catch in the throat.

Another got from Wordsworth's

> Serene will be our days and bright
> And happy will our nature be
> When love is an unerring light
> And joy its own security

First line banal, second a little less so, 'unerring light' loosens the magic which in the last line soars

Little Gidding – read aloud to myself, a good experience providing just the right amount of absorption and of closure of introspection – which can become ill mannered. The sound of my voice made me behave better. And Eliot is good to read aloud. When *The Dry Salvages* came out in 19   , I read it right off at her request to Kathleen Hilton Young and her patient Peter. Oneself as sole listener is even better and I shall repeat the new found pleasure. With Eliot? I feel now to be as far ahead of him as I was once behind. Always a distance – and a respectful one. How I dislike his homage to pain! What a mind except the human could have excogitated it? Of course there's pain on and off through each individual's life, and pain at the end of most lives. You can't shirk it and so on. But why should it be endorsed by the schoolmaster and sanctified by the priest until

> the fire and the rose are one

when so much of it is caused by disease or by bullies? It is here that Eliot becomes unsatisfactory as a seer, as Coventry does as a shrine. That misfire-cathedral has given Christ a green face and the Angel of the Agony matches for legs.

I write the above well aware of Polaris and Co. Extra pain may be ahead for me and millions of others. But its preponderancy won't make it more real. Even if Man is wiped out other forms of life may get comfortable.   4–1–63

Homosexuality is

a couple of hairy old males sitting on each other's knees and liking it.

– Brigadier Terence Clark, M.P. for Portsmouth West, as quoted by Encounter for May 1961

Jules et Jim. Film where a Femme Fatale breaks up a dull friendship – 'twas all that that seemed to me, what moved me was the vast woodlands recalling Dabo. But contemporary criticism rates it otherwise and contemporary young women readily identify themselves with the Femme. The actress, who seemed to me adequate, is France's greatest.   Feb 22 1963

Stay with God

This gracious title to a misty book which says the same thing over and over again.

This type of thing: –

The notion that travel is broadening
the reverse is true because
it ties ever more tightly the knots in the net of the senses,
it causes one to see many things and remember few,
to make many acquaintances and few friends; it leads the imagination
on to tomorrow and prevents mind
      dwelling on the moment of today,
it scatters affection and prevents love from manifesting
it makes meditation difficult and prayer impossible.

Thus Francis Brabazon in America or far est drones on, and one is tempted to throw the book away and perhaps will. But compare it with another mystickish book entitled Hunting the Guru

And you begin to learn.
      Stay with God,
            Francis Brabazon

Don't bother to answer this – I see you are likely getting a little long in the tooth.

– Transatlantic Tribute

Wordsworth

> And from my pillow, looking forth by light
> Of moon or favouring stars, I could behold
> The antechapel where the statue stood
> Of NEWTON with his prism and silent face,
> The marble index of a mind for ever
> Voyaging through strange seas of thought, alone

Luxury to transcribe the above. The lift towards greatness starts with *Newton*, continues with *marble index* and whizzes with *Voyaging*. I nearly transcribed the earlier lines but dismissed them because infected with quaintness

King Lear: old, idle, and trustful, and so far like myself

The need to have someone to be kind to

leads straight into a dubious aspect of Xtianity and has to be watched. I think it was what damaged my mother after Gran's death in that fated year 1911. I heard her moaning "I could have made her so happy." Her vengeful ill-temper auraed each anniversary, setting in soon after the new year and sometimes not clearing off till March. – But I haven't made my point yet, which is that it is *right* to be kind and even sacrifice ourselves to people who need kindness and lie in our way – otherwise, besides failing to help them, we run into the aridity of self-development. To seek for recipients of one's goodness, to play the Potted Jesus leads to the contrary the Christian danger.

– Written about 1961. Entered 1963

George Herbert again and again so arresting me by his felicity of diction that, whatever my mood, I want to copy lines of him down and shall assign all this page for that purpose:

> Then with our trinity of light
> Motion and heat lets take our flight
> Unto the place – – –

> That so amongst the rest I may
> Glitter and curl and mind as they:
> That winding is their fashion
> Of adoration.

———

> He so far thy good did plot
> That his ownself he forgot,
> Did he die, or did he not?

———

> And like a man in wrath the heart
> Stood up and answered "I have felt"

From Tennyson's duel between reason and emotion across the grave. The lines had some magic and power yesterday which now that I copy them out have faded. I should never think of applying them to Rob's death, though I might forty years ago to Mohammed el Adl's. Such love as I can feel no longer asserts or fights. It is bound up with my own impermanence, with the consent I have given to disappear, with the disappearance of the fragile Tennysonian Lincolnshire which I hope to see next week. The death of our countryside [which will *never* be renewed] upsets me more than the death of a man or of a generation of men which be replaced in much the same form.   15–4–63

I can't read any one of the lovely nature-references in In Memoriam or Maud without pain.

Hayden's Creation

listened to yesterday after glancing at a Julian Huxley about the age of the Universe and the accelerating change in it owing to Man's consciousness of him. Hayden has the better artistic wicket. The benevolent creator, struggling only against chaos, makes good, and until the end, when a slight warning is hinted by Uriel, there is nothing about sin and the possibility of a Fall. The happy pair stroll about through the beautiful and powerful forms of life that have preceded them. It is all reasonable and sincere. I wished more and more that our universe could have been like that and spared a religion smirched by Christ's wounds from that tedious cross. The drops of happiness I have just

experienced in France belong to the great unspilled helping that
was bestowed on Hayden. The record-album, with commercial
insensitiveness, contains illustrations from the cieling of the
Sistine. Michelangelo divines the speculations of Huxley. His
last judgment is not necessarily an end. His Adam is created
worried, his Eve worries as soon as she wakes.   27–6–63

Spinoza:

> I have made a ceaseless effort not to ridicule, not to bewail, not to
> scorn human actions, but to understand them

> Remote and pompous but useful as a side-thought.

Henry Kirke White who remains I have just opened wears ill. Why
should Southey and others have helped such a dreary son of a
Nottingham butcher?

> If I choose, I could find a good deal of religious society here [John's]   1806
> but I must not indulge myself with it too much

> Mr Simeon's preaching strikes me much

> I am going to mount the Gog-magog hills this morning in quest of a
> good night's sleep. The Gog magog hills for my body, and the Bible
> for my mind, are my only medicines. I am sorry to say that neither are
> quite adequate.

> Given to my uncle, the Rev. John Jebb by C. G. Curtis, nicely
> and contemporaneously bound with Aunt Laura's bookplate in
> it, but soon likely to disappear.

Dogs which will cope with ban-the-bomb demonstrators and guard air-
fields throughout the world were shown to members of the press at
R.A.F. Debden to day.   – Cambridge News 20/8/63

Van Gogh per Malraux:

> In life and painting I can quite well dispense with God. But, suffering
> as I am, I cannot dispense with something greater than myself, some-
> thing that is my whole life: the power of creation.
>   sympathetic, but means – ?

> [Further evidence that though we should pity suffering and try to
> abate it we must not hold it in respect.]

Astronomy, via Hoyle, can help my outlook. Earth 4000 million years old and coagulated out of cold bodies. Milky Way not much old. Life, or rather the chemicals preludes to it could have started before coagulation. This and other ill apprehended scraps (such as the time it takes travel have an effect on my mind and counsel it that nothing matters for humans but the immediate – error starting when we deduce from it what is likely to happen next. – Throughout the universe other limited "living" objects may be following analogous illusions

Richard III – A creditable film and the cruelty and treachery did not bore, as they do generally, for the reason that Mattei's experience of both is fresh in my memory. Small unkindnesses and little lies are familiar enough in our sheltered lives but we assume that the wicked we encounter won't go much further. They want to and have done in his case. The police, arresting him without cause, beating him up in their car and saying the doctor had gone when he demanded one, make Elizabethan "ranting" comprehensible. One unlucky step and the surface of moderate trobles break and you are neck deep in insults and pain, or over your neck in them and silent. We are all in danger from other men, though their malice may not explode often. The scenes of Clarence and of the Little Princes can occur in a prison, even if it is equipped with computors, and it occurred last week, thus pulling literature and life closer to each other

The film lasted 2½ hours. I saw it first when it came out many years ago. I remember a funny shot of "Behold his grace between two clergymen" which has been cancelled. The entry of the little princes different, and the smile of the younger baby adorable. – Now I must glance through the text – v. fine play, needs less realistic treatment – e.g. the tents of Richard and Richmond should back on each other at Bosworth, to convenience the ghosts.   entered 14–8–64 should have gone in p. 250

Pudendalia

Somebody says that K. Clark points out that when the Greeks sculpted the male nude for aesthetic rather than phallic or ritual reasons they made the pricks too small. They did. The idea that Man at last is shown in his Unveiled Glory is false. And with the growth of Christianisation there the shrinking continues. In Flaxman the Life Giver has shrunk to an intercural pimple. There is also a shrinkage both in area and in thickness of the pubic hair. What is the reason of this dishonesty? And What about the Life Receivers? They are at present doing rather better, anyhow as regards their pubic hairs which are now allowed to romp all over the place without being prosecuted. (For their elimination cf. the elimination of wires and poles in a travel-advert). It is sometimes said (correctly?) that Greek female statues are hairless because prostitutes stood for them and were shaved for sanitary reasons.

Returning to males and to a bather without a costume. If he is sexed big and thick for his own purposes he can be an artist's model, if for someone else's, O.K, but he belongs elsewhere. Desire distracts. I am all for the erotic, but admit that it makes hay-cocks and that the Ancient Greeks, who did not always want them, reacted towards castration

I have written nought but the above all this Sabbath morn, and much of it was meditated in my bath, oblivious of my own charms. I fear it doesnt rise much above fidget level.

Feebleness and fumbling of the above partly due to lumbago and scrappy feeding – both now ameliorated. Also to old age's tendency to think it has grasped what it hasnt; felt quite confident I had thought out something lucid while in my bath and was there over an hour. I remain puzzled by Greek hesitancy in the 6th & 7th cent. B.C. If pudenda at all, why not of the normal size?

1.9.63.

For me this satisfaction of the flesh is the least of pleasures that this world affords. The peace it offers is beyond doubt; the price of renewal and renewal and renewal of this peace is its danger. It transforms itself to a drug or a false religion. Some dearth in, or addition to, my constitution inclines me to asceticism. The inclination remains but I have not always, especially when younger and more polite, when my body was less able to resist the mind's orders, been able – thank God – to follow this inclination.

From "Boys will be Boys" by Hal Porter, a chapter from a forthcoming (?) novel. Printed in the London Magazine Sept 1962. Copied Sept 1963.

Simon Raven has characteristically pinched this title.

Comus – Just rushed through on a whim, to realise that although now incapable of important criticism, I am more sensitive than ever to style. My eyes readily fill with tears. There is a passage (*now can't find it*) quite conventional and ready to bore where this or that is to be hidden in the sea, but Milton because he has style puts 'flat' before sea and all lives

> Virtue could see to do what Virtue would
> By her own radiant light, though Sun and Moon
> Were in the flat sea sunk

> after 7 similar lines

To William Golding   K.C.C. Feb 4 1964

Dear William Golding

I have just had a wonderful pre-read of *The Spire* and it is a wonderful book. I also congratulate you. The last part – anyhow after the Visitor's visit – went away from me, but even then the sense of human individuals was maintained. And all through – and this is its great (literary) merit – there is the sense of weight – stone weight. I have only once come across it before in a novel called *The Nebuly Coat* (author's name forgotten) but there it is only incidental – the central pillars groan to each other despairingly in the night – but in The Spire it's continuous.

But how I do deplore Christianity.

A Hindu or Egyptian building wouldn't have created half that trouble or been so riddled by that sense of sin. We've got to admit that death is inevitable, pain failure and treachery probable, that there's blood in parturition, filth in sex, sex in love and so on. But is the peculiarity of Christianity to emphasise these drawbacks and not to seek earthly emphasis elsewhere. How typical of it not to allow one glimpse of the Spire from the Barsetshire countryside! There, mile after mile, unaware of the spiritual and architectural weaknesses inside it, unaware of the possibilities of an immediate fall, people were seeing it and feeling excited or pleased

The idea of its fall is by itself, a bit of a bogy, isnt it? The real question is *when*. If in Jocelyn's or in Roger's life – appalling. If in the 16th century – not too bad. If to day – the close of a long secular triumph

Yours ever

[Morgan Forster]

To Benjamin Britten   K.C.C. Feb 14 1964

Darling Ben,

     I expect you know all that there is to be know about
               , but he is behaving like such a shit that words of warning
seem advisable.

     He wrote to me a year or more ago asking to call – apparently a
private meeting – came with friends, there was tea, literary talk, and I
thought no more about it. Not he. He thought or pretended to think
that I was contemptuous of him and now takes his revenge. It will not
be published in this country owing to the decency and kindness of
Donald Mitchell who told me about it, and only America will learn
that I am an old queen or more precisely a "governess" with a "toothy
grin."

     Turning to more normal topics, I have helped to give a piece of
Greek stuff to the Fitzwilliam. I think it absolutely lovely and am
delighted beyond words, the experts are likewise content. Attic,
Pentelic marble, date 330 B.C. apparently once attached to a funeral
water bath but quite big enough to put Mr Craft in, but he shall be
left to the crows. Two boys – Lysippean types – play upon it with
their hoops I do hope you will have time to see it when you come
over in June. Whether you will see me – Michelangelesque type – is
less certain, for Bob and May are taking their continental holiday
rather earlier and if I go with them, which I hope to do, I shall miss
you and the Requiem.

     To which I must now address myself. The amount of thoughtful
matter and material thought which Miss Irene Seccombe is bestowing
on it is immense.

               Love as ever
                [Morgan]

Borrow [Lavengro Ch xxi]

How frequently does his form visit my mind's eye in slumber and
wakefulness, in the light of day and in the night watches; but last
night I saw him in his beauty and his strength; he was about to speak,
and my ear was on the stretch, when at once I awoke, and there I was
alone –––

[supposed to be about his elder brother, but reverberates elsewhere and into a prison in Spain.]

Mont Blanc Shelley's lines on incompetent and intolerable. Not so
his letter or letters written from Chamonix in the same 1816. I

was there myself, just over a week ago and nearly 150 years after
him, looking at a greatly changed valley, connected with the
sublimities by many facilities whose overhead twangings could
sometimes be heard. The mountain however seemed inaccessible
and the cairns and directions on its summits unimaginable. (N.B.
do not ever go up a labelled mountain. Remember Mont Ven-
toux.) I think it gains by being so blocky and denying a crisis.
(Everest, seen from a vast distance, cant be compared). It makes
no attempt to dominate with a peak. Shelley's letter gets this and
there is a quelling sentence about icy blood circulating in the stony
veins. How glad I am to have seen it and to have over heard its
echo in our tourist past. The decision to visit it was sudden and
my own. I was so near being stupid about it because millions had
seen it before me, – not then remembering Shelley   20–6–64

Irish Lady dying in New York: –

Lord when my soul flies back to Kerry let it not pass over Cork

Bitter, superstitious, drunken, untruthful, chaste, the Irish do not
please me except through their desire to please.

Is being interested in life a habit, continued when no real interest
survives?

[two entries from a 1952 diary]

A Flake of Blake:

The Spider sits in his laboured Web, eagerly watching for the Fly
Presently comes a famish'd Bird & takes away the Spider
His Web is left all desolate that his little anxious heart
So careful wove & spread it out with sighs and weariness.

From the Lament of Enion.

Scientific American for *July, 1964*

Wish I could read

Radio Waves from Jupiter
The Early Relatives of Man
Germ-Free Isolators
The Chinampas of Mexico
Computor Experiments

all simply-written, and bearing upon the life I am now living. But I haven't the training (which my earlier education ought to have supplied) nor the power to concentrate (which is a defect in my character).

James E. Baxter

––– a job well botched: half of the honey melted
And half the rest young grubs. Through earth-black smouldering
  ashes
And maimed bees groaning we drew out our plunder –
Little enough their gold and slight our joy
Fallen then the city of instinctive wisdom.
Tragedy is written distinct and small;
A hive burned on a cool night in summer,
But loss is a precious stone to me, a nectar
Distilled in time, preaching the truth of winter
To the fallen heart that does not cease to fall.

[– Quoted in introduction to Maurice Shadbolt's short stories *Summer Fires*]

Fartus Name of an Arab marsh community in Mesopotamia, and not ill named judging by a photograph of a boy in it. He is standing in a boat. He has a mild face, a slender figure, and a hanging-garden that almost overbalances him. Hanging and upstanding are said to measure much the same in these parts, but the bulk, the initial erigerous bulk! He has so much more to feel with than most of us. He is scarcely for human approach. May the river gods bruise him into ecstasy and swallow his seed! What a welcome change anyway from the boredom of phalloi or from the moderation of Hellas!

Greek and Latin Main reason for retaining them in education: they remind youths and maidens that there is a civilisation and a way of looking at things which was not and could not be Christian. Other values but this the unique one: Christians can avoid it by Premonition tricks.

Since at 85 I may have to die soon, I should like to emphasise that I am still not Christian and dont want even a memorial service in our friendly chapel.

The Pumpkin Eater. I have struggled into this modern and feminine
novel with some difficulty, but finished it with admiration. The
main male character is so unreal that the women whom he tears
into and puts into pods are not as real as they should be. Masses of
children at first indistinguishable from moving excreta. In the
final chapter they and their begetter close rather grandly upon her
in her tower. Throughout the book the word "Love" occurs
constantly. [Penelope Mortimer, authoress]

Chesterton Church, Cambs.

Inscription on exterior north wall

> Should simple villages rhymes offend thine eye,
> Stranger, as thoughtfully thou passest by
> Know that there lies beside this humble stone
> A child of colour, haply not thine own
> Her father born of Afric's sun-burnt race
> Torn from his native fields, ah! foul disgrace,
> Through various toils at last to Britain came
> Espous'd, so heaven ordain'd, an English dame,
> And follow'd Christ their hope two infants dear:
> But one, a hapless orphan, slumbers here
> To bury her the village children came
> And dropp'd choice flowers and lisp'd her early fame
> And some that lov'd her most, as if unblest,
> Bedew'd with tears the white wreaths on their breast
> But she is gone and dwells in that abode
> Where some of eve'ry clime shall joy in God.

Near this place lies interred Anna Maria Vassa, daughter of Gustavus
Vassa the African She died July 21st, 1797 aged 4 years

I note the year: Marianne Thornton was born in it. The verses,
and the hope in them, have touched me for over 20 years, but the
inscription was too dim to be deciphered. Water runs down it.
This has just been sent me by a Mr Eden.   14–10–64

Anna Karenin

To day (Nov 5 1964) I have finished my second reading of this
great book with due homage and ponderous reservations.
Of the main characters, only *Anna* and *her husband* satisfied me.
They were shown straight through and all round, and I detected

no exterior judgements – no tendency to *punish* Anna for her adultery – her agonies with her son, her snub at the opera, her final decay spring honestly out of the situation.

Amongst secondary characters *Vronsky* and *Dolly* are good, *Kitty* less so.

Levin fails. Tolstoy is much too indulgent and complacent about him. He is so marvellous in his famous early act of working with the peasants, that, enchanted, we forget his later boringness – e.g. his visit to the session of the nobility. Our last glimpse of him is repellant. He actually gets a sense of God, and who the Hell cares? Anna has been crushed by a train, Vronsky has gone senselessly to the wars, but do they enter his mind now or on other occasions? They don't; thanks to the stray remark of a peasant, he has got a sense of God and all will be comprehensible or at any rate tolerable for him in the future

I suppose he represents Tolstoy

He confirms what I have always detested in that great man's and semi-great artist's egoism

I have enjoyed much of this long read, though at my present age parts of it have been a "challenge" and I was often by minor characters – e.g., when two who had scarcely been introduced to me fail to become engaged because of a mushroom. A whole chapter at least goes on this

I hope to go through the above when I have found one or both of the two pens I have lost.

My gouts better.

My powers of attention as good as they can hope to be.

Mahler. 3rd Symphony 4th Symphony Song of Earth per gramophone and in that order of approval. Find little originality in him and seriousness rather than profundity, but wish I had found him sooner. Certainly, like many others, he loves beauty and wishes it hadnt to be left, so his company is congenial and his tediousness easy to condone. What a curse orchestral prolixity was in the early half of this century! Composers were allowed too many instruments and too much time. Size not fully filled and too readily worshipped by Central Europe. Wagner, the leader here, but he *had* something thoughtful to say.

P.S. my submission to the *S. of E.* largely due to Ferrier's singing and though I tried to dismiss as irrelevant her own early death I could not do so.   17–12–64

New Religious Fantasy: Presence of the Mothers of the Innocents at the Crucifixion. It kept recurring to me last Xmas 1964 and I could have made some thing out of it half a century back. "So that's what my baby was killed for." Or: "Serve him right." Coeval with the B.V.M. who would be about 50, though not thus represented in Art. – How insensitive of Christianity to introduce this legend! No wonder it handled it lightly. Is there a parallel in the Krishna legend?

Another fantasy – less original – is Money = God

Do not laugh at money – blasphemy. Do not say 'I have as much as I want" – it = ls "I am saved" and penury may punish you for your spiritual over-confidence.   – 22–1–65

[Mother's Birthday. Her age would be 110. I suppose bones and some muck still remain from her. I have bought her some flowers].

Verrocchio. Sleeping youth, Berlin.

Well developed youthood with hand large enough to cover what it doesnt. The occasional nude honesty so rare both in antique and renaissance art. Provocative but for the usual silly head.

Gombrich: from his Visual Metaphors of Value in Art: –

There was a time – and it is not so very far back – when riches, economic wealth, could feast the eye, when the miser could enjoy the sparkle of his hoard instead of having to inspect balance sheets. The fact that wealth can no longer be seen, that it no longer provides direct visual gratification, belongs with the many dissociations of value from immediate experience which are the price we pay for our complex civilisation.

[excellently put, and clearing up some vague regrets of my own]

Dream of Saint Cerf

Woke this morning (26–2–65) from some welcome landscape
material. I was riding with someone on one horse up grassy
country which fell slightly away to our left. Another rider there
passed us and looked at us, but did not call out – for which I was
glad. We continued and the down ahead of us now became pre-
cipitous and reached up to the sky. But my companion said "We're
nearly there" and the turf on our right now fell away steeply and
ended in a trimming of rocks and some old walls, beyond which
was an immense blue landscape He said *Saint Cerf* and I woke up
and just remembered the word. Much else I forgot or have
dimmed.

I am sure the above is connected with Constable's large Hadleigh
Castle which I peered into yesterday at Burlington House, though
there is no physical resemblance. I had there the advantage of the
company of the friend from Shingle street (name slips me) who
encouraged and explained. I am freshened by this dream, which
was not sexual or even human and brought me towards the
visualness which seems nearer now that my eye sight weakens.

Glad that no one pranced in while I was trying to get down the
above.

Scrap note of period April 1965

It is as if there is something inside me
inciting me to dawdle and not to concentrate

Dates – from Melvin Calvin

Origin of Earth – c 4700 millions back.
Fossils Frequent: 600 millions only.

"Life" – i.e. living molecules – must have started between the
above.

These considerations – like those about space – steady me, and
help me to concentrate upon what's small and immediate. They
compel me to adopt values

Nearly Dying – cf page 231. Must be recorded again. May 3, Bobs house, Coventry. A stroke. Felt odd, and asked not to be driven to station. Doctor soon summoned, but by that time I was unconscious and went through an alarming display. Recovering painless, except when I thrust my left arm under the pillow, found it hot, flung both arms round Bob, shrieked with pain, heard him say '*Your dear Bob*" – words ever to be remembered. May also burnt when she touched me, – This fancy happy a second time, but less violently. Tried to write messages by the 7th – but illegibly. Back in King's on the 29th. – Writing this June 28th

Clemenceau;
answer when asked in his old age

'What will you do now?' was "I am going to live till I die."

I like this answer, July 3rd

Philo – opening whom casually On Dreams, I, 44: –

Those who have failed to make a good voyage under the sails of the sovereign mind can always fall back on the oars of sense-perception. But it is an excellent course even when you have fallen into this plight not to grow old and live your life in it, but feeling that you are spending your days in a foreign country, as sojourners to be ever seeking for removal.

Transcribed with some trouble at the age of 86 and not with complete approval. I would like sense-perceptions to attend me to the end.

Reopened Nov. 11 1968

Doubtful whether I shall write more. Have ordered this book (which goes to College Library)
to go to College Library.

How it rains!

Book

It is wrong to think one has to say something. It may be wrong
to think one has something to say. An old author who is beginning his last book, as here I am, is depressed by the little effect his
opinions have had – he might as well have never expressed them
– and he is tempted to a last-minute emphasis or to a filling up of
gaps, which will make his purpose clearer. Vain effort – actually
due to the shortness of time ahead of him, and to the sense of
time wasted behind him. It is not to extend my influence that I am
writing now, nor even to help. It is an attempt to be more honest
with myself* than I yet have, though such attempts usually defeat
themselves through the self-consciousness they generate

---

* "With myself": misleading words, suggestion Book is a Confessions.
It is not mainly that. It is mainly an account of the world outside me,
as it is, and as it likely to become. I must be aware of my personality in
order to discount it: e.g. a literary man, I must not fall into the
pleasant error of supposing that interest in literature will increase.
Similarly, a sexual man, I must not suppose many others have my
outfit: this error less likely, so constant are the reminders to the
contrary.

Plan of Book: None except that it will be written on one side of
this paper, so that pages can be cut out and rearranged. Opposite
pages for short notes only. Date each entry – noting mood when
powerful.

My life after death is unlikely to come in – though it might be if
I was badly frightened. The belief that I may live after my breath
ceases and my body begins to smell never occurs to me – either
in the simple form cherished by my ancestors, or in the difficult

modern ecclesiastical form, where the spiritual expert rebuffs the
claimants to immortality, and convicts them of crudeness, and of
unspirituality. I think of death as a permanent anaesthetic – to be
reached amidst pain or fear if my luck is bad, and under perfect
hospital conditions if the luck's good. In either case it finishes me
off as a memoirist or an observer. My great extension is not
through time to eternity, but through space to infinity: here: now:
and one of my complaints against modern conditions is that they
prevent one from seeing the stars.

early July 1956

Games without fun might be one of the Sections. cf. Orwell and my
reference to him. And recent book by the Priestleys. And Eric
Fletcher on village boys. History of Games – Homeric, Olympic.
Constantinopolitan: tainted from the first by professionalism, the
presence of audiences, and the desire to win. Yet to condemn the
last would be silly for without that desire there would be no
games. Contrast Dancing which is fun, which was once religious?
Above ¶ shows my lack of knowledge and of equipment. – I am
trying to write a book beyond my powers.

Mem. Resist temptation to maunder more about Family History.
Marianne has been enough. Criticisms of me as spinsterish,
something in them.

Bunny Leff, a young fellow here, medieval philosophy, spoke to
me this afternoon 22–7–56 at a fruitful moment; agreement that
this age *is* different from all the past because of the rapidity of
change. Impossible to know what writers etc. who profess to
interpret it are trying to say.

Fear that the Companions will not continue: that the dogs, cats,
will follow the rabbits whom the horses are already following,
that the little common birds will follow the rare and large ones,
that the barley will follow the silphium and the rose the musk,
that Man will suppose himself the only possible form of life, that
armed and capsuled murderers will penetrate the new regions
accessible above us and beneath us to kill whatever is stirring: the
regions beneath us from which we came.

That infinitely distant cousinhood! There was a time when we –
i.e. what we came from – communicated. Which is clumsily
recognised in Bestiality.

The man-modified surface of the earth is on its way to being man-destroyed. After which will come the man-modification of the waters and destruction of their contents [dead fish from Pest Control in the Cam]. Assuming present processes continue – though it is a risky assumption – nothing will be allowed to survive that does not conduce to human comfort, and the nature of human comfort will be decided by applied-scientists.

P.S. – remember that neither the Companions (dog and horse) or the Rivals (lion and lizard) would have behaved less aggressively than we do, had they got the upper hand. They might never have been able to write these words, even; never have guessed that their victory meant elsewhere defeat. To write etc. and to guess etc. are specifically human achievements.

cf. this withdrawal from us of other forms of life with the withdrawal of the stars from our observations: [last page]. Both accelerated in the past 50 years.

> The Coventry Glass
> Look Back in Anger
> – a good play

Notes

These notes include translations. Except where otherwise indicated, the translations are my own, and I have made them as literal as possible. I gratefully acknowledge help received from my colleagues Professor R. J. Clark and Professor A. R. Chadwick. The numbers on the left refer to the pages of the *Commonplace Book*.

1 Forster's quotation from Carlyle, *Past and Present* (1858), bk. IV, ch. IV ('Captains of Industry') can be found on p. 246 of the Clarendon Press edition (1918). As frequently in his quotations from other writers, Forster is not altogether accurate either verbally or in matters of punctuation: the Clarendon Press edition hyphenates 'ice-palace'; the second 'visible' is followed by a comma; 'did this' is followed by a semi-colon. Among the books found in Forster's rooms in King's College, Cambridge at his death (many of which were subsequently sold by the college) was a copy of the 1872 edition of *Past and Present*. 'Jean Paul' was the pen-name of the German Romantic novelist Johann Friedrich Richter (1763–1825).

John Middleton Murry, editor of the *Athenaeum* from 1919 to 1921, edited the *Adelphi* from 1923 to 1948. There, in July 1924, he published a review of *A Passage to India* which, though admiring and perceptive, Forster might conceivably have found patronising.

2 The Upas Tree, supposed to have existed in Java and thought capable of poisoning all animal and vegetable life within a radius of fifteen miles, was first mentioned in 1783 in the *London Magazine*. This prompted Erasmus Darwin to speak of 'Fell Upas ... the Hydra tree of death' in *The Loves of the Plants*, III, 239. It is called 'This boundless upas, this all-blasting tree' by Byron (*Childe Harolde's Pilgrimage*, canto IV, stanza 126). Blake does not refer to the Upas Tree, but Forster may have been confusing it with the 'Tree of Mystery' mentioned in Blake's *The Book of Ahania*, line

127 and suggested also in 'A Poison Tree' and 'The Human Abstract'.

Pages 2–22 constitute Forster's notes for his Clark Lectures at Cambridge, published in 1927 as *Aspects of the Novel*. In his Diary (12 July 1926) Forster noted: 'Clark Lectures for 1927. Making notes in Bp. Jebb's commonplace book.'

Sterne, *Tristram Shandy*, bk. 1, ch. 11. The World's Classics edition of this (reset, 1951) gives 'pocket-picking', not 'pocket-picket'; 'pretensions', not 'pretentiousness'; 'no better, but often worse', not 'no better and often worse'.

3   The quotation beginning 'It is a singular blessing . . .' is from *Tristram Shandy*, bk. 3, ch. 34. The World's Classics edition has, not 'remissness' but 'renitency against conviction'.

The quotation from Samuel Butler's *Erewhon* (1872) comes from ch. 20 (p. 185 in the 8th edition, 1890, which Forster owned).

The quotation beginning 'I am convinced . . .' is from *Tristram Shandy*, bk. 5, ch. 42.

4   Johnson's comment on *Tristram Shandy* was made on 20 March 1776. See *Boswell's Life of Johnson*, ed. G. B. Hill, rev. L. F. Powell (Oxford, Clarendon Press, 1934), II, 449.

5   *Reg. Palmer*. Entries in Forster's Diary made between 20 September and 17 October 1924 refer to a budding friendship with a 'chauffeur' called 'Tom Palmer (I think that is his name)' to whom Forster had offered cigarettes and who had invited Forster round to his house. Forster also mentioned the relationship in letters to Florence Barger of 2 October 1924 (from which it appears that he was a Weybridge bus driver, married, who reminded Forster of his former lover in Alexandria, Mohammed el Adl) and 28 March 1928. The second letter calls him 'Tom Palmer' but adds ' "Tom" my invention as a matter of fact'. P. N. Furbank (*E. M. Forster: A Life* (1978), II, 133–8) refers to Forster's friendship, and brief affair, with one 'Arthur B—', who seems to be the same man ('there was even doubt about his name: first it was "Arthur", then it was "Sid", now it seemed to be "Ted" '). A visit to 'Reg Palmer's at Addlestone' (near Weybridge), is mentioned by Forster in a letter to the writer John Hampson (13 August 1945), and a letter from Reg Palmer, dated 3 June 1960, thanks Forster for a gift of money which enabled him and his wife to have a trip to France. Another letter to Forster, undated and signed 'Reg', gives an example of the 'Cockney fun' perhaps referred to here: humorously obscene, it makes play with the double-entendres produced when a man telephoning a doctor for medical advice

about his wife is by mistake connected to 'a locomotive engineer who was telling a driver how to make his engine go better.'

6   Woolaston is a village in Gloucestershire, on the Severn between Chepstow and Lydney; but I have been unable to discover its connection with J. R. Ackerley's play *The Prisoners of War*, twice staged in London in 1925 and published by Chatto & Windus that year.

The bracketed passage after '*suspense*' has been transposed. It appears in fact in the original as an afterthought, added after 'Woolaston', and connected with '*suspense*' by an arrowed line.

7   The pattern of *Roman Pictures* is discussed by Forster in chapter 8 of *Aspects of the Novel*. Percy Lubbock's *The Craft of Fiction* was published by Cape in 1921. The phrase Forster quotes is on p. 42, and comes at the end of Chapter Three, devoted to *War and Peace*, about which Lubbock is far more appreciative than Forster grudgingly admits here. Forster's attitude to Lubbock, born 1878 and his contemporary at King's College, Cambridge, is illuminated by an early entry in his Diary (30 December 1911): 'How discomforting Percy Lubbock is. He makes it clear that I am a literary idler. I would not be long with him for nuts.' Forster records having coffee with him (Diary, 20 November 1899), and one book in his library, George Calderon's *Dwala*, was a gift from Lubbock in 1904. Lubbock was also Forster's superior in the Red Cross in World War I.

For 'Ladder of' Forster originally wrote 'Hierarchy of'.

Henry Arthur Jones (1851–1929) wrote about sixty plays; *Saints and Sinners* appeared four years before Matthew Arnold's death in 1888.

8   *Vanbrugh*. Constant is speaking to Lady Brute, act III, sc. 1. *The Complete Works of Sir John Vanbrugh*, ed. Bonamy Dobrée and Geoffrey Webb (Nonesuch Press, 1927), vol. I, p. 143 prints a semi-colon after 'pity' and a comma after 'continence'.

H.C.D. Highest Common Denominator.

The phrase 'because they are written in prose' is in the original connected by a line to the passage on p. 9 beginning 'Then have they also . . .'.

Old Wives Tale is connected by a line to Forster's remark on p. 9 about Louis Couperus's *Old People and the Things that Pass* (a Dutch novel which appeared in English translation in 1919).

9   The passage from *Robinson Crusoe* can be found on p. 216 of the

Oxford English Novels text of 1972, but not in exactly the form given by Forster, whose readings are not recorded as variants by the editor, J. Donald Crowley. He gives: 'I took it by another handle'; 'All things do say O to him'; 'He said, yes, they all went to Benamuckee ...'. Forster's third sentence omits (without indication, as frequently in the *Commonplace Book*) a phrase of Defoe's. The sentence reads in full: 'I asked him then, if this old Person had made all things, why did not all Things worship him?'

10 The verse quotation (which should begin: 'His art ...') is Caliban's view of Prospero (*The Tempest*, I, ii, 372–3).

'Virginia says'. The quoted phrases, and the critical view Forster describes, occur in Virginia Woolf's essay 'Robinson Crusoe', originally published in *The Common Reader: Second Series* in 1932. (Reprinted in Virginia Woolf, *Collected Essays* (London, Hogarth Press, 1966), vol. I, pp. 69–75.)

Memoirs of a Midget was published by Walter de la Mare in 1921, and won the James Tait Black Prize.

11 *The Bible in Spain*, a travel book by George Borrow, appeared in 1843. (Borrow had worked in Spain 1835–40 as a colporteur for the British and Foreign Bible Society.)

Adventures of a Younger Son, by E. J. Trelawney, a friend of Shelley, appeared in 1831.

W. H. Hudson's *Green Mansions*, set in South America, appeared in 1904.

In the first edition of Richardson's *Clarissa Harlowe* (London, 1748), this passage, with slightly different punctuation, occurs on p. 35 of vol. II.

12 'Kath. of Arr.' Presumably Katharine of Aragon in Shakespeare's *Henry VIII*.

The word and passage marked by Forster's asterisks are connected by a line in the original.

13 'The Fiction Factory'. See Appendix B of *Aspects of the Novel* (Abinger Edition, 1974), pp. 138–9. The phrase was Forster's title for his review (published in the *Daily News*, 23 April 1919, under the pseudonym 'a novelist') of Clayton Hamilton's book *Materials and Methods of Fiction*. Forster refers to this book, without naming it, early in *Aspects of the Novel* (see Abinger Edition, p. 7).

The Ambassadors is analysed in ch. XI of *The Craft of Fiction* (pp. 156–71).

The passage in angle brackets was cancelled by Forster in the original.

'*Paris*' is connected in the original by a line to '*Paris*' on p. 14.

The quotations from *The Ambassadors* beginning 'As a child . . .' and 'She was dressed . . .' occur in Book Nine, part III (pp. 260–2 in the Everyman Edition, 1948). In the first quotation, Forster omits after 'parlours' (without indication) James's phrase '(oh Mrs Newsome's phrases and his own!)'. I have not identified the edition to which Forster gives page references. He gave his own copy of *The Ambassadors* to Bob Buckingham.

14 'Eg. art'. i.e. Egyptian art. cf. *Aspects of the Novel*, ch. 8 (p. 164 in the Pelican Edition, 1962).

15 'Fleda.' Fleda Vetch, heroine of *The Spoils of Poynton* (1897). *Nameless* is connected by a line in the original to Forster's 'N.B.' passage. This passage, marked by a square bracket in the original, is in its turn connected by a curved line to the passage (also marked by a square bracket) which begins 'and listen to the uncomfortable words . . .'.

The long quoted passage of H. G. Wells comes from the last section, entitled 'Of Art, of Literature, of Mr Henry James', of *Boon* (1915). Forster quotes it neither accurately nor fully; nor does he indicate the size of his omissions. The dots after 'all at once' represent two omitted sentences; those after 'elaborates' two and a half pages. Since Wells never let *Boon* be reprinted, it is now a rare book; the full text of the passage can be found in *Henry James and H. G. Wells: A Record of their Friendship, their Debate on the Art of Fiction, and their Quarrel*, ed. Leon Edel and Gordon N. Ray (University of Illinois Press, 1958), pp. 245–7.

Forster's blank instead of James's reply (two dignified letters written in July 1915) may or may not be an ironic comment on James. Despite Wells's nervous apology for his criticisms, James was too hurt to be placated, and their friendship ended. See *The Letters of Henry James*, ed. Percy Lubbock (London, 1920), pp. 503–8.

16 Norman Douglas's *D. H. Lawrence and Maurice Magnus: A Plea for Better Manners* was privately printed in 1924. Douglas sent four copies of it to Lytton Strachey in February 1925; perhaps Forster saw one of these. The passage quoted (pp. 30–1) refers to Lawrence's distortions of Douglas and Magnus in an Introduction which Lawrence had supplied to Magnus' *Memoirs of a Private in the Foreign Legion*. Forster omits Douglas's inverted commas around 'useful'; substitutes semi-colon for comma after 'is

eliminated'; and writes 'as far as they go' instead of Douglas's 'so far as they go'.

After Forster's note on 'pseudo-roundness' comes, in the original, the long quotation from *Boon* – an afterthought which I have transferred for the sake of neatness to the end of the section in which Forster discusses Henry James.

17   'The great power of blackness . . .'. Quoted (not quite correctly) from Melville's essay 'Hawthorne and His Mosses' (1850).

Billy Budd, Melville's last work, was finished in 1891, but not published until 1924 (London, Constable). I have not traced the edition whose pagination conforms to Forster's here. His own copies of *Billy Budd* in his library at his death were the editions of 1946 (published by John Lehmann with an Introduction by William Plomer, who gave Forster a copy in 1947) and 1948. In Forster's 1946 edition the first quotation is found on p. 48, the second (about Claggart) on pp. 55–6. In the second quotation Forster omits a sentence after 'is auspicious to it', and substitutes 'character' for Melville's 'depravity'. Both quoted passages (and some others) have vertical ink-lines drawn beside them in Forster's 1946 copy. Early in 1949 Forster and Eric Crozier collaborated in writing the libretto for Benjamin Britten's opera *Billy Budd*.

Forster's quotation from Melville's *Pierre* (1852) comes from the Conclusion to section ii of Book I. (See *The Writings of Herman Melville*, The Northwestern-Newberry Edition (Evanston and Chicago, 1971), vol. VII, p. 8. The correct reading is 'Sons of Men!'.) Forster uses the phrase in his Introductory Chapter of *Aspects of the Novel*.

18   'Mark Rutherford'. Pseudonym of William Hale White (1831–1913), author of *The Autobiography of Mark Rutherford* (1881), *The Revolution in Tanner's Lane* (1887), etc.

'Bunny Garnett'. The novelist David Garnett (b. 1892) son of the influential Edwardian publisher's reader Edward Garnett.

'Heard'. Henry Fitzgerald (Gerald) Heard (1889–1971). Forster first met him in about 1925.

In the original, the phrase '*end of Pt. I*' is connected by a line to the long quotation from *Great Expectations* (p. 19).

19   In the quotation from *Great Expectations*, Forster's dots after 'dear dear friend' represent two omitted paragraphs.

The names of Richardson and David Garnett were interlinear insertions by Forster.

The quotation beginning 'Nor can I go on . . .' comes from

Goldsmith, *The Vicar of Wakefield*, ch. 31 (p. 177 in the Oxford English Novels edition, 1974).

At his death Forster possessed four novels by David Garnett: *Lady into Fox* (1922), which Garnett had given him; *A Man in the Zoo* (1924); *The Grasshoppers Come* (1931); *The Flowers of the Forest* (1955). 'Sailor' is *The Sailor's Return* (1928).

Lolly Willowes (1926). Novel by Sylvia Townsend Warner (1893–1978).

20 *Together* (1923) is by Norman Douglas. *Thaïs*, by Anatole France, is discussed in *Aspects of the Novel*, ch. 8.

In the original, a line connects '*people*' with the passage beginning 'seems obvious yet'; another line connects '*plot or pattern*' with the passage 'say-plot ... Together', which is enclosed in one of Forster's frequent 'boxes'.

21 *Opal Whitely*. Forster is referring to *The Diary of Opal Whiteley* (London, Putnam, 1920). 'Opal Whiteley' purported to be a twenty-one-year old American girl, of totally unknown origin, who had lived in lumber camps and, from the age of six onwards, had written a diary on scrap paper and 'strips torn from bags once containing butcher's meat'. The book reads like a literary hoax, being composed in an extraordinary kind of English which mixes oddity of idiom with the arch use of French and Classical names – s⸺ ⸺h as 'Menander Euripides Theocritus Thucydides' – for trees, ⸺eep etc. Ellery Sedgwick, of the *Atlantic Monthly*, provided a Preface in which he commented that 'an outstanding peculiarity of it is the diarist's knowledge of the names of the good and great'; whether he was deceived or in on a hoax is not clear. Viscount Grey of Fallodon, who wrote an Introduction, treats the book as genuine.

The blank before 'words' (Trollope) represents a number which Forster failed to supply.

H. G. Wells's *The New Machiavelli* appeared in 1911.

Aristotle's comments on character (from the *Poetics*) occupy the left-hand column of p. 36 in the original. The right-hand column, intended for Alain, is left blank. Forster possessed a copy of the reprint of Alain's *Système des Beaux Arts* (Gallimard, Paris, 1926).

Forster had been allowed to see, and to copy, Housman's letter declining to deliver the Clark Lectures for 1926; they were instead delivered by T. S. Eliot. Housman's letter of refusal (with slightly different punctuation) is printed on pp. 227–8 of *The Letters of A. E. Housman*, ed. Henry Maas (London, Rupert Hart Davis, 1971). Forster deeply admired Housman, and owned copies of his three volumes of poetry, together with a copy of *The Name and Nature of Poetry* (1933). Into the fly-leaf of *Last Poems* (1922) Forster gummed a brief but friendly note from Housman, acknowledging Forster's praise of that volume.

At the end of 1927 Forster noted in his Diary the 'success' of his Clark Lectures at Cambridge: 'Big audiences in the Arts Theatre and fellowship at King's in consequence'. He had resided at King's College in November 1927.

22 *Train Talks*. 's.v.' i.e. sotto voce.

23 'Sebastian' was W. J. H. ('Sebastian') Sprott (1897–1971). Forster first met him in 1923, when Sprott was studying psychology at Cambridge and a member of the 'Apostles', as was Forster. In later life Sprott was a Professor of Psychology at Nottingham University and briefly, before his own death, Forster's literary executor.

The quotations are from Matthew Arnold's poem 'Human Life' (first published 1852). 'Fear and fret' should be 'fret and fear'; Arnold has an exclamation mark after 'steering of our way' and a comma after 'design'd'.

24 The second quotation from Ecclesiasticus is chapter 27, verses 19–21.

'It is a tempest . . .'. Ecclesiasticus 16, v. 21.

'He gave them . . .'. Ecclesiasticus 17, vv. 2–3.

25 'And let the counsel . . .'. Ecclesiasticus 37, vv. 13–14. The last part of this quotation, in slightly different form, occurs in *Tristram Shandy*, bk. II, ch. 17.

'*The Party* . . .'. The passage refers to the visit paid in late 1924 and early 1925 by the Duke and Duchess of York to Kenya, Uganda and the Sudan, during which they took part in many shooting trips.

26 Chartres Cathedral (ii). The word 'red' looks, in the original, more like 'rest', which is a possible meaning; but since there is a great deal of red and blue glass in Chartres Cathedral I have preferred the present reading.

'Max to Lytton'. Sir Max Beerbohm to Lytton Strachey. Lady Hester Stanhope (1776–1839), the niece of William Pitt, lived from 1814 in the Lebanon, a legendary figure in her own lifetime.

Dryden. The first quotation is lines 1–8 of 'To my Honour'd Friend, Dr. Charleton, on his learned and useful Works; and more particularly this of Stone-Heng, by him Restored to the true Founders' (1663). See *The Poems of John Dryden*, ed. James Kinsley

(Oxford, Clarendon Press, 1958), vol. I, p. 32. The second quotation is lines 23–30 of 'To Mr. Granville, on his Excellent Tragedy, call'd Heroick Love' (1698). *Ibid.*, vol. III, p. 1434.

27   The third quotation is lines 62–6 of 'To my Honour'd Kinsman, John Driden, of Chesterton in the County of Huntingdon, Esquire' (1700). *Ibid.*, vol. IV, p. 1531. 'Human' appears in Kinsley's edition as 'Humane', and Forster's punctuation differs in part in all three passages.

Forster first met the poet Siegfried Sassoon (1886–1967) in 1919. On 25 August 1927 (about the time of this entry) Forster received a postcard from Sassoon, who had recently visited Bayreuth and Munich and was then with his older friend Frank Schuster, 'hearing Strauss operas in Frankfort.'

Public Bores. F. S. Marvin (1863–1943) was a prolific editor and author of such books as *The Living Past* (1913). Having read Modern History at Oxford, he worked as a teacher in elementary schools, as an extension lecturer, and as an Inspector of Schools. He was Staff Inspector at the Board of Education until 1924, and organised courses, for teachers and others, in modern languages, history and education. Albert Mansbridge (1876–1952), a self-educated working-class man, founded the Workers' Educational Association in 1903, and until the 1920s frequently served on important committees concerned with education, including the Royal Commission on the Universities of Oxford and Cambridge (1919–22). He was made Companion of Honour in 1931. Edward Thompson, the author of books on Tagore (1926), India, and Robert Bridges (1944), published his *Collected Poems* in 1930. He died in 1946. H. M. Tomlinson (1873–1958) wrote about the Thames and the sea; 'Salt Junk' is a depreciatory reference to his book *Old Junk* (1918). 'Edward Eastaway' was the *nom de plume* used by the poet Edward Thomas. Ralph Vaughan Williams's *A Pastoral Symphony* was first performed in 1922; in 1929 he went to live in Dorking, only a few miles from West Hackhurst where Forster and his mother had settled in 1925. During the 1930s Forster and Vaughan Williams collaborated on the *Abinger Pageant* and the pageant *England's Pleasant Land*.

The phrases 'Pope says from Heywood (Dunciad I, 98)' and 'via Lord Morley of Borley' are interlinear additions.

After 'of an *educational* nature and therefore' Forster originally wrote, then cancelled, 'worthless, or anyhow'.

28   Thomas Mann's *The Magic Mountain* (1924) appeared in a two-volume English translation by H. T. Lowe-Porter in June 1927 (published by Martin Secker). This translation was in Forster's

library at his death. The first passage (quoted by Forster inaccurately and incompletely) occurs in vol. I, ch. IV ('Excursus on the Sense of Time'), pp. 135–6. The second (beginning 'her', not 'Music's') is from vol. I, ch. III ('Politically Suspect'), p. 147. *Re* Forster's 'much on the connection', see *The Magic Mountain*, vol. II, ch. VII ('By the Ocean of Time'), pp. 683–91.

Lytton Strachey's last important work, *Elizabeth and Essex*, was finished at the end of April 1928, about six months after Forster made this entry. The book had been started on 17 December 1925. Michael Holroyd notes that none of Strachey's major works 'gave him so much difficulty [as this one] or wore him out so completely . . . he often needed to interrupt his work with short recuperative holidays' (*Lytton Strachey: A Biography* (London, 1973), p. 912). Shortly before finishing it, Strachey wrote to Roger Senhouse: 'I am almost dead with exhaustion from this fearful tussle with the Old Hag' (*ibid.*, p. 963).

29 'M. A. dishes'. For 'dishes' Forster originally wrote 'joints'.

'F.V.'. Frank Vicary, originally a ship's-steward whom Forster had met in Alexandria in 1916, when Vicary was convalescing in Montazah hospital. Forster had befriended him, and in the mid-1920s had bought him a cottage and some land in Alvington, Gloucestershire, where he could run a farm. Instead, Vicary got into debt and mortgaged the cottage (Forster's Diary, 31 December 1928). I have found no material to document the particular reference to 'prison' here.

The word after 'Scotch' is hard to decipher; it could be 'bun' but this seems unlikely in the context.

31 'Si vous partiez . . .' André Gide, *Les Faux Monnayeurs* (Paris, 1925), pt. 2, ch. 3. Forster gives a loose translation of this in ch. 5 of *Aspects of the Novel*.

The poem Forster quotes is the entire text of 'Bahnhofstrasse' by James Joyce. It appeared in *Pomes Penyeach*, first published in 1927 by Shakespeare & Co. (Paris).

Forster was described as an 'elusive' writer in many early reviews of his work. J. B. Priestley, reviewing *A Passage to India* in the *London Mercury* (July 1924) spoke of Forster's 'somewhat elusive philosophy of personal relationships'; but his review was a very favourable one nonetheless. 'D.N.': *Daily News*.

Felday is a hamlet south of the Guildford–Dorking main road and just before Holmbury St Mary.

Lost, lost! The quotation comes from *Oscar Browning* by H. E. Wortham (London, 1927), pp. 204–5.

Oscar Browning, known as 'the O.B.', was a legendary and very influential Fellow of King's College, Cambridge, when Forster was an undergraduate.

32   'L'Annonce fait à Marie' (Claudel): i.e. the Annunciation. Its alternative title is *The Maiden Violaine*.

Passion and scholarship. Not a quotation from Housman but a description of him.

33   In *A New Variorum Edition of Shakespeare, The Sonnets*, ed. Hyder Edward Rollins (1944), vol. I, p. 275, the line is printed as 'Now all is done, have what shall have no end', with the textual note: 'Save what Mal. [Malone] (Tyrwhitt conj.).'.

Lord Vaux was a contributor to *Tottel's Miscellany* (1557). Forster's date is strange: Lord Vaux lived from 1510 to 1556.

'S. K.': South Kensington.

34   'Les amours qui suivent ...'. La Bruyère, *Les Caractères*, 'Du Coeur,' section 11. ('One loves well only once; that is the first time; the loves that follow are less involuntary.') Forster had used the phrase at the end of chapter 24 of *The Longest Journey* (1907), in reference to Agnes Pembroke's feelings for Rickie Elliot.

'Jack'. Perhaps a reference to W. J. H. Sprott, sometimes known as 'Jack', sometimes as 'Sebastian'.

Castle Acre is a Norfolk village just north of Swaffham. I have been unable to discover when Forster visited it, or why.

C. Day. Charlie Day, born 15 July 1900, was a ship's stoker who lived in Charlton in south-east London and worked for the Canadian Pacific Steamship Company. Forster refers to him in his Diary (31 December 1928) as 'the third surprise of my life, and the greatest, though not the most profound.' Their relationship extended from about 1927 to at least 1931, and they corresponded fairly frequently in 1928.

35   Forster's admiration for Ibsen's *Peer Gynt* was reflected during his undergraduate years in the pen-name he chose for an essay on 'The Relation of Dryden to Milton and Pope' which he submitted to examiners at Cambridge: he requested it be returned to 'Peer Gynt', Union Society, Cambridge.

The Great Boyg appears in *Peer Gynt*, act. II, sc. 7.

36   Laura Cowie (1892–1969) was a prominent West End actress in the period 1908–1939; but no performance of Hedda Gabler by her is recorded in the authoritative *Who Was Who in the Theatre 1912–1976* (Detroit, Gale Research, 1978).

Lord Farrer (1859–1940) was the local landowner in Forster's area, and lived in Abinger Hall. His father, T. H. Farrer, had received a peerage in 1893; Forster's mother had in her early days worked for T. H. Farrer's wife as a governess.

37 'Ordnance Map ... names of all the fields'. Forster had in his possession a very large-scale Ordnance Survey map (originally owned by his aunt Laura Forster, for whom West Hackhurst had been designed by Forster's father) showing the area round the house. On it Forster marked all the fields which had names (there were 155 of them) and a list of their names in Forster's hand survives, with the map, in the library of King's College, Cambridge.

38 The first Mauriac quotation is from *Le Désert de l'Amour* (Paris, 1925), ch. XI, p. 230. There should be a comma after 'conformer'. 'It is our sorrow to see the loved one make up before our eyes its own image of us, abolish our most precious virtues, and place in full view this weakness, this absurdity, this vice. . . . And it imposes its vision on us, it obliges us to conform, while it looks at us, to its narrow idea. And it will never know that, to the eye of another, whose affection is valueless to us, our virtue bursts forth, our talent shines out, our force appears supernatural, our face that of a god.' (Mauriac, *The Desert of Love*).

The second (which in the original Forster added in a space on the opposite page, fourteen years later) is from *La Pharisienne* (Paris, 1942), p. 117: 'The night was devoted to the wind and the moon.' (Mauriac, *The Woman of the Pharisees*).

Forster owned a copy of the first book (Paris, 1927). His admiration for Mauriac appears in a letter from Forster to T. E. Lawrence in 1931: 'How good Mauriac is. I am just reading Genetrix.'

Stars and Atoms (first mentioned by Forster on p. 37) was published by The Clarendon Press in 1927. The first quotation (which should begin 'We have seen that spatially . . .') is the start of Lecture III, p. 85. After 'excited atom' Eddington has '(p. 74)', and before 'three score years' he has 'man's'. The second quotation is the conclusion of Lecture II, p. 84, and should begin: 'Under "ordinary" conditions – you will understand my use of the word – matter . . .'

39 The path of the ancient Pilgrims' Way (to Canterbury) runs west to east across the North Downs and passes fairly close to West Hackhurst. For the 'yew wood . . . that I have kidded myself into thinking sinister', compare Forster's entry in his Diary for 24 March 1925: 'I walked on the downs and felt certain paths were sinister, so turned back.'

40   George Meredith, whose novels Forster greatly admired in his
        youth, settled permanently in a cottage near Box Hill above
        Dorking in 1867. For 'better' Forster originally wrote 'good'.

        The Greek letters 'κ.τ.λ.' stand for 'etc.'

        Thomas Deloney lived from 1543 to 1600. Part II of 'The Gentle
        Craft' (shoe-making) was published in 1639. The first passage,
        spoken by Margaret (known as Long Meg of Westminster) to
        'Gillian of the George', comes from chapter 1 of the section
        entitled 'Richard Casteler'. (*The Gentle Craft*, ed. Alexis F. Lange,
        Palaestra XVIII, Berlin 1903, Part II, p. 8). In the second, Margaret
        speaks to Gillian about 'Richard of the Rose, the Wakeful Cock
        of Westminster' (*ibid.*, Part II, p. 11). Between 'a man' and 'a
        Wren', this edition has 'a shrimpe'. The French critic Abel
        Chevalley gave Forster his book on Thomas Deloney (Paris,
        1926) and his French translation of Deloney's *Jack of Newbury*
        (Paris, n.d.).

42   Izaak Walton's quotation from du Bartas occurs in *The Compleat
        Angler* (1653), p. 23. (A facsimile of the first edition was published
        in London by A. C. Black Ltd in 1928.) 'Sent to S.S . . .': This
        phrase, a later addition, was written by Forster obliquely, in a
        very small hand, to the right of the quotation; 'S.S.' is perhaps
        Siegfried Sassoon, who married Hester Gatty in November,
        1933.

43   p. 72. 'Hjordis and D   '. Hjordis and Dagny in Ibsen's *The
        Vikings at Helgeland*.

        The first quotation is Milton, *Paradise Regained*, IV, 368–72. The
        second is lines 8–10 of 'An Epitaph on the Marchioness of
        Winchester'. There should be a comma after 'breath'; 'alas'
        follows a semi-colon and should be uncapitalised.

        Ibsen. In February 1929 Forster gave a Centenary Lecture on
        Ibsen in the Midlands (P. N. Furbank, *E. M. Forster: A Life*, II,
        159). Perhaps these notes, and those on pp. 70–2, were made with
        this in mind.

44   *Charlie Chaplin*. After the first 'or' there is a blank in the original;
        the '*m*' after the second 'or' is presumably a stylised abbreviation
        for 'Medieval'.

        'S.P.W.'. Presumably Sydney Waterlow, an Etonian whom
        Forster first met in 1905; he was the nephew of 'Elizabeth' of
        Elizabeth and her German Garden (later Countess Russell). Forster's
        Diary for 1 October 1928 records: 'Sydney Waterlow, tiresome
        as ever, has just left.'

45   *Horace Walpole*. The quotation is from a letter Walpole sent to George Montagu on 13 November 1760. (See *The Letters of Horace Walpole*, ed. M. Alderton Pink (London, Macmillan, 1938), pp. 112–13.) An adonis is a kind of wig. The third sentence should read: 'Attending the funeral of a father, how little reason so ever he had to love him, could not be pleasant.' Gibbon's Journal has only: '11th [Nov.] We saw the King's funeral.' (*Gibbon's Journal*, intro. by D. M. Low (London, Chatto & Windus, 1929), p. 17). Gibbon, twenty-three at the time, had a commission in the South Hampshire Militia, and attended the funeral with Sir Thomas Worsley, its Lieutenant-Colonel. Forster's essay 'Captain Edward Gibbon' (1931, reprinted in *Abinger Harvest*) begins with a description of Gibbon passing near West Hackhurst in 1761.

A. S. Eddington's *The Nature of the Physical World* was published in 1928, and that year Forster bought it as a Christmas present for himself. He refers to the book in his Diary (31 December 1928): 'Shall be 50 in a few minutes and see on looking back that I have been fiddling in this book for close on 20 years. But Eddington's Nature of the Physical world, though of course I can't understand it, heartens me to take a high hand with time. The hour which I do now hear striking on the village clock, and now in the hall, is said not to be the only one, and perhaps I am his man who travels to the ends of the universe and remains younger than if he sat at home. There seems also a tendency to confusion tempered by occasional recognitions in the Universe which comforted me while I was worrying because I hadn't heard from Charlie [Day]. Indeed I am reading unscientifically as the author feared, – I would rather have Eddington's mind than any I know of, because he understands the limitations of the literary man and is not too proud to explain. If my mind were suppler it would influence it.'

47   *Pee Shit*. An elaborated P.S.

Literature as Compensation. 'Shakespeare' is an interlinear addition.

'Relief from my pain.' In the first two weeks of January 1929 Forster had been suffering 'no end' as a result of difficulties with Charlie Day. 'It's an illness not an affair' (Diary, 12 Jan. 1929).

48   *Guinea Worms*. In December 1928 Forster visited Frankfurt to see his old friend Syed Ross Masood, recently ill with Spanish 'flu. Bijapur is 200 miles west of Hyderabad, where Forster had stayed with Masood late in 1921. Forster failed to specify the worm's length, hence the blank before 'feet'.

W. J. Turner (1889–1946) was an Australian-born poet and journalist and literary editor of the *Daily Herald* from 1920 to 1923. He was also Music Critic for the *New Statesman*.

'Orlando'. Virginia Woolf's book of that title was published in 1926; the character and history of Orlando were modelled on that of Victoria Sackville-West and her ancestors.

H. W. Massingham (1860–1924) was editor of the *Daily Chronicle* and, from 1907 to 1924, editor of the *Nation*. Lady Jane Maria Strachey (mother of Lytton) died in December 1928.

49　'Bully' and 'sex-talk' are interlinear additions. For 'critics' Forster originally wrote 'enemies'.

'Wyndham Lewes'. Percy Wyndham Lewis (1884–1957), author of *Tarr* (1918), *The Childermass* (1927), *The Apes of God* (1928), etc.

The section from 'Gerald Heard' to '26-2-29' is written sideways on the opposite page in the original, and linked by a heavy arrow to 'D. H. Lawrence' and by a lighter arrow to the original conclusion of the section ('comfort or sympathy').

The correct title of the book by Gerald Heard is *The Ascent of Humanity* (London, 1929). The quotation beginning 'Their intelligence . . .' is from p. 207, but the second sentence, after 'the only choice before us is', should continue 'utter destruction or a metamorphosis . . .'. The phrase 'strain-symptom' occurs on p. 204, which also makes the points summed up in Forster's final sentence ('G. H. argues . . .'). Heard's book is dedicated 'to E.M.F. and K.W.'. Chapter V ('The Upper Individuality') does not mention Bloomsbury by name, but discusses two contrasted twentieth-century groups, the 'intellectuals' and the 'emotionalists'. Frances Marshall, the sister-in-law of David Garnett, married Ralph Partridge in 1933; both were close friends of Lytton Strachey. I have not identified Miss MacMunn. She was, perhaps, a relative of Howard MacMunn (1878–1947), a friend of Forster's at Tonbridge and King's, who went into the Church and later became a Canon of Durham.

50　'Civis': citizen/civil person.

The imaginary conversation, and Forster's comment at the end, perhaps constitute cryptic references to his relationship with Charlie Day; or possibly to distress over Frank Vicary, who had shocked Forster by raising a mortgage on the cottage Forster had bought him.

51　*Pigmies.* Both phrases are quotations from *The Kalahari and its Native Races* by Ernest Hubert Lewis Schwarz (London, 1928), pp. 153, 155.

Place. The point is made on pp. 5–7 of Bertrand Russell's *The ABC of Relativity* (London, 1926): 'the whole notion that one is always in some definite "place" is due to the fortunate immobility of most of the large objects on the earth's surface' (p. 7).

St. George's Hill is near Weybridge, where Forster lived until 1925. Forster visited Aligarh on his first trip to India in 1912.

(ii) The phrase forms used for these various 'lands' may owe something to Sterne. *Tristram Shandy* (bk. 8, ch. 1) talks of 'Freeze-land, Fog-land.' After 'steamer-land' Forster added, then cancelled, 'and airoplane-land'.

The quotation from A. N. Whitehead is from *Science and the Modern World* (Cambridge, 1926), p. 5.

52   Forster's essay 'Anonymity: An Enquiry' was written in 1925. It was collected in *Two Cheers for Democracy* (1951).

Raphèle. Raphèle-les-Arles is near St Rémy. Forster went there in June 1926 to visit his friend and translator Charles Mauron.

(*Thought and Logic*) Before 'suspicious' the original has '∴' (i.e. 'because'), which seems unlikely.

Edward Carpenter (1844-1929) had greatly influenced Forster in his youth; Forster's visit to him at Millthorpe near Sheffield in 1913 had triggered the writing of *Maurice*.

53   Carpenter's book of essays, *Civilisation, its Cause and Cure*, was published in 1889.

There is a blank in the original after 'e.g.'. It perhaps represents 'being a homosexual'.

The quotations from T. S. Eliot are from his essay 'Tradition and the Individual Talent', collected in *The Sacred Wood* (1920). The first quotation is on pp. 50-1 (not p. 52); the second on p. 52; the third on pp. 52-3.

Frank Vicary's eldest child, Donald, had died in February 1928, scalded by boiling bath-water. Forster had at that time given Vicary £20. The younger son, Peter, was about eight.

54   'Uprooted' is printed in Chekhov's *The Bishop, and Other Stories* (trans. Constance Garnett, 1919). The quotation is on p. 157, the dots are Chekhov's, but the final sentence should read 'could be found to prove to them that their life ...'.

'Joe' is J. R. Ackerley, whom Forster first met in 1923. They remained close friends all their lives. Ackerley later became Literary Editor of *The Listener*.

55   The phrase 'It takes two to make a Hero' is written in a large firm hand.

Henry Bone had worked at West Hackhurst as gardener since 1919, first for Forster's Aunt Laura, then for Forster and his mother. Wonham was perhaps a gamekeeper for Lord Farrer at Abinger Hall (cf. Forster's use of the name in *The Longest Journey*). Damon was Lord Farrer's shepherd: the 'Abinger Pageant' of 1934, for which Forster wrote the script, began with him 'driving his flock of sheep across the scene' (Ursula Vaughan Williams, *R.V.W.: A Biography of Ralph Vaughan Williams* (London, 1964) p. 202).

'Lambring', which is not in Joseph Wright's *English Dialect Dictionary* (1898–1905), is presumably an error for 'lambing'.

56   'Cold Kitchen' is Cole Kitchen Farm, just north of Gomshall, to the west of West Hackhurst.

The quotation from Vaughan is stanzas 2 and 5 of 'Quickness' (*The Works of Henry Vaughan*, ed. L. C. Martin (Clarendon Press, 1914), II, 538). Martin prints the last line in italics.

The quotation from F. L. Lucas is the opening of 'The Graces', from *Marionettes* (1930); a re-worked version of it forms the first stanza of 'To the Graces' in Lucas's *From Many Times and Lands* (1953), p. 315. Lucas was a Fellow of King's College, Cambridge from 1920 until his death in 1967.

57   Bray was a neighbour of Forster's. Shortly before leaving West Hackhurst for good, Forster noted in his Diary (22 October 1946): 'Tea with Reggie Bray. Two friendly old men, I feeling the younger. He has Jacobean tapestry.' The term for a double elm ('cuckold') was told to Forster by one of the Broyd family, his neighbours at Hackhurst farm.

'I hadnt it three years ago . . .'. In summer 1926 Forster bought from Lord Farrer a piece of woodland called Piney Copse, adjacent to West Hackhurst. He wrote about it in his essay 'My Wood' (1926).

'Heroism consists in not allowing the body to disown the rashness of the mind.' (Maurois).

André Maurois published his two-volume biography *Byron* in 1930. Forster possessed a copy of this.

'Goldie'. Goldsworthy Lowes Dickinson, a Fellow of King's who befriended Forster as an undergraduate. He died in 1932. Forster's biography of him was published in 1934.

58   'Solent Wolf'. *Wolf Solent* (1929) by John Cowper Powys. His novels and those of his brother T. F. Powys are mostly set in 'Wessex', Dorset particularly.

'T.E.': T. E. Lawrence.

'S.P.G.': Society for the Propagation of the Gospel.

'C.M.S.': Church Missionary Society.

59   Forster had taken a dislike to the novelist J. B. Priestley, who had been guest of honour at the annual dinner in 1929 of 'Young P.E.N.', a 'club for unknown writers' formed in 1928 with Forster as president. (P. N. Furbank, *E. M. Forster: A Life*, II, 154–5). Priestley's novel *The Good Companions*, published in 1929, was a best seller.

'Walpole' was the novelist Hugh Walpole, who had praised Forster highly in his study of Conrad, published in 1917. Mrs Marie Adelaide Belloc-Lowndes, who died in 1947, published the first of her many novels in 1904.

Frieda Lawrence visited Forster shortly after the death of D. H. Lawrence in 1930. They had last met in February 1915, when Forster had spent an uncomfortable three days with her and D. H. Lawrence in the Lawrence's borrowed cottage at Greatham in Sussex. Despite Forster's mixed feelings here, he spoke very generously about Lawrence in a broadcast in 1930.

'F.L.L.': F. L. Lucas.

The bracketed phrase '[later note]' refers, I think, to the passage which follows it; whereas '[much later note]' (p. 60) refers to the quotation which precedes it.

60   'T.E.S.': T. E. Shaw (T. E. Lawrence).

K. W. Marshall worked for Boriswood Ltd, who published James Hanley's novel *Boy*, the subject of a prosecution for obscenity. The letter to Marshall containing the sentences quoted by Forster is not included in *The Letters of T. E. Lawrence*, ed. David Garnett (Cape, 1938).

Tennyson. From the first edition (1850) of *In Memoriam*, section II begins with the lines 'Old Yew, which graspest at the stones / That name the underlying dead'. The three stanzas Forster quotes were added, as section XXXIX, to the 1870 edition. The capitalisation of 'yew' is Forster's; there should be a semi-colon after 'flower'.

The two-line quotation is the close of Tennyson's 'A Dedication' (*Poems of Tennyson 1830–1870* (Oxford, 1912), p. 794.) A footnote explains Tennyson's reference as to 'the fruit of the Spindle Tree (Euonymus Europaeus).'

'Flow down, cold rivulet' is Tennyson's 'A Farewell' (*ibid.*, pp. 241–2); as usual, Forster takes liberties with punctuation. For 'alder tree' (stanza 3), compare the Oniton section (ch. 29) of *Howards End*.

61   'Far in a western brookland' is Poem LII of Housman's *A Shropshire Lad* (1896). Forster's own copy was the 1900 Grant Richards edition; the 1898 Grant Richards edition has the reading of line 9 given by Forster. In Housman's *Collected Poems* (Cape, 1939) this was changed to 'He hears: no more remembered.'

These two poems are written side by side in the original.

I have checked Forster's references to Corneille against Corneille, *Oeuvres complètes* (Paris, Editions du Seuil, 1963). There are minor variations of punctuation and accent-use throughout.

A 'soufflet' can be either a slap on the face or a box on the ear.

'Il est historique . . .': *Oeuvres complètes*, p. 219. 'presse trop . . . . . qu'on y donnâit l'ordre'; p. 220. (1) 'It is historically accurate and was approved in its time; but it would certainly be displeasing to ours';

62   (2) 'their conversation is full of such fine sentiments'; (3) 'compresses the incidents too much'; (4) 'It is the inconvenience of the rule; let us pass on to that of the unity of place'; (5) 'One must sometimes help the scene'; (6) 'grant that [the obsequies] were performed before the end of the play, or that the body lay in state in his house, waiting for the order to be given.'

The three short *Discours* passages in small type are connected by lines to earlier passages: the first to 'Infanta' (p. 62), the second to 'King's advice' (p. 61), the third to 'Moors' (p. 62).

The first quotation is from 'Discours de l'Utilité et des Parties du Poème Dramatique' (*op. cit.*, p. 829): 'Aristotle strongly criticises detached episodes and says that bad poets write them from ignorance and good ones in order to give employment to actors. The Infanta is of this number.'

63   The second summarises Corneille's statement: 'le mariage n'est point un achèvement necessaire pour la tragédie, ni même pour la comédie. Quant à la premier, c'est le peril d'un héros qui la constitue, et lorsqu'il en est sortie, l'action est terminée' (*op. cit.*, p. 824): 'Marriage is not a necessary conclusion for tragedy, nor even for comedy. Tragedy is characterised by the peril of a hero, and when he has emerged from this the action is over.'

The third reference is to *op. cit.*, p. 828.

Cinna. The couplet is spoken by Auguste to Livie (IV, iii, 43–4): 'After a long storm one must find a port/And I see only two, repose or death.'

'Dans le seul ... Emilie': (*op. cit.*, p. 269): 'only in Augustus's palace, provided that you will assign a suite of rooms in it to Emilia.'

'ont sans doute ... conduire': (*op. cit.*, pp. 269–70); 'n'ayant ... soutenir': (*Op. cit.*, p. 270): 'no doubt need more intellect to imagine, and more art to conduct [but simple plays] not having the same by way of subject, need greater strength in verse, reasoning and feelings to sustain them.'

Trois Discours 1660. 'And as perhaps I understand it in my fashion, I am not jealous if someone else understands it in his [but] The commentary I make most use of is experience of the theatre and reflections on what I have seen to please or displease there.'

The full title of *Discours I* is 'Discours de l'Utilité et des Parties du Poème Dramatique'. 'P. D. a pour seul but ...' (*op. cit.*, p. 822): 'The dramatic poem has for its purpose simply the audience's pleasure; [but it is impossible to please without introducing] usefulness.'

'L'amour nous donne [not 'vous'] ... inquiétudes' (*op. cit.*, p. 822): 'Love gives you a lot of uneasiness; Love gives a lot of uneasiness to the souls it possesses.'

64 'un usage ... périls' (*op. cit.*, p. 823): 'a habit we have adopted, which each person may depart from at his own risk.'

'Quelque passion ... premier' (*op. cit.*, p. 824): 'Some passion more noble and more manly than love, such as ambition or revenge, and intended to make us fear greater sorrows than the loss of a mistress. It is appropriate to mix love with it ... but it must make do with second place in the poem and leave them the first.' Forster's dots after 'amour' represent two omitted lines.

'Cleopâtre ... partent' (*op. cit.*, p. 826): 'Cleopatra, in Rodogune, is very wicked; but all her crimes are accompanied by a grandeur of soul which has something so elevated in it, that at the same time as one detests her actions, one admires the source they spring from ...' Between 'méchante' and 'mais tous' Forster omits three lines without indication.

'Les sentiments'. Here Forster is summarising a paragraph by Corneille, which concludes as indicated here. (*op. cit.*, p. 827): 'Sentiments: it is never the poet who speaks, and those he makes to speak are not orators.'

'La versification': '[As to] versification, those he makes to speak are not poets.' Another summary; what Corneille says is: 'la versification [doit être] aisée et élevée au-dessus de la prose, mais non pas jusqu' à l'enflure du poème epique, puisque ceux que le poète fait parler ne sont pas des poètes' (*op. cit.*, p. 827): 'The versification [should be] smooth and elevated above prose, but not to the flowery extent of the epic poem, since those whom the poet makes speak are not poets.'

Discours de la Tragedie (Discourse on Tragedy) 'πιθανον ἀδυνατον'. i.e. 'The plausible impossible', which in Aristotle's *Poetics* (ch. 25) is preferred to the possible implausible.

'Cette [not 'la'] reduction . . . vraisemblance' (*op. cit.*, p. 837): 'The reduction of tragedy to the novel is the touchstone for distinguishing necessary actions from those which are true to life. We are hampered in the theatre by place, by time, and by the inconveniences of representation . . . The novel has none of these constraints . . . that is why *it is never free to depart from verisimilitude.*' After 'représentation' Forster omits three lines; after 'contraintes' he omits eight. The underlining (italicization here) is Forster's.

Discours des Trois Unités. (Discourse on the Three Unities). For 'minimised' Forster originally wrote 'avoided'. Corneille says: 'Dans le dénouement je trouve deux choses à éviter, le simple changement de volonté, et la machine' (*op. cit.*, p. 842): 'In the denouement I find there are two things to be avoided, the simple change of will, and the machine.'

65 'Je pousserais . . .' (*op. cit.*, p. 844): 'I should extend it without scruple to 30 [hours].'

'Voltaire comments . . .' i.e. in Voltaire, *Critique des Tragédies de Corneille et de Racine*, collected by B. Bonieux (Clermont Ferrand, 1866): 'If you wish more tears to be spilled, take the day and the night, but go no further: in that case, the illusion would then be too much spoiled.'

'Il est facile . . . théâtre': (Corneille, *op. cit.*, p. 846): 'It is easy for theoreticians to be severe; but if they wished to give ten or twelve poems of this kind to the public, they would perhaps stretch the rules more than I have done, as soon as they have realised by experience how restricting their exactitude is, and how many beautiful things it bans from our theatre.' This passage is marked by Forster in the original by a double vertical line. 'Plus' should be preceded by 'encore'.

The Conquest of Granada. George Saintsbury, in the Mermaid *Dryden* (2 vols, n.d.) says that the play was performed in the winter of 1669–70; George Watson (*Of Dramatic Poesy and Other Critical Essays*, 2 vols (Everyman, 1962)) says it was performed in two parts, in December 1670 and January 1671. Saintsbury and Watson both date the play's publication as 1672. Forster's quotation differs in small details of punctuation, idiom and spelling from Watson's text.

66   'Alm.': Almanzor.

George Saintsbury (*Dryden*, English Men of Letters Series (1881)) describes the play on pp. 46-51.

The Rehearsal (1672) was attributed to George Villiers, 2nd Duke of Buckingham. It satirises the heroic tragedies of its time, including *The Conquest of Granada*.

a. Spoken by Abdelmelech, chief of the Abencerrages.
c. Abdalla speaking of Lyndaraxa.
d. Almanzor speaking of Almahide.
e. 'She' is Almahide; 'He' is Almanzor. 'wonnot' is correct.

67   f. Spoken by Almahide.
g. 'He' is Almanzor; 'She' is Almahide.
h. Spoken by Lyndaraxa. 'from heaven are sent'.

68   'One loose, one sally' (Mermaid *Dryden*).
j. Spoken by Almanzor. Later the Ghost of Almanzor's mother says:
'Far hence, upon the Mountains of the Moon,
Is my abode; where heaven and nature smile,
And strew with flowers the secret bed of Nile.'

The initial letters of 'Very interesting' are written in a large hand.

69   The phrase 'Wit elsewhere defined as a propriety of thoughts and words' was in the original on the opposite page, and linked by a line to 'ii Wit' here.

'In a poet'. Watson (*op. cit.*) has 'in the poet'.

70   The Marquis de St Évremond (1616-1703) spent the years 1662-5 in England, and returned permanently to England in 1670. In 1930 Forster was given a copy of St Évremond's *Oeuvres choisis* (Paris, n.d.) by W. J. H. Sprott. The two quotations are linked to each other in such a way, in the original, that they form a double box surrounding Forster's final comment on Dryden. They are, in fact, one continuous quotation from 'Dissertation sur le mot de Vaste'. (Saint-Évremond, *Oeuvres en Prose*, ed. René Ternois (Paris, 1966), III, 383.) 'We think more forcefully than we write, there is always part of our thought that remains with us. We hardly ever communicate it plainly: and it is by the spirit of penetration rather than by the clear comprehension of words, that we enter fully into an author's thought. Meanwhile, as if we were afraid of fully understanding what others think, or of making our own

thought understood, we weaken the terms which would have the force to express it.'

The date Forster gives for Dryden's *All for Love* is that of its publication.

Point (ii). What Dryden says is: 'If I have kept myself within the bounds of modesty, all beyond is but nicety and affectation, which is no more than modesty depraved into a vice.' Dryden is not speaking so directly about French poets as Forster's phrasing suggests. The next point, however ('are so careful . . .'), is addressed directly to them. Dryden's view is that Racine should have depicted an 'Amazonian' Hippolyte because 'antiquity' has given us this view of him.

(iii) The quotation beginning 'Poets themselves' should close at 'malice'. Forster marks the start of it by a vertical double line.

71   The quotation from the Prologue is lines 29–30; 'would' should be 'could'.

'A & C': Shakespeare's *Antony and Cleopatra*. *All for Love* is analysed in A. W. Verrall, *Lectures on Dryden* (1914), pp. 238–66. The nine-line quotation is III, i, 459–67; there should be a full stop after 'mistress'.

Albion and Albanius was an opera, with music by the French composer Lewis Grabu.

Dryden says (Everyman edition, ed. Watson, II, 34ff): 'Whoso undertakes the writing of an opera is obliged to imitate the design of the Italians', and notes of the French 'their perpetual ill accent'. 'Advantages' should be 'advantage'. 'Meanness of thought' is mentioned on p. 40.

72   The correct title of St. Évremond's treatise is 'Sur les Opera'. 'une sottise . . . sottise': St Évremond, *Oeuvres en Prose*, ed. René Ternois (Paris, Librairie Marcel Didier, 1966), III, 151).

'un travail bizarre . . . ouvrage': *op. cit.*, p. 154; 'J'ai vu . . . que le bon gout y soit rare': *op. cit.*, p. 158: 'a piece of nonsense loaded with music, dances, machines, decorations, is a magnificent piece of nonsense, but still nonsense. . . . a bizarre labour of poetry and music, in which the poet and the musician, equally hampered by each other, give themselves much trouble to create a bad work. . . . I have seen comedies, in England, where there was a lot of music; but, to put it mildly, I have been unable to get used to English song. I came too late to their country to be able to adopt a taste so different from all others. There is no nation which displays more courage in its men and more beauty in its women, and more wit in both sexes. One cannot have everything. Where so many good qualities are common, it is not such a great evil if good taste is rare.'

For 'style' Forster originally wrote 'manners'.

73 'For K's return'. Charles II was invited back to England in 1660.

'Abs. & Ach': *Absalom and Achitophel.*

74 'Farquhar'. George Farquhar (1678–1707), best known for *The Recruiting Officer* (1706) and *The Beaux Stratagem* (1707). His remarks on Dryden's funeral appear in his 'Miscellany of Verse and Letters', *Love and Business* (1702), reprinted in vol. II of *The Complete Works of George Farquhar*, ed. Charles Stonehill (Nonesuch Press, 1930).

Rodogune. The final comment 'Some years later' was added by Forster in a smaller hand. 'Viennent-ils ...' 'Are our lovers coming?'

Gotthold Ephraim Lessing (1729–81) did much to free German literature from the restrictions of French classical drama.

Preface to The Maiden Queen. Forster gives the date of its first performance. Forster's initial question appears in Dryden as: 'Tis a question variously disputed, whether an author may be allowed as a competent judge of his own works'. (*The Dramatic Works of John Dryden*, ed. George Saintsbury (Edinburgh, 1882), II, 418). Forster does not bother to distinguish between where Dryden's words end and his own begin. The first quotation should end at 'may'; the second begins with 'determine'; the next with 'But for ...'. There should be a comma after 'writing'. 'As it properly' should be 'as it is properly'. The next quotation begins 'and fancy', and there should be a comma after 'certain'.

This preface is omitted from *Essays of John Dryden*, ed. W. P. Ker, 2 vols (Oxford, The Clarendon Press, 2nd impression 1926).

75 *Rasselas.* I have checked Forster's quotations against R. W. Chapman's edition (Oxford, Clarendon Press, 1927).

'Whose opinions' should be 'whose interests and opinions' (ch. 10).

'The business of a poet'. Johnson adds 'said Imlac' (ch. 10). 'Only those characteristics': 'Only' is Forster's addition.

'To be a poet ... difficult, returned the prince': ch. 11.

'Human life ... enjoyed'. Spoken by Imlac at the end of ch. 11.

The bracketed phrases after 'Irene' represent a marginal addition of Forster's in the original.

'Their mirth ... abashed them': ch. 17.

76   'A glimpse of pastoral life' is the title of ch. 19. For Forster, perhaps the 'humour' resides in this chapter's debunking of an image of pastoral innocence and content; Nekayah sees shepherds as 'envious savages'.

The quotation from Nekayah in ch. 28 should read: 'the rude collisions of contrary desire where both are urged by violent impulses, the obstinate contests of disagreeing virtues'.

The 'analysis of waning sorrow' (Nekayah's for her lost favourite, Pekuah) is in fact in ch. 35.

'another, ch. 44' is connected by a line to the quotation beginning 'In time' (it comes from ch. 43, not from ch. 44; 'on the mind' should read 'upon the mind'); and by another to the quotation beginning 'No disease of imagination [Johnson adds 'answered Imlac']', which comes from ch. 45, not from ch. 46. These final quotations appear in the original in two parallel columns.

Johnson's *Life of Savage*. 1743 was the year Johnson announced his plan to write it; it was published in 1744. It would be truer to say that it doesn't contain much literary criticism than that it contains none.

'The liberty of the press . . .': *Samuel Johnson: Life of Savage*, ed. Clarence Tracy (Oxford, Clarendon Press, 1971), p. 49.

'The whole range . . .': *ibid.*, p. 65. Tracy's note reads: 'Walpole, according to G. B. Hill (*Lives of the Poets* ii, 372, n. 1). But there is nothing in Johnson's words to point to Walpole in particular.'

'He was an indefatigable . . .': *ibid.*, p. 83. This quotation is connected by a line to the word 'amuses' in the section 'Generalities on Johnson' on p. 77.

Lord Tyrconnel was originally very friendly towards Savage, but they later quarrelled.

Logan Pearsall Smith, an American author and littérateur who settled in Hampshire, was the brother-in-law of Bertrand Russell and also connected to the art critic and connoisseur Bernard Berenson. He was originally the friend, and later the enemy, of Lady Ottoline Morrell.

Cyril Connolly served as Logan Pearsall Smith's secretary in the late 1920s, and dedicated his book *Enemies of Promise* to him in 1938.

77   Johnson. *Preface to Dictionary*.

Forster puts a cross (x) beside 'heart' and connects it to his 'example', from the Notes to Johnson's edition of Shakespeare.

'words are . . .': Johnson's italics.

'words use but . . .' should read 'words are but'.

'the things they denote' should read 'the things which they denote'.

'a poet doomed to wake' should read 'a poet doomed at last to wake'.

In the original, the section 'Against academies . . . roughness of another' starts in the left margin and squeezes upwards to fill a space originally left blank next to the 'example' from *Othello*.

Generalities in Johnson

The quotation occurs very early in Johnson's *Preface to Shakespeare*. 'S's persons' should read 'His persons'.

78   The words 'Generalities/Universal' are in the original enclosed by curly brackets. 'Typical' and 'Mystical' are bracketed on the left only.

Criticism. The opening sentence (only) is Forster's version of sentiments expressed by Henry Home, Lord Kames (1696–1782) in the Introduction to his *Elements of Criticism* (1761). The sixth edition of this (Edinburgh, 1785) was issued in a facsimile version (Garland Publishing Inc., New York) in 1972. On p. 13 Kames refers to 'the gay and agreeable form of criticism'; on p. 14 he says that 'To censure works, not men, is the just prerogative of criticism.'

For 'their colleagues' Forster originally wrote 'one another'.

(i) i.e. 'literature is very wonderful, and it is very kind of geniuses to write'.

'Mr. Richards'. I. A. Richards (b. 1893). His *Principles of Literary Criticism* appeared in 1924, *Practical Criticism* in 1929.

79   The bracketed phrase 'to go home' was crossed out by Forster in the original.

Blindoak Gate is to the north of Abinger Hammer, at the end of a path which runs up from Hackhurst Lane on to Hackhurst Downs.

Johnson on Othello/Macbeth. Forster possessed a copy of *Lives of the Poets* (1781); but I have not discovered which 'original edition' he is referring to here – Johnson's eight-volume edition of Shakespeare's *Plays* (1765), or (for the *Macbeth* comments) *Miscellaneous Observations on the Tragedy of Macbeth* (1745). The book he was comparing with it is *Johnson on Shakespeare*, Essays and Notes selected and set forth with an Introduction by Walter Raleigh

(London, Henry Frowde, 1908). The points in *Othello* and *Macbeth* which Forster notes are omitted by Raleigh.

George Steevens published his own, incomplete edition of Shakespeare in 1766; on its republication in full form in 1773 he made use of Johnson's notes. William Warburton's edition of Shakespeare appeared in 1747.

Othello. 'Naturally J. . . .': Raleigh praised Johnson (pp. xiv–xv), despite Macaulay's earlier criticism of him; Forster's comment would seem to mean not that Johnson was stupid but that Raleigh's praise was overdoing things.

80   *Macbeth.* Johnson's full emendation (Note VIII of *Miscellaneous Observations on the Tragedy of Macbeth*, 1745) reads: 'Time! on! – the hour runs through the roughest day.'

'Mark Antony's was by Caesar'. In vol. 5 of *The Works of Samuel Johnson* (1825), Note XXIV (pp. 75–6), the phrase 'as, it is said / Antony's was by Caesar' is rejected as a player's interpolation. Neither in Johnson's 1745 *Observations* nor in his *General Observations on the Plays of Shakespeare* did he change his mind, as Forster indicates here.

Battle of the Books. Dryden's statement to Swift is, in the original, inserted by Forster in a box above this passage, and linked by a line to 'Dryden'.

'*Criticism*' is in the original linked by a line with 'cf. *Tale of a Tub*' below. The 'Criticism' reference is on p. 241 of *A Tale of a Tub etc.*, ed. A. C. Guthkelch and D. Nichol Smith (Oxford, Clarendon Press, 1920; 2nd edition, 1958), the 'Helicon' reference on p. 255. The quotations from *A Tale of a Tub* are found on p. 93 ('with the caution . . .') and p. 98 ('The Nauplians . . .'). The latter reads 'Argia' rather than 'Argos'.

81   The quotations are from Johnson's *Life of Swift*. 'Pleasure' should be 'delight'.

Boileau. L'Art Poétique.
'Qui ne sait . . .': Canto I, line 63. ('He cannot write who knows not to give o'er'.)

'Avant donc . . .': Canto I, line 150. ('Learn then to think ere you pretend to write'.)

'Dans un roman . . .': Canto III, lines 119–22.
('In a romance those errors are excused;
There 'tis enough that, reading, we're amused,
Rules too severe would there be useless found;
But the strict scene must have a juster bound')

'Ni sans raison . . .': Canto III, lines 137–8. The second line is within quotation marks in Boileau.
('Or tell in vain how "the rough Tanais bore
His sevenfold waters to the Euxine shore" '.)

82   The Shakespeare quotation is *Othello*, III, iii, 453–8; 'returning' should read 'retiring'.

'Machinery of an epic . . .': These matters are discussed in Canto III, lines 193–236.

'C'est un vice . . .': Canto IV, line 144 ('It is a vice that goes with mediocrity')

'B. Lit.': *Biographia Literaria*.

'Don't be just a poet. . . .': Canto IV, lines 121–4.
('Let not your only business be to write,
Be virtuous, just, and in your friends delight.
'Tis not enough your poems be admired,
But strive your conversation be desired.')
The translations of Boileau are by Sir William Soame (1680); they were revised by Dryden and published in 1693. (See *The Art of Poetry: The Poetical Treatises of Horace, Vida and Boileau*, with the translations of Howes, Pitt and Soame, New York, 1926.)

Dante. The translation which Forster appears to have read is *Dante's Treatise 'De Vulgari Eloquentia'*, translated into English with explanatory notes by A. G. Ferrers Howell (London, Kegan Paul, Trench, Trubner & Co., 1890.)

'Subjects for poetry' are dealt with in bk. 2, ch. 2; Forster summarises pp. 50–1 of the translation.

'Fictio rhetorica . . .' (bk. 2, ch. 4, p. 55): a description of Canzone, 'a rhetorical composition set to music'.

83   'adornment . . .': bk. 2, ch. 1 (p. 47).
Vocabulary. bk. 2, ch. 7 (pp. 65–6) mentions words which are (a) 'combed out', such as 'amore', 'virtute', 'salute'; (b) 'shaggy' (Dante gives no examples).

The Latin words 'pexa' and 'hirsuta' which Dante uses ('combed out' and 'shaggy'), and the phrase 'Fictio rhetorica', are not referred to in Howell's notes, so that Forster was reconstructing the original quite accurately. The 1843 edition of Dante's Latin text (made by Alessandro Torri and published in Livorno) has 'Fictio rhetorica in musicaque posita' (bk. 2, p. 108).

84   In the original, a line connects *'excitement'* with 'important, though' lower down this page.

2. 'The property of passion . . .': *Biographia Literaria*, XVII. Coleridge puts 'create' in italics.

3. Forster is inaccurate here. It is 'real' (not 'really') which Coleridge objects to, adding, 'For "real" therefore we must substitute *ordinary* or *lingua communis*' (*BL*, XVII).

'C. pertinacious'. In the original, a line connects 'the poems' in this paragraph with *Ode to Dejection* below.

'Indignation to' should be 'Indignation at'; Coleridge has a full stop after 'stars'.

85   Housman, *Last Poems* (1922): after 'under which' Housman has 'in the early months of 1895'.

'Partition-scheme'. Coleridge recalls this at the start of *BL*, XIV. The quotation should read: 'to procure for these shadows of imagination that willing suspension of disbelief for the moment, which constitutes poetic faith'.

'This breathing house . . .': Lines 8–9 of 'Youth and Age'.

S. S. Koteliansky came from Kiev to England in 1910 to study economics and stayed permanently, making his living from translating Russian writers into English. He was friendly with D. H. Lawrence, Middleton Murry, Katherine Mansfield and Leonard Woolf.

'And I the while . . .': lines 5–6 of 'Work without Hope'.

Ancient Mariner. The quotation is lines 377–9 (pt. V.)

In the original, 'width of sympathy' is connected by a line to 'e.g. flea on Bardolph's nose' on Forster's opposite page, p. 87 here.

Coleridge on Shakespeare. Forster's page numbers in this section refer to *Lectures and Notes on Shakespeare and the Other English Poets* by Samuel Taylor Coleridge: Now first collected by T. Ashe (London, George Bell & Sons, 1884).

'one of the invisible inhabitants . . .': This is not in Coleridge's Lecture IX of 1811, but Ashe has the gist of it (p. 140).

86   'because dead as a poet': Forster originally wrote 'because he had died as a poet'.

'All thoughts, all passions': The first stanza of Coleridge's 'Love'.

'Love is a desire . . .': Ashe, p. 95 (Coleridge's Lecture VII of 1811). Ashe gives the passage as a quotation made by Coleridge; so does T. H. Raysor (Everyman Edition of Coleridge's *Shakespearean Criticism* (1960), vol. 2, p. 106). Raysor adds in a footnote:

'This Platonic definition of love derives directly from the *Symposium*'.)

'Coleridge's 7th and incomparably best lecture': Henry Crabb Robinson's diary (Raysor, vol. 2, p. 171).

'Shakespeare makes it . . .' should read 'Our poet . . . a point for which Shakespeare . . .' (Ashe, p. 98; Raysor, vol. 2, p. 108).

Genevieve is the heroine of Coleridge's poem 'Love' (1799).

'it seems to me . . . possibility': Ashe, pp. 217–18. This is a quotation from a Coleridge lecture of 1818, 'Poetry, the Drama, and Shakespeare'.

The two 'Ode to Dejection' headings (pp. 86 and 87) are placed by Forster in boxes connected by a line.

87   'Flea on Bardolph's nose'. The quotations here, and the reference to Shakespeare's wit, are in Ashe, pp. 73–5.

'Pure morals'. To expand Forster's rather cryptic quotations here, it is worth quoting in full the passage to which he is referring, from Lecture I, 1811: 'Another cause of false criticism is the greater purity of morality in our present age, compared to the last. Our notions upon this subject are sometimes carried to excess, particularly among those who in print affect to enforce the value of a high standard. Far be it from me to depreciate that value; but let me ask, who now will venture to read a number of the "Spectator", or of the "Tatler", to his wife and daughters, without first examining it to make sure that it contains no word which might, in our day, offend the delicacy of female ears, and shock feminine susceptibility? Even our theatres, the representations at which usually reflect the morals of the period, have taken a sort of domestic turn, and while the performances at them may be said, in some sense, to improve the heart, there is no doubt that they vitiate the taste. The effect is bad, however good the cause.' (Ashe, p. 37; Raysor, vol. 2, pp. 34–5.) Elsewhere, Coleridge makes a rather different point (or speaks less obliquely): 'It is my earnest desire – my passionate endeavour, – to enforce at various times and by various arguments and instances the close and reciprocal connection of just taste with pure morality.' ('Poetry, the Drama, and Shakespeare', 1818. Ashe, p. 225.)

Forster's view of Joyce's *Ulysses* (1922) was very mixed. He reviewed it on 12 March 1926 (*New Leader*, pp. 13–14), calling it 'this epic of grubbiness and disillusion' yet conceding it to be 'technically . . . the most remarkable book of our times'. His conclusion was that *Ulysses* was 'a huge and interesting attempt to write a new novel . . . writers have much to learn from it. But it is not a book for readers, and it is not the book of the age. Too narrow-minded for that: too ignorant of goodness; too super-stitious about the body.' His own copy of it (Sixth Printing, Shakespeare & Co., Paris, August 1925) has in Forster's hand, on a blank page near the beginning, this quotation from *Tristram Shandy*: 'There are others again who will draw a man's character from no other helps in the world, but merely from his evacuations; but this gives a very incorrect outline – unless indeed you take a sketch of his repletions too, and by correcting one drawing from the other compound one good figure out of them both. I should have no objection to this method, but that I think it must smell too strong of the lamp, and be rendered still more operose by forcing you to have an eye to the rest of his *Non-naturals*.'

Shaw's *Saint Joan* appeared in 1924. A copy of it (published in Leipzig in 1924) appears to have been the only Shaw work which Forster acquired for himself, though he inherited a copy of *Cashel Byron's Profession* from his Aunt Laura.

John Addington Symonds (1840–93). Cf. pp. 224–7, where Forster copies out material from Symonds's Autobiography.

88 The family tree is that of Forster's family on his mother's (paternal) side. The name 'Richard' (to the left of 'John Whichelo') is very faint, as if Forster had quickly blotted it; he was John Whichelo's brother. (*Vide* the full family tree at the beginning of P. N. Furbank's *E. M. Forster: A Life*. The 'vulgar woman' was Elizabeth Young (b. 1804), whose children are not recorded there.)

The detail about Richard Mayle Whichelo is recorded by Forster in a very small hand at the bottom of his page.

Dulness! The lines are in fact *Dunciad*, I, 145–54. James Suther-land's Twickenham Edition of *The Dunciad* (1943) has 'makes their aim', and a rather different punctuation. One notes another nasty crack at J. B. Priestley.

89 *Henry James.* In *The Letters of Henry James*, ed. Percy Lubbock (London, Macmillan, 1920) the page references are as follows:
(i) vol. I, p. 228 (to Edmund Gosse, 13 December 1894). The underlining is Forster's.
(ii) vol. I, p. 278 (to Grace Norton, 25 December 1897). (The text reads 'My view of his . . .'; there are no commas after 'soul' and 'time'; James places dots after 'screws'.)
(iii) vol. I, pp. 204–5 (to Robert Louis Stevenson, 17 February 1893). The underlining is Forster's.

John Collier published during the 1930s poems, short stories and novels. The 'book of selections' referred to here is *The Scandal and Credulities of John Aubrey*, ed. John Collier (London, Peter Davies, 1931). Collier gave Forster a copy of it in 1931. It prints a selection of Aubrey's Brief Lives, and has an introduction both quirky and very sure of itself.

90 'Nixon'. J. E. Nixon, an eccentric don at King's when Forster was an undergraduate.

'Bob Trevelyan'. R. C. Trevelyan (1872–1951), poet, translator of the classics, and close friend of Forster's since his early days at Cambridge. He and his wife Bessie had a house at Holmbury St Mary, near West Hackhurst. The quotation is presumably from a letter to Forster from Trevelyan, à propos his son Julian (b. 1910), the painter.

Bray is on the Thames near Maidenhead. Siegfried Sassoon first met Frank Schuster in 1917 (when Schuster was already well past sixty), at a luncheon given by Osbert Sitwell. At that time he had an 'elegant house in Old Queen Street, Westminster'; Sassoon describes him as 'wealthy, a superfine gastronomist, and a giver of superb parties'; he was also a lover of concerts and opera. (Siegfried Sassoon, *Siegfried's Journey* (1946), pp. 122–6.)

Love of Animals. G. J. Renier's *The English: Are They Human?* was published in 1931. Chapter Three ('Their Dumb Masters') is concerned with 'Animal Worship in England'; Renier, a Dutch historian and journalist who had spent seventeen years in England, does not really deal with Forster's 'point', but does give plenty of examples of British pro-animal attitudes. Forster reviewed the book (*Spectator*, 27 June 1931), calling it 'acute and witty', also 'astringent': 'The earlier chapters are the more amusing, and I particularly commend them to men who pride themselves on their sense of humour and to women who prefer animals to men.' The poet Victoria Sackville-West, wife of Harold Nicolson and close friend of Virginia Woolf, was a great animal lover.

Voltaire's *Les Singularités de la Nature* appeared in Geneva in 1769. 'It appears above all difficult that the organs of generation may not be destined to perpetuate the species. This mechanism is very admirable; but the sensation which nature has attached to this mechanism is more admirable still. Epicurus has to admit that the pleasure is divine, and that pleasure is a final cause by which are unceasingly produced those sensitive creatures who have not been able to give themselves sensation.'

91 The sentence about Poe is from *The Complete Poems of Edgar Allan Poe*, with a Critical Introduction by Charles F. Richardson (New

York and London, G. P. Putnam's Sons, 1908), p. lii. Richardson was Professor of English at Dartmouth College.

'Ah no, ah no'. Forster included this rhythmic phrase in his 1935 essay 'Word-Making and Sound-Taking' (collected in 1936 in *Abinger Harvest*); there he mentions 'Schumann's piano quintet'.

The Disarmament Conference was in session at this time (February 1932) at the League of Nations Headquarters at Geneva. The *News Chronicle* (25 February 1932) reported that the general debate on disarmament had ended on February 24, with various committee meetings to follow. Contrary to the impression given by Forster's reference, the report was headed 'Geneva Optimism'.

Forster met his lifelong close friend Bob Buckingham in 1930. He writes 'Bob' with two capital B's – perhaps, in the context, a joking reference to 'Bob', the slang word for 'shilling' (present 5p.).

'Florence' was Forster's old friend Florence Barger, the wife of his Cambridge contemporary George Barger. The bracketed '(generous)' is in the original an addition made by Forster below 'reckless'.

92   Dick Sheppard (Rev. Hugh Richard Lawrie Sheppard, died 1937) was a well-known London clergyman who published popular religious books. From 1914 to 1927 he was vicar of St Martin's-in-the Fields, later becoming Canon and Precentor of St Paul's Cathedral and a Chaplain to the King. Sheppard was a noted philanthropist and pacifist: in October 1934 he sent a letter to the press inviting people who objected to another war to write to him saying so; this led to the foundation of the Peace Pledge Union in June 1935.

Maude Royden (b. 1876) was closely involved with the Women's Suffrage Movement and from 1917 to 1920 was Assistant Preacher at the City Temple, London. She also published popular religious books.

The 'offer' made by Sheppard, Maude Royden (and Dr Herbert Gray, a Presbyterian minister) took the form of a letter to the editor of the *News Chronicle* (the new name of the *Daily News* from 1930). It appeared, with their photographs, on the front page of the issue for 26 February 1932, under the headlines 'Startling Stop-the-War Offer, Church Leaders to stand unarmed between combatants'. The war was that between China and Japan; the Japanese had recently attacked Shanghai, and in their letter the three (as summarised by the editor) 'explain that they have offered themselves as the nucleus of a Peace Army to the League of

Nations. *They volunteer to place themselves unarmed between the combatants.* They appeal for volunteers to join them and state that many women are thinking of doing so.' Sheppard, Gray and Maude Royden, all pacifists, believed that the League of Nations could only operate to stop the war by shunning the use of force itself.

Wormwood Scrubs is a prison near Shepherds Bush in West London. I have found no mention of the case Forster refers to in the *News Chronicle* of this period, though each issue carried a 'Law and Police' section.

93 'Birkenhead'. Presumably the first Earl of Birkenhead (formerly F. E. Smith), who died in 1930. He was Lord Chancellor (1919–22) and Secretary for India (1924–8).

Sir Herbert Samuel, later Viscount Samuel, was a Liberal politician. Forster corresponded with him in 1953 on the subject of homosexuality, which he found 'incomprehensible and utterly disgusting', though deserving more public tolerance.

Marjorie Napier (1894–1978) was the daughter of Forster's paternal cousin Mabel and Sir Lennox Napier.

P. N. Furbank relates Forster's references to taking 'someone one loves' to pay a call and to his two years of 'happiness' to the first two years of Forster's friendship with Bob Buckingham, in which Forster came to terms with Buckingham's prospective marriage to May Hockey. In the early summer of 1931 Forster had taken Buckingham on a car trip to the West Country, calling on Lytton Strachey and Dora Carrington at Hungerford, and attempting also to call on John Collier who lived nearby. (P. N. Furbank, *E. M. Forster: A Life*, II, 167–9.)

In the original, the passage 'I have to read . . . The End' is written obliquely across the top of Forster's page.

'hari kari': A standard British corruption of 'hara-kiri'.

94 Humbert Wolfe (d. 1940) was Deputy Secretary at the Ministry of Labour as well as a poet. He was made CBE in 1918 and CB in 1925.

'So frowned he . . .' (*Hamlet*, I, i, 62–3. Shakespeare has 'Polacks'.). Forster visited Cracow (from Rumania) in 1932, meeting a Polish lady whose attentions later became too pressing – which perhaps accounts for his reflections on women on pp. 92–3.

95 Sir Malcolm Lyall Darling (1880–1969) was a friend of Forster's from his Cambridge days onwards. He joined the Indian Civil Service and for a time was tutor to the Indian prince who later

became Rajah of Dewas State Senior (and to whom Forster was private secretary in 1921). He married in 1909; his wife Jessica ('Josie') died in 1932. The passage is about their surviving son, Colin Darling.

Forster discusses the same movement of this Beethoven concerto (no. 4) in his essay of 1935, 'Word-Making and Sound-Taking.'

96   *Pip Pip!* This short collection of topical 'gems' has its modern equivalents in Sunday newspapers' 'Sayings of the Week' or *Private Eye*'s column 'Pseuds' Corner'. Forster's phrase was once middle-class slang for 'goodbye' ('Tootle-oo, pip pip!'); 'the pips' were also a BBC time signal, serving often (as here, ironically) to preface an announcement.

Ralph Straus was a writer and literary agent.

L. A. G. Strong (1896–1958) wrote verse, popular novels and belles-lettres.

97   Among Forster's books at his death was Voltaire's *Histoire de Charles XII et Histoire de Russie sous Pierre le Grand* (Paris, Firmin Didot Frères, 1856); '[E. M. Forster at West Hackhurst]' is written inside the cover, in Forster's hand. The passage about Patkul is in bk. 3, pp. 97–8. The passage (boxed by Forster, italicized here) 'son courage ... des hommes' is linked in the original to 'irony'; 'qu'il avait compté ... au supplice' is linked to 'pathos', as is 'qui l'embrassa ... en pleurant.' The underlinings of 'seigneur très-clement' and 'traître à la patrie' are Forster's; 'le dernier rigueur' should be 'la dernière rigueur'; 'convulsions de frayeurs' should be 'convulsions de frayeur'; 'a haute voix' should be 'à haute voix'; 'l'ordre très' should be 'l'ordre très-exprès'; 'et sauve son roi' should be 'et serve son roi'; 'à la trahison' should be 'de la trahison'; à cause de' should be 'à ceux de'.

'Charles XII, forgetting that Patkul was the czar's ambassador and remembering only that he was born his subject, ordered the council of war to judge him with the utmost rigour. He was condemned to be broken alive and quartered. A chaplain came to tell him he had to die, without telling him the nature of the punishment. Then this man who had braved death in so many battles, finding himself alone with a priest and his courage no longer upheld by glory or anger, sources of human daring, burst bitterly into tears on the chaplain's breast. He was engaged to a saxon lady named Mme d'Einstedel who had birth, merit and beauty, and whom he had counted on marrying at almost the same time as he was to be executed. He asked the chaplain to find her and console her, and to assure her that he would die full of tenderness towards her. When he had been led to the place of execution, and when he saw the wheels and the stakes laid out, he fell into convulsions of fear and threw himself into the arms of the clergyman, who embraced him, threw his cloak around him, and wept. Then, a Swedish officer read in a loud voice a paper in which were these words: – Be it known, that the express order of his majesty our most clement lord is that this man, a traitor to the fatherland, be broken on the wheel and quartered in payment for his crimes and as an example to others. Let each man beware of treason, and serve [not 'save'] his king faithfully!

At these words 'Most clement prince': what clemency, said Patkul; and at these, 'traitor to the fatherland', 'Alas', said he, 'I have served it too well.' He received sixteen blows, and suffered the longest and most frightful punishment imaginable. So perished the unfortunate Jean Reginold Patkul, ambassador and general of the emperor of Russia.

98   George Arliss was a film star of the 1930s who portrayed such historical figures as Napoleon, Wellington and Disraeli.

The couplet is written in a small hand obliquely across the bottom right of Forster's page.

'Deerleap' is Deerleap Wood to the east of West Hackhurst. It lies above Wootton, just south of the railway (Ry) from Guildford to Dorking. Silent Pool is between Albury and Shere. Paddington is a mill pond very near Abinger Hammer.

Ernest Read was the son of the Abinger Hammer butcher, and an amateur archaeologist.

Stephen Tennant (b. 1906) was a nephew of Lady Margot Asquith, and 'a well-known aesthete' (Furbank, *E. M. Forster: A Life*, II, 184). He was a friend of Siegfried Sassoon and lived at Wilsford Manor near Salisbury, where Forster visited him in the Spring of 1931. He suffered intermittently from the effects of tuberculosis in the early 1930s.

As a boy, Forster attended a small preparatory school at Eastbourne, Kent House, whose headmaster was C. P. Hutchinson. The bracketed phrase ('une vie') is presumably a reference to Maupassant's book of that title (1883).

99   *Camilla* (1796), by Fanny Burney. See *Horace Walpole's Correspondence*, ed. W. S. Lewis (New Haven, Yale University Press (1961), vol. 31, p. 403). Lewis's text has: 'I don't care to say how little – alas! she has reversed . . .'; 'its own utility'; 'don't want'; 'Miss B. knew the world,'; 'and now since she . . .'.

'*Remorse* . . .' The quotation is from ch. 15 of Isherwood's *Mr Norris Changes Trains* (1935). (Penguin edition, 1942, p. 167.)

The two quotations from Hemingway are from *A Farewell to Arms* (1929), the first from ch. 27, the second from ch. 34. (In the second, Hemingway's text reads 'at the broken places', and there is no comma after 'too'.)

Prostate Gland. Of the remark 'Oh my God', Oliver Stallybrass in a manuscript note conjectured that 'Forster seems to have shared the widespread belief that a prostate operation results in impotence'.

100   Hardy died in 1928 and was buried in Westminster Abbey (the Church of our Lady and St Peter, hence 'far Peter's monastery'). Robert Bridges (1844–1930) was at that time Poet Laureate and lived on Boar's Hill outside Oxford; he had a reputation, at least at first meetings, for grumpiness. 'Jack and his apes' is presumably a reference to Sir John Squire and his 'Georgian' literary associates. One of Hardy's best-known poems is called 'Drummer Hodge'. 'Roger' is the painter and art critic Roger Fry (who died in 1934), Margery his sister.

'As he laye . . .': *Aubrey's Brief Lives*. Isaac Barrow (1630–77) was a Cambridge professor and, from 1672, Master of Trinity.

Melville. The first quotation ('I will not add . . .') comes at the end of ch. 124 of *Mardi*, Babbalanja speaking. (Vol. 3 of *The Writings of Herman Melville*, The Northwestern–Newberry Edition, Evanston & Chicago (1970), p. 390.)

The second quotation ('Love is sad . . .') comes at the end of ch. 188 of *Mardi*, said by Babbalanja's guide, in his vision. (*Ibid.*, p. 636.)

'I stand for the heart'. Melville, letter to Nathaniel Hawthorne, 1? June 1851. (*The Letters of Herman Melville*, ed. M. R. Davis & W. H. Gilman, New Haven, Yale University Press (1960), p. 129.) After 'head!' the full quotation runs: 'I had rather be a fool with a heart, than Jupiter Olympus with his head. The reason the mass of men fear God, and *at bottom dislike* Him, is because they rather distrust His heart, and fancy him all brain like a watch.' Forster used the quotation later, in the 'Gokul Ashtami' section of *The Hill of Devi* (1953).

'How many avenues . . .' Norman Douglas, *Together* (1923), p. 84, end of Section V, 'Blumenegg'.

101   *Webster*. Flamineo speaking to Vittoria (V, vi, 252–3). Forster reviewed '*The White Divel* at Cambridge' in the *New Statesman*, 20 March 1920 (pp. 708–9). Forster praised the Marlowe Society production as 'one of the best Elizabethan performances that we

are likely to see for a long time'. Webster's works were edited in four volumes (1927) by F. L. Lucas.

'Do you reason yourself with a beast? . . .': These two 'dream-sentences', written obliquely in the right margin of Forster's page, are linked by a line to his 'dream of pissing' on the page opposite in the original, p. 102 here.

102   Osbert Burdett, a fellow member with Forster and Desmond MacCarthy of the Committee of the London Library, published many books about literary figures, including one on Sydney Smith (1934) and the volume on Blake in the *English Men of Letters* series (1926).

103   *C.I.D.:* Criminal Investigation Division (of the police).

The quotation from Malory's *Le Morte d'Arthur* in fact comes from bk. XXI, ch. 3. The second sentence is quoted incomplete; in full it runs: '. . . of serpents, and worms, and wild beasts, foul and horrible; and suddenly the King thought the wheel turned up-so-down, and he fell among the serpents, and every beast . . .' (*Le Morte darthur*, vol. II, Macmillan Library of English Classics, 1900).

'And the yellow-skirted Fayes . . .': Milton, 'On the Morning of Christ's Nativity', stanza XXVI (lines 235–6).

104   'Under the shady roof . . .': Milton, 'Arcades', lines 88–90.

'you demi-puppets . . .': Shakespeare, *The Tempest*, V, ii, 36–8.

'well you know . . .': Shakespeare, *The Merry Wives of Windsor*, IV, iv, 35–8.

The Cerne Giant is a huge figure of Romano-British origin, 180 feet long, carved in a hill-side close to the village of Cerne Abbas north of Dorchester, Dorset.

Ezekiel. 'The creatures', I, iv; 'wheels', I, xv ff.
The 'sword' image: XXI, 10–32.
The 'orgy' covers XXIV, 1–14.
The 'eulogy' (and lamentation) for Tyre is actually XXVII; XXVIII, 12–14 is a eulogy of the King of Tyre.
The 'valley of dry bones' is actually XXXVII.

Zechariah. The 'magic and meaningless' section (though a Christian might not agree with Forster) is I, 8–11.

105   'This morning . . .': Stisted is in Essex, four miles east of Braintree. The rectory there was the home of Forster's grandparents, the Rev. Charles Forster and his wife Laura (Thornton), and his father was born in it. (See Forster, *Marianne Thornton* (1956), pp. 162–6.) Perhaps Forster was revisiting Stisted on the way to

Fritton Hythe, the home near Yarmouth of his friend Edward Hilton Young, later Lord Kennet (1879–1960), Minister of Health, 1931–5.

Subjects (i). 'W. Blunt'. Wilfred Scawen Blunt (1840–1922). *The Lanchester Tradition* was published in 1913; its author, G. F. Bradby (1863–1947), was a housemaster at Rugby School.

'Then went to Brussels . . .': At this time (1936–7) W. H. Auden and Christopher Isherwood frequently travelled to Ostend, Brussels and Amsterdam. Forster presumably passed through Brussels in 1937 on his way to participate in a four-day meeting of writers held in July in Paris, on the subject of 'The Immediate Future of Literature'; here he gave an address in French. He also visited the Paris Exhibition (see his essay 'The Last Parade' (1937), collected in *Two Cheers for Democracy* (1951).

'Christopher's North-West Passage'. The description of volunteers in the General Strike occurs at the end of ch. IV of Christopher Isherwood's autobiography *Lions and Shadows* (1938). Forster's phrase is not used there; perhaps he is thinking of the book, subtitled 'An Education in the Twenties', as (in Sterne's phrase from *Tristram Shandy*) a 'North-West Passage to the Intellectual world'.

Subjects (ii). Lord Grey was presumably Edward Grey, 1st Viscount of Fallodon (1862–1933) who in 1927 published *Charm of Birds*.

Bewick. Thomas Bewick (1753–1828), famous for his wood-engravings, particularly in his *History of British Birds* (1797 and 1804). Forster had inherited bird-books by Bewick from his Aunt Laura.

Peter Scott (b. 1905), son of Capt. Robert Falcon Scott, RN, and Kathleen Scott (later remarried, to Edward Hilton Young, 1st Lord Kennet); bird-painter, author of books on birds, Founder of the Wildfowl Trust.

Subjects (iii). Charles Mauron ('They give nothing and receive nothing'); he lived in St Rémy in Provence.

Sir Max Beerbohm (1872–1956), wit, caricaturist and essayist.

Desmond MacCarthy (1887–1952), Knighted in 1951, writer and journalist and, in the 1920s, Literary Editor of the *New Statesman*.

Subjects (iv). The triad of Hindu deities. Siva and Vishnu are the gods of destruction and preservation respectively, the latter being the most worshipped; Brahma, least worshipped of the three, is also the hardest to define simply, but is connected with the activity of prayer and the notion of success.

Ibsen's Letters. 'I am conscious ...': Written to Björnson 16 September 1864, from Rome (*The Correspondence of Henrik Ibsen,* translation edited by Mary Morison (1904), p. 77. The punctuation here is slightly different from Forster's.)

'An aesthete ...': Written to Björnson 12 September 1865, from Ariccia near Rome. (*Ibid.,* pp. 86–7.)

106 'All that is delightful ...': Written to Brandes 20 September 1870, from Dresden; Brandes was in Rome at the time. (*Ibid.,* p. 205. Between the first and second sentences comes: 'And then the glorious aspiration after liberty – that is at an end now.')

'The state'. Written to Brandes 17 February 1871, from Dresden. (*Ibid.,* p. 209. 'Admiration' should be 'culmination'; after 'all religion will fall' comes: 'Neither the conceptions of morality nor those of art are eternal.')

According to a note by Oliver Stallybrass, Forster had lectured on Ibsen in Scotland and at Manchester in November 1928.

'H.E.': Holy Eucharist.

Cowley to Evelyn. The passage is from Essay No. 5, 'The Garden', dedicated to Evelyn (Abraham Cowley, *The Essays and Other Prose Writings,* ed. Alfred B. Gough, Oxford, Clarendon Press (1915), p. 168). Evelyn had dedicated to Cowley the 2nd edition (1666) of his *Kalendarium Hortense, or The Gardener's Almanac;* this essay is Cowley's 'acknowledgement of the compliment' (*ibid.,* p. 341). The 'hired house' was the Porch House, Chertsey (very near Weybridge). After 'the study of Nature' Forster omits two lines of verse and another sentence.

107 *Bunyan.* The passage describing the death of Mr Badman's wife may be found on p. 275 of the Everyman edition (n.d.) of *Grace Abounding to the Chief of Sinners and The Life and Death of Mr Badman.* This edition has no chapter divisions and its punctuation is slightly different; for 'follow in his steps' it has 'follow his steps'. Forster's dots indicate one omitted sentence.

La Bruyère (1645–96). The quoted passage is from the essay 'Du Coeur', which is the fourth essay (though not so numbered) in his sequence entitled 'Les Caractères ou les Moeurs de ce siècle'. (*Caractères* par Jean de la Bruyère, Paris, Nelson, n.d., p. 174.) Forster owned a two-volume edition published in Paris in 1769. ('One opens a devotional book, and it moves one; one opens another book, which is gallant, and it makes its impression. Dare I say that only the heart reconciles contrary things, and admits things incompatible?')

Death of John Cox. Everyman edition (above), pp. 293–4. Its wording is in five places slightly different from Forster's.

108 *Marx-cum-Engels.* In this section Forster is translating, summarising and commenting on *Sur la Littérature et l'Art: Karl Marx, Friedrich Engels*, trans. and ed. by Jean Fréville (Paris (1936), in the series 'Les Grands Textes du Marxism').

'A man cannot ...' (Marx): Fréville, p. 60 (section called 'Le développement de l'art'). Forster's phrase 'in his own higher conditions' translates 'à un niveau supérieur'. *Re* the Greeks, the French text says nothing about 'healthy': it posits an opposition between 'enfants mal élevés' and 'enfants vieillots'.

Renaissance (Engels): Fréville, p. 69.

Goethe (Engels): Fréville, p. 83; 'to the doing of little jobs' perhaps translates 'des menus plaisirs', which is in French in Engels' original (German) text.

109 Shakespeare (Marx): Fréville, p. 87. The reference to Timon of Athens is Forster's addition.

Comedy (Marx): Fréville, pp. 89–90 (section 28, entitled 'La comédie, dernière phase d'une forme historique'). 'Les dieux de la Grèce [...] eurent à subir une seconde mort dans les Dialogues de Lucien.' ('The gods of Greece had to suffer a second death in the dialogues of Lucian'.) 'Pourquoi cette marche de l'histoire? Pour que l'humanité se separe *joyeusement* de son passé. ('Why this march of History? So that humanity will separate joyously from its past.')

'New masked by the old, ...' (Marx): Fréville, p. 91.

'Les hommes font leur propre histoire [...] mais dans des conditions directement données et heritées du passé.' ('Men make their own history ... but in conditions directly given by, and inherited from, the past.')

'Luther St Paul [etc.]' i.e. the first takes over the role, or borrows the language, of the second.

'Complètement ...': Fréville, p. 92. 'Elle oubliait' should be 'elle avait oubliée'; 'époche' should be 'époque'. ('completely absorbed by the production of wealth and by the peaceful struggle of competition, she forgot that the ghosts of the Roman epoch had watched over her cradle.')

Marx's poems: Fréville, p. 113; 'an unattainable fairy palace' translates 'quelque lointain palais feérique'.

Carlyle (Engels): Fréville, pp. 118–19.

Disraeli (Marx and Engels): Fréville, p. 122. Disraeli's party was actually called 'Young England'.

'Political opinions': Fréville, p. 148.

'Materialist method' (Engels): Fréville, p. 153.

Forster's essay 'The Ivory Tower' was published in *The London Mercury* (Xmas Number, 1938), pp. 119–30.

110 *Hitler* on 'Art is grounded in the people'. (Hitler's actual phrase was 'Denn in der Zeit liegt keine kunst begründet, sondern nur in den Volkern.' That is, literally: 'For no art is grounded in time, but only in peoples.') The speech was given on 18 July 1937 when Hitler opened the House of German Art (which replaced the former 'Glass Palace') in Munich; the *Völkischer Beobachter* published its text the following day. The original is reprinted in *Hitler: Reden und Proklamationen 1932–1945*, ed. Max Domarus (Munich, 1965), I, 705–10; a translation appears in *The Speeches of Adolph Hitler, April 1922–August 1939*, ed. Norman H. Baynes (New York, 1969), I, 584–91.

Re the references to 'asylum/prison' for 'degenerate artists' in Forster's version, Baynes (*op. cit.*, p. 590) translates Hitler thus: 'Here only two possibilities are open: either these "artists" do really see things in this way and believe in that which they represent – then one has but to ask how the defect in vision arose, and if it is hereditary the Minister for the Interior will have to see to it that so ghastly a defect of vision shall not be allowed to perpetuate itself – or if they do *not* believe in the reality of such impressions but seek on other grounds to impose upon the nation by this humbug, then it is a matter for a criminal court'. Forster's 'prison' fits the latter alternative well enough, but 'asylum' is too kind for the former, which is surely sterilisation or even liquidation.

Julian Huxley and A. C. Haddon: *We Europeans: A Survey of 'Racial' Problems* (London, Jonathan Cape, 1935). Forster's suggestion that Hitler's ideas be compared with Huxley's (and Haddon's) is made in order to discredit the former's doctrine of a German racial identity: Huxley and Haddon scout the notion of a 'Nordic race' with superior qualities (p. 276), attributing it to 'self-interest and wish-fulfilment'. They conclude that 'race' is 'a pseudo-scientific rather than a scientific term' with 'no precise or definable meaning' (p. 262).

Much of the material in this Hitler section is used again by Forster in his 'Three Anti-Nazi Broadcasts' of 1940 (collected in *Two Cheers for Democracy*, 1951) and in *Nordic Twilight* (London, Macmillan, 1940).

111   *Coriolanus Ouverture* [*sic*]: The analysis Forster refers to occurs in vol. IV (Illustrative Music), of *Essays in Musical Analysis* (Oxford, 1936, pp. 43–5) by Donald Francis Tovey, Reid Professor of Music, Edinburgh. No reference is in fact made to any 'sweet tune for the ladies'. Vol. I appeared in 1935, and in it Tovey dedicated the entire series to Forster's old friend R. C. Trevelyan.

112   The reference to Carlton House Terrace occurs in *How We Celebrate the Coronation: A Word to London's Visitors* (1937) by Robert Byron (1905–41).

'Mrs. Jeffrey.' P. N. Furbank suggests this may have been the woman who looked after Forster at his London flat.

113   In the original, Forster encloses the quotation from Ruskin with lines in such a way that it looks like a motto (or picture) hanging on a wall. See John Ruskin, *The Stones of Venice* (1851–53) vol. 1, ch. 1 ('The Quarry'), section 38.

At the Alexandria camp . . .': *History of the British Expedition to Egypt*, by Robert Thomas Wilson, Lieutenant Colonel of Cavalry in His Britannic Majesty's Service (London, 1802), p. 61, footnote. Wilson became a general, and was knighted, later. His text differs slightly from Forster in a few details of punctuation; he writes 'however' after 'camp', and 'in a boat' rather than 'on a boat'.

William Gifford, *The Works of Ben Jonson, with a Memoir* (1838). In the new edition (1853) this quotation is found as a footnote to p. 71 (introductory 'Memoirs of Ben Jonson by William Gifford'). Wallington, a very large estate now owned by the National Trust, was the Northumberland home of the Trevelyan family; it is near Kirkharle, twenty miles north-west of Newcastle-upon-Tyne. After the death of the historian G. M. Trevelyan on 21 July 1962, Forster wrote in his Diary (25 July 1962): 'At what date did I visit Wallington [?] When Sir G.O.T. was alive [he died in 1928] and told me he had thrown Madame Bovary out of the train between Piacenza and Palma [*sic*]? On that same date G.M.T. climbed a perpendicular Border Wall, hanging on cracks by his fingers.' Sir G. O. Trevelyan was Lord Macaulay's nephew.

'Tu mihi . . .': These lines, belonging to the 'Sulpicia' sequence, are of uncertain authorship, but generally attributed not to Propertius but to Tibullus: lines 11–12 of a poem variously listed as bk. 3, no. 19 and bk. 4, no. 13 (see *Catullus, Tibullus and Per-vigilium Veneris*, Loeb Classical Library (1913, revised edition, 1950), p. 336). Later editors have not included bks. 3 and 4 in editions of Tibullus, since their place in the canon is dubious. Postgate, the Loeb editor, translates the lines: 'For me thou art repose from cares, light even in night's darkness, a throng amid the solitudes.' They perhaps express something of Forster's feelings for Bob Buckingham.

Kenneth Searight was a young Army officer (also a poet and homosexual) whom Forster met on the boat out to India in 1912, and later visited at his regimental camp in Peshawar. An entry in Forster's Diary (3 July 1920) records the ending of their friendship, which the previous year had been warm but fizzled out in unsatisfactory letters and arrangements to meet.

Early Greek Science. Forster is referring here to Benjamin Farrington's *Science and Politics in the Ancient World* (1939).

'Ionia . . . experimented freely'. In fact, on p. 23, Farrington concedes as 'good as far as it goes' the view that 'the Greeks . . . indulged in much physical speculation but [. . .] did not establish a tradition of systematic experiment'.

114 'Royal Lie' [otherwise called the 'Golden Lie']. See Farrington, p. 130: 'the notorious Royal Lie of the *Republic* in which Plato taught that the human race by divine ordinance was composed of three types, golden men like himself who were to legislate and govern, silver men to be the police and soldiers, and iron men to do the work'.

Farrington on Cornford. Forster is surely arrogant (and ignorant) here. Farrington was Professor of Classics at Swansea; he refers in ch. 10 to F. M. Cornford's *Before and after Socrates*, and is hardly likely not to have known Cornford's *From Religion to Philosophy* (1912).

Plato and Socrates. See Farrington, p. 120. Farrington's view is that Plato's Socrates 'gives us reliable evidence of the painter, not of the subject. The Socrates of the *Dialogues* was the contribution of Plato to thought, not to Socrates.' (For Plato, Socrates' wisdom was 'sound' because Apollo had approved it. But Farrington is sceptical whether the real Socrates was such a divinely approved – i.e. state-approved – thinker.)

Lucretius *De Rerum Natura.* W. H. D. Rouse (Loeb edition, Heinemann, 1924) translates thus: 'Moreover, avarice and the blind lust of distinction, which drives wretched men to transgress the bounds of law, and sometimes by sharing and scheming crime to strive night and day with exceeding toil to climb the pinnacle of power, these sores of life in no small degree are fed by the fear of death.'

'Vulnera vitae'. See Farrington, p. 220: 'For the false doctrines of the state cults . . . Lucretius, with that gift for metaphor in which his genius is so frequently revealed, coined the phrase "wounds of life" (*vulnera vitae*).'4 Farrington's note 4 (p. 233) says: 'See Bk. V, 1197, and Bk. 3, 63'. Forster refers only to the second passage.

Rev. John Newton. The quotation is from *Messiah: Fifty Expository Discourses on the series of Scriptural Passages, which form the subject of the celebrated Oratorio of Handel, Preached in the Years 1784 and 1785 in the Parish Church of St Mary Woolnoth, Lombard Street; by John Newton, Rector* (2 vols, London, 1786), I, 64–5 (Sermon IV – The Lord Coming to his Temple). The punctuation differs slightly from Forster's.

115   *Familiar Conversation.* These remarks are not included in *Letters and Conversational Remarks by the late Rev. John Newton During the last Eighteen Years of his Life*, compiled by John Campbell (London, 1809).

116   *Voltaire.* (i) 'My friend, one must have — in order to create a good tragedy: now at eighty-four one no longer has —'
(ii) 'Woe to the man who doesn't correct himself and his works: one must correct oneself, even at eighty. I don't like old men who say: "I have become set in my ways." Old fool, take another set.'
(iii) 'His intention, apparently, was to be hanged; he is a man who seeks all sorts of elevation.'

Forster owned a six-volume edition of Pope published in 1764; his line-numberings presumably adhere to this, and are the same as the 1751 edition of *The Dunciad* to which I have referred. (In 'O when shall rise . . .', however, 1751 has 'cover' for 'shelter'; and in 'A place there is' it has 'leans' for 'lends'. Dunciad B (1742), in the Twickenham edition (1943), gives the same line-numbering as Forster, but with the readings 'cover' and 'leans' indicated above.

117   Arthur Hugh Clough, *Dipsychus* (1865). The title means 'in two minds'. Forster owned the 1878 edition of Clough's *Poems*; this, and all editions before the OUP one of 1951, had 'mild' in line 214, for which 'good', the reading of Clough's manuscript, was substituted in 1951.

The second quotation is from sc. X, lines 46–51.

The quotations from Lord Acton are from *A Lecture on the Study of History* (1895), originally given as a lecture at Cambridge that year. The first quotation is p. 7 ('Feed' should be 'fed'); the second (p. 118) is p. 13 ('as well as' should be 'as far as'); the last (beginning 'A historian') is p. 42.

118   Hughie Waterston was a local farmer, born at Hackhurst Farm. An entry in Forster's Diary (22 January 1935) indicates that

Waterston strongly attracted him. I have not located Bishop's Cross. In 1943 Waterston was at Oundle in Northamptonshire, where Forster visited him in March (see p. 151).

The passage from Acton marked with Forster's cross (†) is in the original connected to the quotation from *The Prelude*, exactly level on the opposite page (here p. 119). *Above* it, written sideways, is the section 'I glanced in these two books . . . has altered too drastically' (p. 119).

119   I am not sure why Forster refers to 'these two books of the Prelude', since the three quotations from Wordsworth's *The Prelude* all come from bk. XII (in the 1850 edition, which Forster owned.) Bk. XII of 1850 is however bk. XI in the original version of 1805; so perhaps Forster was comparing the two texts.

'inwardly oppressed . . .': *The Prelude* (1850), XII, 3–7.

'even in pleasure pleased . . .': *Ibid.*, 109–11.

'I could no more . . .': *Ibid.*, 60–7.

'Sonnet on Napoleon' (1803). The title, shared with other sonnets, is 'October 1803'; the first line is 'When, looking on the present face of things'. Forster quotes lines 5–7; there should be a colon after 'great' and a semi-colon after 'venerate'.

120   Stephen Spender's long poem *Vienna*, describing the defeat of the Social Democrats in Austria, was published in November 1934.

'*Human felicity*'. I have not traced this passage in Benjamin Franklin's voluminous output. The comment on him is from D. H. Lawrence, *Studies in Classic American Literature* (1924), Phoenix Edition (1964), pp. 13–14. There should be a full-stop after 'venery'.

The Church. This letter from Frank Vicary to Forster was written a month after they met.

Forster owned a six-volume edition of Mme de Sévigné's letters published in Paris in 1738. I have taken my details and pagination from *Lettres de Madame de Sevigné* (10 vols, Paris, 1820), which is different in details of punctuation and (in nine cases) of phrasing.

'Vous me demandez . . .': Letter 235, 16 March 1672, to her daughter, Mme de Grignan (II, 361–2). For 'fille', the 1820 text has 'enfant', for 'les épines qui s'y rencontrent' it has 'les épines dont elle est semée'; for 'vous ne direz' it has 'vous me direz', and it adds 'donc' after 'je veux'.

'You ask me, my dear daughter, if I always like life well: I swear to you that I find smarting sorrows in it, but I am still more disgusted by death; I find myself so unhappy to have to finish all this by it, that if I could go backwards I should ask nothing better. I find myself with an embarrassing commitment; I am embarked on life without my consent; I must leave it, that overwhelms me; and how shall I leave it, where, by what door? when will this be? in what frame of mind? will I suffer thousands of sorrows, which will make me die in despair? will I have a stroke? will I die by an accident? How shall I deal with God? what will I have to present to him? will dread and necessity be my return towards him? will I have no other feeling but fear? what can I hope? am I worthy of Paradise? am I worthy of Hell? What alternatives! What embarrassment! Nothing is so mad as to put one's salvation in doubt; but nothing is so natural, and the foolish life I lead is the easiest thing in the world to understand. I drown myself in these thoughts, and I find death so terrible that I hate life more because it leads me there than because of the thorns to be met with in it. You must not say that I wish to live for ever, not at all; but if someone had asked my opinion, I should have liked it well to have died in the arms of my nurse, it would have spared me many worries and given me Heaven very surely and easily; but let us speak of something else.'

121   'Je me suis . . .': Letter 152, 10 June 1671, to Mme de Grignan (II, 283.) The 1820 text has 'le plus natural du monde', 'et qu'on n'aime point', and 'il faut donc sortir de cet état'.

'I am neither for God nor the devil: this state wearies me, but between ourselves I find it the most natural in the world. One is not for the Devil, because one fears God, and at bottom one possesses a religious principle: one is also not for God, because his law seems hard, and one does not like to destroy oneself. That sums up the lukewarm, whose great number does not astonish me at all; I understand their reasons; but God hates them, one must escape from them, and there's the rub.'

'J'ai acheté . . .': Letter 137, 24 April 1671, to Mme de Grignan (II, 31–2). In the 1820 text the first sentence runs: 'un peu de vert, et c'est le violet qui domine.' This quotation is inserted by Forster at the bottom of his previous page.

'I have bought, to make me a dressing gown, some stuff like your last skirt; it is admirable, there's a little green in it but violet dominates; in a word, I succumbed. People wanted me to line it with fire-red, but I found that that had the air of a final impenitence; the outside is pure fragility, but the underpart would have been a decided flounce, which seemed to be against good manners, I decided in favour of white taffeta.'

Ibsen. Some of these quotations had, in fact, already been entered in the Commonplace Book (pp. 105–06).

'Sometimes' is an interlinear addition.

Quotation 1, 'willingless' [*sic*]; presumably a slip for 'willingness'.

122   Both 'dying' remarks are recorded in R. W. Ketton-Cremer, *Horace Walpole: A Biography* (Faber & Faber, 1940), Sir Robert Walpole's on p. 96, Mann's on p. 288.

'Sir Thomas Mann' is a slip for Sir Horace Mann.

'I almost think . . . now'. Horace Walpole to George Montague, 5 January 1766. (See *Horace Walpole's Correspondence*, ed. W. S. Lewis, vol. 10, Yale U.P. (1941), p. 192.) Lewis has 'Catherine de Medicis'.

'Squabbles and speeches'. This passage, with slightly different punctuation, is the last paragraph of a letter from Horace Walpole to George Montague, 4 (not 1) November, 1762. (See *The Letters of Horace Walpole*, ed. Mrs Paget Toynbee, vol. 4 (1904), p. 271.)

123   'Mr. Doddington . . . England.' Horace Walpole to the Earl of Strafford, 7 June 1760. (See *Horace Walpole's Correspondence*, ed. W. S. Lewis, vol. 35, Yale U.P. (1973), pp. 301–2.) Lewis has 'more than ever they had'.

'*Bigotry*'. Ernest Hemingway, *For Whom the Bell Tolls* (Cape, 1941), p. 159 (ch. 13). There is no comma after 'right'.

Wordsworth on Machinery. The quotation is in fact from Poem XLII (Sonnet on 'Steamboats, Viaducts, and Railways') of Wordsworth's 'Itinerary Poems of 1833', lines 4–8. 'A prophetic sense' should be 'that prophetic sense'; 'you' should be 'ye'.

'Salimmo su . . .': The last four lines of Dante's *Inferno*; the final line ends 'a riveder le stelle.' John D. Sinclair (*The Divine Comedy of Dante Alighieri* (Oxford University Press, 1971), vol. I, 'Inferno', p. 427) translates thus: 'We climbed up, he first and I second, so far that I saw through a round opening some of the fair things that heaven bears; and thence we came forth [to see again the stars.]'

124   Malherbe. (a) 'Wasn't that a fine start?'; (b) 'Speak to me no more of them; your bad style makes them disgusting to me.'

Dolly Winthrop, speaking to Silas Marner: George Eliot, *Silas Marner* (1861), ch. X.

Ralph the Heir, by Anthony Trollope.

125   Mme de Sévigné, letter to Mme de Grignan, 7 August 1675. 'What! I've said nothing of St Marceau to you, while speaking of St Genevieve! I don't know what I was thinking of. St Marceau came to take St Genevieve as far as her house; without that one could not make her go. It was the Goldsmiths who carried St

Marceau's shrine; there were two million francs' worth of precious stones. It was the loveliest thing in the world. St Genevieve came after, carried by barefoot children with extreme devotion. Coming out of Notre Dame the good saint [Marceau] went to conduct the good saint [Genevieve] as far as a marked place where they always separate; but do you realise with what violence? Ten more men were needed to carry them, because of the effort they made to rejoin, and if by chance they approached each other, neither human power nor human force could separate them. Ask the best citizens and the common people; but something prevents them, and they only make a gentle inclination one to the other, and then every one goes home.'

'Non non, mon du Périer, aussitôt que la Parque': Stanza 7 of 'Consolation à Monsieur du Périer, sur la Mort de sa Fille' (1607): Malherbe, *Oeuvres*, ed. Éd. Mignot, Paris (n.d., La Renaissance du Livre), p. 35: 'As soon as the Fate takes the soul from the body, age vanishes on this side of the ship and does not follow the dead.'

'Toutes les autres morts . . .': Stanza 32 of 'Pour le Roi, allant chatier la Rébellion des Rochelois' (1628): *ibid*, p. 162: 'All the other dead have neither merit nor mark, / This one alone wears a radiant brightness / Which revives man, and takes him from the ship / To the table of the Gods.'

'Donner un sens . . .': line 2 of Stanza 2 of Mallarmé's 'Le Tombeau d'Edgar Poe' (1876): 'To give a purer meaning to the words of the tribe.'

The quotation from Gerald Heard is from *The Creed of Christ: An Interpretation of the Lord's Prayer* (1941), p. 12.

'Like other priests': On p. 34 Heard describes himself as 'a layman'. 'Mis-prayer' is dealt with at length in ch. 2. The first quotation (Heard, p. 144) should read: 'But the idea of being mildly inoffensive, gently in good taste, keeping one's religion to oneself . . .'; the second (p. 145) ends at 'ourselves'. The 'diabolic' men were convicts on Alcatraz.

126   The hierarchy (in upward order) of 'Servants–Friends–Sons' is dealt with on p. 24, also p. 36 ('Friends' = Saints).

Hugh Ross Williamson's *A.D. 33: A Tract for the Times* also appeared in 1941. The title refers to one proposed date of the Crucifixion, not 28 but 33 A.D. In his foreword Williamson states that he wants to consider '*why* these forces [Pilate, the Sanhedrin, the 'Jerusalem mob', Judas] were inimical to Jesus', and by so doing 'estimate the nature of his own teaching', as revealed particularly in relation to 'the "Kingdom of Heaven" and the revolutionary doctrine of Love'.

Kiev fell on 17 September 1941. 'Op. 101' is a Beethoven piano sonata: early in the war, encouraged by Charles Mauron, Forster had been working through the Beethoven piano sonatas, playing them himself and on record, and writing analyses of them. (See P. N. Furbank, *E. M. Forster: A Life*, II, 252–3.) A card to Forster from Marie Mauron, undated but probably late 1940, indicates that Charles Mauron had just gone permanently blind.

E. K. Bennett (1887–1958), originally a clerk with the firm of Crosse & Blackwell, had been a pupil of Forster's in about 1908 at the Working Men's College, Crowndale Road, London. They met again in Egypt during World War I, by which time Bennett had studied Modern Languages at Gonville and Caius College, Cambridge. Later Bennett became a Fellow, and for a time President, of Caius, and University Lecturer in German. Forster kept Bennett's later letters (1945–58) in an envelope he marked 'Keep. Precious. E.K.B.' (usually he put on letters simply 'keep', if anything at all), but this one has not been preserved. Forster quoted this passage from it again when he wrote an obituary piece about Bennett in *The Caian* (Michaelmas term, 1958).

127   *The Vision of the Cross.* See G. M. Trevelyan, *History of England* (1926), p. 67. What Trevelyan in fact quotes is *The Dream of the Rood*, in verse translation:

> Stripped himself then the young hero,
> that was God Almighty,
> Strong and brave:
> he mounted the high cross
> courageously in the sight of many,
> when he wanted to set mankind free.
> I trembled when the hero embraced me.
> I dared not bend to the earth.

Perhaps Forster is quoting a prose translation read elsewhere, and means simply that the same *work* is quoted by Trevelyan; who certainly says nothing himself about 'a 10th century manuscript'.

'Our tough redeemer . . .': Forster's parody of Harriet Auber's hymn beginning:

> Our blest redeemer, ere he breathed
>   His tender last farewell,
> A guide, a comforter beqeathed
>   With us to dwell.

'Written when the Russians . . .': In the original, this is written vertically in the left margin of the entries from 'Our tough redeemer . . . .' to 'Bob on Blessed are the Meek.' Mojaisk (Mozhaisk/Mozhaysk) is sixty miles west of Moscow; it was retaken around January 1942.

Sylvia's Lovers. The passage quoted is from ch. VII. (See *The Works of Mrs. Gaskell* (Knutsford Edition, 1906), VI, 78–9.) The novel, described by Wendy Craik (*Elizabeth Gaskell and the English Provincial Novel* (London, 1975), p. 140) as 'one of the greatest novels in the English tongue', is set in Whitby. The main characters are Sylvia Robson, her cousin Philip Hepburn, and the sailor Charley Kinraid.

128   Jean-Jacques Olier founded the Seminary of St Sulpice. A life of him by the Abbé Faillon was published in Paris in 1853, an English life by Edward Healy Thompson in London in 1861. The quotation can be found at the end of ch. 4 of Aldous Huxley's *Grey Eminence* (1944).

The quotation from Bakunin is one of the four epigraphs to Herbert Read's *The Philosophy of Anarchism* (1940). (Another occurs on p. 141.)

129   'Disgusting Death' is written in very large letters.

'Gerry'. Gerald Heard, presumably.

H. A. L. Fisher's *A History of Europe* was originally published in three volumes in 1935. In 1938 a revised and enlarged edition appeared in three volumes, and was reissued in 1943. In this, Forster's quotation appears in vol. I, Preface, p. vi. Fisher says 'I can see only'; 'following upon another'; 'as wave follows upon wave'; 'generalizations'; 'recognize'; 'contingent and unforeseen'; he also has a colon, not a dash, after 'historian'.

Ruskin, re-appointed Slade Professor of Fine Art at Oxford in 1883, gave only five lectures of his seven-lecture series 'The Pleasures of England'. 'The Pleasures of Deed' was Lecture III, given in November 1884. (See *The Works of John Ruskin*, ed. E. T. Cook and Alexander Wedderburn (George Allen, 1908), XXXIII, 473.) Forster omits five of Ruskin's commas.

The two quotations from Courier are from his 'Petition pour les Villageois que l'on empêche de Danser' (1822). See Paul-Louis Courier, *Oeuvres Complètes* (Paris, 1951), pp. 135–6. It is not indicated in this Pléiade edition whether the petition was addressed to the Chamber of Deputies. (1) 'Policemen have multiplied in France considerably more than violins, however less necessary for the dance.' (2) 'The people are wise, whatever our secret ones say.'

The Shaw/Hegel is written vertically in the left margin, alongside the quotations from Fisher to Courier. See Bernard Shaw, *Collected Plays with their Prefaces*, vol. V (The Bodley Head, 1972), p. 55. What Hegel said is: '. . . what experience and history teach is this – that peoples and governments never have learned any-thing from history, or acted on principles deduced from it'. (G. W. F. Hegel, Introduction, *Lectures in the Philosophy of History*, trans. J. Sibree (New York, Collier, 1902), p. 49).

Valéry: 'History is the most dangerous product that the chemistry of the intellect has elaborated. Its properties are well-known. It produces dreams, it makes peoples drunk, engenders in them false memories, exaggerates their reflexes, maintains their old wounds, torments them in their sleep, leads them to the delirium of grandeur or of persecution, and makes nations bitter, haughty, insupportable and vain.'

130 N.G.: The National Gallery in London.

Bapu Sahib: The Maharajah of Dewas Senior, to whom Forster was Private Secretary in 1921. His remark is recorded, in a slightly different form, in the 'Colonel Wilson' section of *The Hill of Devi* (1953), Penguin edition (1965), p. 146.

131 '194 ': There are four figures, the fourth difficult to decipher: it looks like a very hasty '3', but this seems odd in view of the reference in the next section to 'May 1942'.

Penetrabis ad Urbem. For this general title, see the quotation from Claudian on p. 132. Below it an earlier phrase – apparently 'Easter 300' – has been scratched out – a mistake perhaps for 'Easter 400' (which Oliver Stallybrass conjectured to be a com-panion title for 'Easter 1942' on p. 130). In the events surrounding the fall of Rome to the Goths (23 August 410 A.D.) Forster saw a parallel with Hitler's attempts in Europe in World War II. (It is interesting that the poem by Sidney Keyes entitled 'Rome Remember', written in August 1942, draws an implicit parallel between Rome and contemporary Europe/Britain.)

Commodian was a Third Century Christian Latin poet in Africa. This is a tricky and perhaps corrupt passage. A possible translation might run: 'She for her part used to rejoice; but the whole earth groaned. / Nevertheless the man came: that retribution was deserved. / She is mourning for eternity who used to boast herself eternal.'

St Augustine. 'Is the translation correct?' Oliver Stallybrass, in a note on this passage, answers: 'The question takes us into deep waters. The translation in question is that by John Healey (1610, republished in the Temple Classics in 1903 and again in 1931), except that Forster has taken a number of liberties, substituting "The intrepid city" for "the Great Western Babylon" (itself a colourful rendering of *imperiosa civitas*), "the wider" for "this large", "produces still" for "procured", "remember" for "consider", "these" for "those", and "feelings" for "feeling".' In an earlier version of his note he says that Healey's version takes 'enormous liberties with Augustine's text'.

132   Claudian was a Greek-speaking Alexandrian who came to Rome in 395 A.D. The Loeb editor of his work, Maurice Platnauer, describes him as 'the last poet of Classical Rome'. The title of his poem should be *De Bello Gothico* (though in fact it is referred to in the *Classical Dictionary* as *Bellum Gothicum*.) The lines (546-7) are translated by Platnauer as: 'Away with delay, Alaric; boldly cross the Italian Alps this year and thou shalt reach the city'. (*Claudian*, vol. II (Heinemann, Loeb Classical Library, 1922), p. 164). The (italicization) underlinings of letters – to make ROMA – are Forster's.

'The innocency . . .': This quotation from St Augustine does not occur in this place in E. B. Pusey's Everyman translation (1838) of the *Confessions*. There it is found on p. 7 as 'Bk. 1 [VII] 11: The weakness then of infant limbs, not its will, is its innocence'. Presumably Forster was using a different edition, differently subdivided.

St Jerome, 'extracted from Hodgkin': Forster derives his material from Thomas Hodgkin, *Italy and Her Invaders 376-476* (London, 1880), I, 377-81. 'Quid salvum est . . .': Hodgkin translates, in his text (p. 378), as 'What can be safe, if Rome in ruins fall?', giving the Latin in a footnote.

'Urbs antiqua . . .': (*Aeneid*, ii, 363). Hodgkin gives Conington's translation in his text (p. 379): 'An ancient city topples down/ From broad-based heights of old renown'.

'Into such times . . .': Hodgkin, p. 380; Hodgkin has 'playthings' rather than 'toys', and 'yearn only for the future'.

'Docks on fire'. Forster described this sight in his Diary, 8 Sept. 1940: 'London Burning! I watched this event from my Chiswick flat last night with disgust and indignation, but with no intensity though the spectacle was superb, I thought It is nothing like the burning of Troy. Yet the Surrey Docks were ablaze, at the back with towers and spires outlines against them, greenish yellow searchlights swept the sky in futile agony, crimson shells burst behind the spire of Turnham Green church. This is all that a world catastrophe amounts to. Something which one is too sad or sullen to appreciate. Perhaps we are really behaving heroically, as I remarked to Tony Butts [a friend of the poet William Plomer] this morning. Some one else will have to say. Now and then tracts of the horizon flashed a ghastly electric green. Or the fire ahead burst up as I hoped it was dying down, 'Oh!' I cried once faintly, then returned to my bed and read Middlemarch. God help us all – help us to feel and not to be matey. In the morning a crimson valance of cloud hung above the fire itself.'

Notes on St Jerome, extracted from W. E. H. Lecky, *History of European Morals from Augustus to Charlemagne*, 2 vols. (1869), one-volume edition (1911).

'severely flagellated . . .': Lecky (1911 edition), p. 115.

'St. Paula : Lecky, p. 133 (the Latin – 'overcoming piety towards her children by piety towards God – is quoted in a footnote).

133   'In this matter cruelty . . .': Lecky, p. 134.

The book is in fact *well*-indexed, with 'subject' sub-heads added to 'name' entries.

134   The doggerel couplet on Pelagius is presumably Forster's own.

The Pelagius article is in Michaud's *Biographie Universelle Ancienne et Moderne* (Paris, 1834–?1880), XXXII, 381–2. It states that Pelagius came from Great Britain, that his family name was Morgan (meaning 'born beside the sea'), and that he changed this name to its Latin equivalent.

The matters referred to here are discussed in John Neville Figgis, *The Political Aspects of S. Augustine's 'City of God'* (Longman, 1921). The first two questions asked by Forster are stated by Figgis on pp. 3–4. The first also begins ch. II (p. 32 ff); ch. III (pp. 51 ff.) deals with St Augustine and the State, and he and the Donatists are discussed on pp. 56–7; Augustine's views on Imperialism are discussed on p. 58: 'as many States in the world as there are families in a city' are Figgis's words. Figgis makes no reference to Salvian's and Jerome's views of the Fall of Rome, though the Fall itself is touched on briefly on p. 6.

135   Forster's third Latin quotation (*De Civ. Dei*, IV.4) should begin 'Remota' not 'remotu'. In the second, 'requiritur' should be 'adquiritur'. William M. Greene (Loeb edition, Heinemann, 1963, vols I and II) translates thus: (1) ['Ut magnum . . .']. 'Why should it have been necessary in order to be a great empire, to be turbulent?' (2) ['An latitudo . . .'] 'Whether extent of rule, acquired only by war, should be counted among the blessings of the wise or

happy.' (3) ['Remota itaque . . .'] 'And so if justice is left out, what are kingdoms except great robber bands? For what are robber bands except little kingdoms?' (4) ['An congruat . . .'] 'Whether good men can consistently seek to extend their rule.'

St Jerome's Letters: See *Select Letters of St Jerome*, with English translation by F. A. Wright (Heinemann, Loeb Classical Library, 1933).

Letter 22 (pp. 67-8), written to a woman called Eustochium, daughter of Paula: '. . . I often found myself . . .'. There is a small omission before 'the fires of lust'.

'I praise wedlock, I praise marriage; but it is because they produce me virgins'. (Forster's alteration follows the Latin, 'sed quia', more literally than Wright.)

For 'heretical virgins' see p. 149: 'not virgins, but prostitutes'.

Letter 45: 'Was I ever attracted . . . painted faces, display of gold? No other matron in Rome could dominate my mind but one who mourned and fasted, who was squalid with dirt, . . .' (p. 183).

'You belch after a meal of wild duck and boast of the sturgeon you devour; I fill . . .' (p. 185).

136   'Mel meum . . .': Wright translates (p. 205) as 'My honey, my light, my darling.'

Letter 77: 'With us [Christians] what is unlawful for women is equally unlawful for men, and as both sexes serve God they are bound by the same conditions' (p. 315).

Letter 117: What Forster translates as 'major-domo' ('clericos') is given by Wright as 'clerical director'.

'desire, which in the case of virgins is the sharper set because it thinks that anything of which it knows nothing is especially delightful [. . .]' (p. 385).

'if your vest be slit on purpose to let something be seen within [. . .]'.

'over your ears. Your shawl sometimes drops . . .' (p. 387).

'My volubility . . .' etc. (p. 397). Forster's word 'vigour' could just possibly be 'rigour'; but judging from the length and speed of the letter (written, as St Jerome says, 'in the space of one short night') 'vigour' seems more likely.

Letter 60: 'For twenty years and more the blood of Romans has every day been shed . . .' (p. 301).

'Romanus orbis ruit et . . .': Wright translates (p. 302) as: 'The

Roman world is falling, and yet we hold our heads erect instead of bowing our necks.'

'It is by reason of our sins that the barbarians are strong . . .' (p. 305).

137   Letter 107: pp. 339–371. 'Getarum . . .': p. 342. Wright translates: 'The ruddy, flaxen-haired Getae carry tent-churches about with their armies . . .'.

Letter 127: 'but to the church of St Paul', see p. 465. The word which I have transcribed as 'palace' is almost illegible in the original; Wright's note (p. 438) mentions Marcella's 'house on the Aventine', Appendix I (p. 484) refers to Albina's 'palace on the Aventine' (Marcella was Albina's daughter).

Forster commented on his reading of St Jerome in a letter of 10 June 1942 to the writer John Hampson (John Simpson): 'I am reading *The Death of the Moth*. I feel rather tired of Virginia [Woolf] for the moment, and prefer the letters of that old scream St Jerome. He was a terrific (suppressed) womaniser, and writes from a cave in Palestine pages and pages to a young lady whom he has never seen in France, rebuking her severely for things which she has never done so far as he knows, but which she might have done, such as allowing her arm to be held by a slightly-bearded young man.'

Apollinaris Sidonius (Bishop of what is now Clermont-Ferrand in the Auvergne). Forster's material is derived from vol. II of *Italy and Her Invaders 376–476* by Thomas Hodgkin (Clarendon Press, 1880).

'Euric a cid of Toulouse': The use here, of 'cid' for nobleman, is odd, but appears to be what Forster wrote. Euric, who killed his brother Theodoric II to get the throne, was king of the Visigoths, whose territory centred on Toulouse.

'Smith's Dictionary' is presumably the *Dictionary of Christian Biography* (1877–87) by Sir William Smith (1813–1893).

'Egypt may be lost to me . . .': Tobruk fell on 20 June 1942; by 1 July the German forces had reached El Alamein, sixty miles from Alexandria, where they were finally held by General Sir Claude Auchinleck.

138   *Art:* There were two versions of the book Forster refers to here. The first, *Byzantine Art* by Hayford Peirce and Royall Tyler, was published in London in 1926; the second, *L'Art Byzantine* by the same authors, was published in two volumes in Paris (1932, 1934). Forster looked at the first volume of the latter, whose format is

twice the size of the 1926 volume, and contains twice the number of plates.

Bronze statue: The 'profile' is plate 31, the only one also in the 1926 volume (plate 9), where it was thought to be Theodosius the Great, Leo the Great, 'or even Anastasius'. By 1932 it was surmised to be Valentinian I.

Valens medal, plate 33. 'Badly executed' is the view of Peirce and Tyler.

Marble relief, plate 33. Forster's comment is just.

Silver disk of Theodosius, plates 35, 36, 37. Arcadius and Honorius are conjectured by Peirce and Tyler. 'His fit': 'Theodose est mort hydropique en Janvier 395'.

Base of Theodosius' obelisk, plates 41, 42. At this time Arcadius was eighteen, Honorius eleven.

Silver disk of Valentinian II, plate 43. 'Decorative': the guards' shields are very large and make a symmetrical decoration right across the centre of the disk.

Diptych from Monza, plate 52. The son is called Eucherius; Forster's '(?)' is his abbreviation of Peirce and Tyler's 'presque certainement' for the identities of all three.

Traprain Treasure, plates 62 (a) and (b), also plate 60. The place the treasure came from was called Traprain-Law, belonging to 'le comte de Balfour'.

Woodchester Pavement, plates 65 (a) and 68 (b): a mosaic.

Mural painting, Catacomb of Priscilla, plate 51.

Mural Mosaic, Mausoleum of Galla Placidia, Ravenna, plate 115.

La Patène de St Denis, plate 117. This is a communion plate; the 'mystery' concerns its material, style and date.

Wilpert. Forster is referring to Joseph Wilpert, *Die Romische Mosaiken und Malereien du kirchlichen Bauten Vom IV – XIII Jahrhundert* (Freiburg im Breslau, 1917). This consists of four exceptionally large-format, separately-boxed, volumes of text and illustrations, very handsomely printed on glossy paper. The illustrations are in colour, and very faithful to their originals; Forster's description of the work as 'superb' is an understatement. On the title-page, under the title, is printed: 'Unter den Auspizien und mit Allerhöchster Forderung Seiner Majestät Kaiser Wilhelms II.'

139   The Mosaic illustrations compose vol. III.

St Costanza, Constantine's Mausoleum, plates 4, 5, 6.

Sta Maria Maggiore, plates 8–26.

Baptistery ('Taufkirche'), S. Giovanni, plates 29–39.

St Pudenziana, plates 42–4 (these fold out complete, and are very fine).

Childhood of Christ, plates 57–60, 63–5.

St Ambrogio, plates 83–5.

Ravenna, Galla Placidia, plates 48–52 (52 is 'Deer Drinking', the one referred to by Pierce and Tyler as 'over-restored').

Lateran, St John the Evangelist, plate 86 (both magnificent and delicate).

Ravenna, Baptistery of the Orthodox, plate 78 (splendid deep blue tiles are used to depict a very human and realistic head; Forster's 'etc.' refers to a mosaic of St Agnes depicted on the same plate).

St John of the Studium: not an illustration in Wilpert.

'Why did Rome fall?': The book from which Forster got his reasons is Thomas Hodgkin's *Italy and Her Invaders 376–476* (1880), II, 545–638. Hodgkin was a Fellow of University College, London rather than a 'quaker banker'; but he may have come from a banking family, and the Hodgkins are an English clan long connected with Quakerism. (George Lloyd Hodgkin (1880–1918), a Quaker friend of Forster's at King's, had briefly worked in a branch of Barclays Bank in Banbury.)

'Because it had completed . . .': Hodgkin, p. 545. The 'subsidiary causes', discussed by Hodgkin at length, are summarised by Forster. 'It was the diffusion . . .': p. 556.

140 'Bad finance': Hodgkin's text (p. 627) reads: 'the true business of a banker – the acting as a broker between those classes of the community which desire to lend and those classes which desire to borrow – cannot have been understood'.

'The ruin . . . Morning': This is Forster's quasi-poetic rearrangement of Hodgkin's prose (p. 634). Hodgkin has 'State', 'alien peoples', a comma after 'lands', 'oh', 'morning' followed by an exclamation mark.

141 Sebastopol fell to the Germans in July 1942, after a siege lasting 250 days.

See St Basil's *Letters* (4 vols., Heinemann, Loeb Classical Library, 1929), translated by Roy J. Deferrari. The bracketed passage represents Forster's interlinear addition.

Letter 135, to Diodorus, Presbyter of Antioch: II, 307–11. The phrase Forster quotes is on p. 309.

'A perfect society . . .': This, from St Basil, is one of the four epigraphs used by Herbert Read at the start of *The Philosophy of Anarchism* (Freedom Press, London 1940).

Letter 14, to Gregory of Nazianzus: I, 107-11. The Loeb text has 'the Pontus' ('Τον Πόντον'), i.e. Pontus Euxinus, the Black Sea. Letter 11 (so written) is an error for Letter 2 (II), to Gregory of Nazianzus: I, 21. 'On Monastic Rule' is Forster's title. There are minor variations of punctuation; 'affect' is Forster's correction of the translator's 'effect'. In the original, the passage is written in the left-hand margin, vertically, with an arrow connecting it to the word 'chastity' (page 140, last paragraph).

142   *St Gregory of Nyssa*: After 'brother to the above' the original has 'and also a Father?', which Forster cancelled.

St Cyril of Alexandria: The reference to 'my Guide' is to Forster's *Alexandria: A History and a Guide*, published in Alexandria in 1922, and reprinted there in 1938. It was most recently reprinted in Woodstock, New York in 1974, and in London in 1981.

143   *St John Chrysostom*. Evidently Forster's interest flagged at this point: there is a blank space instead of his intended note.

Forster's family trees of Emperors can be found, in fuller form, at the beginning (unpaginated) of Thomas Hodgkin's *The Dynasty of Theodosius* (1889). Flocilloi appears there as Aelia Flacilla.

144   Forster's material on the Sophists and others is drawn from part III ('Byzantium A.D. 313-565') of F. A. Wright's *A History of Later Greek Literature* from the Death of Alexandria in 323 B.C. to the Death of Justinian in 565 A.D. (Routledge, 1932).

Himerius: Wright, pp. 356-7.

Themistius: Wright, pp. 357-8; though Wright doesn't have the reference to Gratian. After 'the soul will escape' Wright has 'even though the tongue be constrained'.

Libanius: Wright, pp. 358-62.

Eunapius: Wright, pp. 368-9.

Proclus: Wright, pp. 380-1.

Quintus Smyrnaeus: Wright, pp. 369-72. *Posthomerica* is the title of a poem by him. Forster's note is a vertical insert in the left margin, connected by an arrow to the text.

Nonnus: Wright, pp. 351-4. He is described as 'born at Panopolis, the ancient Chemnis, a town of the Thebaid in Egypt'. Wright calls him 'an Ovid writing in Greek'; his *Dionysiaca* was an epic in 48 books, twice the length of the *Iliad*. Books 10, 11 and 12 deal with Dionysus' 'passion for the fair youth Ampelos', Book 48 with 'the god's amours with Pallene and Aura,' in which there occurs a naked wrestling scene which 'descends to physical details which may bring a blush to the cheeks of modern readers'. If Forster did, in fact, look up 'these timely indecencies', perhaps this scene was in his mind when he came to write 'Little Imber' in November, 1961.

Palladas: Wright, pp. 374–9. The two poems of his which Forster proposed to look up in the Greek Anthology (A.P. x. 78 and A.P. x. 45) are given in translation by Wright on pp. 377–8. They are hostile to human pride and pessimistic about human hopes. Man's 'life is but a fleeting dream' (78) and he is a 'poor crawling worm / . . . sprung from lust and one foul drop of sperm.'

145   After Trèves, Forster did not describe the other two cities (Milan and Ravenna); instead he left a blank, filled seventeen years later by his description of his visit to Trèves in 1960. The earlier time sequence resumes with 'Socrates of Constantinople' on p. 145.

Ausonius: Roman poet (*c*. A.D. 310–390) born at Bordeaux; tutor to the Emperor Valentinian's son Gratian. He wrote a poem describing the Moselle, together with its wine and its trout.

146   *Socrates of Constantinople*. Forster referred to his reading in a letter to John Hampson (John Simpson), undated but contemporary with this entry: 'I have been reading Socrates – not the philosopher, but a 4th century Christian Ecclesiastical Historian, and he has succeeded in making me laugh quite a lot over a Purity Drive which the Emperor Theodosius organised in Rome. There was a terrific menace in the Night Clubs: they were built over bakeries and provided with machines, which tipped the bright young people out of their beds on to the ovens, where they were trapped and obliged to bake bread for the rest of their lives. Theodosius rescued them. He also arranged an alternative punishment for adulteresses. Hitherto they had been obliged to become prostitutes, and, all the time they were being had, little bells rang so that the people in the street outside could imagine what was happening. Theodosius thought this a bad plan.'

Prudentius is dealt with on pp. 37–51 of Benjamin Farrington, *Science and Politics in the Ancient World* (1939).

Trelawney Dayrell Reed, *The Battle for Britain in the Fifth Century: An Essay in Dark Age History* (Methuen, 1944). Reed's 'tendentious' argument is stated on p. 38 and summed up in the last paragraph of p. 202.

Reed (p. 197) says that Ambrosius 'was acknowledged as head-king of all the kings of Britain' in 472, and gives the period 465–470 for the building of Wansdyke (p. 155). Reed also gives the date of Nennius' History of the Britons as 828 (i.e. ninth century).

The 'Alleluia Victory' is mentioned on pp. 64 and 192. I have not found in Reed the 'curious anecdotes' mentioned by Forster, nor the list of British Gods, but as Reed's book was published after this entry (1942/1943) was made, presumably Forster saw the gist of its material in a magazine, together with items not reprinted.

In the original, the pages numbered 154 to 158 (following the 'British gods' entry) are entirely blank.

E. H. Carr, *Michael Bakunin* (Macmillan, 1937). 'Pitiless and ungenerous account'. As with Forster's phrase 'sordid and absurd' (p. 147), this is not entirely fair to Carr. His last paragraph of Book 5 (p. 440) describes Bakunin as 'one of the completest embodiments in history of the spirit of liberty . . . which is almost universally felt to be an indispensable part of the highest manifestations and aspirations of humanity.'

147 'States cannot be made . . .': The dots after the second 'States' represent an omitted half-sentence. 'Good, just, and moral State.' (Carr's punctuation.) After this Forster omits four sentences without indication. 'Only a weak State can be a virtuous State . . . and its desires': Carr, p. 343, quoting Bakunin's address to the Second Congress of the League of Peace and Freedom, Berne, 1868.

Carr, p. 356: 'Bakunin . . . defined the seven degrees of happiness as: "first, to die fighting for liberty; second, love and friendship; third, art and science; fourth, smoking; fifth, drinking; sixth, eating; and seventh, sleeping".'

'The passion for destruction . . . passion!': Bakunin on 'Reaction in Germany' (Carr, pp. 110 and 434).

'All exercise of authority . . .'; 'Every State . . . assumes man to be fundamentally bad and wicked'; 'a herd of animals . . . . life.': Carr, p. 436.

'Everything will pass . . .': Carr, p. 487.

'Nechaev, the Tiger-Boy': '[Bakunin] began to call young Nechaev by the tender nickname of "Boy" ' (Carr, p. 377). He also called him a 'young tiger' (p. 389). Nechaev's opinions, Carr says on p. 375, displayed 'vigour and ferocity'. Forster's bracketed '(1)' is linked in the original by a line to the opinion of Nechaev quoted later, but printed here between rules: 'We recognise no other activity . . .': Carr's wording, quoting Nechaev's pamphlet *Principles of Revolution.* (Carr, p. 380.)

148 Quotation from Weitling: Carr, p. 122 ('govt.' is Forster's abbreviation).

'Music heard so deeply . . .': T. S. Eliot, *The Dry Salvages* (*Four Quartets*, 1944), section V, lines 27–9. Forster had a separate copy of *Little Gidding* (1942), but no other single Quartet is recorded in the catalogue of Forster's books (King's College, Cambridge). His copy of *Four Quartets* (1952 printing) was given to Bob Buckingham.

Proust. Forster owned Proust's *A la Recherche du Temps Perdu* in the eight-volume edition published in Paris by Gallimard in 1919. In his diary (1 March 1922) Forster recorded, while on the boat returning from India, his early impressions of Proust: 'Bought Du Côté de Chez Swann at Marseilles and note how cleverly Proust uses his memories and experiences to illustrate his state of mind. A rich outlook is presented incidentally. His work impresses me by its weight and length, and sometimes touches me by its truth to my feelings. Would that I had the knack of unrolling such an embroidered ribbon. Yet even then I should not be content. The little sip of pure creation that I have been granted has spoilt me.'

I have checked Forster's quotations from *Le Temps Retrouvé* against the Pléiade edition of Proust, vol. III (Paris, 1954). The translations given are from *Time Regained*, trans. Andreas Mayor (Chatto & Windus, 1970).

'[Or] les aberrations . . . la tare maladive . . . encore': Pléiade edition, vol. III (1954), p. 840. ('Perversions . . . are like loves in which the germ of disease has spread victoriously to every part. Even in the maddest of them love may still be recognised'. Mayor, p. 188.)

'Une oeuvre . . .': Pléiade text, p. 882. ('A work in which there are theories is like an object which still has the ticket that shows its price'. Mayor, p. 244.)

'Theories . . .': The Pléiade text (p. 881) reads: '. . . diverse théories littéraires qui m'avaient un moment troublé – notamment celles que la critique avait développées au moment de l'affaire Dreyfus et avait reprises pendant la guerre, et qui tendaient à "faire sortir l'artiste de sa tour d'ivoire", et à traiter . . . sentimentaux, mais peignant . . . et, à défaut . . . foules . . . [bracketed phrase between 'oisifs' and 'mais' omitted by Forster] . . . intellectuels, . . . héros.'

The passage as quoted by Forster is translated by Mayor (p. 243) thus: 'Theories . . . taken up again during the war, according to which "the artist must be made to leave his ivory tower" and the themes chosen by the writer ought to be not frivolous or sentimental but rather such things as great working-class movements or – in default of crowds – at least no longer as in the past unimportant men of leisure . . . but noble intellectuals or men of heroic stature.'

'Les chagrins . . .': Pléiade, p. 910. The French text has 'mènent,' 'pour qui,' 'a sonné,' 'mort!' ('Sufferings are servants, obscure and detested, against whom one struggles, beneath whose dominion one more and more completely falls, dire and dreadful servants whom it is impossible to replace and who by subterranean paths lead us towards truth and death. Happy are those who have first come face to face with truth, those for whom, near though the one may be to the other, the hour of truth has struck before the hour of death!' Mayor, pp. 281–2.)

'Mais d'abord, il en est . . . mort. Quelques-uns . . . non pas parce qu'ils . . . moins d'imagination': Pléiade, p. 930. A footnote to 'moins' (p. 1140) indicates that Proust's manuscript has 'plus', which presumably was printed uncorrected in earlier editions. ('Old age, in this respect, is like death. Some men confront them both with indifference, not because they have more courage than others but because they have less [not 'more', as in Forster's version] imagination.' Mayor, p. 309.)

'Car nos plus grands craintes, . . . au-dessus . . . forces, . . . les autres': Pléiade, p. 1035. ('For neither our greatest fears nor our greatest hopes are beyond the limits of our strength – we are able in the end both to dominate the first and to achieve the second.' Mayor, p. 455.)

'I sit under a tree . . .': Hardy's Diary, 28 November 1875. See *The Life of Thomas Hardy 1840–1920* by Florence Emily Hardy (2 vols, 1928 and 1930), one volume (1962), p. 107.

The Johnson quotation is not verbatim. See *Boswell's Life of Johnson*, ed. G. B. Hill, rev. L. F. Powell (Clarendon Press, 1934), I, 467: 'At supper this night he talked of good eating with uncommon satisfaction. Some people (said he,) have a foolish way of not minding, or pretending not to mind, what they eat. For my part, I look upon my belly very studiously, and very carefully; for I look upon it, that he who does not mind his belly will hardly mind any thing else' (5 August 1763).

149   The second Darwin quotation is the final sentences of ch. 19 of *The Voyage of the Beagle* (1839 and later: Everyman Edition,

Dent, 1906, p. 434). Forster quotes it again (minus the last sentence) on p. 201. It is dated 14 March 1836 in Nora Barlow's edition of *Charles Darwin's Diary of the Voyage of H.M.S. "Beagle"* (Cambridge University Press, 1933), p. 394. This text has 'rising infant', not 'rising child'.

The Swinburne quotation ('Hymn to Man,' originally published in *Songs before Sunrise*, 1871) can be found in *The Poems of Algernon Charles Swinburne* (6 vols., Chatto & Windus, 1904), II, 98. Forster cavalierly omits or alters Swinburne's punctuation. The word he could not remember in line 2 is 'forces'.

A. P. Wavell, *Allenby: Soldier and Statesman* (2 vols., 1940 and 1944), one-volume edition (Harrap, 1946), p. 74. Wavell has: 'that Boer prisoners'; 'fraternization'; 'to ending'.

No sensuousness: Forster owned copies of Mrs Gaskell's *Cranford*, *Mary Barton*, *North and South* and *Ruth*, but not, apparently, a copy of *Sylvia's Lovers*; so I have been unable to determine to which edition his pagination refers.

150   I have not been able to find the first five of these quotations from Cocteau in the very comprehensive *Cocteau's World, An Anthology of Writings by Jean Cocteau*, edited and translated by Margaret Crosland (Peter Owen, 1972). The sixth, however, is referred to on p. 475 in the section 'Beauty Secrets' (*Secrets de Beauté*, in vol. X of Cocteau's *Oeuvres Complets*, 1946–   ): 'When I wrote "Victor Hugo was a madman who believed he was Victor Hugo", this was not a witticism. Hugo's greatness is that he was mad and nobody in the world suspected it.' The other five can be translated as:

(1) I admire God's lack of success: it is the lack of success of masterpieces. Which does not prevent them being famous and being feared.

(2) The world accepts dangerous experiences in the domain of art because it does not take art seriously, but it condemns them in life.

(3) Perfect bodies rigged with muscles as a ship with cordage and whose limbs seem to open out in a star shape around a fleece where rises, whereas a woman is built to deceive, the only thing about a man which cannot lie.

(4) I suppose that many journalists do not wish to lie but that they lie by means of the mechanism of poetry and of History, which slowly mis-shapes things in order to produce style.

(5) It is amusing and significant that Bergson never speaks of the unjust laugh, the official laugh when confronted with beauty.

One more novel?: 'Diverted to unimportancies'. Throughout the war Forster broadcast regularly to India; in 1943 he briefly resumed the Presidency of the National Council for Civil Liberties, whose first president he became in 1934.

151   'the shallowness of Shostakovitch': Not a depreciatory reference; in a letter to John Hampson (John Simpson) on 23 August 1942 Forster wrote that he had 'bought with pleasure a record of Shostakowitz's [*sic*] Piano Concerto', presumably the light-hearted Concerto for Piano, Trumpet and Strings of 1933.

Agriculture: The visit to the Rockingham Forest area (between Corby and Oundle) is referred to in two of Forster's letters of this period. On 24 February 1943 he wrote to John Hampson: 'I hope to visit Jack Sprott at Nottingham and Hughie Waterston at Oundle'; and in a letter to Hampson of 21 March 1943 he referred back to the visit: 'I don't myself dislike the look of land under plough. What is depressing is when all the hedges are rooted up, as by Hughie Waterston in Northamptonshire.'

'W.L.A.': Women's Land Army.

152   'Dassera!': An Indian festival (also written 'Dessera' and 'Dussehra') which marks the opening of the cold weather season; the most important Hindu festival of the year. In associating it with his 'tools' (those of the writer, presumably) Forster is perhaps remembering his participation in the ceremonies for Dassera at Dewas in 1921: 'During the festival, Forster had to officiate as a priest. Under the direction of his clerk, he first worshipped a pen, an inkpot and a wastepaper basket, offering them and his clerk a sacrament of cocoanut' (P. N. Furbank, *E. M. Forster: A Life*, II, 96–7.

Charles Mauron's letters: A letter from Forster to John Hampson (21 March 1943) indicates the mood Forster was in during the period in which he copied these letters into his Commonplace Book: 'I am all ruffled by Churchill's hideous heartless shifty speech, too much of which has come through our wireless, and must comfort myself by a line to you before I go to bed. I was a bit wrought up anyhow, as I have been transcribing and destroying Charles Mauron's letters for most of the day, and realising I shall never see him again, and then I have to endure this dentured dotard telling me I live in a glorious age.' Contact was in fact re-established with the Maurons late in 1944, after the liberation of France. Not all the letters were in fact destroyed; the originals of three of those transcribed here are among Forster's papers at King's College, Cambridge.

Snow: 'Write to me my dear friend. And make the spring come quickly. It doesn't seem to be hurrying – we are in the midst of snow, ice and frost. The meadows are pure white, the clocks striking are all muffled – a tone of a clock with a cold, old, cracked, ridiculous – Last night I went out on the road to see the snow-flakes flying around the electric lamp. I had frozen feet, but I was very happy: I have an absurd love of snow, a love stripped of all ordinary sentimentality, but very profound. The touch of the flakes on my face always gives me immense pleasure. Write.'

Winter: 'Winter's starting again. My big empty room is still as you have known it, and already I spend long hours writing, smoking, and walking the length and breadth of it. Only in the evening, from time to time, as it is raining hard outside, a mouse comes from God knows where and scratches at the door. We have taken in a neighbour's cat, but disdainful of mice it is happy to drop something unsuitable in the rubber tub. The harp strings snap. Our two pigeons – we have two pigeons – are unwilling to love each other tenderly. Sometimes a relative arrives with a basket full of grapes, of salad herbs, and of anecdotes: the latest deaths in St Rémy, the latest cuckolds. This evening Marie read *War and Peace* to me. Here it is peace, complete peace.' [Forster has perhaps omitted a comma after 'raisins'.]

Spring: 'The weather was fine enough till yesterday: the almond trees are in flower; the stove is warm: peace, good humour and disorder reign uncontested: Marie plays the harp and I my very dear piano.'

Civilisation: 'As for what awaits our civilisation, here it is: it will become a civilisation of other men, and it will appear very young to them: in fact it will always be very old: at the very end it will freeze, according to Carnot's principle. At this (? period), far in the future, you and I will be treated as barbarians or as decadents, or as barbarous decadents, or as nothing: but all that will be a matter of utter indifference to us. I should love to see you in order not to speak to you of our civilisation.'

153   T. E. Lawrence: The original of this letter at King's has 'T. E. Lawrence' written at the top of it in Forster's hand. Near the end, Mauron has a comma after 'il les adorait'. The letter is undated; Michael Halls, King's College Library archivist, conjectures it as early 1936. 'This Lawrence drains me and I must get finished with it – in a fortnight I suppose. For five months I have been living exclusively with him, cheek by jowl, and as there are few styles as revealing as his, I think I am beginning to get to know him. I don't say that I understand him – there are always difficul-ties with him whereas I never have any – but I know how he has suffered and triumphed and suffered again. At bottom he was duped, by himself, by others and by circumstances – and he has

paid dearly for a book much too 'raw meat' in certain respects and 'sunset-ish' in others to be truly satisfying. Yet one feels a breadth of shoulders, a mastery. But this being duped is too cruel: poor man! to adore the 'fine movements of the chin' of Allenby! to adore, detest, adore, detest, without much knowing why and to receive in exchange many bitter pills, little joy, and an infinity of indifference. For the Arabs could surely be, however unbearable, sometimes noble; but the generals didn't give a damn, and dropped him when he had served their purposes; and in the last analysis he worked for the generals or their fellows; and he knew it; and he adored and detested them *truly*, without being able to help it, I think. A sad life, for which only lofty literary works would have compensated: the sufferings of Beethoven, seen close up, would have to be absurd.'

Charles Mauron had presumably been reading the edition of *Seven Pillars of Wisdom* 'first published for general circulation' in 1935 (London, Jonathan Cape).

Clive Bell: 'For a whole evening I have had the vanity of Clive Bell under my eye. It seems that he was under a cloud; but truly he presented a superb spectacle of hollow infatuation, of false intelligence, of fake wit; all Bloomsbury around me trembled before this image of its own ideal – in an imitation.

Poem: The original of this letter at King's has 'What is a poem' pencilled in Forster's hand at the top. The section quoted is the second half, down the side of which Forster has pencilled a line. 'Modern' should be 'moderne'; 'tentatives' is perhaps 'tentateurs' in Mauron's letter; 'même pas de la precedente'; there should be a full stop after 'magnifique'; 'J'enviens à Valery'; comma after 'toujours'; 'cherchent à etouffer'. 'I am studying modern French poetry or rather some attempts at it. Let me first explain what for me is poetry, relying on a poem of Baudelaire. A poem – know this, Morgan – is a being which likes to remember, which takes pleasure in resemblances and echoes. I study the surrealists and I see that their poems forget everything, everything. A sentence does not remember even the one before. I salute Proust in passing and I perceive that if he often remembers in a magnificent way, he also has strange slips of memory – I come to Valéry and I notice that he remembers very well, but that often he takes no pleasure in it – those memories don't count as art. Lastly, I speak of Duhamel, Romains, Vildrac, a group who are often moved by quite other things than echoes. My conclusion is that, now and always, many big things, chaos, intelligence, sentiment, seek to smother the little poem and prevent it playing with its memories.

But the little poem defends itself – it is never smothered. And so
the world goes on.
And I go on thinking you my friend.
Marie sends you her love.'

154   Mrs. Zangwill: The original letter is headed 'Raphele les Arles';
at the top Forster has written 'Epicureanism'. The quoted passage
is the last paragraph of a total of three pages. The dots are
Mauron's; there should be a comma after 'd Octobre'. Israel
Zangwill (1864–1926) was a Jewish novelist and playwright who
lived in England; *Ghetto Tragedies* was published in 1893. 'A
young publisher, Mr Hazan, having noticed a beautiful translation published by Plon in October, asked me to translate Zangwill's *Ghetto Tragedies* for him. I don't like Zangwill but I have no
money. I agreed. Madame Zangwill turned a deaf ear: she didn't
know Mr Charles Mauron and she feared that he did not sufficiently honour the memory of her Jew of a husband. The young
publisher crisply declared that the translation would be made by
Mr Mauron or he wouldn't publish the book. (Heavens! why do
all life's events turn heroic around me, who am so peaceful!)
Madame Zangwill gave way. But listen, my dear Morgan, to the
noise she made when she gave way:'

Marie Mauron's Great-Uncle. In the original, the date given for
Forster's visit is 'the 1930s'; overlaid on the '3' is a '4', which
presumably was added by Forster to celebrate a return visit after
the war. The word 'or' follows 'vegetables' at the end of a line,
and has no obvious purpose – except perhaps as an elliptical
transition to the snatch of speech which follows it.

155   *Le Silence de la Mer*, a short novel of forty-two pages, was written
in October 1941 not by Jean Schlumberger but by Jean Bruller, a
pacifist artist and carpenter. It was printed and circulated clandes-
tinely, no one knowing at the time who 'Vercors' was, not even
Bruller's wife. (André Gide and Roger Martin du Gard were the
two most popular guesses at his identity.) It was eventually
published in London in 1946 in French, in the series 'Editions
Penguin'. Raymond Mortimer (1895–1980) was a well-known
writer and reviewer.

The story by the French novelist Jean Giono is 'Prélude de Pan',
first published 1 November 1929 in *L'Almanach des Champs* and
reprinted in *Solitude de la pitié* (Paris, Gallimard, 1932). The dance
culminates in a coupling of humans and beasts.

Forster referred to reading *Illusions Perdus* in a letter of 24 July
1947 (apparently a slip for 1943) to John Hampson: 'Am reading

Balzac (Illusions Perdus). Admiration at last exceeds dislike.'
(See p. 161.)

Gide's Journal, which spanned the years 1889–1949, was published in six volumes in Paris between 1946 and 1950. Volume 5,
incomplete editions of which appeared in New York and Algiers
in 1944, covers the years 1939–42; presumably sections of it
appeared earlier in journals, since Forster's entry was made before
25 July 1943. Gide's reading recorded in it was indeed voluminous, taking in, *inter alia*, Racine, *Mansfield Park*, Eckermann's
Conversations with Goethe, *Faust*, Zola, Kafka, Tourneur, Stein-
beck, St Evremond, Faulkner's *Sartoris*, Pearl Buck's *The Good
Earth*, books on Euripides and Aeschylus, Thomas Mann's *Lotte
in Weimar* and Aldous Huxley's *Beyond the Mexique Bay*.

'Charles' is Charles Mauron, who had gone completely blind
three years earlier.

156 Mussolini did not resign; he was dismissed from his post by the
King of Italy on 25 July 1943.

Barbe Baker: Richard St Barbe Baker (1899–1982) took a Diploma
in Forestry at Cambridge after World War I and worked from
1920 with the Colonial Office as a Forestry Officer in Kenya. In
1922 he founded a society he named 'The Men of the Trees',
which was dedicated to the planting and protection of trees. In
1929 he resigned from the Colonial Office to pursue his society's
work full-time. One of his ambitions was to reclaim the Sahara
Desert.

James Burnham's *The Managerial Revolution* was published in
1941. In it, Burnham 'forecast a change towards not a classless
society but one dominated by a new class of managers, whose one
object is to manage in its own interest, without ethical considerations.' (See Robert Hewison, *In Anger* (1981), p. 43.)

The verse quotation is the final stanza of Gerard Manley Hopkins's
'Inversnaid' (1881). There should be a comma after 'left' and a
semi-colon after 'wet'.

157 The poem is the last in Stefan George's volume *Das Neue Reiche*
(1928). See Stefan George, *Werke*, vol. I (Munich and Düsseldorf,
1958), p. 469. This edition employs no punctuation at the ends of
lines; 'ein quell' (lines 4 and 14) appears as two words; line 7 has
'im schatten'. Forster's friend E. K. Bennett published a book on
Stefan George in 1954, and presented Forster with a copy. A
translation of the poem appears in *The Works of Stefan George*,
trans. Olga Marx and Ernst Morwitz (2nd Edition, revised and
enlarged, University of North Carolina Press, 1974), p. 410:

You like a flame, unflawed and slender,
You flower sprung from Crown and Spear.
You like the morning, light and tender,
You like a spring, withdrawn and clear,

Companion me in sunny meadows,
Encompass me in evening haze,
And where I go, you shine through shadows,
You cool of wind, you breath of blaze.

You are my thoughts and my desire,
The air I breathe with you is blent,
From every draught I drink your fire,
And you I kiss in every scent.

You like the morning, light and tender,
You flower sprung from Crown and Spear,
You like a flame, unflawed and slender,
You like a spring, withdrawn and clear.

158   The poem by Baudelaire is not in the 1957 text of *Les Fleurs du Mal*, but appears as no. VI ('Hymne') of 'Supplément Aux Fleurs du Mal' in Charles Baudelaire, *Les Fleurs du Mal*, ed. Édouard Maynial (Paris, 1929), p. 241. Line 6: 'imprégné'; line 12: 'la nuit,'; line 19: 'A l'ange, . . . immortelle,'.

To the most dear, to the most lovely,
Who fills my heart with light,
To the angel, to the immortal idol,
Greetings in immortality!

She breathes upon my life
Like a salt-laden breeze,
And in my insatiable soul
Pours the taste of the eternal.

Ever fresh sachet scenting
The atmosphere of a dear retreat,
Forgotten censer smoking
Secretly through the night.

How can I, incorruptible love,
Express you truthfully?
Musk-grain that lies, invisible,
At the bottom of my eternity?

To the most good, to the most lovely,
Who makes my joy and health,
To the angel, to the immortal idol,
Greetings in immortality!

Forster's reference is to *The Ordeal of Mark Twain* by Van Wyck Brooks (London, 1922).

159   In the original, the phrase 'unlike to them' is an interlinear addition placed by Forster in square brackets above 'am I removed'.

160   R. C. Trevelyan and his wife Bessie, old friends of Forster's, were also near neighbours of his.

Two Events. 'Chesfield' (either Chesfield Park or Chesfield Manor) is a house near Forster's early home, Rooksnest in Hertfordshire. I cannot certainly identify Neil Stuart, but conceivably 'Stuart' is Forster's version, here, of 'Steward': it was a family called Poyntz Steward who (according to a talk Forster gave to the Memoir Club in the early 1930s) turned Forster and his mother out of Rooksnest, which they wanted for a friend of theirs, who died soon after. (Mrs Poyntz Steward, whom Forster had visited a year before he gave his talk, lived at Chesfield, 'her bald white house'.) It was evidently on a recent visit to his friends the Postons, who had taken over Rooksnest in 1913, that Forster encountered Neil Stuart again.

Lionel Trilling's important critical study of Forster's fiction (*E. M. Forster*) was published in America in 1943, and in England in 1944.

161   *Balzac: Illusions Perdues* (published in three parts, 1837, 1839, 1843). Among Forster's books at his death was Kathleen Raine's translation of this (*Lost Illusions*) published by John Lehmann Ltd in 1951, with an introduction by Raymond Mortimer. The passage quoted comes in part II, 'A Provincial Celebrity in Paris', and is rendered thus on pp. 312–13 of the translation: 'As she spoke these words that cut Camusot to the quick, Coralie felt for Lucien's leg, and pressed it between hers; she took his hand and squeezed it. Then she was silent, and seemed lost in one of those moments of infinite delight that recompense poor girls like herself for all their past troubles, all their sufferings, and that in their hearts take on a poetry unknown to other women, to whom these violent contrasts are, happily, unknown.' (Coralie, an actress, is the mistress of Camusot, a wealthy tradesman. She falls in love with Lucien de Rubempré, a young provincial who becomes a great success on a Paris newspaper, as poet and journalist.) The sequel to *Illusions Perdues*, *Splendeurs et Misères de Courtisanes*, appeared in 1847.

162   The fourth quotation from Gide, beginning 'Cette méprisable comédie', occurs in his Journal entry for 12 March 1938. Translations:

(1) 'This torpor is sometimes insupportable. But I believe that nothing has better enabled me to sympathise with beings of inferior intelligence than these depressions, these diminutions of value. Something is lacking in Valéry for not having, on some mornings, woken up feeling like an idiot.'

(2) 'Some rot and others ossify; all age. Only great intellectual fervour triumphs over the fatigue and withering of the body.'

(3) 'Indignation certainly, but not hatred. I am and shall remain incapable of hating. Even in the most frightful times of the war. And no doubt it is a great weakness, or it will become so when action calls; but nothing can be done about it.'

(4) 'This contemptible comedy which we all play, more or less; to which I should wish to lend myself less than so many others, and in such a way that my writings find in the very refusal their principal value.'

The quotation from Baudelaire is lines 3-4 of *Les Fleurs du Mal*, XL, 'Semper Eadem'. 'Vendage' should be 'vendange'; there should be a comma after 'connu'; there is no accent on 'a'. Gide quotes the lines in his Journal entry for 21 August 1938: 'When our heart has once reaped its harvest/To live is a sickness. It is a secret known to all.'

163   The quotation from the Lay of the Battle of Maldon (991) is one of the epigraphs on the title-page of vol. I (1934) of Arnold Toynbee's *A Study of History* (12 vols.). Forster omits the commas at the end of the first three lines.

'On Hydon's top . . .': The rhyme is about Hydon Ball, the highest point of Hydon Heath near Burgate, on the route from Woking to Haslemere. See p. 178 of *A Handbook for Travellers in Surrey, Hampshire and the Isle of Wright* (4th edition revised, John Murray, 1888). Forster possessed a copy of this bought by his aunt Laura Forster in 1897. (After 1888, Surrey was dealt with in a separate Murray Guide.) After lines 1, 2 and 3 there should be a comma, a colon, and a comma respectively.

Among Forster's books was the 1871 edition of Carlyle's *The Life of John Sterling* (1851). Sterling (1806-44) founded in 1838 a literary club called the Sterling Club whose members included Carlyle, Tennyson and J. S. Mill. J. A. Froude (1818-94) acted as Carlyle's literary executor, and brought out various biographical remains of Carlyle and his wife, as well as writing a life of him. Lady Ashburton, a friend of Carlyle's, is linked by Forster to Lady Ottoline Morrell, famous for her literary entertaining at Garsington Manor. The bracketed phrases represent cancellations in the original text.

164   Bede, *Ecclesiastical History*, bk. 5, ch. 13 (Loeb translation, Heinemann, 1930, II, 273). J. E. King's translation reads: 'two most wicked sprites having ploughshares in their hands rose up and struck me, the one in the head, the other in the foot; the which strokes now with great anguish creep into the inward parts of my body, and as soon as they meet together I shall die'.

Amiel. I have failed to trace this quotation ('To die all at once is a privilege; you will die by inches'), but it is presumably from Henri-Frédéric Amiel's *Fragments d'un Journal Intime* (1883/84). Forster had an edition of this published in Geneva in 1887. A new edition, in two volumes, appeared in Paris in 1927.

Melville. The quotation comes near the end of 'Bridegroom Dick', published in 1888 in *John Marr and other Sailors*. The first line begins: 'Doff hats to Decatur!' Forster quotes the lines again on p. 189. In April 1943 William Plomer presented Forster with a copy of his *Selected Poems of Herman Melville* (Hogarth Press, 1943), describing Forster in his inscription as 'an earlier investigator of Melville'. The selection does not contain this poem.

Waterton. Forster possessed the third edition (1836) of Charles Waterton's *Wanderings in South America*. I have checked the fourth edition (1839); this quotation appears on pp. 185–6. 'Best of time' (p. 165) should be 'best part of his time'. Waterton, while in Dutch and British Guiana, rode on an alligator, which hardly seems 'stupid obscene cruelty'; but he also got an Indian to kill a five-foot cayman by shooting an arrow in its eye (p. 169), and himself killed a Coulanacara snake (fourteen feet long) by cutting its throat (p. 194). He also killed a cayman (p. 220), and on various of his voyages tried the effects of Indian poison on animals, though not on reptiles.

165   *Seeing this house*: An interesting premonition, since Forster's mother died in 1945 and he himself was obliged to quit West Hackhurst in 1946.

166   *Areopagitica*: In August, 1944, Forster presided at a five-day conference, organised by PEN, celebrating the tercentenary of Milton's *Areopagitica*. His talk, 'The Tercentenary of the Areopagitica', was reprinted in *Two Cheers for Democracy* (1951). The quotations here occur on pp. 705–6 of *Milton: Complete Poetry and Selected Prose*, ed. E. H. Visiak (Nonesuch Library, 1938).

The first dots represent an omitted phrase ($1\frac{1}{2}$ lines); the second $2\frac{1}{2}$ sentences (14 lines); the third $1\frac{1}{2}$ sentences (10 lines).

Abdollatiph: The quotation is from Appendix no. 2, by Samuel Henley (pp. 137–8), to *The Tomb of Alexander: A Dissertation on the Sarcophagus Brought from Alexandria and now in the British*

Museum, by Edward Daniel Clark, LL.D., Fellow of Jesus College, Cambridge (Cambridge University Press, 1805). Forster possessed a copy of this book.

167   The quotation from Ruskin is the conclusion of Ruskin's introduction to his notes on the Turner drawings, owned by him, which were exhibited in 1878 at the Fine Art Society's Galleries, 148 New Bond Street, London. The date given at the end is: 'Brantwood, 12 Feb. 1878.' (See *The Works of John Ruskin*, ed. E. T. Cook and Alexander Wedderburn (London, 1904), XIII, 409–10.)

In the original, the underlined phrase here italicized is linked by a line to 'Oh that someone . . .' in Forster's comment below. This comment is in very small handwriting, and I have been unable to decipher a word after 'attentive to'.

'The Walls . . .': Henry Miller, *Tropic of Cancer* (1934), third printing, Grove Press, New York (1961), pp. 87–9.

After 'Indian Empire' Forster omits two sentences; 'fecundity that' should be 'fecundity which'; there should be a comma after 'virile'.

168   Forster visited the famous temples at Khajraho while staying with the Maharajah of Chhaturpur in 1921.

'Gently and happily . . .': With small alterations, this passage was reprinted, in the section 'The Last of Abinger', in *Two Cheers for Democracy* (1951). (This section also reprints a number of other *Commonplace Book* passages relating to the Abinger area.) In *Two Cheers* 'Edwards' becomes 'Empson', 'fishes' backs' becomes 'fishes' tails', and the word 'wrongs' is omitted. Forster also punctuates more precisely. Paddington is a mill pond just south of the road from Abinger Hammer to Wotton. In the original, a straggly oblique line is drawn beside the indented passages from 'Have done so' to the end.

169   When he and his mother had to leave Rooksnest in 1893 on the expiry of the lease, Forster drew a detailed map of its garden too. This is preserved at King's College, Cambridge, in a small notebook containing Forster's recollections of his early years at Rooksnest.

170   'The world is too much with us . . .': From William Wordsworth, *Poems* (1807). There should be a comma after 'soon', a colon after 'powers', and a comma after 'away'.

After 'the sea' Forster originally wrote 'has to' and then cancelled it.

'The Blake' was presumably Forster's first edition of Blake's *Songs of Innocence*, inherited from his aunt Laura. He presented this to King's College, Cambridge, on 9 January 1959, on the occasion of a luncheon given by the college in honour of his eightieth birthday.

'10.70 p.m.' seems likely to be a slip for '10.07 p.m.'

'There you may wither': This elegiac couplet occupies the centre of an otherwise blank page. Much searching has failed to track it down; conceivably – since he wrote poetry occasionally – it is by Forster himself, though the archaic-sounding 'his spring' argues against this.

172 'Poetry lifts the veil ...': Shelley, *A Defence of Poetry* (1821) (p. 131 in *Shelley's Literary and Philosophical Criticism*, ed. John Shawcross (London, Henry Frowde, 1909)).

The quotation from Clare is the last stanza of 'Adieu': *The Poems of John Clare*, ed. J. W. Tibble (Dent, 1935), II, 511–12. Various commas are omitted; 'yellow cup' should be 'yellow cups.' The poem was written in Northampton Asylum.

173 *Dream Sentences*: The lines 'I will pull down Hastings ...' were used by Forster at the beginning of his essay of 1949, 'An Outsider on Poetry' (a review of Geoffrey Grigson's anthology *Poetry of the Present*), reprinted in 1951 in *Two Cheers for Democracy*. There he calls them 'two lines of modern poetry ... poetry because they scan and modern because they are obscure and minatory'.

Joseph Conrad: Morton Dauwen Zabel's *The Portable Conrad* (New York, Viking Press, 1947) contains *Heart of Darkness* (1899), to which Forster's remark applies well; but not 'Karain: A Memory', published in *Tales of Unrest* (1898). The square brackets and the marginal '?' were added by Forster later, in a different ink.

Dream Sentences: Agnes Dowland had been the Forsters' maid at West Hackhurst. A number of these 'dream sentences' are out-of-sequence additions, added by Forster at the bottom of two facing pages (186 and 187 in the original) presenting 1947 material.

174 'The Kangra Miniature': Forster had revisited India in 1945, and an entry (15 October 1945) in the diary which he kept on this visit sheds light on this reference: 'I ... saw many miniatures at the Lahore museum ... K. and R. [Krishna and Radha] in the rains, a yellow mass hurrying under his umbrella through blacks, greys and greens.' Eric Dickinson, Principal of the Government College, with whom Forster stayed in Lahore, owned some Kangra and other miniatures, and had discovered 'a local school of painters at Kishangarh.' Forster's entry concludes: 'These

Kangra and Kishangarh things have enlarged my feeling for Hindu art, and I think of them with love.'

'Mr Shire': E. S. Shire, a Fellow of King's College, Cambridge, later Vice-Provost.

'Maimie' was Maimie (Mary) Preston, who had married Inglis Synnot, a cousin of Forster's father, then after his death married an older man called Aylward, with whom she lived in a house above Salisbury where Forster often stayed in his youth. She died during the First World War.

175   *Lord Chartley*: The quotation is found in *The Farington Diary*, by Joseph Farington, R.A., edited by James Greig (8 vols, Hutchinson, 1922–8), vol. IV, 1924 (20 September 1806 to 7 January 1808), p. 223. 'Sometimes' should be 'sometime'; there should be a comma after 'ago'. Forster was a member of the Reform Club, hence 'Reform Club paper'.

Presumably Forster had the story of the six policemen from Bob Buckingham, who was in the police. 'D.D.I.' i.e. Deputy Director of Investigations. The blank space after 'Even' is in the original.

Alain-Fournier: see David Paul, 'The Mysterious Landscape: A Study of Alain-Fournier', *Cornhill* no. 972 (Autumn 1947), pp. 440–9. The essay ends with a comparison of Alain-Fournier's *Le Grand Meaulnes* with *A Passage to India*. Paul refers to Forster as 'a writer of genius who refuses to write'.

176   Talleyrand: 'She is all assertion, but when one asks for the evidence, that's her secret.'

'*Give me birds*': The 'grandmother' would be Forster's maternal grandmother, Louisa Graham Whichelo (1827–1911).

'*The years seem to fly . . .*': Ruth Goldsmith had been the Forster's cook.

'Everything depends . . .': This entry was made after the death in 1947 of the Ulster novelist Forrest Reid (b. 1876), a friend of Forster's since 1912. The quotation is from ch. 10 of *Uncle Stephen* (1931, revised edition 1945), p. 416 in *Tom Barber*, containing *Young Tom*, *The Retreat* and *Uncle Stephen* (New York, Pantheon Books, 1955). For this edition, the first American publication of these three novels, Forster provided an introduction.

In the passage quoted, Uncle Stephen is speaking to the adolescent Tom Barber; 'always' is underlined by Reid. Deverell is a lower-class young man who makes friends with Tom, his social superior; a countryman who poaches, he has a touch of Forster's Alec Scudder in *Maurice*.

177   Henry James, *The Princess Casamassima* (1886).

'I haven't ... dance': bk. I, ch. 2 (Mr Vetch speaking to Miss Pynsent about Hyacinth Robinson as a boy), p. 58 in vol. X of *The Bodley Head Henry James* (1972). After 'badly' Forster omits '; that's not the worst thing in the world!'; 'it' should be 'the world.'

'The people ... of the people myself': bk. I, ch. 37 (Mr Vetch speaking to the Princess Casamassima), p. 476. 'Those you used to plead for' should be preceded by 'She hesitated.'; semi-colon after 'plead for'; 'everything' should be 'every one, everything.'

'He changes ... We can at least try': bk. IV, ch. 37 (Princess Casamassima speaking), pp. 478–9. 'In his heart' should be 'on his heart'; semi-colon after 'told you'; comma after 'well'. 'He needn't ... happen.': Mr Vetch replying.

'Paul was looking off toward London ... in it, that ...': bk. IV, ch. 35, p. 460. 'Firm' should be 'fine'; semi-colon after 'people'; 'sturdy newness' should be preceded by 'powerful'. The dots after the final 'that' represent the continuation of James's sentence.

178   Lionel Trilling's article 'The Princess Casamassima: An Introductory Essay' appeared in *Horizon*, April 1958, pp. 267–95. It is hard to see why Forster calls it 'wrong-headed'; Trilling praises the novel as 'a first-rate rendering of social reality'.

I have not traced the source of this quotation, but part of it is also quoted (with 'common wretches' instead of 'worst wretches') in Angus Calder, *Revolutionary Empire* (Cape, 1981), p. 543; he notes that 'a Duchess complained' in these terms, but gives no footnote.

Left Ankle: 'May & Bob' i.e. Buckingham.

179   *Belly*: Eric Fletcher was a miner's son who had come to King's as an undergraduate in 1945. From 1948 (in the summer of which this note was written) to 1950 he was an Education Officer in the RAF.

'Hinchinbrooke' is Hinchingbrook House outside Huntingdon; it had been until 1943 the home of the 9th Earl of Sandwich, a friend of Forster's and a Trustee of the Tate Gallery from 1934 to 1941.

Thomas Gray: The first quotation is from a letter of Gray to William Mason (21 September 1753). See *Correspondence of Thomas Gray*, ed. Paget Toynbee and Leonard Whibley (Clarendon Press, 1935), I, 381. 'Nor wish you should' should be 'nor would wish you should'.

The second quotation is from a letter of Gray to Norton Nicholls

(26 August 1766). *Ibid.*, III, 926. There should be a full stop after 'too late'.

Forster owned a 1925 edition of Gray's Letters, given to him in 1937 by his mother.

180 'E. Fitzgerald.': Edward Fitzgerald (1809–83), author of the *Rubáiyát of Omar Khayyám* (1859).

'3 Trumpington Street': After the death of his mother in 1945, Forster was elected an Honorary Fellow of King's and (unusually) invited to reside there. For his first seven years, however, he did not have sleeping accommodation in College but lodged nearby, in a house belonging to a Fellow of the College, L. P. Wilkinson, and his wife Sydney. An entry in Forster's Diary (31 December 1947) describes his circumstances: 'Time: 11.40 P.M. Place: Cambridge, 3 Trumpington Street, the upper of the two rooms I rent there, the small armchair covered with ragged red Morris chinz [*sic*], a good electric light, a good gas fire, the house empty for the Wilkinsons are seeing the New Year in in College, an occasional car in the street. Above the gas fire, on the cream-yellow wall, the best of the Japanese prints Masood gave me, stuck above the frame a little piece of holly from West Hackhurst, i.e. from Piney Copse, for I have lost West Hackhurst since this book was opened last.'

Notes on a talk with Bob [Buckingham]: The last word was originally 'weak', the 'ened' being added a little later.

181 Ruskin, *Praeterita* (1885–9), vol. I, ch. 6 (London, Rupert Hart-Davis, 1949, p. 107.)

For 'uncritical of' Forster originally wrote, then cancelled, 'indifferent to'.

182 *Toma and Tinka*: These were Forster's two cats at West Hackhurst, Tinka, the younger, being the gift of John Hampson in January, 1937. For Toma, cf. Forster's Diary, 22 October 1946: 'Toma's last night. Much affection during drawing room supper and returned for more. How little I mind his cankered ear. Yesterday morning this very sweet cat, disliking Tinka on my bed, but desirous to honour me, sat on my knee and clawed my pyjamaed breast. What pleasure these cats have been and felt – years of purring, my creation. Tomorrow he will "sleep" in "mother's pocket." Rubbishy word, sleep.'

Emma: Forster had this in the R. W. Chapman edition, but also possessed his mother's copy, which had been given her by Forster's father in 1878. Forster had written in it 'In my mother's room, West Hackhurst, 1946.' Since the previous entry is a dream involving his mother which ended 'in misery', it is tempting to imagine Forster later read his mother's copy of *Emma* to restore something of his 'lost stability'.

Keynes: The quotation is from a paper (dated 9 September 1938) which Maynard Keynes read to the Bloomsbury 'Memoir Club'. (In it, later, he referred to Forster as 'the elusive colt of a dark horse'.) Keynes is speaking of himself at Cambridge in 1902-3, when G. E. Moore's *Principia Ethica* appeared. See Maynard Keynes, *Two Memoirs*, introduced by David Garnett (London, Rupert Hart Davis, 1949), p. 81.

Cocteau. See Jean Cocteau, *Le Mythe du Greco* (1943), vol. X of *Oeuvres Complets* (Geneva, Marguerat, 1946-51). In *Cocteau's World* (1972), p. 263, the passage is translated: 'Poetry forms on the surface of the world like iridescence on the surface of a marsh. The world should not complain. It comes from the depths.'

William Plomer, *Sado* (Hogarth Press, 1931), pp. 118-19. 'She also came'; 'at sea for a flag'; 'game-of-skill in sporting'; 'game-of-chance'. 'She' is Iris Komatsu, an English girl married to a Japanese; the 'also' relates her to Lucas, an English painter.

Ben Jonson: The works referred to are in *Ben Jonson*, ed. C. H. Herford, Percy and Evelyn Simpson (Clarendon Press, 1941), vol. VII.

The first passage is lines 30-73 of *Lovers Made Men* (1617); Lethe questions; Mercury states or answers. Herford *et al.*, pp. 454-5: these editors state that 'Gifford, not knowing the Quarto, renamed the piece *The Masque of Lethe*' – so Forster presumably knew the Gifford version. Herford *et al.* print the passage in its stanza form, like Forster, though they also assign separate lines to each new speaker.

183   Forster quotes lines 9-10 of the 'Panegyric' (Herford *et al.*, p. 113). Its full title is 'A Panegyric, on the Happy Entrance of James, Our Sovereign, to His first High Session of Parliament, in this His Kingdom, the 19 of March, 1603'.

Ruskin, *Praeterita*, vol. I, ch. 12 (Rupert Hart-Davis, 1949, p. 206).

'I find myself in nothing whatsoever *changed*'; '. . . me, I am but the same youth,'.

184   *Ordinance*: Perhaps Forster picked up this example of confused English during his American trip in 1947. 'Norphelt' should be 'Norphlet'.

Purcell: A slightly different version of this catch (with 'same' instead of 'game' in line 6) is printed on the record sleeve of

Vanguard Record BG 602, *Tavern Songs Vol. 2*, sung by Alfred Deller and the Deller consort. (Vanguard Record Society Inc., New York, n.d.)

'Seen at Ben's': In March, 1949 Forster spent sixteen days at the home of Benjamin Britten in Aldeburgh, working with Eric Crozier on the libretto of *Billy Budd*.

Who is Sylvia?: Simon Raven refers to Forster's seeing this play in his article 'The Strangeness of E. M. Forster' (*Spectator*, 225 (1971), p. 237): 'One belief [Forster] most certainly and sincerely held was that everyone must be allowed freedom in his sexual affairs; and some friends who took him to the theatre were therefore very surprised when he started grumbling because, as he said, the play was about "immorality flats".' gta: great actor.

185   'Il donne aux fleurs . . .': This is not in *Esther* but in *Athalie* (1691), I, iv, 13: 'He gives the flowers their lovely colours.'

Recent evening train: For 'Sneers' Forster started to write 'Vulgar s', then cancelled it.

186   See Hector Bolitho, *A Biographer's Notebook* (Longmans, 1950), pp. 164–5. The quotation comes from the final section of Bolitho's book, entitled 'Mowbray Morris: A Late Victorian Man of Letters'. There are, as always, minor differences of punctuation.

'When a man . . .': The quotation occurs on pp. 277–8 of *Hindu Infanticide: An Account of the Measures adopted for suppressing the Practice of the Systematic Murder by their Parents of Female Infants*, edited by Edward Moor F.R.S. (London, 1811). (Dr Leyden was describing a custom in Sumatra). Forster possessed a copy of this book, originally the property of Sir John Lubbock (1834–1913), a Victorian devotee of natural science.

The Bull (which actually begins 'Munificentissimus Deus') was translated in *The Tablet* by Monsignor Ronald Knox (23 December 1950, pp. 553–6).

188   The quotation from Capetanakis is on p. 133 of *Demetrios Capetanakis: A Greek Poet in England* (London, John Lehmann Ltd, 1947). Capetanakis 'died of an incurable disease in Westminster Hospital on March 9, 1944'. The book collects poems and essays by him, and essays on him by John Lehmann, Edith Sitwell, William Plomer and Panayotis Canellopoulos. The reference to *Troilus and Cressida* is on p. 132, and comes from Capetanakis' essay 'A View of English Poetry'.

'The proofs of my own book': *Two Cheers for Democracy* (1951).

'Wordsworth on Londoners': *The Prelude*, bk. VII (1850), lines 725–8.

'The Fitzwilliam': The Fitzwilliam Museum in Cambridge, opposite Forster's lodgings in Trumpington Street.

189   Denton Welch's 'unpublished journal' was published the following year (*The Denton Welch Journals*, edited with introduction by Jocelyn Brooke (London, Hamish Hamilton, 1952)). Denton Welch died 30 December 1948; his journal, 11 May 1942 (p. 66) records 'A fine letter from E. M. Forster full of very *sensible* praise for the book' (*Maiden Voyage*, which had just appeared). Forster referred to Welch's death in his Diary (10 January 1949): 'Denton Welch has died "after a long illness" at 31. Shock and regret that often come to me in the case of someone who hasn't mattered to me. I have been re-reading this evening his Maiden Voyage – so desultory and egotistical, but so first hand. He would not have gone far, but decadence such as his is always welcome and badly needed. Poor chap – hurt his back I think. He wrote to me once, very impassioned and straight, about an agent provocateur, and later on there was a little literary correspondence. I feel so sorry about him, and somehow guilty. Yet there was nothing I could have given him or done for him.'

'I think really . . . joyless way': *Journals*, p. 160 (13 July 1945).

'In my heart . . . Freindship': *Journals*, p. 145 (8 January 1945).

'It becomes more right . . . enjoyed': *Journals*, pp. 224–5 (13 September 1946).

The other two quotations are not in the published book, which cut down the Journal to 'a little over half its original length' (Brooke, p. xiv.)

190   Quotations from Gerald Brenan, *The Face of Spain* (Turnstile Press, 1950).
'Flying induces . . . beside him': pp. 21–2.
'I imagine . . . know him': p. 27 (the speaker is the Spanish guide who showed Brenan round the Church of Nuestra Señora de Almudena in Madrid).
'The feeling of affection . . . faculties?': p. 120 (Brenan talking of his house at Churriana near Malaga). 'Human spirit' should be 'feudal spirit'.

The passage from Ian Stephens, which Forster must have read in manuscript, was eventually published in Stephens's *Unmade Journey* (Stacy International, 1977), p. 274. Stephens, who had worked for many years in India and Pakistan, was at the time a Fellow of King's.

191   'In 1851 . . .': See Reginald L. Hine, *Hitchin Worthies: Four Centuries of English Life* (Allen & Unwin, 1932), p. 367. Rev.

John Alington (1795–1863) owned Letchworth Hall; he figures in Hine's chapter 'A Group of Eccentrics'. Hitchin is the next town to Stevenage, so Forster may have gone there while on a visit to Rooksnest.

'Imagination may consecrate ...': This is the beginning of ch. XI of George Douglas (Brown), *The House with the Green Shutters* (1901): Memorial Edition (Andrew Melrose Ltd, 1923), p. 90. There should be commas after 'that' and 'perfect'.

192 'Writers ought to write ...': Tony Hyndman was a friend of the poet Stephen Spender from 1933 onwards. He appears in Spender's autobiography, *World Within World* (London, Hamish Hamilton, 1951) under the name 'Jimmy Younger'. Fulbourn (Mental) Hospital is just outside Cambridge. 'Patrick and Sydney': i.e. Wilkinson.

Natasha (Litvin) Spender, concert pianist, wife of the poet Stephen Spender.

Don Windham: Donald Windham, American writer whom Forster first met in New York in 1947, when Windham was eighteen. Nick Furbank: P. N. Furbank, later Forster's official biographer; at this time he was Fellow and Director of Studies in English at Emmanuel College, Cambridge. The 'Arts' is the Arts Theatre Restaurant. Norman Routledge was a Mathematical Fellow of King's (1951–60), later a housemaster at Eton. This story certainly does not relate to Dr Routledge's 'Girton hostess', Mrs H. W. Leakey. She cannot recall telling the story of anyone else, although some of her experiences as a wartime billeting officer could have amused Forster.

193 Thomas Babington Macaulay, *The History of England* (10th edition, Longman, 1854), ch. V, pp. 623–4.

Sydney Smith's letter to Bishop Blomfield (of London) was published in *The Times*, 5 September 1840. See *The Letters of Sydney Smith*, ed. Nowell C. Smith (Clarendon Press, 1953), II, 707. Forster owned this two-volume edition. (Cf. Commonplace Book, p. 200.)

194 Eric Bentley, *The Cult of the Superman: A Study of the Idea of Heroism in Carlyle and Nietzsche, with Notes on Other Hero-Worshippers of Modern Times*: first published in America, 1944 (London, 1947).

'No man ever wanted ...': London edition, p. 143.

'Lawrence is to be understood ...': p. 230. 'Modern' should be 'recent'.

'The modesty ...': p. 263.

'Although the naked body . . .': This passage was eventually published in Kenneth Clark, *The Nude* (1956), the first sentence on p. 4; then six sentences which Forster omits; 'it is ourselves . . . false morals', p. 6. (Two sentences are omitted between 'bad morals.' and 'And since . . .'.)

195   Lydia Keynes (formerly the ballerina Lydia Lopokova) was the wife of John Maynard Keynes.

'Disorderly conduct . . .': Four writers called Bonald, all French, are listed in the British Library Catalogue. The likeliest author of this phrase is perhaps the third, Viscount Louis Gabriel Ambroise de Bonald, the nineteenth-century historian and man of letters. Did Forster perhaps see the remark in a book on him, Mary H. Quinlan's *The Historical Thought of the Vicomte de Bonald* (1953)?

'All are as busy . . .': This letter of J. R. Ackerley is not included in *The Ackerley Letters*, ed. Neville Braybrooke (Harcourt Brace Jovanovich, New York and London, 1975).

196   The book Forster was looking at was L. P. Wilkinson, *Ovid Recalled* (Cambridge University Press, 1955). Wilkinson quotes Yeats, italicising the phrase from 'gaily' to 'mind', on p. 125; he gives the source as Yeats, *Autobiographies* (1926 edition), p. 401. (It is on p. 326 of the Macmillan edition of 1955.)

The Ovid quotation (*Tristia*, I, iii, 27–34) is slightly misquoted by Forster: 'cernans' should be 'cernens'; 'nostra' should be 'nostro'; 'diqui' should be 'dique'. (The 1924 Loeb translation is: 'Now the voices of men and dogs were hushed and the moon aloft was guiding her steeds through the night. Gazing up at her, and by her light at the Capitol, which, all in vain, adjoined my home, I prayed: "Ye deities that dwell near by and ye temples never henceforth to be seen by my eyes, ye gods of this lofty city of Quirinus, whom I must leave, receive from me this my salutation for all time." ')

Wilkinson, in a footnote on the passage (p. 313), says: 'Goethe, on his last night in Rome, paced the Colosseum in the moonlight declaiming this passage (*Italienische Reise*, III, pp. 336–7, Sophien Ausgabe, Bd. 32.)'

Proust: 'Old age at first makes us incapable of attempting but not of desiring. It is only in a third phase that those who live to a great age have renounced desire, just as they have had to abandon action.'

'*L'art n'est pas rêves . . .*' 'Art is not dreams but possession of dreams.'

197   Tom Coley was an American actor friend of Forster's. His

'impressions of British adverts' are written down the left margin of Forster's page.

198   Proust: I have not discovered to what edition of *Du Côté de Chez Swann* Forster's pagination refers. It is not that of the Paris edition of 1919 (Gallimard) which was in Forster's library at his death. 'He had for so long given up aiming his life at an ideal goal and turned it towards the pursuit of everyday satisfactions, that he believed, without ever precisely saying so to himself, that this situation would continue unchanged until his death: moreover, no longer conscious of high ideas in his mind, he had ceased to believe in their reality, without being able completely to deny it. Also he had adopted the habit of escaping into unimportant thoughts which allowed him to leave to one side the depths of things.'

'No, thou art come too late . . .': Matthew Arnold, *Empedocles on Etna* (1852), act II, lines 16–18, Empedocles talking to himself.

The Shield of Aeneas is described in Virgil, *Aeneid* VIII, lines 625–732. The lines quoted are 731–2. In 1906 Forster provided an Introduction and Notes for the two-volume Dent edition of *The Aeneid of Virgil*, translated by E. Fairfax Taylor. Taylor translates these lines, which begin with 'Miratur', as: 'He sees, and gladdening at the gift divine,/Upbears aloft the fame and fortunes of his line.' In his Introduction, Forster says that 'the last six books [i.e. 7–12] are less attractive' (p. xvi.)

199   'Secretosque pios . . .': line 670. ('Distant shine/The just, where Cato stands, dealing the law divine.')

Lord Brooke: The first quotation is stanzas 9, 10, and 11 (lines 1–2) of 'A Treatie of Warres' (Fulke Greville, Lord Brooke, *Complete Works in Prose and Verse*, ed. Alexander B. Grosart (4 vols, 1870, Fuller Worthies Library), vol. II, pp. 106–7.) Grosart's text has 'human hope and feare', 'laid on our neckes', 'chang'd:', 'Pride will no more', 'rang'd;' 'For Warre never did love' (stanza 9); 'monuments of mind', 'tyrannise;', 'Wisdom oftimes', 'again;' 'men do beastly raine' (stanza 10).

The second quotation is from section 1, stanza 1, of 'A Treatise of Monarchy' (vol. 1, p. 5). Grosart has 'by united hearts'.

Copulation. For 'estimated', Forster originally wrote 'classified', then cancelled it.

200   Dorothy Parker on Forster. See *Writers at Work: The Paris Review Interviews* (1st series, New York, 1967).

Hippocratic Oath: Forster went on a cruise in the Aegean, with Bob and May Buckingham, in March–April 1956. He referred to it in his Diary (31 December 1956) as one of the '3 good things of 1956', the others being 'the appearance and success of 'Marianne Thornton' ' and 'my autumn week in Leiden'.

201 *Proust to Paul Morand*: 'What desolates me is to see intelligent people placing taste above all else, or at least what they call taste, and denying in advance all that the ages to come will produce.'

202 'The Bursarial Business in Congregation.' This was one of the regular meetings (held once or twice a term) of the King's College Governing Body; at this meeting the re-appointment of the Second Bursar was debated.

Inscription: A fuller version of this appears on p. 252 (see later note).

203 *Shelley*: The first quotation is from *Queen Mab*, part I, lines 85–93. (*The Complete Poetical Works of P. B. Shelley*, ed. Neville Rogers (Clarendon Press, 1972), vol. I, p. 234.) For 'dwelling' in Housman, see *Last Poems* (1922), VII, last stanza: 'And down the distance they/With dying note and swelling/Walk the resounding way/To the still dwelling.'

The only poem by Cavafy which bears any resemblance at all to the 'last two lines' of Shelley quoted here is 'To Call Up the Shades' ('ΓΙΑ ΝΑΡΘΟΥΝ-'):

> One candle is enough. Its gentle light
> will be more suitable, will be more gracious
> when the Shades come, the Shades of Love.
>
> One candle is enough. Tonight the room
> should not have too much light. In deep reverie,
> all receptiveness, and with the gentle light –
> in this deep reverie I'll form visions
> to call up the Shades, the Shades of Love.

(C. P. Cavafy, *Collected Poems*, trans. Edmund Keeley and Philip Sherrard, ed. George Savidis. (Princeton University Press, 1975), p. 199.) The poem was published in August, 1920. Forster first met Cavafy in Alexandria in 1916; when conversations became lively Cavafy had the habit of lighting candles in his room.

For 'crumbled' Forster originally wrote 'fallen away', then cancelled it.

The second Shelley quotation is lines 1027–30 of *Hellas, A Lyrical Drama*. 'Fly far' should be 'flee far'; 'folding star' should be 'folding-star'. Ralph Vaughan Williams's Symphony No. 6 in E minor was first performed in 1948.

'Beesley' is Sir John Davidson Beazley (1885–1970), Professor of

Classical Archaeology at Oxford from 1925 to 1956 and the great authority on ancient Greek vases and vase-painting. Forster is confusing two of Sir Maurice Bowra's books, *The Creative Experiment* (1949) and *The Greek Experience* (1957); he means the latter. 'I.G.': Inscriptiones Graecae.

204 William Cooper, *The Ever-Interesting Topic* (Cape, 1953), p. 189 (ch. II of pt. IV, 'What is Natural is Wicked'). Forster omits two sentences after the first one; the second quoted sentence should end 'much of a darker side'.

St Remy: For 'during' Forster originally wrote 'after', then cancelled it.

205 'Little Laura'. Perhaps Forster's maternal cousin Laura Whichelo (1898–1975).

Rogue Elephant: Forster visited Jaipur in October 1945 to attend a conference of writers organised by the All-India branch of PEN. See his essay 'India Again' (1946), printed in *Two Cheers for Democracy* (1951).

Forster's references are to Harold Kurtz, *The Trial of Marshal Ney* (Hamish Hamilton, 1957).

'Je suis frog . . .': See Kurtz, p. 303: 'Oui, je suis Français – je mourrai Français!' (Ney at his trial).

E. K. Bennett died in 1958.

206 'The artist . . .': Quoted (but no reference given) by Harold Acton in *Memoirs of an Aesthete* (Methuen, 1948), p. 178.

'Kathleen is so optimistic . . .': Kathleen Scott, after the death of her first husband Captain Robert Falcon Scott R.N. ('Scott of the Antarctic') married Hilton Young, 1st Baron Kennet. Their house, Fritton Hythe, was in Suffolk near Lowestoft. E. V. Thompson, the nephew of the pre-Raphaelite artist William de Morgan, had been a fellow-undergraduate and friend of Forster's at King's. The definition of a Capitalist, one who 'knows the ropes', recalls the Schlegel sisters' early view of Henry Wilcox in *Howards End*.

Letter to Benjamin Britten: Britten's 'new surroundings' were his new home in Aldeburgh, The Red House, where he lived from 1957 until his death in 1976. (Previously he had lived at Crag House on the Aldeburgh sea-front, where Forster had worked with him and Eric Crozier on Britten's opera *Billy Budd*.) See photographs 286 and 323 in *Benjamin Britten: Pictures from a Life 1913–1976*, compiled by Donald Mitchell and John Evans (Faber & Faber, 1978). For 'another human being' Forster originally wrote, then cancelled, 'someone else'.

NOTES TO PAGES 207–210

207 'Peter': Britten's friend, the tenor Peter Pears.

See Duff Cooper, *Talleyrand* (Cape, 1932), pp. 362–75. For Forster, Talleyrand's death was 'depressing' because before it he renounced previous anti-church attitudes and acts.

'Siegfried': Siegfried Sassoon.

Forster's remark about Harold Kurtz does not reproduce Kurtz's view accurately. In *The Trial of Marshal Ney* (Bibliography, p. 325, in a note on Duff Cooper's book) he says: 'This imperishable work was hailed as a "work of art" when it first appeared. So it is, but is the sitter worthy of it?'

Forster's quotation from Hardy is from *The Dynasts* part 2, act I, sc. VII (Hardy's opening description). Forster possessed a copy of the 1921 edition of *The Dynasts* inscribed for him by Hardy.

208 David Horner was a close friend of Edith Sitwell's brother Osbert; Edith Sitwell was jealous of the friendship. (See Victoria Glendinning, *Edith Sitwell: A Unicorn Among Lions* (New York, Knopf, 1981), p. 314.)

The verses by Sassoon were sent to Forster for his eightieth birthday, to celebrate which King's College organised a luncheon for him and many of his friends on 9 January 1959. A sidelight on the verses is given in a letter from Sassoon (16 February 1961) to Dame Felicitas Corrigan, a nun at Stanbrook Abbey: 'Morgan Forster – O dear, I love him, but he is dreadfully antichurchdom and needs no help from me, living as he does in an apotheosis of adulation'. (D. Felicitas Corrigan, *Siegfried Sassoon: Poet's Pilgrimage* (Gollancz, 1973), p. 207).

Auden's telegram. Forster quoted this in his birthday luncheon speech, adding: 'I certainly don't want to be a sacred anything, and may be going a little further than Wystan here.'

209 W. B. Yeats, 'The Magi' (first published in *Responsibilities*, 1914). 'Depths' should be 'depth'; there should be a comma after 'stones' but none after 'find'. The 'famous vision of the New Birth' refers to Yeats's 'The Second Coming' (in *Michael Robartes and the Dancer*, 1921). Forster owned a copy of Yeats's *Collected Poems* (1933). It is tempting to wonder whether the last line of 'The Magi' influenced Forster when in November 1961 he wrote his last story 'Little Imber': in this, the wrestling of two men produces a live 'enigmatic mass' on the floor between them.

210 'Half mast . . .': A. C. Pigou (1877–7 March 1959) was a Fellow of King's and (1908–43) Professor of Political Economy at Cambridge. He published many books, including *The Theory of Unemployment* (1933) and *Socialism versus Capitalism* (1937). In old

age he used to recline, as Forster notes, in a deck-chair in the Great Court of the College. The passage in brackets is, in the original, a vertical addition in the margin.

'Addenbrookes': Addenbrookes Hospital, then on Trumpington Street a few hundred yards from King's.

'Gibbs': Gibbs Building, which faces the main entrance of the college.

The Reading professor was Professor Percival Allen (b. 1917), Professor of Geology at Reading from 1952 and previously a Lecturer in Geology at Cambridge. He had concocted a story to the effect that diamonds had been discovered in the Thames Valley. His Vice-Chancellor, Sir John Wolfenden, reprimanded him for this hoax.

William Grey Walter (b. 1910), educated at Westminster and King's; Director, Physiological Department, Burden Neurological Institute, Bristol; author of *The Living Brain* (1953) and other books.

'Pagan minimum'. The phrase 'After many pleasant . . . son of Menon' is surrounded by one of Forster's 'boxes'.

211   *Pigou's Funeral*: 'Noel': Noel Annan (later Lord Annan), at this time Provost of King's.

The Donne passage occurs in *Devotions Upon Emergent Occasions* (1624). Sebastian Halliday (b. 1937), the son of the Shakespeare scholar F. E. Halliday, came up to King's in 1957.

Eastern Sunset: The 'Jumbo House' is the large central archway of Gibbs' Building in the Great Court of King's College, so called because an elephant was allegedly once housed there. The Screen is the long stone arcade dividing the college from King's Parade.

Sir Frank Ezra Adcock (1886–1968) Fellow and (recently) Vice-Provost of King's; earlier, Professor of Ancient History at Cambridge.

'My death . . . a minor boo-hoo': In the summer of 1959 Forster gave the Presidential Address to the Cambridge Humanists; speaking at the end of it about whether his Humanism would help him when he was dying, he said 'I should be glad if it did. I do not want to recant and muddle people. But I do not take the hour of death too seriously. It may scare, it may hurt, it probably ends the individual, but in comparison to the hours when a man is alive, the hour of death is almost negligible'. (Printed in *The Bulletin of the University Humanist Federation*, no. 11 (Cambridge Number), Spring 1963.)

212   *Western Radiance*: The Combination Room, whose windows look westward to the Backs, is the college's senior common room.

Jasper Rose was at this time a Fellow of King's in History. In the 1960s he became a Professor in the University of California.

'the Michael Schweetz': The same picture is referred to in Forster's Essay 'Not Looking at Pictures' (1939): 'Colour is visible when thrown in my way – like the two cherries in the great grey Michael Sweertz group in the National Gallery.' Both Forster's spellings are incorrect: it should be Michiel (or Michael) Sweerts (Flemish painter, 1624–64). I did not find this painting in the National Gallery in 1982, and have been unable to identify it.

'Arthur Snatchfold's canary-coloured shirt': See Forster's story 'Arthur Snatchfold', *The Life to Come* (1972).

At the bottom of this passage (original, p. 228) Forster drew a small circle.

'And now behold me . . .': E. H. W. Meyerstein (1889–1952) was an independent, eccentric scholar who lived in Oxford; he admired Forster and had, in November 1944, sent him a copy of his essay 'The problem of evil and suffering in Beethoven's Pianoforte Sonatas'. Forster possessed a copy of *Some Letters of E. H. W. Meyerstein*, ed. Rowland Watson (Neville Spearman, 1959). This letter occurs on p. 117; it was written to R. N. Greene-Armytage on 17 December 1929 from Tunis. The Turkish bath ('Bain Maure') referred to in it was at M'darouch, a village six miles from Madura, the birthplace of Apuleius; to visit Apuleius' birthplace, Meyerstein says earlier in this letter, was 'the real motive for my coming to this country'. Forster transcribes the letter with some minor errors.

213   'After this day . . .': The names mentioned are those of under-graduates who had come up to King's in 1956. Christopher Bacon had been to Tonbridge, Forster's old school.

Jumping Spider: John Earle Raven (1914–80) was a classical philosopher and from 1948 Fellow in Classics at King's. He had also a great knowledge of botany and helped to administer the Cambridge Botanic Garden. Donald Parry (b. 1915), Fellow of King's since 1948 and Lecturer in Zoology at Cambridge, later became Vice-Provost of the college and (initially in that capacity) one of the Trustees of E. M. Forster's estate.

214   'Fear that the Companions . . .': This entry (as Forster belatedly realised) had already been copied into the Commonplace Book, in longer and slightly different form, in 1956. It appears, on un-numbered pages, after the main body of the text.

Smells: The quotation is from John Knowles, *A Separate Peace* (Secker & Warburg, 1959), p. 128. 'Devon' is the name of the New Hampshire preparatory school in which the novel is set; it is modelled on Knowles's own school, Phillips Academy, Exeter. Forster's 'blurb' does not appear in the British edition of the book.

The Kind Ghosts. Poem by Wilfred Owen, dated 30 July 1918 (See *The Collected Poems of Wilfred Owen*, ed. C. Day Lewis (Chatto & Windus, 1963), p. 102). Forster had been given by Siegfried Sassoon on 15 May 1922 a copy of Wilfred Owen's *Poems* (1920). There should be a comma after 'glooms' and 'pall', and a full-stop after 'hall'.

215 After the comment on the Owen quotation, a passage of half a page in the original is omitted.

Yeats: 'For meditations upon unknown thoughts/Make human intercourse grow less and less': from stanza 8 of 'All Soul's Night' (*The Tower*, 1928). 'Repentance . . . impure;' line 6 of 'Stream and Sun at Glendalough' (June 1932), in *The Winding Stair* (1933).

Il Gattopardo. Forster owned both the translation (*The Leopard*, 1960) and the original Italian novel (Milan, 1958). Forster spoke of the novel in the introduction which he wrote for Lampedusa's *Two Stories and a Memory* (Collins/Harvill, 1962): 'Prince Giuseppe di Lampedusa has meant so much to me that I find it impossible to present him formally. His great novel *The Leopard* (Il Gattopardo) has certainly enlarged my life – an unusual experience for a life which is well on in its eighties. Reading and rereading it has made me realise how many ways there are of being alive, how many doors, close to one, which someone else's touch may open' (p. 5). Forster also spoke of being soothed by the 'astronomical passages' in *The Leopard* (p. 7).

After the 'Oct. 19, 1959' entry one line in the original is omitted.

'I heard from Elizabeth Poston . . .': Forster's old friend, the composer Elizabeth Poston, who had lived at Rooksnest since 1913, wrote to him on 3 October 1960 to inform him that land around Rooksnest was now wanted as the final phase in the development of Stevenage, scheduled as a 'New Town' in 1946. Compulsory purchase orders had been served, and she begged Forster to intervene. He replied immediately, offering financial help, and on 8 October (after another letter from Elizabeth Poston) wrote to Henry Brooke, the Minister of Housing, concluding his letter: 'I do trust that a locality which I found so inspiring in the past and so essentially English will be spared urbanisation, and will survive unspoilt to give pleasure to the English people who come after me.' Brooke's reply, cleverly pointing out that Rooksnest itself was not in danger, did not greatly please Forster, and in any case was not sent until 31 October, by which time the necessary public enquiry (19 October) had already been held at Stevenage. A report of the matter, with a photograph of Rooksnest, appeared in the *Manchester Guardian* (19 October), also a letter of protest signed by, among others, Auden, John Betjeman, Lord David Cecil and Victoria Sackville-West. They wished the area (160 acres) to be protected particularly because it was 'the Forster country of "Howards End", which it is felt by literate people the world over should be preserved in its original setting as one of our great literary landmarks.' The dispute aroused strong feelings locally. The conservationist viewpoint was presented at the hearing by Thomas Sharp c.b.e., Past President of the Town Planning Institute.

216   'The dear little Clive . . .': One of the children of the Buckinghams' son Robin (see p. 220).

'Slowly . . .': Stanza 6 of Wilfred Owen's poem 'Exposure'. There should be colons after 'rejoice' and the first 'closed'; commas after 'fires', 'doors', and the final 'closed'. (*Collected Poems of Wilfred Owen*, ed. C. Day Lewis (Chatto & Windus, 1963), pp. 48–9.)

Half a page is left blank in the original after the Wilfred Owen quotation.

Sidgwick Lecture: The comment at the end marked by Forster's asterisk is in the original written at the bottom of the opposite page.

217   *Boswell on Slavery.* Said by Boswell on 23 September 1777. (*Boswell's Life of Johnson*, ed. G. B. Hill, rev. L. F. Powell (Oxford, Clarendon Press, 1934), III, 204.)

Forster was in Tesserete in Switzerland in August, 1911; after it he went on to Orta, arriving back in England on September 17. His diary entry for 31 December 1911 sheds light on Syed Ross Masood's involvement: 'Tesserete (August). The first week was incoherent joy, though the detail escapes me. Towards the end Masood grew tired of the place and it was less pleasant, but it was clear he liked me better than any man in the world, so I did not mind. Near the beginning, I spoke, seeing that after all he did not realise. He was surprised and sorry and put it away at once. It has made either no difference, or a good difference. I have seen the worst of him, but all is well. I bear his going better now, for we shall never be nearer, and do seem firm at last. – A happy but uncreative holiday.'

'Ugliesh' is presumably Forster's way of writing 'ugly-ish'.

The photograph Forster refers to can be seen opposite p. 176 of P. N. Furbank, *E. M. Forster: A Life*, vol. I (1977).

Forster had published four novels by 1911; though he once referred to *Where Angels Fear to Tread* (1905) as 'my novelette'.

The Orkney-born poet Edwin Muir died in 1959; he had lived a few miles from Cambridge in his last years. See Edwin Muir, *An Autobiography* (Hogarth Press, 1954).

218 'I had acquired ... difficult': p. 205.

'I do not know ... inclusion': p. 114. In Forster's bracket the phrases 'that distinction ... burden' and 'that substance ... transmuted' are quoted from Muir's preceding sentence.

'I had reached the stage ... house': p. 83. Forster's bracket, left blank, was no doubt intended for the insertion of a date, or age. The date was c. 1900, when Muir was thirteen.

'The age ... the arts': p. 47. There should be a semi-colon after 'conceive it'; the dots after 'into it' represent two omitted sentences. The 'war' referred to is that between men and animals.

'I do not much admire ... bores us': p. 181. A half-sentence is omitted after 'personalities'; there should be a semi-colon after '*made*'; the passage should end 'ultimately it bores us'. Muir is comparing A. R. Orage, editor of *The New Age* and later *The New English Weekly*, with his greater friend John Holms, who 'had hardly any personality at all'; instead, he had a 'nature', in Goethe's sense of the word.

'The gentleness ... cleanliness': p. 212.

Drowned in Cam: Albert Lindsay Heather (b. 1937) entered King's as a Choral Scholar in 1957, later becoming a freelance singer and choral conductor. In his diary entry for 29 December 1959 Forster lists his friendship with him as one of his four 'most important events' of the year.

C.D.N.: *Cambridge Daily News*.

Hal Dixon: H. B. F. Dixon, Fellow of King's.

219 The Rev. Ivor Erskine St Clair Ramsay, Dean of King's, committed suicide on 22 January 1956 by throwing himself from the roof of King's College Chapel.

Peacefulness: For 'human earshot' Forster originally wrote 'our', then cancelled it.

220 Henri Gaudier-Brzeska (1891–1915), French sculptor, killed in World War I. He came to London in 1911, was a friend of Ezra Pound and Wyndham Lewis, and was involved with Vorticism and Cubism.

Clive and Paul were the children of Bob and May Buckingham's son Robin.

221   *A week in Rome*: Forster recorded his '2nd Italian visit' as one of his four 'most important events' of 1959. (Diary, 29 December 1959.)

Enzo Crea was a friend Forster made on this visit to Rome. Crea photographed Forster, in November, in a restaurant at Palestrina near Rome, and gave it to Forster as a token of friendship. It is now in the collection of Forster photographs at King's.

Boredom: Initials and a place, in the original, are omitted here. The passage 'an explanation . . . my malais' [*sic*] is enclosed in a box and connected by a line to 'why' in the preceding comments.

222   *The Nude*, by Kenneth Clark, was first published in 1956, by John Murray, not in 1936. The page references to pp. 124, 127 and 213 are correct; but p. 130 should be p. 139.

'The vast crowds.' The top half of Forster's page in the original, above this entry, has been left blank.

223   'You're getting . . .': 'C.D.' is presumably a reference to Charlie Day.

Hansard: In November 1960 Forster appeared as a defence witness in the 'Lady Chatterley' trial, in which Penguin Books were prosecuted under the new Obscene Publications Act (1959) for publishing the unexpurgated text of *Lady Chatterley's Lover*; so he was no doubt amused by the views of his 'betters'. At Forster's death his library contained vol. 596, no. 22 (26 November 1958) of *Hansard* (which included the debate on the Wolfenden Report on homosexuality and the law), but not the issue quoted here.

224   *R. A. Furness*: Sir Robert Allason Furness (1883-1954), an old King's College acquaintance of Forster's. He worked for the Egyptian Civil Service (1906-23), during which time Forster knew him in Alexandria, and from 1945 to 1950 was British Council Representative in Egypt. In 1931 he published *Translations of the Greek Anthology* and *Poems of Callimachus*. P. N. Furbank has suggested that 'Everard' may be someone called Everard Digby. Another possibility is the Hon. Everard Feilding, who was in Alexandria at the same time as Furness. Feilding lived there with D. A. Winstanley, Forster's colleague in Red Cross work.

John Addington Symonds (1840-1893): Material from the memoirs quoted here was made use of (but not verbatim) by Phyllis Grosskurth in *John Addington Symonds: A Biography* (Longman, 1964). Her preface (p. ix) indicates that the manuscript memoirs were bequeathed by Symonds's literary executor, Horatio F. Brown, to the London Library in 1926, 'with a fifty-year embargo on their release for publication'. An entry in Forster's diary (12 October 1939) indicates his involvement with them: 'L.L. meeting on Monday to decide whether Dame Katherine Furse should be allowed to see her father's autobiography. Desmond [MacCarthy], in the chair, said yes. Harold Nicolson asked for further information, although he had already made up his mind. "What do you think, Morgan?" he called unexpectedly. Morgan said, and then turned to my neighbour, Hake, director of the National Portrait Gallery, to find the Dark Ages'. (Dame Katherine Furse got permission.) On the blank page opposite this Diary entry, Forster added a later note relevant to the passages in the Commonplace Book: 'Over 20 years later – 1961 I think – I was allowed to read this, all facilities provided, and have made notes on it in my Commonplace Book, pp. 246, 247, 250.'

225   'Worcester': Phyllis Grosskurth (*op. cit.*) has 'Rochester'.

'Soapy Sam' is Samuel Wilberforce, Bishop of Oxford.

226   'Katherine' appears in Grosskurth (*op. cit.*) as 'Catherine'.

227   *Death-Dream*: 'Shallow', 'Skulls like pickled cabbages' and 'red' are interlinear additions in the original.

'd'Annunzio': Gabriele d'Annunzio (1863-1938), Italian poet and novelist.

228   Henry Sidgwick (1838-1900), author of *Methods of Ethics* (1874), and from 1883 Professor of Moral Philosophy at Cambridge.

229   *Sforza*: Presumably quoted from J. Burkhardt, *The Civilisation of the Renaissance in Italy* (1904), of which Forster possessed a copy.

Tennyson: The first quotation is from *The Princess*, VII, lines 294-7. The second is from *Maud*, XXI, lines 841-3 (the quotation should end with a semi-colon).

Bacilli: Michael David Yudkin (b. 1938) had come up to King's from Eton in 1956. He obtained his Ph.D. in 1963 and became a lecturer in Biochemistry at Oxford.

230   *Bironic Entry*: i.e. made with a Biro – the only such entry in the Commonplace Book. Visiting J. R. Ackerley's flat in London, Forster had fallen on the threshold and broken his wrist (see bottom of this page); for the next few weeks he was in and out of hospital, first for his wrist, then for possible damage to his heart and lungs, then for blood deficiency.

Charles Richard du Vivier (b. 1938) came up to King's in 1958.

His injuries were sufficiently serious to lead to an Aegrotat Degree later in 1961.

Illnesses (April 4th): 'Barry' was a Welsh male nurse. F. R. Iredale was Head Porter at King's from 1954 to 1968.

231   *April 25*: Forster had a copy of Hardy's *Collected Poems* (1919), with Hardy's signature; Forster dated it '27–1–20' in pencil on the fly-leaf. On the back fly-leaf Forster copied out Hardy's poem 'Surview' (first published in *Late Lyrics and Earlier*), omitting the last stanza. Presumably this entry explains why.

April 26: For 'Public', Forster originally wrote 'Private', then cancelled it.

June 3rd: The Buckinghams, who had previously lived in Shepherds Bush, London, moved to a suburb of Coventry in 1953.

Nearly Dying: For 'approach', Forster originally wrote 'accept', then cancelled it. Forster's life was in danger for a day or two before his blood-deficiency was diagnosed. (See P. N. Furbank, *E. M. Forster: A Life*, II, 315.)

232   The Arab general Amr conquered Egypt and entered Alexandria in 641 A.D. Forster quoted his reply in *Alexandria: A History and a Guide* (1922), and described him as 'one of the ablest and most charming men that Islam ever produced'. (See first UK edition (1982), pp. 63/60.)

'I feel now . . .': Forster's 'now' is an interlinear addition.

233   *Burning Words*: Forster presumably read them in a newspaper. William John Carron (1902–69), knighted in 1963, made a Life Peer in 1967, was President of the Amalgamated Engineering Union from 1956 to 1967.

234   *Katanga*. There was much tension at this time between the Central Government of the Congo and the province of Katanga led by Moise Tschombe. Katanga was invaded by Government forces but these were repelled.

'The Rubens': Rubens's *Adoration of the Magi*, painted in 1634. On the death of the Duke of Westminster in 1959, it was sold at auction for £275,000. In March, 1961 the new owner, Mr A. E. Allnatt, gave it to King's College as an adornment for the Chapel; it was finally incorporated in the Chapel as the new altar-piece in the mid-1960s.

'How peaceful . . .': Forster transferred a number of items from West Hackhurst to his rooms at King's, including the elaborate mantel-piece from the drawing-room. (See photographs opposite p. 269 in P. N. Furbank, *E. M. Forster: A Life*, vol. II, 1978.)

Forster's satisfaction here may derive partly from his having finished (with some effort) his last story, 'Little Imber', a month earlier. He mentioned it in his diary for 1 December 1961: 'He [J. R. Ackerley] woke up to help over *Little Imber* which occupied me all November, and might see the light of night after my death . . . No doubt this story, remarkable both [for] its originality and length, has taken much out of me and contributed to my present drowsiness.'

'From letter . . .': Forster originally wrote, then cancelled, 'F.W.' (Florence Whichelo?). One infers from her letter that Forster had sent her money to help mend the roof.

235   *The Woodlanders*: The first quotation is from ch. XVII (Macmillan Library edition, 1949, p. 143); it is spoken by Grammer Oliver to Grace Melbury. 'Any' should be 'Ay,'. The second is also from ch. XVII; it describes the situation of Dr Fitzpiers, living at Hintock.

Forster got to know Thomas and Florence Hardy as a result of his friendship with Siegfried Sassoon. This letter records the first of a number of visits to Max Gate.

236   (ii) Emma Lavinia Hardy, *Some Recollections*, edited by Evelyn Hardy and Robert Gittings (London, 1961).
(iii) Forster's attitude to Florence Hardy is a little ungenerous; she had inscribed a copy of Thomas Hardy's *Winter Words* (1928) for him.
(iv) Arthur Elliot Felkin (1892–1968) came up to King's College in 1911, read Modern Languages and History, and formed a close friendship with Goldsworthy Lowes Dickinson. After World War I he became a member of the Secretariat of the League of Nations in Geneva, and later worked for the United Nations. He retired in 1955 to a beautiful farm-house near Grasse. Throughout his life he kept a Journal (now at King's), extracts of which, entitled 'Days with Hardy' – were published in *Encounter* (April, 1962, pp. 27–33). He was a brilliant conversationalist, an excellent cook, and a devotee of the arts.

Vaughan, 'The Queer': See *The Works of Henry Vaughan*, ed. L. C. Martin (Oxford, Clarendon Press, 1918), p. 539. Martin's text has a comma after 'eyes' and a semi-colon after 'down'.

Heroic Nude: The English painter Keith Vaughan (b. 1912) was fond of painting nude figures in a landscape. Forster's diary (3 January 1952) records the Christmas gift of a Keith Vaughan painting from Christopher Isherwood.

237   W. H. Auden's 'Hammerfest' (first published in the *London Magazine*) was collected in *About the House* (Faber & Faber, 1966),

pp. 57–8. Auden capitalises 'Reptilian Empire' and 'Horse', and has commas after 'nothing' and 'flowers'. The 'scented flowers' that went down at Actium were Antony and Cleopatra, defeated by Octavius.

The unfortunate Ashton: *The Annual Register, or, A View of history, politicks and literature* was originally founded by Edmund Burke and Robert Dodsley in 1758, to record each year's events. It continued to appear until 1954.

238   *The Tables of the Law* (1945, translation of *Das Gesetz*, 1943) is a novella in twenty chapters, written as the introduction to a book containing pieces by ten other writers on each of the Ten Commandments.

Old Age: Forster's Introduction, dated 14 May 1962, was printed in William Golding, *Lord of the Flies* (New York, Coward-MacCann, 1962), pp. ix–xiii. In it Forster describes Piggy as 'the brains of the party', and also as possessing 'the wisdom of the heart . . . He is the human spirit, aware that the universe has not been created for his convenience, and doing the best he can.' (Essentially, he is Forster.) Forster concludes: 'At the present moment (if I may speak personally) it is respect for Piggy that seems needed most [in the world]. I do not find it in our leaders.'

Bertrand Russell (1872–1970) had his ninetieth birthday on 18 May 1962.

239   'Je suis protestant . . .': 'I am a protestant, since I protest against all religions.' Remark by Pierre Bayle (1647–1706), made on meeting the Abbé de Polignac in Rotterdam. The anecdote is recorded, in a slightly different wording, in Louis Thomas (ed.), *L'Esprit du XVIIIᵉ siècle*, vol. II (Paris, Aux Armes de France, 1942), p. 7.

J. F. Millet: The quotation is from a letter Millet wrote (probably just after settling in Barbizon near Fontainebleau in 1849) to his friend Alfred Sensier. See *Jean François Millet: His Life and Letters*, by Julia Cartwright (London, Swan Sonnenschein, 1896), p. 104: 'If you could but see how beautiful the forest is! I run there whenever I can, at the end of the day when my work is done, and each time I come back crushed. The calm and grandeur are tremendous, so much so, that at times I find myself really frightened. I do not know what the trees are saying to each other.'

'May this and the Giver . . .': The name in fact is Pitt-Rivers; the father of 'Michael P.R.', George Henry Lane Fox Pitt-Rivers (1890–1966), described himself in *Who's Who* as 'Owner-Director of the Pitt-Rivers museum, Farnham, Blandford, Dorset.'

The Gibbon passage is the early part of *The Decline and Fall of the Roman Empire*, ch. XLV (Modern Library edition, New York, n.d., pp. 383–4). The capitalising of 'Justin' is Forster's.

240 'Since last September . . .': George Meredith died in 1905, Leslie Stephen on 22 February 1904. Meredith's letter was written 14 February 1904. (See *The Letters of George Meredith*, ed. C L. Cline (Oxford, Clarendon Press, 1970), III, 1490–1, letter 2167.) Forster's dots indicate an omission of five sentences.

241 *Edwin Muir*: Forster quotes the last four lines of 'The Journey Back', first published in *The Labyrinth* (1949). (*Collected Poems*, 1963, p. 172.) The lines should begin with capitals. Forster possessed a copy of Edwin Muir's *Collected Poems 1921–1958* (1960). The quotation is lines 17–20 of Wordsworth's 'Ode to Duty' (1804). Commas should end the first three lines, a full stop the last one.

Little Gidding: With 'And' at the beginning, the line Forster quotes is the last line of *Little Gidding* (1942). There is a further reference to Eliot in Forster's Diary for 28 August 1964: 'Eric [Fletcher] and I played T. S. Eliot reading the 4 Quartets, and despite his priestliness he held us.' *The Dry Salvages* was published in 1941.

242 *Jules et Jim*, starring Oskar Werner, Henri Serre and Jeanne Moreau. Dabo is in France, twenty-five miles west of Strasbourg.

Francis Brabazon, Australian author. *Stay with God* appeared in 1959. Before 'Brabazon' Forster originally wrote 'King', then cancelled it. (Francis King, born 1923, is an English novelist who spent some years in Japan, knew Forster, and published a book on him in 1978.)

243 *Wordsworth*: *The Prelude* (1850), bk. III, lines 58–63.

'Gran's death': that of Forster's maternal grandmother, Louisa Graham Whichelo.

244 *George Herbert*: The first quotation is stanzas 5 and 7 of 'The Star' (from *The Temple*). The full text of stanza 5 reads: 'Then with our trinity of light,/Motion, and heat, let's take our flight/Unto the place where thou/Before didst bow.' The second quotation is stanza 9 of 'Businesse' (from *The Temple*). 'Ownself' should be 'own self'. After these two quotations (side by side in the original, p. 270) Forster left the rest of the page blank.

Tennyson: *In Memoriam* CXXIV, lines 15–16.

'Rob's death': Robin Buckingham (b. 1933) died of Hodgkin's Disease in September 1962. Despite what Forster says here, he was deeply upset.

Hayden's [*sic*] *Creation*. For 'accelerating' Forster originally wrote 'increasing', then cancelled it.

245   *Henry Kirke White* (1785–1806): Forster's copy, which had belonged to Laura Mary Forster, was the third edition (1855) of his *Poetical Works*. I have checked Forster's references against *The Life and Remains of Henry Kirke White of Nottingham, late of St John's College, Cambridge* (1825). (Kirke White was a senior sizar of the college.) Southey encouraged him to publish a second edition of *Clifton Grove, and Other Poems* (1802), which had been harshly criticised in the *Monthly Review*; he was also helped by Wilberforce and by Charles Simeon. Since Kirke White died young of consumption and was a 'deserving' member of the working class, one might expect more sympathy from Forster; but he is churchy and rather priggish, and tends to 'put on the style'.

'If I choose . . . strikes me much': From a letter to Ben Maddock from Cambridge, 26 October 1805 (p. 309); the sentences follow each other, despite Forster's separation of them.

'I am going . . . quite adequate': Letter to Ben Maddock from Cambridge, 17 February 1806 (p. 333).

I have corrected Forster's error in 'bookplate'; he wrote 'book-place'.

246   *Astronomy*: The reference is partly to Fred Hoyle, *Astronomy* (Macdonald, 1962), where Hoyle says: 'the Earth was aggregated out of a large number of small, cold bodies' (p. 25). But the estimate of the age of the earth does not occur there, but in a number of places (including p. 62) in Hoyle's *Frontiers of Astronomy* (Heinemann, 1955). 'For humans' is an interlinear addition.

Richard III: The version with Laurence Olivier in the leading role. Mattei Radef was a young antique dealer in London.

For 'princes' Forster originally wrote 'babe', then cancelled it.

247   *Pudendalia*: For 'sexed big' Forster originally wrote 'furnished hard', then cancelled it; for 'an artist's model' he originally wrote 'a subject for art'.

No novel of this name by Hal Porter appeared.

Simon Raven (b. 1927), educated at King's (1948–52). Author of many novels, including those in the 'Alms for Oblivion' sequence. His book *Boys will be Boys* appeared in 1963.

248   *Comus*: The quotation is lines 372–4 (*Milton: Complete Short Poems*, ed. John Carey (Longman, 1968), p. 194). It is connected by a line to '*now can't find it*'.

William Golding: *The Spire* was published in 1964. On 24 June 1964 Forster visited Golding in Salisbury and was driven by him to Figsbury Rings, the 'Cadbury Rings' of *The Longest Journey* (Diary, 26 June 1964).

The Nebuly Coat, by John Meade Falkner, was published by Edward Arnold (Forster's own publishers) in 1903.

249 *To Benjamin Britten*: A name in the original has been omitted here. 'A piece of Greek stuff . . .' See P. N. Furbank, *E. M. Forster: A Life*, II, 316: 'He gave several thousand pounds to the Fitzwilliam Museum in Cambridge towards the buying of a Greek sculpture'. 'The Requiem': Britten's *War Requiem* (1961), which was performed by the Cambridge University Musical Society in King's College Chapel on 9 June 1964. Irene Seccombe was secretary of the C.U.M.S.

Britten's reply to Forster's letter was sent from Venice on 16 February 1964: 'Morgan dearest, You are quite right 'shit' is the only word for [   ]. Having wrecked one great man (admittedly the weakest of Great men) he now tries to harm another great man by cheap pin-pricks. Luckily Donald Mitchell realises it, and won't sully Faber's name by publishing such stuff – and your reputation in the States is so high and strong that no one can take this more seriously than his other rot. But doesn't it make one furious? My blood is still boiling although your letter arrived an hour ago. You mustn't let it worry you, my dear – secure in your position of the greatest influence for good, intelligence, tenderness and wit of our times . . . You know what you mean to all of us, of every generation.'

George Borrow, *Lavengro* (1851), ch. XXI. 'For how frequently . . .'; 'and in wakefulness'. The final dashes are Forster's; Borrow's sentence continues normally.

Mont Blanc: Shelley's poem 'Mont Blanc' is dated 23 July 1816; one agrees with Forster's comment – the description lacks particularity and sharpness. The letters, a sequence of four (dated 22, 24 and 25 July and 2 August 1816), were written from Chamonix to Thomas Love Peacock. The sequence is collectively numbered 358 in vol. 1 of *The Letters of P. B. Shelley*, ed. Frederick L. Jones (Oxford, Clarendon Press, 1964), pp. 495–502. The phrase Forster refers to is in the third letter: 'One would think that Mont Blanc was a living being and that the frozen blood forever circulated slowly thro' his stony veins' (p. 500).

The letters are better than the poem: graphic and observant, as well as 'sublime'.

250   *A Flake of Blake.* The lines occur in the 'First Night' section of
      Vala, or The Four Zoas (1797); immediately after them comes the
      line from which Forster derives his own title: 'This was the
      Lamentation of Enion round the golden Feast.' (See *Poetry and
      Prose of William Blake*, ed. Geoffrey Keynes (Nonesuch Press,
      1927), p. 297.)

251   *James E. Baxter*: correctly, James K. Baxter, New Zealand poet
      (b. 1926). His poem is not quoted in the introduction of *Summer
      Fires and Winter Country* by Maurice Shadbolt (Eyre & Spottis-
      woode, 1963), since there is no introduction. It is in fact the
      epigraph preceding the 'Summer Fires' section in this two-block
      book of short stories. There should be a comma after 'groaning';
      and a stanza division between lines 4 and 5.

      Fartus: Forster is commenting on a photograph (plate 41, 'A
      Fartus boy in the reed beds') in Wilfred Thesiger, *The Marsh
      Arabs* (Longman, 1964), between pp. 106–7. The pose is rather
      ungainly, with protruding stomach and buttocks. The boy, naked
      except for a head-cloth, has a circumcised penis (not erect) which
      is the same length as his scrotum. Forster somewhat exaggerates
      his endowment. The next to last sentence originally read: 'Do the
      river gods bruise him into ecstasy and swallow his seed?'

      Greek and Latin: When Forster died, there was no memorial
      service in King's College Chapel; instead, a memorial concert
      was given in the college hall on 22 November 1970, attended by
      (among others) more than fifty of Forster's friends from else-
      where.

252   *The Pumpkin Eater*, by Penelope Mortimer (Hutchinson, 1962).
      Forster's description of the final chapter (ch. 25) is quite a reason-
      able one. The 'tower' is a real one, to which the wife of the 'main
      male character', Jake Armitage, retires to live alone; Jake and the
      children 'join' her there, but at first the children seem 'like
      beaters' closing in on her.

      Chesterton Church: The inscription, quoted by Forster minus its
      first four lines on p. 202, is just by the entrance to St Andrew's
      Church, Chesterton, Cambridge. Neither Forster nor 'Mr Eden'
      gets it quite right; there are water marks still on the left of the
      inscription, but when I checked it (25 August 1981) it seemed
      recently cleaned and was not at all difficult to decipher. Line 1:
      'offend' should be 'attract'; line 2, comma after 'by'; line 4, no
      comma after 'colour', full stop after 'own'; line 6, no dash or
      exclamation mark, semi-colon after 'disgrace'; line 7, comma after
      'toils', full stop after 'came'; line 9, semi-colon after 'Christ',
      comma after 'dear'; line 10, full stop after 'here'; line 11, comma

after 'came'; line 12, comma after 'flowers', semi-colon after 'fame'; line 14, 'wreath', semi-colon after 'breast'; line 16, 'some' (Eden), not 'sons' (Forster).

253   *Anna Karenina*: For 'scarcely', Forster originally wrote 'never', then cancelled it.

Mahler: The famous contralto Kathleen Ferrier died of cancer of the throat on 8 October 1953 at the age of 41. She recorded Mahler's *Das Lied von der Erde* in 1952 with the Vienna Philharmonic Orchestra under Bruno Walter. The date I have transcribed at the end is actually written, in a 'box', after the words 'too readily'.

254   *New Religious Fantasy*: '=ls' i.e. 'equals'.

Gombrich: 'Visual Metaphors of Value in Art' (pp. 12–29) is the second essay in E. H. Gombrich's collection *Meditations on a Hobby Horse and Other Essays on the Theory of Art* (Phaidon Press, 1963). The quotation is on p. 15; 'could thus feast the eye'; 'admire balance sheets'; 'civilization'; comma after 'hoard'.

255   *Saint Cerf*: I have not located an actual place of this name.

Constable painted two large pictures (dated 1828–9) of Hadleigh Castle in Essex; both are large (c. 48 × 65 inches.) They appear (plates 121 and 122) in Basil Taylor, *Constable: Paintings, drawings and Watercolours* (Phaidon Press, 1973). Taylor calls plate 121 (which is very similar to plate 122) Constable's 'most tragic work, the picture most strongly charged with an unequivocal and fierce passion' (introduction, p. 31). Despite Forster's disclaimer ('there is no physical resemblance'), the landscape of Constable's picture does have similarities to that of Forster's dream. Forster refers to the painting in his diary (27 February 1965): 'A little note to say that I have been enjoying the official Second World War Pictures in All Saints Passage [Cambridge] this afternoon – looking back at the Pipers and Moores and even at the Ardizzones. This, following on a much greater experience two days ago with the Constables at Burlington House [in London, the home of the Royal Academy], shows that visual objects can remain if beckoned. I would like to preach this truth to others, but preaching dims, – I have touched on Hadleigh Castle in the other book.'

The 'friend from Shingle Street' (a hamlet twelve miles south of Aldeburgh, on the Suffolk coast) was Norman Scarfe, once a lecturer in history at Leicester University, later Editor of the Shell Guides to regions of Great Britain.

Melvin Calvin, chemist and author of various books including *Chemical Evolution* (Oxford University Press, 1969).

256 *Nearly Dying*: For 'left' Forster originally wrote 'right'; 'happy' is presumably a slip for 'happened'.

Philo: *On Dreams*, I, 44–5. Forster (significantly or otherwise) does not transcribe the whole of Philo's last sentence, which concludes: 'as sojourners to be ever seeking for removal and return to the land of your fathers.' (*Philo*, Loeb Edition, 1934, vol. V, trans. Colson Whitaker, p. 319.)

257 Pages 292–300 in the original are blank. The entries headed 'Book' were made on later, unnumbered pages, the entry marked 'x' (here between rules) and the two titles (p. 259) being written on otherwise blank pages opposite. These entries all date from about 1956. What the 'Book' was intended to be – other than a set of comments separate from the Commonplace Book proper – is not clear.

For 'author' Forster originally wrote 'person'.

258 Orwell. Forster is referring to his review of *Shooting an Elephant* (1950), published in *The Listener*, 2 Nov. 1950, p. 471.

'Recent book by the Priestleys': *Journey down a Rainbow*, by J. B. Priestley and his wife Jacquetta Hawkes (Cresset Press, 1955).

'Marianne has been enough': *Marianne Thornton* (1956).

'Bunny Leff': Gordon Leff (b. 1926) was a Fellow of King's from 1955 to 1959. He later became Professor of Medieval History at the University of York.

For 'kill' (in 'The Companions' section) Forster originally wrote 'destroy'.

259 For 'guess' Forster originally wrote 'speculate'.

'The Coventry Glass': Forster possessed a copy of *Windows for Coventry* [Cathedral] by Robin Darwin, Basil Spence *et al.* (1956).

John Osborne, *Look Back in Anger* (1956).

Index

Numbers in italics signify quotations

Ackerley, J. R., 54, 157, 158, *195–6, 230*, 262, 275, 342, 353, 355
Acton, John Emerich Edward Dalberg Lord, *117–18, 119*, 159, *162*, 304–5
Adcock, Sir Frank Ezra, 211, 347
Adventures of a Younger Son (Trelawney), 11, 263
Alain, 266
Alain-Fournier, 175, 335
Albion and Albanius (Dryden), 71–2, 282
All for Love (Dryden), 70–1, 282
Allen, Percival, 347
Ambassadors, The (James), 13, 14, 263, 264
Amiel, Henri-Frédéric, *164*, 332
Anna Karenina (Tolstoy), 252–3, 361
Annan, Noel, 211, 347
Aristotle, *21*, 62, 63, 266
Arliss, George, 98, 295
Arnold, Matthew, 7, *23, 198*, 267, 343
'Arthur Snatchfold' (Forster), 348
Aspects of the Novel (Forster), 22, 261, 262, 263, 264, 265, 266
Aubrey, John, 89–90, 291, 296
Auden, W. H., *208, 237*, 298, 346, 355–6
St Augustine, *131, 132, 133, 134, 135*, 311, 312, 313
Ausonius, 319
Austen, Jane, 12, 15, 19, 124, 182, 337–8
Aylward, 'Maimie', *174*, 335

Bacon, Francis (Lord Verulam), *43, 200*
Baker, Richard St Barbe, 156, 328
Bakunin, Michael, *128, 146, 147*, 320
Baldwin, Mrs Stanley, 25
Balzac, Honoré de, *161*, 327–8, 330
Barger, Florence, 91, 261, 292
St Basil, *141*, 318
'Battle of Maldon, The', *163*
Baudelaire, Charles, 156, *158, 162*, 329, 331
Baxter, James K., *251*, 360

Bayle, Pierre, *239*, 356
Beaumont and Fletcher, *170–1*
Beazley, Sir John Davidson, 203, 344–5
Bede, the Venerable, *164*, 332
Beerbohm, Sir Max, 26, 105, 267, 298
Beethoven, Ludwig van, 95, 111, 158, 160, 222, 294, 309
Bell, Clive, 153
Belloc Lowndes, Marie Adelaide, 59, 277
Bennett, Arnold, 59, 69
Bennett, E. K., *126*, 205, 309
Benson, E. F., 18
Bentley, Eric, 194, 341
Berenson, Bernard, 284
Bewick, Thomas, 105, 298
Bible in Spain, The (Borrow), 11, 263
Bijapur, 48, 273
Birkenhead, Lord, 93, 293
Blake, William, 2, 170, *250*, 260–61, 334, 360
Bleak House (Dickens), 20
Bloomsbury, 48–9
Boccherini, Luigi, 209
Boileau, Nicolas, *81–2*, 286–7
Bone, Henry, 55, 160, 169, 276
Borrow, George, *249*, 359
Boswell, James, *217*, 350
Bowra, Sir Maurice, 203, 345
Brabazon, Francis, *242*, 357
Brahms, Johannes, 32
Bray, Reginald, 57, 276
Brehmer, Robert G. Jr., 197
Brenan, Gerald, *190*, 340
Bridges, Robert, 100, 296
Britten, Benjamin, 184, 208, 249, 265, 339, 345, 346, 359
Bronte, Charlotte, 18, *21*
Bronte, Emily, 8, 12
Brooks, Van Wyck, 330
Brothers Karamazov, The (Dostoievsky), 7
Browning, Oscar, 31, 32, 270

Buckingham, Bob, 91, 127, 130, 144, 149, 150, 178, 180, 181, 192, 202, 220, 231, 232, 234, 249, 256, 292, 293, 303, 335, 337, 343, 354
Buckingham, Robin, 350, 352, 357
Buckingham, Duchess of, *178*
Bunyan, John, *107, 108*, 299
Burdett, Osbert, 102, 297
Burney, Fanny, 3, 295
Burnham, James, 156, 328
Butler, Samuel, 3, 25, 27, 55, 156
Byron, Robert, *112*, 302

Caine, Hall, 112
Calvin, Melvin, 255, 361
Cambridge, 49–50
Capetanakis, Demetrios, 158, *188*, 189, 339
Captain Singleton (Defoe), 9
Carlyle, Thomas, *1*, 32, *163*, 194, 260, 331
Carpenter, Edward, 52–3, *163*, 278
Carr, E. H., 146, 147, 320–21
Carron, William John, *233*, 354
Castle Acre, 34, 270
Cavafy, C. F., 202, 213, 344
Chamberlain, Neville, 105
Chaplin, Charlie, 44, 272
Chartres Cathedral, 26, 267
Chekhov, Anton, *54*, 275
Chesterton Church, inscription on, 202, 252, 360–61
Chevalley, Abel, 272
Cinna (Corneille), 63, 278–9
Clare, John, *172–3*, 334
Clark, Kenneth, 162, *194–5, 222–3*, 237, 246, 342, 352
Clark, Brigadier Terence, *242*
Clarissa Harlowe (Richardson), 11, 12, 263
Claudel, Paul, 32, 270
Claudian, *132*, 312
Clemenceau, Georges Eugène Benjamin, *256*
Clough, Arthur Hugh, *117*, 304
Cocteau, Jean, *150, 182, 206*, 323, 338
Cole, Leslie, 231, 232
Coleridge, Samuel Taylor, 83, *84–7*, 180, 288–9
Coley, Tom, 197, 342–3
Collier, John, 89, 93, 290–91, 293
Colonel Jack (Defoe), 10
Commodian, 131, 311
Connolly, Cyril, 56, 76, 284
Conquest of Granada, The (Dryden), 65–8, 280–81
Conrad, Joseph, 8, 12, 18, 30, 59, 173, 334

Constable, John, 255, 362
Cooper, Duff, 207
Cooper, William, *204*, 345
Corneille, Pierre, *61–5*, 278–80
Cornford, F. M., 114, 303
Couperus, Louis, 9, 262
Courier, Paul-Louis, *129*, 310–11
Coventry, 232
Coventry Cathedral, 241, 259, 362
Cowie, Laura, 36, 270
Cowley, Abraham, *106–07*, 299
Cowper, William, *115*
Crabbe, George, 151, *194*
Craft of Fiction, The (Lubbock), 7
Cranford (Mrs Gaskell), 12
Crea, Enzo, 221, 352
Crozier, Eric, 265, 339
Cunningham Graham, R. B., 27
St Cyril of Alexandria, 142
St Cyril of Jerusalem, 142

D'Annunzio, Gabriele, 227, 353
Dante Alighieri, 39, *82–3*, 123, 287, 307
Darling, Malcolm, *95*, 293–4
Darwin, Charles, *149, 201*, 322–3
Day, Charlie, 34, 223, 270, 273, 274, 352
Defoe, Daniel, *4–6, 9*, 10, 12, 21
de la Mare, Walter, 20, 74, 161
Deloney, Thomas, *40–1*, 272
Dewas Senior, Maharajah of ('Bapu Sahib'), 130, 293–4, 311
Dickens, Charles, 4, 12, 16, 18, *19*, 192
Dickinson, Eric, 334
Dixon, H. B. F., *351*
Donne, John, *211*, 347
Dostoievsky, Fyodor, 12, 17, 18
Douglas, Norman, *16*, 20, *100–01*, 105, *213*, 264–5, 266
Douglas (Brown), George, *191*
Dowland, Agnes, 173, 334
Dryden, John, 26–7, *65–8, 69–72, 74*, 267–8, 281, 282, 283
Du Bartas, Guillaume Salluste, *43*, 272
du Vivier, Charles Richard, 230, 353–4

Ecclesiasticus, Book of, *24*, 267
Eddington, Sir A. S., 37, *38–9*, 45–7, 271, 273
el Adl, Mohammed, 213, 227, 244, 261
Eliot, George, 18, *124*, 307
Eliot, T. S., *53*, 148, 241, 266, 275, 278, 321, 323, 357
Engels, Friedrich, *109*, 300, 301, 303
Erewhon (Butler), 10
Ezekiel, Book of, 104, 297

Farquhar, George, 283
Farrer, Lord, 36, 37, 271, 276
Farington, Joseph, *175*, 335
Farrington, Benjamin, 113, 114, 303–4
Feilding, Everard, 352
Felkin, Arthur Elliott, 236, 355
Ferrier, Kathleen, 254, 361
Fielden, Lionel, 156
Fielding, Henry, 8, 11, 12
Figgis, John Neville, 313
Fisher, H. A. L., 129, 310
Fitzgerald, Edward, 74, 180, 337
Fletcher, Eric, 179, 195, 258, 336
Fond du Lac (Wisconsin), 198
FORSTER, Edward Morgan, topics mentioned or discussed by: resentment, 1–2, 166; character, story and pattern in the novel, 6–7, 12; time in the novel, 8–9, 20, 28; English versus foreign novels, 12; 'round' and 'flat' characters, 15–16; evil in fiction, 17–18, 58; boredom, 18, 221–2; bores, 27, 28; writers' aims, 20–1; love, 23, 33–4, 39, 93, 201, 226–7; animals, 25, 90, 102, 105, 118, 181–2, 191, 214, 258, 259; 'a *middle-aged* novel', 29–30; his mother, 30, 40, 55, 176, 243, 254; his elusiveness, 31; moments of heightened awareness, 31, 95–6, 105, 150, 155, 168, 172, 185, 211, 212, 228, 234; forgetfulness, 32, 224; music, 32, 91, 95, 111–12, 126, 158, 160, 184, 203, 209, 215, 222, 244, 294; West Hackhurst and the surrounding area, 36–8, 39–40, 55, 56, 58, 79, 98, 112, 159, 165, 168, 169; astronomy, 38–9, 187, 221, 246; death, 41, 95, 102, 218–19, 231–2, 254, 258; character-reading, 44–5; literature, 47–8; sense of place, 51; thought and logic, 52; dreams, 54, 92, 102, 103, 112–13, 165, 173–4, 181–2, 197, 227, 234, 255, 256; old age, 55, 57, 58, 160, 187, 188, 224, 238, 247; trees, 56–7; women, 59–60, 92, 93, 149, 173, 175, 226, 227; criticism, 78; his own character, 85, 97–8, 101, 103, 105, 159, 238, 258; his own writing, 87, 150–1, 188, 219, 230, 238, 257–8; *Howards End*, 203–4; money, 91–2; own letters transcribed (to Goldsworthy Lowes Dickinson, 92; to Stephen Tennant, 98–9; to Benjamin Britten, 206–07, 249; to the Mistress of Newnham, 216–17; to William Golding, 248); happiness, 94, 95; his health and physical state, 99–100, 171–2,

178–9, 192, 230–3, 253, 256; Robert Bridges, poem on, 100; India and matters Indian, 168, 174, 205, 233, 254; tourists, 181; copulation, 199–200; honour, 201–02; resistance to death-bed conversion, 207, 251; nearly run over, 213; children, 220, 246
Forster, Laura, 271, 276, 290, 331, 334
France, Anatole, 13
Frankfort, 48
Franklin, Benjamin, *120*
Froude, J. A., 163
Fry, Roger, 100, 163, 296
Fulke Greville, Lord Brooke, *199*, 343
Furbank, P. N., 192, 261, 272, 277, 290, 293, 295, 302, 309, 324, 341, 352, 354, 359
Furness, Sir Robert Allason, 224, 352

Gandhi, Mahatma, 156
Garnett, David, 18, 19, 265, 266
Gaskell, Elizabeth, *127–8*, 323
Gaudier-Brzeska, Henri, *220*, 351
Geneva, 91, 292
George VI, King, 103
George, Stefan, *157*, 194, 328–29
St Germain d'Auxerre, 146
Gibbon, Edward, 45, *239–40*, 273, 357
Gide, André, 155, *162*, 269, 327, 330–31
Gifford, Walter S., *54*
Gifford, William, *113*, 302
Giono, Jean, 155, 327
Goldsmith, Oliver, 11, *19*, 265–6
Goldsmith, Ruth, 176, 335
Gombrich, E. H., *254*, 361
Gray, Thomas, *179–80*, 336–7
Great Expectations (Dickens), 18, 19, 265
Green, Julien, 58
Green Mansions (Hudson), 11, 263
St Gregory of Nazianzen, 142
St Gregory of Nyssa, 142
Grey, Edward (Viscount Fallodon), 266, 298
Gulliver's Travels (Swift), 10, 11

Halliday, Sebastian, 211, 347
Hamilton, Clayton, 263
Hampson, John (John Simpson), 261, 315, 319, 324, 327–8, 337
Hansard, *223–4*, 352
Hardy, Emma, 236, 355
Hardy, Florence, 236, 355
Hardy, Thomas, 7, 12, 100, 124, *148*, *207–08*, 209, 231, *235*, 296, 322, 346, 354, 355

Hawthorne, Nathaniel, 17, 18
Haydn, Joseph, 244, 245, 358
Heard, Gerald, 18, *36*, 37, *49*, 52, 53, 92, *125*, 127, 129, 133, 265, 274, 308
Heart of Midlothian, The (Scott), 12
Heather, Lindsay, 218, 351
Hedda Gabler (Ibsen), 36
Hegel, G. W. F., 311
Heine, Heinrich, 47
Hemingway, Ernest, *99*, *123*, 296, 307
Henley, Samuel, *166*, 332–3
Herbert, George, *244*
Hill of Devi, The (Forster), 296
Himerius, 144
Hine, Reginald L., *191*
Hippocratic Oath, 201
Hitler, Adolf, *110*, 301
Hodgkin, Thomas, 137, *140*, 317
Hölderlin, Friedrich, 32
Holroyd, Michael, 269
Home, Henry (Lord Kames), 285
Hopkins, Gerald Manley, *156*, 328
Horner, David, 208, 346
Housman, A. E., *21–2*, 32, 47, *61*, 84, 85, 105, 203, 266–7, 270, 278, 288, 344
Howland, Allan, *123*
Hoyle, Sir Fred, *187*, 246, 358
Hudson, W. H., 27
Hutchinson, Hilton, 98–9
Huxley, Aldous, 163
Huxley, Sir Julian, 110, 244, 245, 301
Hyndman, Tony, 192, 341

Ibsen, Henrik, 23, *35*, 43–4, *105*–6, 109, *121*–2, 222, 270, 299
Isherwood, Christopher, *99*, 105, 295, 298, 355
Ithen, Pino, 217
'Ivory Tower, The' (Forster), 109

James, Henry, 7, *13–14*, 18, 19, 29, 62, 74, *89*, *177*, 178, 290, 336
'Jean Paul' (Johann Friedrich Richter), 1, 260
Jebb, Bishop John, 1
St Jerome, *132*, *133*, *135*, *136*, 312, 313, 314–15
Johnson, Samuel, 4, *75*–7, 78, *79–80*, *148*, 261, 283–6, 322
Jonson, Ben, *182–3*, 338
Jones, Henry Arthur, 7, 262
Journal of the Plague Year, A (Defoe), 11
Joyce, James, 3, *31*, 49, 58, 87, 269, 289–90
Jules et Jim (Film), 242, 357

Keyes, Sidney, 311
Keynes, Lydia (Lydia Lopokova), *195*, 342
Keynes, John Maynard, *182*, 338
King Lear, 243
King's College, Cambridge, 260, 262, 267, 270, 276, 333, 334, 346, 347, 348, 360
Kirke White, Henry, 245, 358
Knowles, John, *214*, 349
Koteliansky, S. S., 85, 288
Kurtz, Harold, 205, 345, 346

La Bruyère, Jean de, *34*, *107*, 270, 299
Lady Chatterley's Lover (D. H. Lawrence), 223–4, 352
Lampedusa, Prince Giuseppe di, 349
Lanchester Tradition, The (Bradby), 105, 298
Lawrence, D. H., 49, 50, 60, *120*, 163, 264, 277, 305
Lawrence, Frieda, 59, 277
Lawrence, T. E., 58, 60, 105, 153–4, 163, 271, 277, 325
Le Cid (Corneille), 61–3
Leff, Gordon, 258, 362
Lenin, V. I., *36*, *110–11*
Lessing, Gotthold Ephraim, 283
Lewis, Percy Wyndham, 49, 274
Leyden, Dr, 186, 339
Libanius, 144
Little Eyolf (Ibsen), 42
'Little Imber' (Forster), 346, 355
Lolly Willowes (Sylvia Townsend Warner), 19, 266
Longest Journey, The (Forster), 270
Lord of the Flies (Golding), 356
Look Back in Anger (Osborne), 259, 362
Lowes Dickinson, Goldsworthy, 92, 102, 104, 114, 117, 158, 163, 180, 181, 182, 197, 230, 236, 276
Lubbock, Percy, 7, 262
Lucas, F. L., *56*, 59, 276, 277, 297
Lucretius, 113, *114*, 303–4

McCarthy, Desmond, 102, 105, 297, 298
Macaulay, Thomas Babington Lord, *193*, 341
Macchiavelli, Niccolo, 101
Mahler, Gustav, 40, 253–4, 361
Malherbe, François de, *124*, *125*, 307, 308
Mallarmé, Stephane, *125*, 308
Malory, Sir Thomas, *103*, 297
Mann, Sir Horace, *122*, 307
Mann, Thomas, 28, 29, 30, *238*, 268–9, 356

Mansbridge, Albert, 27, 268
Marius the Epicurean (Pater), 11
Mansfield, Denis, 20
'Mark Rutherford' (William Hale White),
  18, 265
Marlowe Society, 210, 296
Marshall, Frances (Frances Partridge), 49,
  274
Marshall, K. W., 277
Marvin, F. S., 27, 268
Marx, Karl, *108*, 109, 300, 301
Masood, Syed Ross, 51, 217, 273, 337
Masood, Syed Ross, 51, 217, 273, 337,
  350
Massingham, H. W., 48, 274
Maugham, W. Somerset, 157, 200
Mauriac, François, *38*, 271
Maurois, André, *57*, 58, 276
Mauron, Charles, 52, 105, 126, *152–5*,
  155, 204, 205, 275, 298, 309, 324–27,
  328
Mauron, Marie, 154, 309
Melville, Herman, *17*, 18, *100*, *164*, *189*,
  265, 296, 332
Memoirs of a Midget (de la Mare), 10, 263
Meredith, George, 7, 8, 40, 59, *240*, 272,
  357
Meyerstein, E. H. W., *212*, 348
St Michael's Church, Coventry, 24
Middleton Murry, John, 1, 2, *96*, 118, 260
Mill, John Stuart, *162*
Miller, Henry, *167*, 333
Millet, Jean François, *239*, 356
Milton, John, *43*, *103–04*, *166*, *248*, 272,
  297, 332, 358
Mirza, Baber, 48
Mitchell, Donald, 249
Moby Dick (Melville), 6, *20*
Moll Flanders (Defoe), 4
Montague, C. E., 27
Moore, George, 74
Moore, G. E., *233*
Morrell, Lady Ottoline, 163, 284, 331
Morris, Mowbray, *185–6*, 339
Morris, William, 53
Mortimer, Raymond, 155
Mosley, Sir Oswald, *96*
Muir, Edwin, 217, *218*, *241*, 351, 357

Napier, Marjorie, 93, 293
Nebuly Coat, The (John Meade Falkner),
  248, 359
Newton, John, *114–15*, 304
Ney, Marshal, 205–06, 345
Nicolson, Harold, 207

Nietzsche, Friedrich, 194
Nixon, J. E., 90, 291
Nonnus, 144, 318–19

Oedipus Tyrannus (Sophocles), 101
Old Wives' Tale, The (Bennett), 8, 20
Olier, Jean-Jacques, *128*, 310
Orwell, George, 258, 362
Our Mutual Friend (Dickens), 18
Ovid, *196*, 342
Owen, Wilfred, *214–15*, *216*, 349, 350

Palladas, 144, 319
Palmer, Reg, 5, 182, 261–2
Parker, Dorothy, *200*, 343
Parry, Donald, 213, 348
Paul, David, 335
Peacock, Thomas Love, 20
Pears, Sir Peter, 207, 208, 346
Peer Gynt (Ibsen), 35, 270
Peirce, Hayford, 137, 315
Pelagius, 313
Peregrine Pickle (Smollett), *256*, 362
Philo of Alexandria, *256*, 362
Pigou, A. C., 210, 211, 346–7
Pilgrim's Progress, The (Bunyan), 11
Pitt-Rivers, Michael, 239
Pius XII, Pope, 186, 339
Plato, 114, 303
Plomer, William, 156, *182*, 265, 332,
  338
Poe, Edgar Allan, 91, 291–2
Pope, Alexander, 27, *88–9*, *116–17*, 290,
  304
Porter, Hal, *247*, 358
Poston, Elizabeth, 215, 349
Poston, Ralph, 161
Powys brothers, 58, 276
Priestley, J. B., 31, 59, 88, 157, 258, 269,
  277, 290, 362
Prisoners of War, The (Ackerley), 6, 262
Proclus, 144
Propertius, *113*, 302
Proust, Marcel, 3, 8, 12, 16, *148*, 161, 181,
  196, *198*, *201*, 321–2, 342, 343, 344
Proverbs, 33
Pumpkin Eater, The (Penelope Mortimer),
  252, 360
Purcell, Henry, 184, 338–9

Racine, Jean, *185*, 339
Radef, Mattei, 246, 358
Rakshit, Indu, *96*
Raleigh, Walter, 79, 285–6
Ramsay, Ivor Erskine St Clair, 219, 351

Rasselas (Johnson), 11, *75–6*, 283–4
Rattigan, Sir Terence, 184–5
Raven, John, 213, 348
Raven, Simon, 247, 339, 358
Read, Ernest, 295
Read, Sir Herbert, 310, 318
Reed, Trelawney, Dayrell, 145, 319–20
Rehearsal, The (Duke of Buckingham), 66, 281
Reid, Forrest, 18, 102, *176*, 177, 335
Renier, G. J., 90, 291
Richard III (film), 358
Richards, I. A., 285
Richardson, Charles F., 91
Richardson, Samuel, *11–12*, 18, 19, 24
Robinson Crusoe (Defoe), 9, 11, 262–3
Rodin, Auguste, *148*
Rodogune (Corneille), 74, 279, 283
Rome, 221
Rooksnest, 215, 333
Rose, Jasper, 212, 348
Routledge, Norman, 192, 341
Roxana (Defoe), 6, 9, 10
Royden, Maude, 92, 292–3
Rubens, Peter Paul, 234, 354
Ruskin, John, *113*, *129*, 156, *167*, *180*, *181*, *183*, 310, 333, 337, 338
Russell, Bertrand, 45, 51, 102, 238, 274–5, 284, 356

Sackville-West, Victoria, 90, 274, 291
St Evremond, Marquis de, *70*, 71, *72*, 281, 282
St Rémy, 105, 204–05
Saintsbury, George, 280
Samuel, Viscount, 293
Sassoon, Siegfried, 43, 90, 207, *208*, 268, 272, 291, 346
Scarfe, Norman, 361
Schopenhauer, Friedrich, *113*
Schumann, Robert, 91
Schuster, Frank, 90, 268, 291
Schwarz, Ernest Herbert Lewis, *51*, 274
Scott, Sir Peter, 105, 241, 298
Scott, Sir Walter, 11, 12, 18
Searight, Kenneth, *113*, 303
Seccombe, Irene, 249, 359
Sévigné, Marquise de, *120–1*, *125*, 305–6, 307–8
Sforza, Ludovico, *229*, 353
Shakespeare, William, *10*, 47, 68, 69, 81, *82*, 85–7, *94*, 95, 103, *104*, 210, 263, 270, 282, 285, 286, 288, 289, 295, 297
Shaw, George Bernard, 60, 87, *129*, 311
Sheppard, Dick, 92, 292–3

Shelley, Percy Bysshe, *172*, *203*, 334, 344, 359
Shire, E. S., 174, 230, 335
Shostakovich, Dmitri, 151, 324
Sidgwick, Henry, 353
Silence de la Mer, Le ('Vercors'), 155, 327
Sitwell, Dame Edith, 207, 208
Smith, Logan Pearsall, 76, 284
Smith, Sydney, *193*, *200*, 341
Smollett, Tobias, 3, 11
Smyrnaues, Quintus, 144, 318
Socrates of Constantinople, 146, 319
Spender, Natasha, 192, 341
Spender, Stephen, 120, 201, 305
Spinoza, Baruch, *245*
Spire, The (Golding), 248, 359
Spoils of Poynton, The (James), 15
Sprott, W. J. H. ('Sebastian'), 23, 267, 270, 281, 324
Stalin, J., 111
Stallybrass, Oliver, 296, 299, 311–12
Stanhope, Lady Hester, 26, 267
Stephens, Ian, 190, 340
Sterne, Laurence, *2–4*, 8, 11, 12, 20, 261
Stevenson, Robert Louis, 7
Stisted, 105, 297
Strachey, Lytton, 28, 123, 267, 269, 293
Straus, Ralph, *96*, 294
Strong, L. A. G., 294
Stuart, Neil, 160, 161
Sweerts, Michiel, 348
Swift, Jonathan, 3, *10*, 11, *80*, *81*, 117, 286
Swinburne, Algernon Charles, *149*, 323
Sylvia's Lovers (Mrs Gaskell), 149, 310
Symonds, John Addington, 53, 74, *87*, 88, *224–6*, *228*, 229, 290, 352–3
Synesius, *143*

Talleyrand (-Perigord), Charles Maurice, *176*, 207, 335, 346
Taylor, Sherwood, *176*
Tennant, Stephen, 98, 295
Tennyson, Alfred Lord, *60–1*, *229*, 244, 277, 353, 357
Tesserete, 217, 350
Thackeray, William Makepiece, 12
Thaïs (Anatole France), 20, 266
Themistius, *144*
Thomas, Edward, 27, 268
Thompson, Edward, 27, 268
Thompson, E. V., 206, 345
Thornton, John, 115
Thornton, Lucy, *187*
Thornton, Marianne, 252, 258

Tibullus, 302–3
The Times, *25*, *96*
Together (Norman Douglas), 20, 266, 296
Tolstoy, Alexei, 12, 15
Tomlinson, H. M., 27, 268
Tonbridge School, 198
Tovey, Donald Francis, 111, 302
Treasure Island (Stevenson), 9
Trevelyan, Sir G. M., 207, 302, 309
Trevelyan, R. C., 90, 160, 291, 302, 330
Trèves, 145, 319
Trilling, Lionel, 161, 178, 330, 336
Tristram Shandy (Sterne), 11, 12, 267, 275, 298
Trollope, Anthony, 20, 307
Turner, W. J., 48, 273
Twain, Mark, 158–9
Tyler, Royall, 138, 315

Valéry, Paul, *129*, 311
Vanbrugh, Sir John, *8*, 262
Van Gogh, Vincent, *239*, *245*
Vaughan, Henry, *56*, *236*, 276, 355
Vaughan, Keith, 236, 237, 355
Vaughan Williams, Ralph, 27, 203, 268, 344
Vaux, Lord, *33*, 270
Verrall, A. W., 71, 282
Verrochio, Andrea del, 254
Vicary, Frank, 29, 53, 116, *120*, 269, 274, 275, 305
Virgil, *198*, 343
Voltaire, 90, *97*, 98, *116*, 280, 294–5, 304
Von Gaertringen, Friedrich Hiller, 203

Walpole, Horace, *45*, *99*, *122*, *123*, 273, 307
Walpole, Hugh, 59, 277
Walter, William Grey, 210, 347
Walton, Izaak, 272
Wagner, Richard, 194, 254

War and Peace (Tolstoy), 6, 7, 8
Waterlow, Sydney, 44, 272
Waterston, Hugh, 118, 151, 304–5, 324
Waterton, Charles, *164–5*, 332
Watson, George, 280, 281
Wavell, Field Marshal Earl, *149*, 323
Webster, John, *101*, 296–7
Weitling, 148
Welch, Denton, *189*, 340
Wells, H. G., *15*, 16, 21, 37, 264, 266
When We Dead Awaken (Ibsen), 41, 42
Where Angels Fear to Tread (Forster), 351
Whichelo, Louisa Graham, *176*, 335, 357
Whichelo family tree, 88, 290
Whitehead, Alfred North, *51*, *196*, 275
Whiteley, Opal, 21, 266
Whitman, Walt, 37, 53
Wilkinson, L. P., 192, 196, 337, 341, 342
Williamson, Hugh Ross, 126, 308–9
Wilpert, Joseph, 138, 316, 317
Wilson, General R. T., 302
Windham, Donald, 192, 341
Wolfe, Humbert, 94, 293
Woolaston, 6, 262
Woolf, Leonard, 31
Woolf, Virginia, 10, 54, 105, 263, 274, 315
Wordsworth, William, 83–4, *119*, *123*, 163, *170*, *188*, 189, 209, *241*, 243, 305, 307, 333, 339, 357
Wortham, H. E., *31–2*, 269

Yeats, W. B., 74, *196*, 209, *215*, 234, 342, 346, 349
Young, Edward Hilton (Lord Kennet), 105, 206, 298, 345
Yudkin, Michael David, 229, 353

Zangwill, Israel, 153, 154, 327
Zechariah, *104*, 297
Zuleika Dobson (Beerbohm), 11

Publishers' acknowledgements

The *Commonplace Book* contains extracts from the work of a number of authors still in copyright. The Publishers are grateful to them, their publishers, agents or executors for allowing their work to appear in this form, and wish particularly to acknowledge the help of the following:

The Bodley Head Ltd, for J. D. Sinclair, *The Divine Comedy of Dante Alighieri, volume 1: Inferno*.

Curtis Brown Ltd, for Christopher Isherwood, *Mr Norris Changes Trains*; William Cooper, *The Ever-Interesting Topic*; and H. A. L. Fisher, *History of Europe, volume 1*.

John Calder (Publishers) Ltd, and Grove Press, Inc., for Henry Miller, *Tropic of Cancer*: copyright Grove Press, Inc., 1961.

Jonathan Cape Ltd, for Ernest Hemingway, *For Whom the Bell Tolls*, and R. A. Furness.

Cassell Ltd, for Gerald Heard, *By Any Other Name* and *The Creed of Christ*.

Chatto and Windus Ltd, for Aldous Huxley, *Grey Eminence*; Norman Douglas, *Experiments*; and Marcel Proust, *À la recherche du temps perdu*.

Constable and Co. Ltd, for H. E. Wrotham, *Oscar Browning*.

Editions Gallimard, for Paul Valéry, *Works*; Marcel Proust, *À la recherche du temps perdu*; André Malraux; André Gide, *Journal*; Jean Cocteau, *Works*.

The Executor of the Estate of Sir Malcolm Lyall Darling, for the unpublished diary.

Faber and Faber Ltd, London, for the lines from *Four Quartets* by T. S. Eliot; 'Hammerfest' by W. H. Auden; and *Collected Poems* by Edwin Muir.

Gordon Press Inc., for *The Speeches of Adolf Hitler* translated by N. H. Baynes, volume 1.

Harcourt Brace Jovanovich Inc., for T. S. Eliot, *Four Quartets*.

Harrap Ltd, for A. P. Wavell, *Allenby: Soldier and Statesman*.

Rupert Hart-Davis Ltd/Granada Publishing Ltd, for G. L. Keynes, *My Early Beliefs*; and A. E. Housman, *Letters*.

Rupert Hart-Davis and The Hogarth Press Ltd, for William Plomer, *Sado*.

David Higham Associates Ltd, for Denton Welch, *Journals*, published by Hamish Hamilton.

The Literary Executors of the Estate of H. G. Wells, for H. G. Wells, *Boon*.

The London Magazine for Hal Porter, *Boys will be Boys*.

Macmillan (Publishers) Ltd, for Edward H. Carr, *Biography of Michael Bakunin*.

Michael B. Yeats and Macmillan London, for the extract from W. B. Yeats, *The Magi*; reprinted with the permission of Macmillan Publishing Company, copyright 1916 by Macmillan Publishing Co., renewed 1944 by Bertha Georgie Yeats.

Methuen and Co. Ltd, for T. S. Eliot, *The Sacred Wood*; and François Mauriac, *Le desért de l'amour*.

Gavin Muir and The Hogarth Press Ltd, and Norwood Editions, for Edwin Muir, *An Autobiography*.

John Murray (Publishers) Ltd, for Kenneth Clark, *The Nude*.

University of North Carolina Press, for Stefan George, translated by O. Marx and E. Marwitz.

Oxford University Press, for *The Oxford Chekhov*, translated by Robert Hingley; and *Stars and Atoms* by A. S. Eddington.

Oxford University Press, Inc., for Edwin Muir, *Collected Poems*.

Phaidon Press Ltd, for Professor E. H. Gombrich, *Meditations on a Hobby Horse*, copyright 1963 Phaidon Press Ltd.

Princeton University Press, for C. P. Cavafy, *Collected Poems*, translated by Edmund Keeley and Philip Sherrard, copyright 1975 Princeton University Press.

Routledge and Kegan Paul, and Princeton University Press, for *The Collected Works of Paul Valéry*.

George Sassoon, for Siegfried Sassoon.

Martin Secker and Warburg Ltd, and Curtis Brown Ltd, New York, for John Knowles, *A Separate Peace*.

Martin Secker and Warburg Ltd, and Alfred E. Knopf Inc., for Thomas Mann, *The Magic Mountain*, translated by H. Lowe-Porter.

Martin Secker and Warburg Ltd, and Viking Penguin Inc., for Dorothy Parker in *The Paris Review*.

The Society of Authors, as the literary representative of the estate of Norman Douglas, *A Plea for Better Manners*, and as the literary representative of the estate of John Middleton Murry.

Neville Spearman Ltd, for E. H. W. Meyerstein, *Letters*.

The author, for Ian Stephens, *Horned Moon*.

The Times, for two extracts, 17 March 1925 and 29 September 1934.